T0392740

The Financial Statecraft of Borrowers

As China rises to prominence as a global lender, what impact does this have on borrowing countries? In a context of deepening global financial integration and rising powers, this book examines how developing countries, specifically in sub-Saharan Africa, can use borrowing relationships to their advantage. Alexandra O. Zeitz reveals how these countries, once reliant on traditional donors, may now leverage Chinese loans and international sovereign bonds to enhance their bargaining power in aid negotiations – a strategy she terms the "financial statecraft of borrowers." Grounded in extensive interviews with senior officials from recipient countries and donor agencies in Ethiopia, Ghana, and Kenya, and complemented by the statistical analysis of aid agreements, *The Financial Statecraft of Borrowers* offers a comprehensive understanding of how aid relationships are changing along with the shifting landscape of international finance.

ALEXANDRA O. ZEITZ is Assistant Professor in the Department of Political Science at Concordia University in Montréal, Canada. Her research focuses on international finance, sovereign debt, and foreign aid, with an emphasis on the developing world. She held a Max Weber postdoctoral fellowship at the European University Institute and received her doctorate in International Relations from the University of Oxford.

The Financial Statecraft of Borrowers

African Governments and External Finance

ALEXANDRA O. ZEITZ
Concordia University

CAMBRIDGE
UNIVERSITY PRESS

CAMBRIDGE
UNIVERSITY PRESS

Shaftesbury Road, Cambridge CB2 8EA, United Kingdom

One Liberty Plaza, 20th Floor, New York, NY 10006, USA

477 Williamstown Road, Port Melbourne, VIC 3207, Australia

314–321, 3rd Floor, Plot 3, Splendor Forum, Jasola District Centre,
New Delhi – 110025, India

103 Penang Road, #05–06/07, Visioncrest Commercial, Singapore 238467

Cambridge University Press is part of Cambridge University Press & Assessment,
a department of the University of Cambridge.

We share the University's mission to contribute to society through the pursuit of
education, learning and research at the highest international levels of excellence.

www.cambridge.org
Information on this title: www.cambridge.org/9781009475068

DOI: 10.1017/9781009475075

When citing this work, please include a reference to the DOI
10.1017/9781009475075

First published 2025

A catalogue record for this publication is available from the British Library

*A Cataloging-in-Publication data record for this book is available from the
Library of Congress*

ISBN 978-1-009-47506-8 Hardback
ISBN 978-1-009-47504-4 Paperback

Cambridge University Press & Assessment has no responsibility for the persistence
or accuracy of URLs for external or third-party internet websites referred to in this
publication and does not guarantee that any content on such websites is, or will
remain, accurate or appropriate.

In memory of my mother

Contents

Contents ix

Figures

Tables

Acknowledgments

Like all research projects, this one would not have been possible without the input and support of many people. I am especially grateful for the generosity and openness of all those who agreed to speak with me in Nairobi, Accra, Addis Ababa, New York, and Washington D.C. about the relationships between governments and their donors and creditors. This project was borne out of a curiosity about how transformations in the global financial system were playing out in the aid negotiations in developing countries, and I would not have been able to understand this if it were not for the willingness of those with first-hand knowledge of these negotiations to take the time to talk to me. The relationships and dynamics they told me about were sometimes sensitive, and I appreciate the trust they placed in me by sharing their experiences and insights.

This book has benefited from the feedback and intellectual support of many scholars at different stages of its development. At the University of Oxford, I was extremely lucky to work with Ricardo Soares de Oliveira and Ben Ansell, who helped me to develop the foundations of this project and carry it out in my thesis. I also thank Nic Cheeseman, David Doyle, Robin Harding, and Karolina Milewicz for their feedback. At Oxford, the Global Economic Governance (GEG) Programme cemented my interest in the relationship between developing countries and the global economy, and I am grateful to Emily Jones and others at GEG for their input, including Peter Knaack, Peace Medie, Folashadé Soulé-Kondou, Taylor St. John, Camila Villard Duran, and Ngaire Woods. For their friendship, feedback, and intellectual exchange during the years of the DPhil, I thank Quentin Bruneau, Michaela Collord, Barnaby Dye, Claire Elder, Jakob Hensing, Ivo Iaydjiev, Jure Jeric, Miles Kellerman, Hanna Notte, Brett Rosenberg, Sam Rowan, Thom Wetzer, and Nina Yancy. For welcoming me during fieldwork, facilitating invaluable connections, and helping me to put new knowledge in context, I thank the following: Gabrielle Lynch, Radha Upadhyaya, and the team at the British Institute in Eastern Africa, Nairobi; Abdul-Fatawu Hakeem and researchers at the University of Ghana, Accra; Nahom Teklewold, Biruk Terrefe, and scholars at the Ethiopian Development Research Institute, Addis Ababa. While finishing my dissertation, I was hosted as a visitor at Princeton University by Helen Milner and at the University of Heidelberg by Axel Dreher; I am grateful to both. As the examiners at my doctoral defense, Robin Harding and Layna Mosley raised important questions about the project and first helped me to think about how to develop it into a book.

The European University Institute provided a welcoming and stimulating environment as I was first developing the book from my dissertation during my postdoctoral fellowship, and I am grateful to the community of Max Weber fellows for their friendship and advice during this time, especially Elizabeth Banks, Caitlin Procter, and Eleanor Woodhouse. For feedback, I thank Dorothee Bohle, as well as Lachlan McNamee, who provided comments on early chapters of this book. At Concordia University, where I have been since 2020, I have been lucky to work with supportive and thoughtful colleagues. For their feedback and advice on book publishing, I especially thank Elizabeth Bloodgood, Patrik Marier, Mireille Paquet, and Marlene Sokolon.

Conversations at my book workshop in September 2021 were crucial for honing my argument, sharpening my analysis, and bringing my findings into dialogue with the literature. I am enormously grateful to Sarah Bermeo, Jonas Bunte, Mark Copelovitch, Saori Katada, Peter Lewis, and Haley Swedlund for their generosity in reading the whole manuscript, their constructive criticism, and their creativity in helping me think though how to improve the book. They spent a long day on Zoom, spanning nine time zones, and I was touched by enthusiasm and openness with which they approached the project, which motivated me during the revisions that followed. I thank Laura Sofía Rivera for her support in organizing the book workshop.

Parts of the book received feedback in various iterations at numerous conferences, including at the meetings of the American Political Science Association in 2015 and the International Studies Association in 2016–2019, and 2021, as well as the 2017 Tracking International Aid and Investment from Development and Emerging Economies workshop at the University of Heidelberg, the 2017 International Political Economy Society meeting, the 2018 Oxford University China–Africa Network meeting, the 2018 Princeton Summer International Political Economy meeting, the 2019 Oxford Politics of African Economic Policy workshop, and the 2019 European University Institute Workshop on the Future of Capitalism. For their comments on earlier versions of papers and chapters that became part of the book, I thank Gerda Asmus, Pritish Behuria, Daniela Campello de Costa Ribeiro, Elizabeth Cobbett, Christopher Cramer, Alexandra Guisinger, Surupa Gupta, Juliet Johnson, Noel Johnston, Silvia Marchesi, Natalya Naqvi, Lauren Prather, Andrew Walter, and Lindsay Whitfield, in addition to those named earlier. In the final stages of revising the manuscript, I received invaluable comments on the Ethiopia case study from Biruk Terefe, Kenya case study from Radha Upadhyaya, and Ghana case study from Kofi Gunu. I apologize to anyone whom I have unintentionally excluded from this list of those who commented on the project along the way.

I have been fortunate to work with smart and talented coauthors on related topics while working on this book, and I have learned an enormous amount from them, hopefully making me a better researcher in the process. My thanks to Jonas Bunte, Richard Clark, Lindsay Dolan, Lauren Ferry, Geoffrey Gertz, Emily Jones, David Leblang, Layna Mosley, Isabel Rodriguez-Toribio, and Sam Rowan.

I gratefully acknowledge financial support that made this research possible during my doctorate, including from the UK Economic and Social Research Council, the University of Oxford Q-Step Quantitative Methods Graduate Scholarship, the Charterhouse European Bursary, the Cyril Foster and Alastair Buchan funds, and St. Antony's College.

At Cambridge University Press, I am very grateful to John Haslam for his support of this book and to the editorial staff for their work. I am greatly appreciative to the two anonymous reviewers for their thorough and perceptive reading of the manuscript and their constructive suggestions that helped me to uncover a better version of my argument. I thank Jessica Stilwell for her help in editing the text in the final stages.

On a personal note, I would like to thank my partner, Sam, who has enthusiastically supported me since the earliest phases of this research, commented on every iteration, taught me so much with his own research and curiosity, and helped me to think deeper and more clearly. I could not ask for a better partner, both intellectually and in life. My family, including my grandparents, Elfriede Kroeger, Arthur Kroeger, Inka Eckermann, and Wolfgang Zeitz, encouraged my curiosity from an early age, and their support put me on the path to doing the research I do today. My father, Frank Zeitz, has been my stalwart champion, even if sometimes bemused that our shared interest in finance has led me to academic research. My mother, Liza Kroeger, was my role model in her zeal for knowledge, enthusiasm, and precision. I am grateful that she was able to see me finish my doctorate, and I wish she had been able to see the book completed. I dedicate this book to her memory.

1 | *Introduction*

In 2001, Sufian Ahmed, Ethiopia's finance minister, confronted a vanishingly narrow set of options. For a developing country, Ethiopia carried a heavy public debt burden – government debt amounted to almost 100 percent of GDP – and could find few willing lenders besides the World Bank and the International Monetary Fund (IMF). The country's leadership, having taken power in the 1990s after sixteen years of civil war, had publicly rejected liberalizing reforms and instead advocated for active state intervention to deliver development. Now, facing a severe funding shortage and with few sources of financing, the country turned to donors to request debt forgiveness and a loan program. The 2001 agreements secured $150 million from the World Bank and $112 million from the IMF. The political price, however, was steep. The agreement with the World Bank included twenty-seven separate reform requirements, including preparing thirty-four state-owned companies for privatization, reducing the authority of the central bank, and restructuring the civil service. Given the government's political orientation, this was a difficult pill to swallow.

A mere twelve years later, Ethiopia's circumstances had changed dramatically. Still Ethiopia's finance minister, Sufian Ahmed now faced a different task: juggling negotiations with a diverse array of creditors in order to finance projects in Ethiopia. In 2013, the Ethiopian government signed an agreement with a consortium of Chinese banks for a $3.3 billion loan to fund a railway connecting the capital, Addis Ababa, to the port in neighboring Djibouti, giving landlocked Ethiopia a vital trade link. A year later, Sufian Ahmed's team traveled to London and New York to meet with private investors before issuing the country's first ever international bond in December 2014, raising $1 billion. At the same time, the World Bank continued to provide loans to the Ethiopian government, supporting the government's infrastructure priorities with more than $700 million in transport-sector projects in 2014.

In little over a decade, Ethiopia went from being seen in Western capitals as a byword for famine and conflict with few credible funding options to borrowing from a diverse array of creditors. As one of the African continent's longest serving finance ministers, in office from 1994 to 2016, Sufian Ahmed personally witnessed this transformation. While Ethiopia is one of the starkest examples of the dramatic expansion of financing options between the early 2000s and the mid 2010s, the country's experience is part of a broader trend that saw African governments expand their access to external finance over this period.

In the late 1990s, the majority of African governments carried large public debt burdens and could find few financiers beyond Western donors and international financial institutions. By the 2010s, emerging donors, especially China, became prominent lenders to countries on the continent. In addition, private investors in international bond markets had become an important source of finance for many African countries. Governments that previously had few options could now assemble a diverse portfolio of external finance.

What happens when a government goes from having few choices for external funding to selecting from a varied menu of lenders? This book investigates if and when such access to a wider set of creditors increases a government's bargaining leverage with its existing donors. I argue that borrowing from a more diverse array of creditors enhances borrowers' negotiating power, giving them greater influence over the terms of aid they receive from traditional donors. Further, new borrowing relationships are most likely to enhance bargaining leverage with traditional donors if the recipient country is an important partner for the donor and if the donor trusts the recipient will uphold its aid agreements.

The empirical context for this analysis is specific to the early decades of the twenty-first century and the changing external finance portfolios of African countries during this time. However, the argument also speaks to long-standing questions in international politics on the relationship between interdependence and power. I argue that developing countries can extract negotiating leverage from their borrowing relationships with new creditors, a phenomenon I term the *financial statecraft of borrowers*. The reference to financial statecraft links my argument to broader claims that countries can use financial interdependence to their advantage, helping them to achieve foreign policy goals.

However, the focus on borrowing countries sets this argument apart from most other research on power and financial interdependence. Rather than examining the bargaining leverage of strong states in the international financial system, I consider the bargaining leverage of the weak, namely developing countries that are often reliant on outside sources of finance. Unlike larger economies that exploit the dependence of other states to achieve foreign policy goals or even reshape global governance, borrowing governments exercise financial statecraft by using borrowing relationships to *reduce* their dependence on any one donor or creditor. This more modest application of financial statecraft highlights the possibility for developing countries to use asymmetric relationships of interdependence to their advantage.

Developing countries' ability to borrow from external creditors is determined largely by dynamics external to the borrowing government. For this reason, developing countries' access to external finance has tended to be cyclical, with expansion of lending during periods of abundant liquidity, followed by crises when finance becomes yet again more scarce. This cyclical pattern has played out in different regions over recent decades: Latin America in the 1970s and 1980s, East Asia in the 1990s, and more recently in sub-Saharan Africa in the 2010s. For African countries, the expansion of foreign finance brought opportunity but also enabled the accumulation of large debt burdens that made them especially vulnerable to crisis when the COVID-19 pandemic and global economic shutdown hit in 2020. This book focuses on the impact of the earlier phase of abundant liquidity on relations between governments and their creditors and donors, examining the upswing rather than the downswing of the global capital cycle. Nevertheless, better understanding the political dynamics during this phase of expanding credit also sheds light on how countries accumulated the debt that later left them vulnerable to crisis.

1.1 The Argument in Brief: The Financial Statecraft of Borrowers

The core argument of this book is that a wider and more diverse pool of creditors can increase borrowing governments' negotiating power with the industrialized countries and multilateral development banks that have traditionally provided the majority of foreign aid.[1] The outcome of interest in this study is the aid agreement between a developing country government and a donor, specifically the extent to which the agreement aligns with the interests of the recipient government. Aid agreements vary along several dimensions, both formal and informal. The most basic dimensions of aid agreements are the amount of aid that donors provide and which projects or programs will be funded with that aid. Moreover, agreements vary in the reform or performance conditions the recipient must meet to access the aid. Donor–recipient relationships also differ in their informal characteristics, with some involving extensive donor scrutiny of recipient policy. Fundamentally, donor–recipient relationships vary in the extent of influence that donors have on development policy in the recipient country.[2]

Variation in the terms of aid agreements is a central outcome in the literature on the politics of aid, with research seeking to explain why some countries receive aid on more generous terms than others. Much scholarship has attributed differences in aid agreements to donors' interests, demonstrating that donors extend more attractive aid to countries that are in some way important to donors. Most of this research has operationalized the generosity of aid in terms of the amount of aid that countries receive, revealing that donors allocate more aid to important trading partners,[3] countries that are more likely to generate spillovers for the donor,[4] major strategic partners, or past colonies.[5] Others have shown a relationship between donors' interests and the conditions attached to foreign aid, showing that the World Bank offers more flexible loans to developing countries that are more ideologically proximate to the United States.[6]

The argument in this book similarly seeks to explain variation in aid agreements. However, rather than explaining these differences primarily with reference to donors' interests, the argument of debt-based financial statecraft is that recipient countries' portfolios of external

---

[1] As a shorthand, I refer to advanced economy bilateral donors and the major multilateral donors, including multilateral development banks, as "traditional donors" or "donors."

[2] Swedlund 2017b, pp. 25–27.

[3] Barthel et al. 2014.

[4] Bermeo 2017.

[5] Alesina and Dollar 2000.

[6] Clark and Dolan 2020.

finance can shape their bargaining power and thus the terms of the aid relationship. The expectation is that countries that broaden and diversify their sources of external finance, becoming less reliant on traditional donors, will secure more attractive terms in their aid agreements. The argument connects recipient countries' portfolios of external finance to the interests of donors in the "marketplace" of foreign aid to explain why some governments receive aid from traditional donors that is more aligned with their interests. My focus is on the impact of a broader range of external finance on governments' relationships with traditional donors, since the latter are the actors that long held a monopoly in the marketplace of foreign aid.

The argument proceeds in a number of steps. First, borrowing from alternate creditors reduces a government's reliance on traditional donors. Second, this reduced reliance encourages traditional donors to provide resources that are more in line with the government's preferences. Finally, some governments extract more leverage from their diversified portfolios of external finance than others due to donors' interest in the borrowing government and their trust that aid agreements will be upheld.

To illustrate the first step, take the example of the Zambian government, which in 2010 announced a $1 billion loan agreement with China to fund key infrastructure investments, followed the same year by a $2 billion agreement to develop a hydroelectric dam.[7] These commitments eased the government's dependence on traditional donors, including the World Bank, which funded infrastructure projects in road construction and electricity generation around this time. By diversifying away from previously prominent sources of financing, the Zambian government became less reliant on traditional donors to continue providing funds into the future. As one commentator noted, "The combined effects of less aid dependence and new donors imply that the impact of traditional aid and donor conditions now play a less significant role in Zambian public debate."[8]

The claim that borrowing from a wider range of sources lowers a government's reliance on individual donors or creditors may be uncontroversial. However, the second step of the argument, the impact of

---

[7] Kragelund 2014.
[8] Rakner 2012.

this reduced dependence on the negotiations between the government and traditional donors, is more counterintuitive. Why would donors offer preferred terms to developing countries that are less reliant on their aid? Would donors not simply be happy that others are providing development finance and move on?

In fact, donors have good reasons to offer attractive terms to borrowing governments that reduce their dependence on donors' development finance: Donors have an interest in shaping recipient government policy, and development finance allows them to shape policy conversations with the recipient government.[9] Scholars have debated whether donor countries are motivated to provide aid out of an altruistic concern for developing countries or for self-interested foreign policy ends.[10] More recent scholarship suggests that bilateral donors act out of an enlightened self-interest, using foreign aid to encourage development with spillover benefits for themselves.[11] What is common across different motivations, however, is that donors seek to have some influence over the policy of recipient countries and that they gain influence in connection with the aid they provide.

Donors are therefore competing in a marketplace for foreign aid, seeking to provide attractive development finance that gives them access to and influence with the recipient government. Historically, major bilateral donors and multilateral development banks have largely had the same broad approach to development aid, even coordinating among themselves in their approach to recipient countries. As borrowing governments diversified their portfolios of finance, borrowing from China or in international bond markets, recipient countries became less reliant on these traditional providers of development finance. Since they operate within a marketplace for aid, I suggest traditional donors do not exit the market when confronted with recipients' greater autonomy but instead innovate and offer recipient governments aid closer to the latter's preferences. My contention that access to additional sources of finance strengthens the government's negotiating strength rests on insights from the bargaining literature on the benefits of outside options. By establishing new borrowing relationships,

---

[9] Whitfield 2009b.

[10] Alesina and Dollar 2000; Berthélemy 2006; Gulrajani and Calleja 2019; Schraeder et al. 1998.

[11] Bermeo 2017, 2018.

developing countries can become more influential with their traditional donors. Recipient influence grows even though the government's new debtor relationships are unequal, with the government being far more reliant on China and private creditors than these creditors are on the borrower.

This claim distinguishes the financial statecraft of borrowers from alternative perspectives on developing countries' integration into the international economic and financial system, especially "dependency" style arguments. Dependency perspectives see developing countries' unequal integration into the international financial system as self-reinforcing. These theories suggest that exploitative and extractive relationships between rich and developing countries make it impossible for poorer countries to develop and instead perpetuate these countries' structurally weak position in the international economy.[12] My concept of debt-based financial statecraft does not deny that borrowing relationships are unequal nor claim that governments can overturn their structural position in the world economy. Instead, it highlights the potential for developing countries to use asymmetric financial ties as a basis for leverage, enhancing their power in negotiations with donors, relatively modest though this outcome is.

In stressing the benefits that developing countries can extract from their borrowing relationships, I draw on a tradition of scholarship on interdependence and economic statecraft.[13] Analysis of economic and financial statecraft has largely seen it as a tool of large and wealthy states, which can capitalize on the economic dependence of others by applying trade sanctions or restricting access to currency or financial systems.[14] While more recent work has expanded the concept to include defensive statecraft aimed at resisting foreign influence,[15] the focus has been on emerging economies that occupy increasingly prominent positions in the international financial system and can benefit from their greater size and centrality. By contrast, I analyze financial statecraft "from below," arguing that developing countries that rely on creditors for continued access to external finance can use these economic ties as a basis for leverage.

---

[12] Taylor 2014.
[13] Baldwin 1985; Hirschman 1945; Keohane and Nye 2001.
[14] Drezner 1999; Steil and Litan 2006.
[15] Armijo 2019.

The final step of the argument is explaining why some governments are more likely to derive negotiating benefits from borrowing from alternative sources than others. I suggest differences across recipient countries are driven both by donors' interest in the relationship with the recipient government and donors' trust in the government's willingness and ability to uphold aid agreements. Donors are more likely to respond proactively to the government's reduced dependence on their aid if the relationship with this government is especially valuable, meaning alternative finance should do more to enhance the bargaining power of recipient countries when this is the case.

Separately, when considering whether to offer more attractive terms in response to a recipient country's diversified portfolio of finance, donors' trust in the government's credibility is key. Since government–donor negotiations are in large part over the extent of flexibility granted to the government in the implementation and oversight of development programs, donors' willingness to meet the government's preferences for flexibility depends on the extent to which donors trust that the government will uphold its part of the agreement. Moreover, if donors do not trust government institutions for implementing and overseeing development programs, they may also worry about the government's uses of alternative finance, fearing that this spending could put their own projects or repayment at risk. In these cases of limited donor trust, governments that borrow from alternative creditors may find donors to be even less accommodating, rather than finding alternative finance a useful source of bargaining leverage in aid negotiations. Donor trust in the recipient government can vary based on the government's past performance in implementing development programs or donors' appraisal of government institutions for budgeting and financial management. Moreover, I suggest that donors base their trust on the domestic politics in the recipient country, with greater distrust in countries where clientelist spending pressures or widespread corruption make the government's spending promises less credible.

1.2 Situating the Argument

This book's focus on how a government's portfolio of external finance impacts relationships with aid donors bridges the often separate literatures on the politics of international finance and development aid. It intervenes in debates about the consequences of a country's choice of creditors and the rise of emerging economies as donors and lenders. Moreover, it highlights the agency of African governments in navigating often asymmetrical relationships with foreign creditors and donors.

1.2.1 Countries' Choice of Creditors

In arguing that the composition of a developing country's set of creditors affects its relationship with aid donors, this book builds on research in international political economy on governments' choice of creditors. For a long time, the conventional understanding was that governments, especially developing country governments, exercised very little choice over who they borrowed from. In this understanding, developing countries are so reliant on international financial institutions and foreign creditors for access to finance that they will accept whatever aid or finance is offered to them, only really discriminating on price, preferring lower cost loans to more expensive ones.

However, recent research shows that governments, including those in developing countries, do make choices about when to borrow and who to borrow from.[16] In the most substantial contribution to this strand of research, Bunte (2019) examines the full range of financing choices available to developing countries in the contemporary era and theorizes the political underpinnings of governments' choice of loans from international financial institutions, traditional creditors, emerging economies, or private markets.[17] Bunte demonstrates not only that developing countries exercise agency over the composition of their debt, but also that this choice reflects the balance of political influence among domestic interest groups, representing finance, industry, and labor. Where finance and industry are most influential, for example, the government will prioritize private lenders.

I build directly on the work of Bunte and others to argue that the diversity of countries' portfolios of external finance matters for their negotiations with donors. I turn from governments' choice of creditors to the *consequences* of those choices, arguing that countries that diversify their portfolio of external finance can increase their bargaining leverage. Inspired by the literature on creditor choice, I bring together

---

[16] Ballard-Rosa et al. 2019; Cormier 2022, 2023; L. Mosley and Rosendorff 2023.
[17] Bunte 2019.

the often separate literatures on debt and aid to argue that governments of developing countries choose from a broad range of external finance, extending from grant aid to market-rate loans. Considering this portfolio as a whole reveals how governments can spread their reliance for external finance from one set of donors to a broader range of creditors, reshaping their negotiations with donors.

1.2.2 *The Rise of China as a Global Lender*

The rise of China, and, to a lesser extent, India and Brazil, has reshaped the global landscape of development finance. As China's economy rapidly grew, various public agencies and banks – including the Ministry of Finance and Commerce, China Development Bank, and China Export-Import Bank – expanded overseas aid giving and lending, often connected to the larger policy of the Belt and Road Initiative. By some estimates, China had become the world's leading official creditor by the end of the 2010s.[18] Scholars have explained China's aid and loan programs as motivated by ambitions for greater influence in recipient countries,[19] a desire for increased international status,[20] or a mix of commercial and geopolitical objectives.[21] Public commentary about China's lending has sometimes raised the alarm that Chinese development finance supports authoritarian governments and undermines good governance advocated by traditional donors and that Chinese lending is an effort to entrap borrowing countries with unsustainable debts that allow China to exercise greater geopolitical influence.[22] However, there is little evidence of a deliberate strategic effort by China to ensnare borrowing countries with unsustainable debts, and Chinese lending seems largely to be motivated by commercial objectives.[23] Research unpacking the heterogeneity of Chinese finance reveals that the low-cost concessional funds most akin to foreign aid are allocated to poorer and more geopolitically aligned recipient countries, following similar patterns as traditional donors' aid allocation.[24] By contrast,

[18] Horn et al. 2021.
[19] Rotberg 2008; Taylor 2014.
[20] Armijo and Katada 2014.
[21] Brautigam 2011; Kaplan 2021.
[22] Chellaney 2017; Naim 2007.
[23] Jones and Hameiri 2020.
[24] Dreher et al. 2018.

more expensive finance is allocated in line with commercial objectives, flowing to countries that are rich in natural resources and suitable for commercial projects involving Chinese firms.[25] The main motivation for Chinese lending appears to be cultivating closer diplomatic relations with borrowing countries and supporting Chinese firms in their expansion to new markets.

The feature of Chinese aid and loans that is most relevant for my argument is its relative flexibility compared with the aid and loans of traditional donors and international financial institutions, especially the lack of reform conditionality. Though funds from Chinese policy banks usually require the recipient government to procure goods and services from Chinese firms and are often priced close to market rates, with more expensive financial terms than traditional donors' development finance, they do not require the government to undertake institutional or policy reforms.[26] Moreover, given the commercial focus of much of this lending, Chinese loans are more likely to fund infrastructure projects.[27] Chinese lenders' approach and focus thus add diversity to the mix of development finance available to developing countries, giving them a greater range of choice.[28]

This book focuses on how the rise of China, among other alternative creditors, changes the bargaining relationship between recipient governments and traditional donors. As such, it builds on previous work that studies how traditional donors respond to the increasing volume of Chinese loans.[29] The results of this previous research cut in different directions, with some finding evidence that loans from nontraditional creditors alter traditional donor aid and others finding little effect. What I add to these analyses is a consideration of how Chinese loans fit within developing countries' broader portfolio of external finance, including private finance and foreign aid from traditional donors. Moreover, prior work has primarily focused on the potential for competition among donors.[30] By turning the lens to recipient governments and theorizing how external finance affects their

---

[25] Kaplan 2021.
[26] Hernandez 2017; Taylor 2011.
[27] Kaplan 2016; Zeitz 2021a.
[28] Greenhill et al. 2013; Kragelund 2012; Woods 2008.
[29] Hernandez 2017; Humphrey and Michaelowa 2019; Swedlund 2017a; Zeitz 2021a.
[30] Bueno de Mesquita and Smith 2016.

reliance on traditional donors, this book sheds light on the conditions under which new development finance – including Chinese finance – is likely to affect traditional donors' aid.

1.2.3 Developing Countries and Private Finance

My account of debt-based financial statecraft builds on several strands of the literature on developing countries in the international financial system. One such strand examines the political consequences of debt composition and another focuses on the impact of sovereign debt on countries' policy autonomy and the cyclical nature of countries' access to private finance. While the emphasis of the creditor-choice literature on governments' preferences over the full range of private and public creditors may be quite recent, there is an earlier wave of scholarship that considers the political consequences of the composition of countries' debts to private creditors. In the 1990s, governments, including in middle-income countries, increasingly shifted their borrowing from a smaller set of banks to dispersed investors in international bond markets, with implications for their relationships with creditors. Copelovitch (2010) finds that countries with higher levels of bond debt received larger but more stringent IMF programs, which the Fund deemed necessary to restore access to bond markets. I build on this work on debt composition, arguing that access to private external finance reshapes countries' relationships with their traditional donors.

Separately, a long-standing debate in international political economy examines the constraints that bond markets impose on borrowing countries' policy choices.[31] While advanced economies appear to have maintained substantial policy discretion despite borrowing in international markets, developing countries are more likely to face bond market discipline in response to policies, or political orientations, that investors fear will put repayment at risk.[32] It may therefore be surprising to argue that private finance acts as a flexible alternative to traditional aid that gives borrowing governments greater autonomy in negotiations with traditional donors.

---

[31] Drezner 2001; Garrett 1998; L. Mosley 2000; L. Mosley et al. 2020.
[32] L. Mosley 2003; Wibbels 2006.

However, I draw on research on global liquidity cycles and developing countries' market access to argue that during phases of widespread lending, investors exercise less scrutiny, even of developing countries.[33] Shifting global allocations of capital in the period after the 2007–2008 global financial crisis gave poorer developing countries, including many African ones, access to international bond finance for the first time. Investors' exuberance and search for returns gave governments access to finance that, while more expensive than traditional donor aid, had no formal performance or reform requirements.[34] In this way, bond market finance gave governments greater autonomy and potentially greater bargaining leverage with traditional donors.

1.2.4 Foreign Aid, Negotiations, and the Donor–Recipient Relationship

I pick up an important insight from the literature on aid agreements, which emphasizes that aid agreements are the outcomes of negotiation. If development aid is understood as a form of charity or a purely humanitarian undertaking, it can be surprising to describe that aid as the outcome of bargaining. However, even if donors and the recipient government share an interest in economic development, their bureaucratic structures, ideological orientations, or broader policy objectives can lead them to have diverging preferences that must be reconciled through negotiation. Whitfield and Fraser (2009) and Swedlund (2017b) each analyze aid agreements through the lens of negotiation, arguing that donors and recipients draw on available resources to influence the design and implementation of aid agreements in line with their preferences. Drawing on these claims, I argue that for developing countries, new borrowing relationships are a resource they can use to increase their bargaining leverage in negotiations over aid.

Within development policymaking, a preoccupation of the last decades has been the extent to which donor-funded projects support the domestic policy priorities of recipient countries. Responding to concerns about the ineffectiveness of aid, in the 2000s the development community declared in the Paris Declaration on Aid Effectiveness that donors should "align behind [recipient countries'] objectives and use

---

[33] Ballard-Rosa et al. 2019; Bauerle Danzman et al. 2017; Naqvi 2018.
[34] Cormier 2023; Zeitz 2021b.

local systems."[35] However, as critics pointed out when these new principles were introduced, the push toward "alignment" offered a mostly bureaucratic solution to a political challenge, namely that recipients and donors can have divergent preferences and that recipients are often reliant on donors, allowing donors to advance their own interests.[36] By analyzing whether access to alternative finance allows recipient governments to push for their preferred outcomes, this book responds to a gap in the policy proposals for aid alignment, examining the political preconditions that enable recipients to achieve negotiating outcomes that are more consistent with their preferences.

1.2.5 African Foreign Policy and the Politics of Extraversion

While my argument about how borrowing relationships affect aid negotiations is a general one, the empirical context in which I develop and test the argument is specific to sub-Saharan Africa in the early decades of the twenty-first century. I focus on countries in the region because, as I explain later in this chapter, the transformations in African countries' access to external finance were abrupt and dramatic, providing an ideal setting to compare an earlier reliance on traditional donor funds to a later diversity of external finance. Moreover, the literature on African politics and international relations has insights for how governing elites can use external ties to their advantage. The literature on "extraversion" in African politics argues that political elites in postcolonial African countries have used relationships with foreign entities – former colonial powers, international organizations, and multinational firms – to achieve personal and political aims.[37] Peiffer and Englebert (2012) conceptualize African governments' different forms of engagement with the outside world as an "extraversion portfolio" and argue that countries with narrow extraversion portfolios, for instance those that depend on a single donor, are less effective at resisting pressures for institutional reform.

This approach is helpful for my analysis, highlighting how ties of seeming dependence, such as an increasing reliance on China for bilateral loans, can be a potential source of strength. While I am more

---

[35] OECD 2005.
[36] Chandy 2011; Rogerson 2005; Sjöstedt 2013.
[37] Bayart 2000, 2009; Clapham 1996.

focused on the implications of diversified finance for borrowing governments, rather than individual elites, I take from the literature on extraversion a focus on African states' agency in managing financial interdependence. On its own, however, an extraversion framework offers little account of how external actors are likely to respond to strategies of extraversion or when these efforts are likely to be successful. To understand how African governments' access to alternative forms of finance affects their relations with donors, one also needs an understanding of these donors' and creditors' motivations. My argument brings together donor and recipient motivations to understand how negotiations change under conditions of diversified finance.

1.3 A Diversified Portfolio of External Finance

While I focus my analysis of debt-based financial statecraft on sub-Saharan Africa[38] in the first decades of the twenty-first century, earlier phases of financial globalization saw other regions gain access to diverse sources of finance. From the late 1960s onward, developing countries in Latin America expanded their access to private finance, experimenting with "indebted industrialization" while they benefited from easy credit from recycled petrodollars and private lenders.[39] Many of these countries subsequently experienced debt crises when access to finance dried up and accumulated debt burdens proved too much to carry.[40] This historical parallel invites caution about the long-term economic sustainability of countries relying on private and market-rate finance, since the accumulation of expensive debt makes countries especially vulnerable to shocks. However, the focus of this book is not on the macroeconomic consequences of external borrowing, but rather on how borrowing in a time of plenty affects countries' foreign relations, specifically their relations with foreign donors.

---

[38] Regional boundaries necessarily entail somewhat arbitrary distinctions. I focus on sub-Saharan Africa and exclude North African countries in line with the common practice of international development agencies. This distinction follows on from different legacies of colonialism and decolonization, as well as differences in contemporary patterns of integration into the international economy.

[39] Devlin 1990; Frieden 1981.

[40] Frieden 1991.

For governments in sub-Saharan Africa, the expansion of financing options in the 2000s and 2010s was especially pronounced when contrasted with countries' earlier reliance on foreign aid from traditional donors. The greater array of financing options available to these countries was the result of three developments: widespread debt forgiveness, China's rise as an official lender, and abundant global liquidity that led private investors to lend to "frontier markets."

More than half of all sub-Saharan African countries received debt relief from international financial institutions and bilateral creditors in the 2000s.[41] Most African countries had accumulated large public debt burdens in the 1970s and 1980s, due to limited accountability for either borrowing governments or official lenders, extensive bilateral lending by advanced economies, and price shocks to resource exports that left government coffers empty and countries getting by on credit. By the 1990s, African governments had amassed large volumes of external debt, most of it owed to public lenders, for which they negotiated repeated payment extensions and delays. After concerted activist campaigns, Western governments and international financial institutions confronted the reality that developing countries' debt service was hampering economic development.[42] In 1996, multilateral institutions and creditor countries began a decade-long process of writing off portions of the debt of thirty-nine highly indebted poor countries, of which more than thirty were in sub-Saharan Africa.

Due to debt relief and the economic growth experienced by many African countries in the 2000s, the external debt of sub-Saharan African countries declined from a height of an average of 115 percent of GDP in 2000 to 41 percent of GDP in 2010 (see Figure 1.1). The substantial reductions in public debt made African governments more attractive to potential lenders. It may be surprising that debt relief enabled governments to borrow, if debt cancellation indicated that borrowers had been unable to meet their debt obligations. Yet, debt relief was explicitly framed as a one-time reduction in unsustainable and unproductive debt, with the intention of freeing up borrowing space for future loans.

The second phenomenon that dramatically increased the availability of external finance to African governments in the 2000s was the

---

[41] Birdsall et al. 2002; Bunte 2018.
[42] Blackmon 2017; Busby 2007.

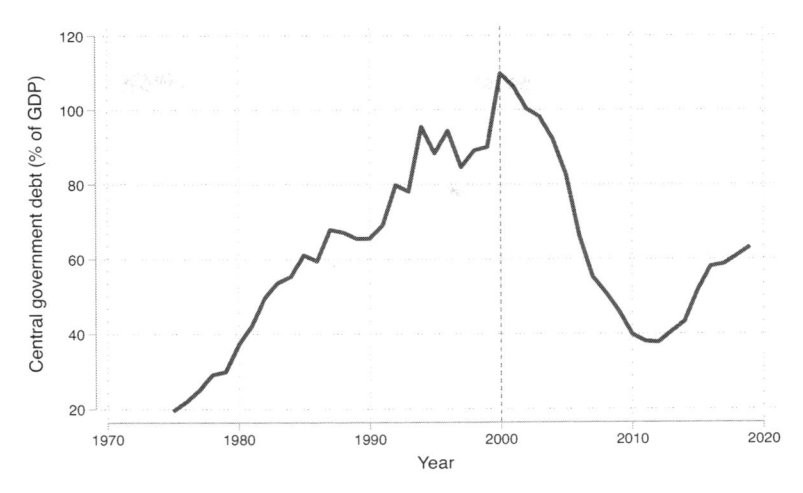

Figure 1.1 Average government debt in sub-Saharan Africa (% of GDP), 1975–2018.
Source: IMF Global Debt Database.

rise of emerging economies as bilateral lenders.[43] Brazil, China, India, Turkey, and various Gulf States all increased their loans to developing countries over the course of the 2000s (see Figure 1.2). Of these emerging lenders, China provided by far the largest amount of financing, using foreign exchange earnings accrued during decades of export-led economic growth to fund its lending program and deploying loans to support domestic firms' interests abroad.[44] Though other emerging donors may become more important in the future, China has been the only meaningful global alternative to traditional lenders and therefore this book focuses on China as the prominent new bilateral lender. While China has extended aid and loans to countries all over the world, sub-Saharan Africa has received the largest share of Chinese finance. Given sub-Saharan governments' previous dependence on traditional donors, the availability of Chinese aid and loans marked a stark change.

The third and final development reshaping African countries' access to external finance in 2000s and 2010s was international bond

---

[43] Brautigam 2011; Horn et al. 2021; Mawdsley 2012.
[44] Dreher et al. 2022; Horn et al. 2021; Kaplan 2021.

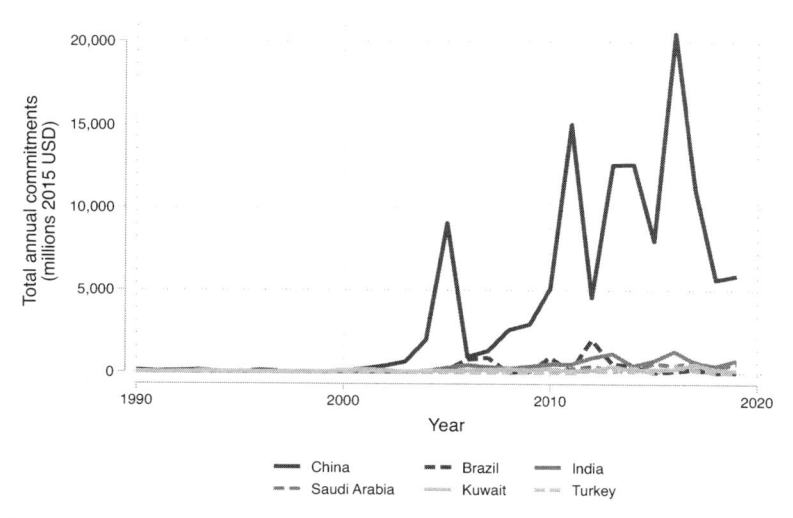

Figure 1.2 Nontraditional bilateral lenders' total annual commitments to sub-Saharan African countries, 1990–2019.
Source: World Bank International Debt Statistics.

markets investors' newfound willingness to lend to African governments.[45] As the yields on government bonds of wealthy countries plummeted with the accommodating monetary policy adopted during and after the global financial crisis (2007–08) and the Eurozone crisis (2009–mid 2010s), bond investors went on a "search for yield," looking for assets that would still generate sizable returns. Investors became willing to lend to first-time and riskier borrowers, dubbed "frontier markets." This greater risk appetite meant that investors exercised less scrutiny over institutions and policies in borrowing countries. Before this change in investor sentiment, the only sub-Saharan African country that had borrowed in international bond markets was South Africa. By 2018, sixteen African countries had issued international bonds (see Figure 1.3). Many of these countries issued repeatedly, returning to markets a number of times to take advantage of attractive interest rates. Not only were African governments able to borrow in global bond markets from which they had previously been excluded, but they also borrowed at appealing interest rates. As the *Financial Times* noted when Ethiopia issued its debut bond in 2014, the "relatively low yield

---

[45] Mecagni et al. 2014; Tyson 2015.

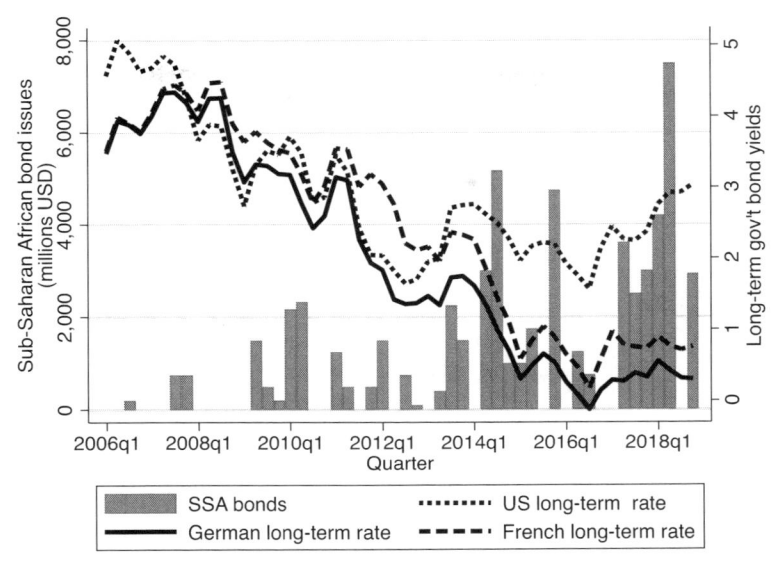

Figure 1.3 Quarterly volume of bond issues by sub-Saharan African countries and long-term yields of leading advanced economies, 2006–2018.
Sources: Capital IQ Database, *Bloomberg, Financial Times, Reuters*; Federal Reserve Bank of St. Louis.
Figure reproduced with permission from Zeitz (2021b) © Cambridge University Press.

of 6.625 per cent ... shows how years of ultra-lax monetary policy in the US, Europe and Japan is allowing countries on the fringes of the frontier market category to tap the international capital market at relatively low cost."[46]

The cumulative impact of these three trends – debt forgiveness, the rise of Chinese lending, and access to international bond markets – has been that traditional development finance, from bilateral donors in the Organisation of Economic Cooperation and Development's Development Assistance Committee (OECD DAC), the World Bank, and other multilateral development banks, has decreased as a share of developing countries' external finance. Figure 1.4 reports snapshots of low- and middle-income countries' composition of external finance in 1990, 2005, and 2018. The figure shows that traditional sources of external finance have been displaced by the two major alternative sources

[46] Blas 2014.

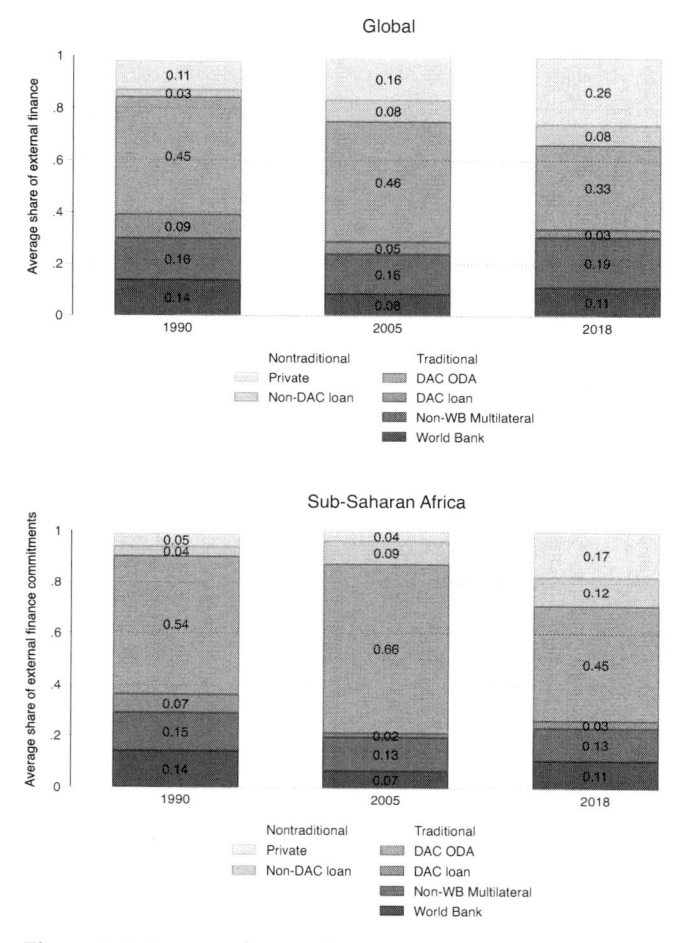

Figure 1.4 Average shares of external finance commitments by creditor and donor type in 1990, 2005, and 2018.
Sources: World Bank Debtor Reporting System; OECD Creditor Reporting System.

of finance: private loans and credit from non-DAC countries, primarily China. Globally, private finance has been the most important new source of finance for developing countries, increasing from an average of 11.3 percent of total external finance in 1990 to 25.5 percent of total external finance in 2018. For African countries, the rise of non-DAC lending has also been important in expanding the portfolio of external finance, with the share of finance coming from non-DAC lenders increasing from an average of 3.7 percent in 1990 to 11.7 percent in 2018.

Debt relief, China's loan program, and increased private lending were global trends. Nevertheless, there are good reasons to focus on the change in bargaining relationships in the African context. First, the increase in available finance was most dramatic for African countries. They were the greatest beneficiaries of debt relief and received the majority of Chinese-financed projects. Though developing countries in other regions were also able to borrow at attractive rates in international bond markets, sub-Saharan Africa had the largest number of first-time issuers during the bond boom. Furthermore, African governments' negotiations with traditional donors are a hard test of the argument that borrowing from alternate sources enhances negotiating power, since the agency and capacity of African governments is often assumed to be low, especially in relations with donors and creditors.[47] If these governments have been able to convert their greater variety of creditors into negotiating strength, it is likely that other governments also have this ability.

Moreover, the period from 2000 to 2018 is attractive for studying the consequences of countries' borrowing choices, since the increase in amount and diversity of finance was largely determined by factors outside of African governments' control. While not all African countries borrowed in global bond markets and China lent more to some African borrowers than to others, the transformation in available finance was the outcome of forces not under the direct influence of African governments. Similarly, governments had to meet set criteria to qualify for debt relief, but the timing of debt reduction was set by the schedules of global debt relief initiatives and almost all countries assessed as having unsustainable debt burdens were granted relief. The fact that the availability of finance was largely shaped by external shocks makes it easier to evaluate whether the diversity of a given government's creditors has an impact on the government's negotiating power, since it is less likely that a government's ability to attract varied sources of external finance is a function of the same underlying capacity that makes it more effective at negotiating with donors.

The year 2000 marks the beginning of this time of expanded access to finance. The Jubilee campaign for debt relief called for developing

[47] W. Brown and Harman 2013; Mohan and Lampert 2012.

countries' debt to be canceled by the start of the new millennium, and though debt relief fell far short of this goal, 2000 was a turning point in bilateral and multilateral debt relief efforts.[48] The dawn of the millennium also saw an initial increase in Chinese lending. In 1999, China announced its "Going Out" strategy, which heralded a step-change in China's overseas financing efforts.[49]

Two decades later, the window of opportunity for borrowing governments appeared to be closing. In March 2018, the IMF released a report sounding the alarm that low-income countries faced an increased risk of debt crisis, in large part due to new, commercial sources of finance.[50] A year later, the Chinese government announced debt sustainability concerns for a number of borrowers, saying it would adopt international standards on project screening and preparation in response, suggesting a slowdown in Chinese lending and potential convergence in official creditor practices and potentially reducing the diversity of financing.[51] Moreover, the volume of Chinese bilateral lending declined after 2018, as an economic slowdown in China combined with borrower repayment difficulties to lead to fewer loan agreements.

The final and unexpected shock that brought the period of plenty to an end came in 2020, when the COVID-19 pandemic plunged the global economy into turmoil. Countries that had accumulated large amounts of debt in the preceding decades were especially vulnerable to the sudden stop of capital flows to developing countries prompted by the economic shutdown. Within months of the onset of the pandemic, Zambia defaulted on its bond debt, becoming the first African country to default in the pandemic era.[52] Analysts that had cautiously warned of debt accumulation in the years leading up to the pandemic now worried about a full-blown debt crisis.

The expansion of credit to African governments in the 2000s and 2010s made debt-based financial statecraft possible, offering a window of opportunity in which new creditors were an alternative to traditional donors, increasing governments' autonomy and potentially

[48] Busby 2007.
[49] Fuchs and Rudyak 2019.
[50] IMF 2018.
[51] Dreher et al. 2022.
[52] Smith 2020.

their bargaining strength. At the same time, the accumulation of debt made countries more vulnerable to crisis. The fragility of countries that expanded and diversified their portfolio of external finance makes clear the economic and political risks associated with this strategy. As the head of the World Bank's economic forecasting unit observed in 2022, "Market access is a wonderful thing to have when there is cheap money out there, but there might be a different view as conditions tighten."[53] By focusing on the consequences of diversified finance during a time of plenty, this book can also help explain why countries accumulate debt burdens that leave them vulnerable in a downswing of the global capital cycle.

1.4 Contributions

This book contributes to the literature on economic interdependence, international finance, and development aid. It argues that countries can – under certain conditions – use asymmetric interdependence to their advantage and shows this phenomenon at work. Expanding the understanding of the consequences of economic interdependence for developing countries thus constitutes the book's first contribution. Without being overly sanguine about the terms on which developing countries are integrated into the international financial system, the book suggests these countries can benefit from relationships of asymmetric interdependence. Specifying and illustrating how developing countries can use these tools, despite their weaker position in the international economy, advances scholarship on economic and financial statecraft. The analysis of African countries' debt-based financial statecraft opens the way for other analyses of countries using asymmetric interdependence to their advantage.

Second, by drawing attention to the role of private finance in developing countries' portfolios of external finance, this book contributes to a growing literature on systemic dynamics in international political economy.[54] Changes in the composition of global capital flows have knock-on effects, including for crisis management and political development.[55] In this case, the rise of private finance for African borrowers

---

[53] Wheatley 2022.
[54] Ballard-Rosa et al. 2019; Bauerle Danzman et al. 2017; Oatley et al. 2013.
[55] Copelovitch 2010; Queralt 2022.

was caused in large part by investors' greater risk acceptance during a phase of loose monetary policy in advanced economies. The evidence in this book points to a surprising spillover of advanced economies' monetary policy, namely that it enhanced developing countries' bargaining power with donors. More broadly, the book highlights the importance of systemic factors – global liquidity conditions, the rise of emerging powers, and the composition of global capital flows – in shaping donor–recipient negotiations.

Third, the book examines the effect of countries' *portfolios* of external finance, reflecting the full diversity of developing countries' sources of external finance, from grant aid to market-rate loans. The literatures on sovereign debt and foreign aid have largely evolved separately, since the motivations of lenders and donors are very different. The former are primarily interested in being repaid, while the latter are interested in development outcomes and dialogue with the recipient government. And yet, from the perspective of a recipient government, loans and aid are different ends of the same spectrum, with trade-offs between them. By investigating the consequences of diversity within the portfolio of external finance, this book adds to a growing literature on borrowing governments' agency in choosing among sources of external finance.

Finally, with respect to foreign aid and development policy, the book describes the consequences of a more diverse financing landscape from the perspective of recipient countries. Much scholarship and commentary has focused on the emergence of new donors, but a large share of it has focused on the motivations and behaviors of these new donors or the implications of their emergence for traditional donors.[56] By contrast, this book builds on research on countries' choice of creditors and turns the focus to recipient governments themselves, identifying how the rise of new donors affects their negotiating leverage.[57] This focus on borrowing countries enriches our understanding of the changing development finance landscape and economic multipolarity, contributing perspectives from outside the expanding core of the international economy.

[56] Dreher et al. 2018; Strange et al. 2017; Swedlund 2017a.
[57] Bunte 2019; Greenhill et al. 2013.

1.5 Plan of the Book and Preview of Findings

The book is structured as follows. **Chapter 2** presents the theoretical argument. It explains how donor and recipient preferences interact in negotiations over foreign aid and outlines the argument that borrowing from alternative creditors can increase a recipient government's leverage in aid negotiations. I describe the mechanism underpinning the financial statecraft of borrowers, namely that recipients' reduced reliance induces donors to offer more attractive aid, and contrast it with alternative arguments based only on geopolitical competition among donors. Moreover, I develop my argument for when developing countries are most likely to benefit from relations with new creditors in their negotiations with traditional donors, which is when a donor especially values the relationship with the recipient government and when donor trust in the recipient is high. When these two conditions – importance to donors and donor trust – align, and a developing country diversifies its portfolio of external finance, then the recipient government is likely to be able to shift the relationship with traditional donors in line with its preferences.

To test this argument, the book combines different sources of evidence across the remaining chapters. Cross-national data on aid flows from OECD bilateral donors and major multilateral donors allows for tests of the association between a recipient country's portfolio of external finance and the terms of their aid from traditional donors, as well as tests for heterogeneity based on recipient importance and donor trust. I complement this analysis with three in-depth case studies of Ethiopia, Kenya, and Ghana, in which I trace how the agreements reached with donors did, or did not, change as the country diversified its sources of finance.

The statistical analysis is reported in **Chapter 3**. The chapter first provides an overview of the changes in developing countries' portfolios of external finance from the 1990s to the late 2010s, demonstrating that while countries in sub-Saharan Africa continued to receive large volumes of traditional aid, these countries also experienced the greatest reduction in their reliance on traditional sources of development finance. Drawing on this data, I assemble indicators of developing countries' reduced reliance on traditional donors, measured as the share of a country's total external finance coming from China, private creditors, or both. To capture outcomes in the relationship between developing countries and traditional donors, I use three measures: the total volume of aid provided by a donor to a recipient, the share of donor aid allocated to the infrastructure sector, and the number of conditions attached to World Bank projects. I show that developing countries that increase the share of finance coming from alternative creditors receive higher volumes of aid from traditional donors, more infrastructure funding, and fewer conditions attached to aid. These broad patterns hold across developing countries but are most pronounced among sub-Saharan African countries. To investigate heterogeneity among developing countries, I use measures of recipient country importance, namely temporary UN Security Council membership and the presence of US military bases, as well as donor trust in the recipient, including budgeting performance scores, corruption perception, and a categorization of the recipient country's political settlement. The results indicate that recipient importance, and especially donor trust, lead to a stronger association between borrowing from alternative creditors and more generous aid terms.

Having shown that borrowing from alternative creditors is associated with preferred aid terms across developing countries, I turn to the case studies to test the mechanisms by which this happens. **Chapter 4** introduces the comparative case analysis, explaining the rationale for case selection, describing the approach to data collection, and providing context on each of the three cases. I focus on three countries – Ethiopia, Kenya, and Ghana – that all borrowed from China and in international bond markets.

I selected these cases based on two attributes that, in my argument, should enable debt-based financial statecraft: significance to donors and donor trust in recipient credibility. There is variation across and within the three countries on these attributes in the period between 2000 and 2018. Broadly, Ethiopia was a case with high importance to donors and high donor trust, while Kenya was characterized by high importance and low donor trust, and Ghana was of declining importance to donors and had low donor trust. Variation in these perceptions over time and across different donors generates different combinations within each case that reveal how recipient-country attributes interact with the recipient's portfolio of external finance to shape aid negotiations. Though none of the case study countries is solidly in the category of low importance and high trust, one or another of the cases does hold this status with certain donors at specific points in time, as with donors in Ethiopia that are less sensitive to the country's geopolitical importance, or donors in Ghana that were less distrustful of the government's credibility. Comparison across the cases and over time thus tests expectations about conditions that enhance or inhibit debt-based financial statecraft.

Analysis within each case tests the mechanism at the heart of debt-based financial statecraft, investigating whether borrowing from alternative creditors altered the donor–recipient relationship because the government reduced its reliance on traditional donors and donors were willing to accommodate the government's preferences to retain the relationship. The data for this analysis comes largely from interviews with government and donor negotiators conducted during fieldwork research in Accra, Nairobi, Addis Ababa, New York, and Washington D.C. in August–October 2013 and January–August 2017. More than 170 elite interviews reveal aspects of aid negotiations that are not always documented in official publications, allowing me to trace how the dynamics and outcomes of negotiations shifted as the governments borrowed from alternative creditors.

A benefit of the case studies for the research design of the book is that they allow for a more fine-grained measure of the outcome variable. To best capture the outcome of interest – the extent to which aid agreements align with the recipient government's preferences, rather than donors' interests – it is necessary to identify the recipient government's priorities and which areas of recipient–donor negotiations were most contentious. In each of the cases, I draw on interviews, public documents, and media reporting to ascertain which areas of negotiations were the most sensitive and what each side's preferred outcomes would have been. I then trace outcomes in these issue areas over time, identifying whether variation in the outcomes is attributable to the recipient government's reduced reliance on donors and to donors' assessments of the recipient's importance and the credibility of recipient commitments.

In broad terms, three issue areas recurred in negotiations across all the cases: governance and democratization, macroeconomic and development policy, and financial management. Table 1.1 shows the pattern of outcomes across the cases in these three areas. In Ethiopia, where all three areas were contentious in negotiations with donors, the government was largely successful in aligning the terms of aid agreements

Table 1.1 *Main negotiation areas and outcomes across the three cases*

Issue	Ethiopia	Kenya	Ghana
Governance and democratization	⇑	⇑	
Macroeconomic and development policy	⇑		⇓
Financial management	⇑	⇓	⇓

Outcomes are denoted as follows:
⇑ indicates an outcome aligned with recipient government preferences.
⇓ indicates an outcome diverging from recipient government preferences.

with its interests during the period when it enjoyed the greatest access to alternative finance. As reported in the Ethiopian case in **Chapter 5**, these outcomes were sometimes informal, as when donors avoided discussions over issues of governance and democratization to avoid antagonizing the government, and other times formal, as when donors agreed to fund the construction of industrial parks that were core to the government's development plans. The Ethiopian government's relative success in shifting the relationship with donors in line with its interests during a time of diversified finance was largely due to the significance donors attached to their relationship with the government, as well as donors' confidence that the government would adhere to aid agreements.

The Kenyan case, presented in **Chapter 6**, shows an uneven track record of debt-based financial statecraft. Here, the issue areas where donors and the government were far apart were governance and democratization, as well as financial management. While donors moderated their criticism of governance issues in an apparent response to the government's increase in borrowing from alternative sources, donors did not accommodate the government's preference for flexibility around financial management. These differences across issue areas are attributable to donors' assessment of Kenya's strategic importance and their concerns about the government's credibility in upholding aid agreements and development plans. For most donors, especially large bilateral donors, Kenya is an important regional security partner. These donors were especially sensitive to Kenya's reduced reliance on donor funds and inclined to moderate their stances on governance issues in response. When it came to financial management, however, Kenya struggled due to limited donor trust in the government's credibility.

Although Kenya diversified its portfolio of external finance and articulated a preference for greater donor flexibility on financial management issues, donors were reluctant to accommodate this preference because of their concerns about corruption and weak institutional capacity.

In Ghana, the government had even more difficulties than the Kenyan government in translating its access to alternative finance into preferred outcomes in negotiations with traditional donors. As described in **Chapter 7**, the main areas of negotiation between the government and donors were over macroeconomic and development policy and financial management. Though the government secured a few victories in traditional donor support for priority development projects as it diversified its external finance to include Chinese loans and bond market finance, it ultimately struggled to shift relations in line with its preferences, with donors at one point withholding their aid funds to persuade the government to accept economic reforms. Despite reducing its reliance on traditional donor funds, Ghana did not see a consistent increase in its negotiating leverage with donors because of the country's reduced importance to donors and donors' concerns about the government's credibility. Historically, Ghana's close relationship with traditional donors has been buoyed by the strength of Ghana's democratic institutions and its progress in economic reforms. When donors attributed Ghana's economic crisis to government mismanagement, the country's symbolic value to several donors began to wane, leading those donors to place less of a priority on maintaining favorable relations with the government. Moreover, donors' lack of trust in the credibility of the government's commitments made them cautious about meeting the government's preferences for flexibility with respect to economic policy and financial management, despite the government's increasing autonomy from donor funds.

The conclusion in **Chapter 8** draws together the evidence from across the case studies and the quantitative analysis and provides additional illustrations of debt-based financial statecraft in Uganda, Senegal, and Laos. The conclusion highlights implications for policymakers, both in developing countries and in donor agencies. The findings indicate that governments that cultivate greater donor confidence will have more success in translating alternative finance into bargaining leverage. Moreover, the case studies highlight the benefits of a clear strategy for the diversification of external finance and a deliberate negotiation approach that deploys any increased bargaining leverage for specific priorities. For donor officials, the findings suggest the benefit of identifying areas where donors can be especially valuable to recipient governments, which can include specializing in distinct market niches.

The conclusion ends with a reflection on future prospects for debt-based financial statecraft. The period of expanding finance in the 2000s and especially the 2010s has been followed in subsequent years by sharp contractions in lending, government defaults, and fears of a widespread debt crisis in the developing world. I suggest that while some of the lessons from a time of abundance are transferable to a time of scarcity, debt crises also reveal the risks and possible limitations of debt-based financial statecraft. Moreover, to appropriately address the realities of countries' diverse portfolios of external finance in a time of vulnerability to debt crisis, the sovereign debt regime will need to be broadened and strengthened.

2 | Theory: The Financial Statecraft of Borrowers

In late 2002, the Zambian government was locked in tense negotiations with its donors. The two sides worked to finalize a debt relief deal, haggling over an agreement that would reduce the mountain of public debt hampering Zambia's economic growth. To receive relief, Zambia had to agree with donors on a wide range of reforms, the most sensitive of which were privatizations of state-owned companies in electricity, banking, telecommunications, and copper. Elected in 2001 on a "New Deal" platform after a slate of privatizations had already been agreed upon, the government of Levy Mwanawasa faced widespread public protests against the proposed privatizations. Responding to the protests, Mwanawasa declared he would renegotiate the terms of debt relief and aid. Yet those renegotiation efforts proved difficult. The country was heavily reliant on donors for external finance, giving these donors an upper hand in negotiations. The IMF resident representative in Lusaka at the time dryly spelled out the country's lack of alternatives, saying "If they don't sell, they will not get the money."[1] Ultimately, the government backed down, agreeing to privatize each of the state-owned firms.

A decade later, Zambia's more diverse portfolio of external finance created possibilities for the government to assert its preferences in negotiations with donors. With more alternative finance available, the Zambian government revisited and reversed some of the privatizations of the early 2000s, including the telecommunications company Zamtel, which was renationalized in 2012. Observing this policy shift, one scholar attributed it to "the availability of money for 'homegrown' development projects" from new creditors, especially China.[2] At the same time, Zambia appears to have benefited less from its reduced

---

[1] Fraser 2007, p. 23.
[2] Kragelund 2014, p. 158.

reliance than might be expected. A different analyst concluded "there is little evidence that the [Zambian government] has used the emergence of [alternative finance] to bolster its negotiating influence."[3] The government was hampered by corruption scandals that "weakened [traditional donors'] perception of Zambia as a responsible aid recipient" and by a domestic political context that meant the country "struggled to articulate clear priorities or take a strategic approach to managing donors."[4]

The Zambian example illustrates both the potential and the challenge of debt-based financial statecraft. As the government borrowed from new lenders, it reduced its dependence on traditional donors and, with that greater autonomy, was able to implement policies that donors had previously questioned. However, the government appears also to have been constrained by donors' lack of trust and its own domestic politics.

The core argument of this book is that borrowing relationships have the potential to enhance developing countries' bargaining leverage. As countries diversify their portfolios of external finance, they are able to bargain more assertively with traditional donors, obtaining greater influence in aid negotiations. I use the shorthand of "donors" or "traditional donors" to refer to the Western, industrialized countries that have historically provided the vast majority of development assistance and are members of the Organisation of Economic Cooperation and Development's Development Assistance Committee (OECD DAC), as well as leading multilateral donors including the World Bank, African Development Bank, and the United Nations (UN).[5] The focus on traditional donors is because these donors long held a monopoly on the provision of external finance, meaning that recipients' turn to alternative finance reduces traditional donors' influence, thereby encouraging these donors to offer more attractive aid to retain their relationship.

I suggest that developing countries' ability to use new borrowing relationships as a source of bargaining leverage is a form of financial statecraft, building on the concept of economic statecraft, which

---

[3] Prizzon 2013, p. 16.

[4] Prizzon 2013, pp. 7, 6.

[5] Though it is not a provider of long-term development finance, the International Monetary Fund (IMF) is also an important actor in the broader relationship between developing countries and their donors, since the IMF provides assessments of macroeconomic and development policy that guide the approach of other donors, especially in crisis contexts.

refers to countries using relationships of economic interdependence to achieve foreign policy goals. While this strategic deployment of economic or financial ties is usually seen as a tool of economically powerful and central states, I highlight how developing countries reliant on external finance can use their borrowing relationships as a source of leverage.

A borrowing country's move to diversify its portfolio of external finance has an impact on relations with donors because donors compete in a *marketplace* for aid. Donor agencies exist to disburse aid and to cultivate close relationships with recipients; this purpose is threatened if recipient governments choose to source more of their development finance from alternative sources. Confronted with competition from alternative creditors, donors will not simply close up shop, but will innovate to retain market share. As a result, I expect that developing countries that borrow from a wider range of creditors will have greater leverage to push for their preferred aid agreements from traditional donors.

Greater autonomy from donor funds is especially likely to increase bargaining leverage when donors place a high value on their relationship with a particular recipient government, whether because the recipient is a strategic ally or reliably delivers development results. In those cases, recipients are more likely to be able to convert their diverse portfolio of external finance into greater leverage with traditional donors. The inverse is also true. Developing countries that are not particularly significant to donors or that do not have donors' trust will struggle to translate alternative finance into greater negotiating leverage with donors.

This chapter presents this argument in a number of steps. First, I draw on the literature on foreign aid to introduce a schematic framework of aid negotiations based on what donors and recipients want in the aid relationship. Then, I introduce my argument for how, given these preferences, aid negotiations change when developing countries borrow from alternative creditors and diversify their portfolios of external finance. I explain how both bilateral loans and private market finance reduce developing countries' reliance on traditional donors, leading to negotiation outcomes more aligned with the recipient's preferences. I then set out why some countries are more successful at debt-based financial statecraft than others. The chapter concludes by situating the argument within the broader literature on economic statecraft.

2.1 Aid Negotiations

When the government of a developing country and an aid donor negotiate, each side brings their own interests to the table. The interplay of those interests shapes the terms of aid agreements. Understanding what each set of actors wants from the other helps to explain when recipient governments are more influential in negotiations, as well as how the relationship changes when the government borrows from a wider variety of lenders.

2.1.1 What a Donor Wants

My argument begins from the premise that donors have strong motivations to provide aid and to maintain the relationship with developing countries that their aid affords them. As I will explain, constraints on the recipient government's time, range of policy choices, and ability to absorb external funds mean that donors compete in a marketplace for aid, seeking to provide attractive aid that preserves their access to the recipient government. The reasons for giving aid to developing countries differ by donor country and institution. Some donors are interested primarily in improving development outcomes. Others may be concerned with having the government's ear on security issues. In both cases, donors require a close relationship with the recipient government, one that allows them to have some say on recipient policy. A key part of the aid relationship for the donor is the access it affords to the recipient country. A donor's wish to exercise some influence makes the donor at least partly dependent on the governments to which they give aid. The bargaining framework underpinning debt-based financial statecraft assumes that donors want to maintain their influence with the recipient government, which can emerge out of various motivations.

Conventionally, scholarship on foreign aid has suggested two sets of reasons that rich countries give aid.[6] First, there are motivations grouped under a heading of "altruistic" aid. In this understanding, donors give aid because they want to reduce poverty and support economic growth in developing countries. A second set of donor motivations can be grouped under the category of "self-interested" aid.

---

[6] Alesina and Dollar 2000; Dreher et al. 2013; Fuchs et al. 2014.

Donors may provide aid because they hope it will yield benefits for the donor country.[7] These benefits can be indirect, as when donors hope that giving aid improves their global "soft power," or they can be direct quid pro quo benefits, as when large sums of aid are committed to military allies or important trading partners.

Recent research suggests that a dichotomous understanding of donor motivations – driven either by recipient need or donor self-interest – is not appropriate for contemporary development aid. Instead, it is often in donors' self-interest to consider recipients' need and pursue "targeted development."[8] Advanced economies can be directly affected by the spillovers of underdevelopment, whether by mass migration arising from instability in fragile states or climate change accelerated by carbon-intensive development.[9] The increasing interdependence of the contemporary era only heightens advanced economies' susceptibility to the spillovers of underdevelopment. Therefore, it may be in rich countries' self-interest to support development in poorer countries.[10]

Regardless of a donor's ultimate motivation, whether enlightened self-interest through targeted development or straightforward self-regard, the important point for the purpose of understanding donor–recipient negotiations is that the donor want some influence over recipient country policy. While it might seem obvious that donors driven by self-interested motivations want to shape recipient policy, it can be more controversial to suggest that donors interested in supporting development also want to influence recipient government policy. And yet, even donors that primarily seek to encourage growth and poverty reduction in developing countries will expect some say in government policy.[11] These donors want to foster the institutions and policies they believe will achieve long-term improvements in development. Contemporary foreign aid rests on what development practitioners call "policy dialogue" between the government and donors, in which donors provide policy advice together with their aid.[12] Donors such as the World Bank or African Development Bank have amassed

---

[7] Kilby and Dreher 2010.
[8] Bermeo 2017.
[9] Bermeo 2018.
[10] Bermeo 2017; Gulrajani and Calleja 2019.
[11] Swedlund 2017b, pp. 26–27.
[12] Molenaers 2012; Swedlund 2017b, pp. 60–62.

experience across developing countries, and their aid programs rest on the expectation that they can extend this expertise to recipient governments, improving development policy in the process. Thus, even donors that are primarily motivated to improve development outcomes want access to and influence with the recipient government.

However, influence with the recipient government is a finite resource. There are limits to the numbers of donors that recipient officials can meet with and, more importantly, there are constraints on the amount of development finance that a recipient government can take on. Moreover, in some areas, a developing country's policy choices can be zero-sum, such that the choice to pursue one donor's preferred policy precludes the recommended policy of another donor.[13] Given these constraints on the side of the recipients, donors are engaged in something like a marketplace for aid, wanting to provide attractive that preserves their relationship with and access to the recipient government. Donors' reasons for wanting access to the recipient government vary depending on the ultimate motivation for providing aid, but foreign aid can reasonably be seen as an instrument of foreign policy, as well as development policy.[14] Competing to provide attractive aid is thus part of broader competition in foreign policy. For instance, research has found that donors compete with one another for access to export markets in developing countries, leading them to offer larger amounts of aid to outweigh the influence efforts of other donors.[15]

Competition in the marketplace for aid is further compounded by the bureaucratic and institutional incentives of aid agencies.[16] Bureaucrats working for donor agencies are evaluated on their ability to implement aid programs. The success of these programs is assessed based on their concrete achievements, but there is also a simple baseline expectation that programs be completed and funds disbursed.[17] This means that donors have an interest in maintaining their relationship with the recipient government so they can continue to operate aid programs and disburse funds. Furthermore, there are incentives for donors to carve out areas of the aid relationship where they can

---

[13] Bueno de Mesquita and Smith 2016.
[14] Lancaster 2007.
[15] Barthel et al. 2014.
[16] Svensson 2003.
[17] Yanguas and Hulme 2015, p. 214.

demonstrate the impact of their aid to domestic audiences, encouraging donors to compete to defend their specialized relationship with the government.

Recognizing that competition among donors can undermine development objectives, some donors have endeavored to coordinate their aid efforts. Industrialized donors have used the OECD DAC to set shared standards for their aid. DAC donors also often actively coordinate their aid within recipient countries. In a given area, such as health, education, or energy, donors may establish sector working groups to coordinate with the government and develop shared programming. In the 2000s and 2010s, many DAC donors even pooled large quantities of their aid and provided it as joint budget support to developing country governments.[18] This coordination among DAC donors reduces transactions for recipient governments, but it also limits the possibilities of securing attractive aid offers from rival donors. This "cross-conditionality" among traditional DAC donors can make it harder for developing country governments to push for their preferred aid deals.[19] Despite these efforts at coordination, aid "harmonization" among traditional donors has often faltered because donors nonetheless wish to establish a distinct profile for themselves, carving out aid projects where they can signal their value to the recipient government and demonstrate their impact to domestic audiences.[20] Even among like-minded donors, the difficulties of coordination thus show the marketplace for aid at work. Emerging providers of development finance, including China, have not participated in coordinating mechanisms.

Donors also take different approaches in the aid relationship depending on the recipient country in question. I suggest that two factors – the importance of the recipient country to the donor's specific goals and the donor's trust in the recipient government – shape the donor's approach to the aid relationship and impact how bargaining changes when the government diversifies its portfolio of finance, as I explain later in this chapter. Some donors have an interest in extracting strategic quid pro quos, other in improving development outcomes, and others in demonstrating the public value of their aid,

[18] Swedlund 2017b.
[19] Rogerson 2005.
[20] Sjöstedt 2013.

and they are all reliant on access to recipient governments to achieve these outcomes. Recipient countries differ in the extent to which they can help donors meet their specific goals. Due to geographic location, for instance, one developing country might be much more important than another for a donor hoping to achieve security objectives with their aid. Alternatively, a recipient country with a well-organized bureaucracy may be better placed to deliver on development policy, helping a donor achieve its objective of improving development outcomes. Recipients that are particularly valuable to a donor can expect that donor to offer more attractive aid to retain their relationship and influence with the government.

When donors place strategic value on their relationship with a particular recipient country, they are more likely to accede to the government's requests, providing more aid or extending it on more flexible terms.[21] This is especially true for bilateral donors, where aid policies are shaped by national politics. By contrast, multilateral donors such as the World Bank are expected to overcome national pressures to extend aid on the basis of self-interest, by pooling resources and delegating decisions over aid allocation to international bureaucrats.[22] Although multilateral institutions combine the interests of many shareholders and may be expected to be more neutral toward recipient countries, research shows that powerful shareholders can influence the decision-making of multilateral donors such that these agencies give preferential treatment to recipient countries.[23] For instance, when recipient countries are politically aligned with the United States, they receive loans from the World Bank even when they have weak macroeconomic conditions.[24] Both bilateral and multilateral donors thus place some value on maintaining their relationships with strategically important countries.

In summary, what donors want out of their negotiations with recipient governments is to have access to the recipient government and some influence over recipient policy, which helps them to achieve their goals in foreign aid. Aid is a tool of foreign policy as well as development policy, and donors are thus incentivized to provide attractive aid

[21] Alesina and Dollar 2000.
[22] Milner 2006.
[23] Clark and Dolan 2020.
[24] Kilby 2009.

in order to secure access to the recipient government. Competing for access to the government's scarce time and influence over policy choice, donors are engaged in a marketplace for aid. Traditional donors' efforts at donor coordination are, in part, attempts to overcome this competition, but alternative creditors operate outside these coordinating mechanisms, introducing the potential for greater competition that may be to the recipient's advantage.

2.1.2 *What a Recipient Wants*

If the unifying theme of donors' diverse motives for providing aid is a desire to shape recipient policy, what is it that recipient governments want out of the aid relationship?[25] Most immediately, the relationship with donors provides recipient governments with access to aid resources. Broadly speaking, recipient governments would prefer to receive more aid funds, rather than fewer. Foreign aid, even when structured as loans rather than grants, is cheaper than loans from banks or sovereign bond markets, and it supplements the often scarce tax revenue to help governments pay for development expenses and other spending. Even when donors bypass the government and distribute aid through NGOs, higher quantities of foreign aid free up government spending. When donors and recipients negotiate over aid, therefore, one dimension of the negotiations is the amount of aid that the donor extends to the country in question.

Though recipient governments would prefer to receive more aid than less, they also want to limit the political price they pay for this aid. The second dimension that recipient governments and donors bargain over in aid negotiations is the flexibility granted to the recipient government in implementing policies covered by the aid agreement. Tensions can arise because donors and recipients have different policy preferences or

---

[25] In characterizing aid negotiations, I describe the interactions between donor agencies and the recipient government. Which precise institution or agency represents the recipient government in negotiations will vary by country, though it is usually the Ministry of Finance that takes the lead. There is obviously heterogeneity within the recipient country on preferences with respect to donors, and the opposition or civil society organizations may have different preferences from the ruling government. I focus on the preferences of the government in power.

frameworks for how to achieve economic development.[26] A developing country government, for instance, might want to expand and subsidize electricity generation to support an emerging manufacturing sector, while donors would prefer to support sustainable agricultural practices among smallholder farmers. Negotiations over which projects to fund with donor aid are thus negotiations over how much to bring donor resources in line with government preferences and how much flexibility to give recipient governments in defining their own policy priorities.

Different approaches to foreign aid over time have given recipients more or less flexibility in setting development priorities. From the mid 2000s to the mid 2010s, donors' use of budget support – in which donors transfer resources directly to the recipient's budget, helping to pay for a share of the government's spending – was intended to align aid most closely with the recipient's policy goals.[27] However, given donors' desire for oversight and their need to be accountable to domestic publics, negotiations around budget support often required recipients to make substantial policy commitments to access this flexible form of finance. Even when the format of aid is intended to give recipients substantial autonomy and flexibility, recipient governments and donors still bargain over the policies and initiatives that aid will support. A central feature of negotiations between aid donors and recipient governments is the effort to reconcile donors' preference for influence with recipient governments' preference for autonomy.

Donors and recipients find themselves negotiating over the extent of control exercised by each side even when both sides agree on the goals of development, such as the weight given to economic growth or social inclusion, or the appropriate policies for achieving these goals. Even when the government and a donor have similar approaches to development policy, the government can have a more foundational interest in retaining discretion and autonomy. Governments are reluctant to acquiesce to outside authority that might undermine their status, as Kahler describes in his work on negotiations between the IMF and developing countries in the 1980s, observing, "governments will seek to preserve their policymaking autonomy against external directives;

[26] Whitfield and Fraser 2009, pp. 37–38.
[27] Swedlund 2017b.

the appearance of subordination to such directives may lower their legitimacy and therefore their ability to implement chosen policies."[28] The recipient government's preference for autonomy and discretion could manifest as pushing for donors to provide budget support, to fund government priority projects, or to limit their public commentary on the government's policies. This dimension of recipient–donor negotiations is, at root, about the extent of autonomy or control, even if the substantive content of negotiations differs between countries and over time. Recipients and donors rarely have diametrically opposed preferences, and it may even be in the recipient government's interest to attribute unpopular reforms to the influence of external actors.[29] Nevertheless, in relationships between developing country governments and aid donors, there is an underlying tension over the extent of autonomy over policy, even if this is only manifest in contentious issue areas.

Some developing countries are better than others at achieving flexibility and autonomy in their relationships with donors. These differences among recipient countries partly due to the donor's interest in the aid relationship, as explained earlier. When donors place a particular value on their relationship with the recipient government, they are likely to offer the recipient more attractive aid to preserve the quality of the relationship, granting the recipient greater discretion in aid negotiations. Donor valuing of the relationship is not, however, the only factor to affect recipient success in negotiation. Attributes of the recipient government also affect whether recipients tend to be more or less successful in negotiations.

Crucially, recipients differ in the extent to which they rely on donor aid. For some developing countries, aid makes up a very large share of public spending in the recipient country. For instance, in Malawi, aid amounted to 127 percent of government expenses in 2016.[30] When recipients are more dependent on donor aid, they cannot afford to be selective about which foreign aid they will accept. With little leverage in negotiations, these governments are more likely to agree to aid terms that grant them less flexibility over development policy. By contrast, developing country governments that collect larger amounts of domestic revenue, whether from natural resource wealth or a larger tax base, are less reliant on foreign aid, even if they continue to receive aid. These governments can be more selective about the aid they accept, negotiating more assertively with donors over the terms of aid, insisting that aid agreements grant them greater flexibility and discretion. Since donors operate in a marketplace of aid, they have incentives to respond by accommodating recipients' preferences. As I explain later in this section, donors' concern for market share is the main channel by which borrowing from alternative creditors affects negotiations between recipients and donors; recipients that diversify their portfolio of external finance become less reliant on traditional donors and better able achieve preferred terms in their aid agreements.

2.1.3 How Donor and Recipient Preferences Interact in Negotiations

Knowing what donors and recipient governments want out of aid relationships helps to generate expectations about when aid agreements are more likely to satisfy recipients' preferences. To simplify, the issues at stake in an aid negotiation can be collapsed into a single dimension, namely the amount of control each side exercises over policy in the recipient country. Of course, ultimate authority for domestic policy rests with the recipient government, but conceptualizing aid negotiations as bargaining over influence captures the extent to which donors or the recipient government shape policy in areas where donors provide aid. This framework builds on an extensive and diverse literature in foreign aid that has analyzed the relationship between donors and recipients through a bargaining lens.[31]

With preferences collapsed into the single dimension of donor versus recipient influence, the interaction between a recipient and a given donor can be analyzed in a simple bargaining framework, as illustrated in Figure 2.1. In these diagrams, the important points are each side's reservation and ideal points. The donor is marked "D," while the recipient government is marked "R." The reservation point is the least favorable outcome an actor is willing to accept, while the ideal point is

---

[31] Bueno de Mesquita and Smith 2009; Kahler 1993; P. Mosley 1986, 1987; Swedlund 2017b; Whitfield 2009b.

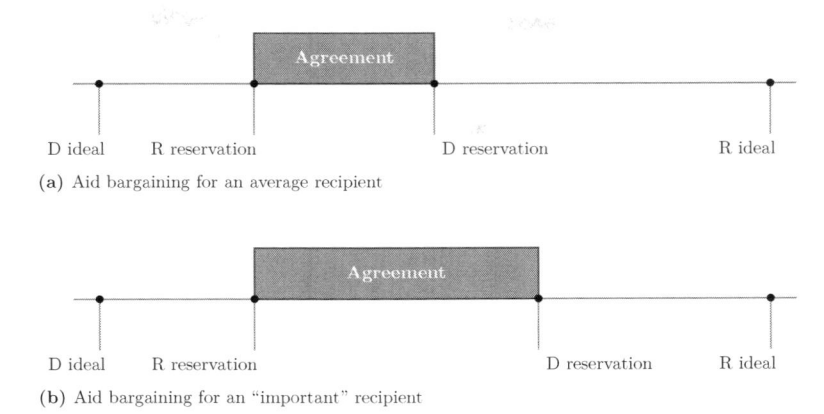

(a) Aid bargaining for an average recipient

(b) Aid bargaining for an "important" recipient

Figure 2.1 Donor–recipient negotiations.

their preferred outcome.[32] An actor's reservation point is determined by what other options they have available if they walk away from these negotiations. The area between the two sides' reservation points shows the area of possible agreement; the outcomes within this area would be acceptable to both sides.

Panels (a) and (b) of Figure 2.1 shows a bargaining dynamic where the recipient country has few alternatives to traditional donors as sources of external finance. This was the situation of most developing countries during the 1990s and early 2000s, and some developing countries even as access to alternative finance expanded in the 2000s and 2010s. In both panels, the recipient government's reservation point is far from its ideal point. The government is willing to accept many possible aid agreements, including ones that are far from its preferred outcome. The asymmetry in the relationship is reflected in the differences in willingness to compromise. The donor's reservation point – the most the donor is willing to compromise – is closer to the donor's ideal point than the recipient's reservation point is to its ideal point.

Despite the donor's greater influence, the bargaining setup also reflects the government's partial leverage in aid negotiations. First, the government is not willing to accept *all* negotiation outcomes. While not particularly selective, the government is not entirely reliant on the

[32] Muthoo 2000.

donor's development finance and is willing to turn down some aid packages that are too far from its ideal point. Second, in both panels, the donor is willing to accept a range of outcomes that are further from its ideal point, reflecting the donor's acceptance of outcomes that accommodate the government's preferences.

The contrast between panels (a) and (b) of Figure 2.1 illustrates how the value the donor places on the relationship with a particular recipient government affects aid negotiations. Figure 2.1(a) shows possible aid agreements for an average recipient country, where the donor places some value on the relationship with the recipient government, but the relationship is not a particular priority for the donor. The zone of possible agreement is close to the donor's ideal point, meaning that aid agreements are likely to reflect the donor's preferences. Figure 2.1(b), by contrast, shows a scenario where the donor places particular value on its relationship with the recipient government. In those cases, because the donor wants to maintain a good relationship with this recipient, the donor is inclined to accept outcomes that are closer to the recipient's preference, so the total range of possible agreements is larger and includes outcomes that are closer to the recipient's ideal point. However, note that simply being important to the donor is not enough for the recipient to turn down many aid offers. The recipient still has few alternatives to traditional donor aid, and its reservation point remains low. Even for "important" recipients, therefore, it is possible that aid agreements hew more closely to donors' preferences, if the recipient has few alternatives to traditional donor aid.

Having stylized the relationship between the recipient and donor in these bargaining terms makes it easier to understand how borrowing from alternative sources increases the recipient government's leverage in negotiations with donors, as I outline in Section 2.2.

2.2 How Alternative Finance Changes Aid Negotiations: The Financial Statecraft of Borrowers

When developing countries borrow from China, other emerging donors, or international bond markets, they reduce their reliance on traditional donor aid. I suggest that in response, donors offer more favorable aid agreements, since they want to retain their relationship and influence. Not only do alternative creditors provide additional funding that leaves recipient countries less reliant on traditional donors, but alternative creditors also offer finance on different terms and conditions than traditional donors. My argument builds on work that has examined how the rise of China as a lender impacts traditional donors but broadens the analysis to include the full range of borrowing countries' portfolios of external finance, including private finance, and develops an account of why some countries may benefit more from alternative finance than others. Earlier research on the impact of the rise of alternative lenders has generated diverging results, with Hernandez (2017) finding that Chinese lending is associated with the World Bank reducing the number of conditions attached to loans to African borrowers, while Humphrey and Michaelowa (2019) find that Chinese loans lead to an increase in multilateral lending only among wealthier African countries eligible for non-concessional finance. Swedlund (2017a) uses data from a survey with donor officials to show that these officials do not perceive China's lending as undermining their own bargaining power, largely because Chinese loans are very different from traditional donors' aid.

However, I suggest that where alternative finance has features that recipient governments find more attractive – such as greater flexibility or speed – these differences can allow recipients to "drive up" the bargain they strike with traditional donors. Moreover, Chinese loans are not the only way that recipient countries can diversify their external finance and reduce their reliance on traditional donors. Examining the full portfolio of recipient countries' external finance and considering the mechanisms by which alternative finance impacts the relationship with traditional donors sheds light on when developing countries are able to translate alternative finance into greater negotiating leverage. The use of new borrowing relationships to achieve preferred aid outcomes is a form of financial statecraft, since borrowing countries use borrowing to alter their relationships with foreign donors, thus achieving broader foreign policy goals of greater autonomy and flexibility in aid agreements.

Below, I briefly describe the two main alternative creditors from which developing country governments, and African governments in particular, borrowed in the early twenty-first century, namely Chinese lenders and international bond markets. I then explain the mechanisms that lead alternative forms of finance to influence negotiations with traditional donors – reduced dependence and geopolitical competition – before introducing my general expectation for how a country's portfolio of external finance impacts aid negotiations.

2.2.1 Chinese Loans as Alternative Finance

China is the leading bilateral lender outside of the traditional donors of the OECD DAC.[33] Chinese bilateral loans and aid are a mix of grants, concessional loans, and commercial finance, including export credit, extended by the China International Development Cooperation Agency, China Development Bank, and the Export-Import Bank of China, among others. Compared to the development finance provided by traditional donors, Chinese loans are attractive to recipient governments for a number of reasons. First, China has emphasized "non-interference" in its approach to development finance, meaning that Chinese loans do not require policy commitments or institutional reforms in recipient countries.[34] Instead, most Chinese loans consist of project financing that funds infrastructure projects carried out by Chinese contractors. Loans are thus tied to the procurement of services from Chinese firms but also enable governments to implement infrastructure projects that might otherwise be difficult to fund. With less intensive review requirements than traditional bilateral and multilateral donors, such as environmental or social safeguards, Chinese-financed infrastructure projects are implemented very quickly, making them attractive for governments wanting to demonstrate tangible development achievements. Moreover, Chinese bilateral loans, especially export finance loans, are often very large, outstripping the amounts that traditional bilateral and even multilateral donors provide.[35]

For recipient governments negotiating with traditional donors, borrowing from China offers several bargaining advantages. For one, the large size of Chinese loans can free up government resources and make the governments less reliant on traditional donor funds. Moreover, the design of Chinese loans reflect many recipient governments' preferences about development finance, involving few, if any, policy

---

[33] Horn et al. 2021.
[34] Brautigam 2011.
[35] Morris et al. 2020.

concessions and giving the government considerable discretion over its development policy.

Chinese development finance is also notable as an alternative because of the geopolitical and commercial competition between China and many bilateral traditional donors. Though this backdrop of global competition may be less relevant for recipient countries' choice to borrow from China than the flexibility of the terms of Chinese development finance, it shapes how traditional donors respond to a country's choice to borrow from China. Many donors and observers in developing countries understand Chinese aid as part of a broader Chinese effort to increase influence in developing countries. While others might question this interpretation, instead seeing Chinese aid as comparable to traditional development finance in its effort to curry diplomatic favor, viewing Chinese finance in terms of strategic competition will likely shape some donors' responses. All donors are engaged in some competition in the marketplace of aid, but traditional donors may react more strongly to aid they perceive as directly undercutting their strategic interests.

2.2.2 *International Bond Markets as Alternative Finance*

Private market finance similarly offers developing country governments an alternative to development finance from traditional donors. As described in Chapter 1, global market conditions in the late 2000s and 2010s allowed many developing countries to borrow extensively in international bond markets, with many African governments, in particular, borrowing in these markets for the first time. Much like with Chinese loans, the appeal of market finance is the flexibility and discretion that it offers recipient governments. When issuing a sovereign bond, the government must provide international investors with information about the country and its finances but need not commit to any specific policies. Market finance is even more flexible than Chinese loans, with bonds not tied to any specific project. These loans have more expensive financial terms than traditional development finance and some Chinese project loans, with higher interest rates and shorter maturities, but they offer recipient governments considerable autonomy. Moreover, borrowing in international bond markets is often seen as a sign that the country has "arrived," attaining a sufficient level of development and stability to be seen as creditworthy.

The relevance of private bond market finance to negotiations with traditional donors may be less readily apparent. After all, the IMF and World Bank encourage reforms to increase macroeconomic stability, making it easier for countries to borrow from international creditors. Donors and private creditors are often thought to reward similar economic outcomes, suggesting that private creditors might not act as much of an alternative for borrowing governments. Bond markets have been shown to impose substantial policy constraints on developing countries, by increasing the cost of borrowing in response to policy changes that put repayment at risk, thereby encouraging convergence on similar macroeconomic policies as those recommended by donors.[36] Moreover, some donors provide technical assistance geared toward deepening governments' access to private finance, whether by deepening domestic bond markets or improving their access to foreign capital.

However, private creditors impose no explicit policy requirements on borrowers at the time of borrowing, instead pricing loans based on an evaluation of creditworthiness. As such, private finance can come with far greater flexibility at the time of borrowing than traditional development finance. This attribute of private finance was very pronounced during the period of abundant global liquidity in the 2010s, when creditors went on a "search for yield" and became less discriminating among borrowers.[37] As L. Mosley notes in her assessment of financial market influence on emerging markets, investors are less responsive to fundamentals in their decisions whether to lend and how to price their loans during "mania" environments in global markets.[38] In this context, borrowing in sovereign bond markets offered governments a flexible form of financing that, while still more expensive than traditional development finance, was relatively accessible.[39]

* * * * * * * * *

Both private bond finance and Chinese loans reduce the recipient government's reliance on traditional donors. First, these creditors provide additional funds. Second, while both bond market finance and Chinese

---

[36] L. Mosley 2003.
[37] Ballard-Rosa et al. 2019; Naqvi 2018.
[38] L. Mosley 2003, pp. 151–152.
[39] Cormier 2023; Zeitz 2021b.

bilateral loans come at a higher financial cost than traditional donors' loans and grants, they both offer greater flexibility on development policy than most traditional donor aid. Both forms of finance, in different ways, act as alternatives to traditional donor aid that enhance the recipient government's ability to push for flexibility. Third, these alternative creditors and donors do not coordinate their funding with traditional donors, unlike OECD DAC donors that explicitly coordinate their approach to the recipient government. By operating outside of the conventional arrangements of traditional donor aid, these creditors offer recipient governments an alternative to the traditional aid on offer.

2.2.3 How Does Alternative Finance Impact Aid Negotiations?

Reduced Dependence

The main mechanism by which alternative finance impacts aid negotiations is by reducing the government's reliance on traditional donors. By diversifying its portfolio of external finance, the borrowing government ensures that each individual lender and donor is less important as a source of finance. In turn, the access and influence that a donor can expect to exercise with their aid will decline. To remain relevant and retain a close relationship with the government, the donor will be encouraged to provide more attractive aid. The donor's interest in maintaining a relationship will enable the recipient government to push for policies closer to its own priorities. For instance, a confidential 2010 US diplomatic cable quotes a South African diplomat noting that traditional donors had "changed their attitude" after seeing Chinese finance commitments in the mid 2000s: "They recognized that they had to measure up to China and 'came calling'."[40] To remain in dialogue with the recipient government about its policies, donors must offer more appealing funding.

A donor does not necessarily need to perceive an alternative creditor as a competitor or geopolitical threat for alternative finance to enhance the recipient government's bargaining leverage. In general, traditional donors do not see countries' borrowing in international markets as a source of ideological competition in the same way that

---

[40] February 10, 2010. Section 01 of 02 Beijing 000367. EO 12958.

some OECD DAC donors express anxiety about China's influence through its aid and loan program. Nonetheless, I expect that borrowing in international bond markets enhances recipients' negotiating strength with traditional donors. Bond market borrowing should matter for recipient leverage both because this finance reduces the recipient government's reliance on traditional donors and because bond finance offers recipients greater flexibility. Donors that want to preserve a close relationship with a recipient that has diversified its portfolio of external finance to include private market finance may need to offer the recipient more attractive and flexible aid to maintain their close relationship with the government.

This dynamic unfolds because of a donor's interest in their relationship with the recipient government and institutional incentives to disburse aid. Operating in a marketplace for aid, a donor will not simply respond to a recipient's reduced reliance on their aid by exiting the market. Instead, a donor will respond to the competitive threat of alternative finance by offering a better product, namely more attractive aid.

Skeptics might object that developing countries have such great need for external finance they will never turn down donor funds. However, access to alternative finance can in fact affect negotiation outcomes even when recipient governments have a considerable need for external finance. Even governments that need large amounts of finance are limited in how much external funding can take on. Especially when the finance in question is non-concessional lending, concerns about debt sustainability mean that, at the margin, a choice for one lender is a choice against another.[41] There are also limits to how much grant aid and concessional finance a recipient government can absorb, given the transaction costs associated with receiving grants. Thus, even with "free" or concessional financing, there are limits on the financing governments can take on, which makes trade-offs between different funding sources possible. These constraints on the government's ability to absorb external funds means that governments may in fact turn down funds they see as significantly worse than their fallback option.

---

[41] Bunte (2019) makes a similar point in explaining why choices for one creditor or another are meaningful choices.

More importantly, returning to donors' interests in shaping government policy, the constraint that matters is the limit on recipient governments' time and policy choices. A donor values their access to the recipient government to influence government policy, access they receive in connection with the development finance they provide. When recipient governments turn to alternative forms of finance, they commit some of their time to arranging and securing this alternative finance. They also potentially make policy commitments that go in different directions from those desired by traditional donors. These alternate commitments limit the government's availability for traditional donors' policy recommendation. Donors are therefore encouraged to provide more attractive financing, aligned more with recipient preferences, to ensure their continued access to government policymaking processes.

Geopolitical Competition

A second mechanism by which alternative finance impacts aid negotiations between the recipient and traditional donors is by playing on geopolitical competition. Aid relationships can be a sign of proximity between donor and recipient. When a developing country establishes a closer relationship with a donor, geopolitical rivals of the new donor are likely to worry about strategic competition. Alternative finance always risks diminishing a donor's influence as the recipient becomes less reliant on the donor, but some forms of alternative finance are more likely to support policies that directly counter the donors' preferences. In those cases, the very fact that the recipient borrows from an alternative creditor may increase the value of the recipient government to the donor. In other words, since donors have an interest in countering the influence of other donors, a recipient may become more important to the donor simply because they have borrowed from particular creditors.

This explains why donors may react more strongly to a recipient country's choice to borrow from China than to borrow in international bond markets. In general, donors can assume that when a recipient borrows from international investors, this finance broadly reinforces the policy guidance that donors provide. Investors are likely to prefer macroeconomic prudence, political stability, and transparency, much like traditional donors, though investors are unlikely to carefully scrutinize compliance with these expectations during phases of abundant global liquidity. More importantly, unlike a bilateral creditor or donor, bond investors are not a single united force looking to sway recipient policy. By contrast, donors are more likely to interpret loans from China as influence attempts. Where alternative finance appears to challenge traditional donors' influence, the very act of borrowing from that creditor may enhance the value of the recipient government to the donor.

My argument for why alternative finance affects the negotiations between donors and recipient governments differs from alternative accounts that begin with competition among rival donors.[42] The debt-based financial statecraft framework begins with the fact that when recipient governments borrow from alternative sources, they improve their outside options and become able to make greater demands of their donors. Recipient governments can exercise greater leverage by diversifying their portfolio of external finance even when their creditors are not geopolitical competitors, so long as creditors do not coordinate their expectations of the recipient. However, geopolitical tension between creditors nonetheless matters. A donor is likely to become more motivated to retain its relationship with a recipient government when the recipient country borrows from a geopolitical competitor. While both Chinese loans and private finance increase the government's leverage, borrowing from China may do more align aid agreements with the recipient's preferences.

2.2.4 Expectations

Returning to the bargaining framework from the previous section, we can incorporate the government's access to alternative finance to see how these outside options enhance the government's bargaining leverage with a donor. Figure 2.2(a) replicates the initial bargaining setup introduced in Figure 2.1. In this scenario, the government has few other sources of finance and will accept terms from donors that are far from its ideal outcome. Figure 2.2(b) shows how borrowing from alternative creditors changes the negotiations between the donor and the recipient. The recipient government can now access attractive outside options, which increases the recipient's reservation point, making the recipient less likely to accept aid agreements that are further from

---

[42] Bueno de Mesquita and Smith 2016.

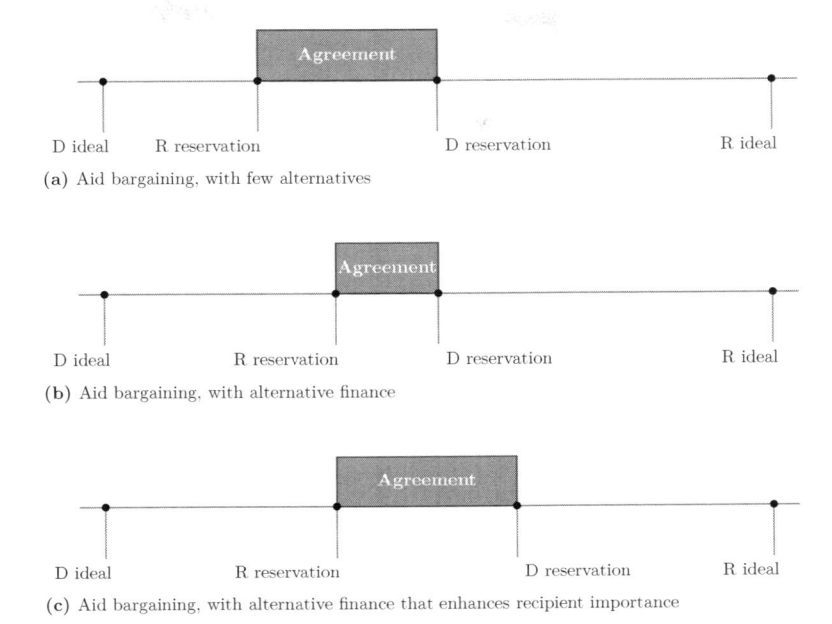

Figure 2.2 Alternative finance and donor–recipient negotiations.

its ideal point. While the zone of possible agreement shrinks, reducing the likelihood of an agreement, the area of possible agreement shifts closer to the recipient's ideal point, making it more likely that any agreement that is reached will align with the recipient's preferences. In practice, closer alignment with the recipient's preferences could mean that the final aid agreement will be more likely to include funding for the government's preferred sectors, have fewer reporting requirements, or have more flexible terms.

Crucially, Figure 2.2 shows that the donor still has an interest in the relationship with the recipient; the donor will not simply walk away from the relationship when the government diversifies its portfolio of external finance. Instead, the donor's reliance on the relationship with the recipient government to achieve the goals of foreign aid means the donor will continue to provide aid, but that the terms of that aid will no longer be as far from the recipient's preferences. This expectation can be expressed as follows:

Recipient governments that borrow from alternative creditors will receive aid agreements from traditional donors that are more aligned with their preferences.

Panels (b) and (c) of Figure 2.2 illustrate how differences among alternative creditors play out in the bargaining framework. All forms of alternative finance increase the recipient government's reservation point. However, when a recipient borrows from creditors that are geopolitical rivals of traditional donors, the donor also attaches greater value to the relationship with the recipient. Perceiving the recipient to be at risk of falling into a rival's orbit, the value of maintaining access to the recipient increases. The donor's reservation point decreases, since reaching an aid agreement is more important to the donor, as Figure 2.2(c) shows. When donors are not only interested in preserving their relationship but also motivated to counter the influence of another creditor, then the recipient can increase their value to the donor by borrowing from competitor creditors. In Figure 2.2(c), the whole zone of possible agreement has moved closer to the recipient's ideal point, with the recipient less willing to accept aid agreements that are far from its preferences and the donor more willing to compromise.

2.3 Variation among Recipient Countries

The main expectation is that developing countries that borrow from a wider range of creditors will achieve preferred aid agreements with traditional donors. However, given both donors' and recipients' interests in the aid relationship, some recipient countries will achieve more bargaining leverage from their diversified portfolio of external finance than others. For one, recipient countries that are more important to donors will extract greater leverage from borrowing from alternative sources. For another, recipient governments are likely to derive greater negotiating leverage when donors have greater trust that the recipient government will uphold aid agreements. Moreover, since a recipient country's importance and credibility vary among their donors, a recipient may also enjoy greater leverage with some donors than others.

2.3.1 Recipient Importance

There are key differences in how an average versus an "important" recipient country experiences the effect of alternative finance on donor–recipient negotiations. Recipient countries that enjoy a "donor darling" status already find many of their donors more willing to compromise on aid agreements. When these countries borrow from alternative sources, they are more likely to benefit from their reduced dependence. In the foreign aid literature, there are three main ways in which developing countries can be especially important to donors: geopolitical significance, commercial ties, and development effectiveness. I expect that these different forms of importance enhance the recipient's ability to turn alternative finance into greater bargaining leverage.

The archetypal "valuable" recipient is a country that is geopolitically important to a donor. At the height of the Cold War, aid was a tool explicitly deployed for strategic ends, used by donors to reward allies and shore up support. Even well into the twenty-first century, security interests remain pivotal for many donors determining favored aid recipients. In the 2000s, the "Global War on Terror" helped define which countries were seen as strategic partners for many Western donors, likely to receive favorable treatment for contributing to counterterrorism efforts in their region.[43] A developing country may be important for a donor's security interests because they cooperate militarily with the donor or because they lend support to the donor's priorities in international organizations. Research has found that donors, acting bilaterally or through multilateral institutions, extend more generous aid to recipients in the years those countries are temporarily on the UN Security Council.[44] Aid donors also often see their relationships with former colonies as diplomatically and strategically important, and donors have tended to allocate higher volumes of aid to their former colonies.[45]

When a recipient country that is geopolitically important to a specific donor diversifies its portfolio of external finance and becomes less available for policy dialogue, the donor is likely to respond by accommodating the recipient's interests. This effect is likely to be compounded if donors worry that alternative creditors, such as China, are using their creditor relationship with the recipient to enhance their strategic influence. As a donor is evaluating where to provide greater flexibility to meet recipient preferences, they are likely to prioritize an aid relationship that offers strategic benefits.

[43] Fleck and Kilby 2010.
[44] Vreeland and Dreher 2014.
[45] Bermeo 2017; Berthélemy and Tichit 2004.

In addition to security-related motivations, a donor may have special commercial interests in a particular recipient country. If a recipient is a source of natural resources, a base for the donor's firms, or an important export market, the donor will prize their relationship with the recipient government for managing those commercial relations. Research has shown recipient countries receive more aid if they are importers of capital goods from donor countries or are important trading partners.[46] Countries also receive more aid when there is trade competition among donors for the recipient's domestic market.[47] Though DAC donors have gradually reduced the use of tied aid, wherein foreign aid is explicitly connected to the procurement of goods and services from the donor country, many donors still justify aid programs on the grounds that they generate more diffuse commercial benefits for domestic companies and workers. If a recipient country that is a meaningful commercial partner develops closer relationships with alternative creditors, donors are more likely to respond to preserve their access to the recipient government.

Even if donors are primarily driven by altruistic motivations, they value their relationships with some recipient countries more than others. The success of donors' development programming depends on the capacity and effectiveness of the recipient government in implementing this programming. For this reason, development practitioners refer to the relationship between donors and the government as a "partnership," with donors termed "development partners" working in collaboration with the government. This reliance on the government for the success of development programming means that donors prefer to work with more effective governments, where aid projects and development programs are more likely to be successful. The same also happens at a subnational scale, where development practitioners prefer to allocate aid to regions where they believe it will be more effectively implemented.[48] Donors' preference for countries that are seen as effective aid implementers is closely related to donors' trust in the recipient government, described in Section 2.3.2. A country's reputation for development effectiveness will often spread to multiple donors, giving the recipient a "donor darling" status. If a country

---

[46] Berthélemy 2006; Younas 2008.
[47] Barthel et al. 2014; Fuchs et al. 2015.
[48] Briggs 2021.

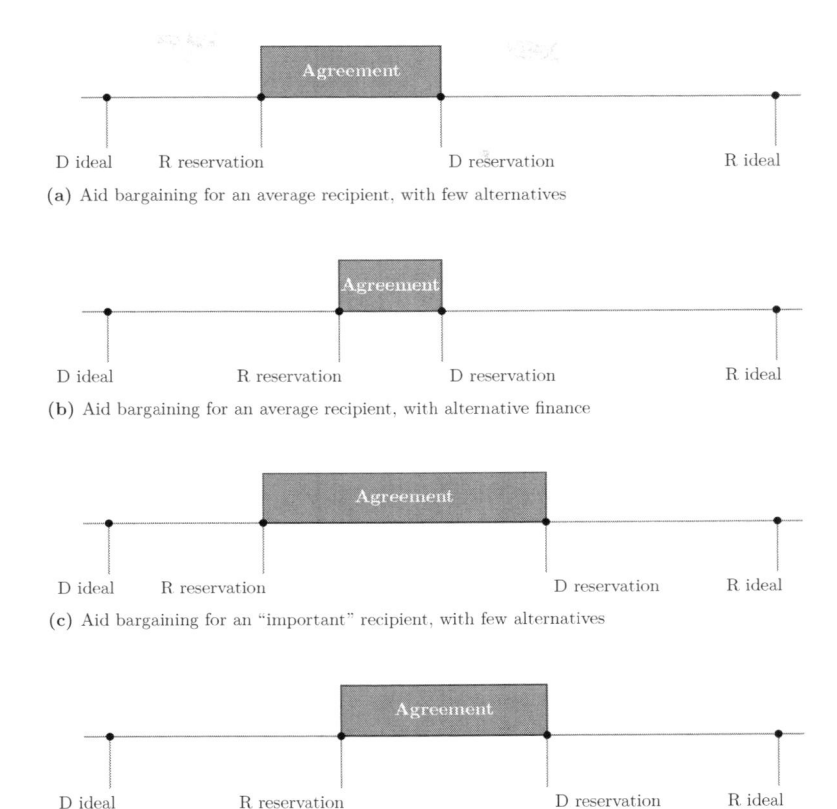

(a) Aid bargaining for an average recipient, with few alternatives

(b) Aid bargaining for an average recipient, with alternative finance

(c) Aid bargaining for an "important" recipient, with few alternatives

(d) Aid bargaining for an "important" recipient, with alternative finance

Figure 2.3 Alternative finance and donor–recipient negotiations, by recipient significance.

enjoying this status diversifies its portfolio of finance, donors may be especially worried about losing access to the government.

Countries that are important to a donor in these different ways will experience a greater impact of their diversified portfolios of finance on their relationship with that donor. Figure 2.3 illustrates this dynamic. Panels (a) and (c) of Figure 2.3 repeat the initial bargaining setup in Figure 2.1, where the borrowing government has few alternative sources of funding. Panels (b) and (d) of Figure 2.3 depict the recipient increasing its reservation point as it becomes less dependent on traditional donors. This dynamic is by now familiar from the account above. The difference between the panels (b) and (d) reveals how the negotiation outcomes are likely to differ when a donor places particular value on the relationship with the government. When a recipient is strategically important to the donor, the zone of possible agreement remains fairly large even when the recipient's reservation point increases due to the availability of outside options. By contrast, for the average recipient, while an increase in outside options raises the recipient's reservation point and precludes agreements far from the recipient's ideal point, the zone of possible agreement also shrinks considerably, and the recipient may find it more difficult to reach an agreement and to substantially alter negotiation outcomes or to reach agreement with the donor.

I therefore expect that recipient countries that are particularly significant to their donors will achieve greater leverage when they diversify their portfolio of external finance. For these countries, borrowing from alternative creditors should do more to align negotiation outcomes with the government's preferences. This expectation can be expressed as follows:

Recipient governments that are important to donors will see a stronger effect of borrowing from alternative creditors on the alignment of aid agreements with their preferences.

2.3.2 Donor Trust in the Recipient Government

For a borrowing country to translate alternative finance into bargaining leverage, a donor needs to not only value the relationship with the borrowing government but also *trust* the government will abide by its commitments in aid agreements. If a donor fears the government will renege on its commitments, the donor will be less likely to respond to the borrower's reduced dependence by offering greater discretion and flexibility. Instead, the donor may worry that the government will use greater flexibility to engage in spending and policies that contravene the overarching agreements the government has made with the donor. Distrust in the government's commitments can cause a donor to respond to the recipient's greater autonomy by applying greater scrutiny and oversight.

My claim that donors are sensitive to the credibility of recipient governments and will adjust their response to alternative finance accordingly builds on the work of Swedlund (2017b), who argues that donors and recipients both face commitment problems in the aid relationship.[49] For donor agencies, concerns about the reliability and predictability of the recipient government come from fears about the misappropriation of aid funds, which can lead to scandals that harm the reputation and autonomy of the agency, as well as undermining the effectiveness of aid. Research has shown that donors are sensitive to the quality of governance in the recipient country, preferring to allocate aid to NGOs and bypass the government in countries' where governance institutions are seen as weak.[50] Moreover, donors are highly sensitive to corruption in the recipient country. While corruption involving aid funds is especially explosive and usually leads to the withdrawal or redesign of aid programs, corruption involving the government's own resources also undermines donor trust and makes donors less willing to give the government greater discretion.

In calibrating their trust in the recipient government, donors pay special attention to institutions for managing public resources, including mechanisms for budgeting, reporting spending, and auditing, or what are collectively known as institutions of public financial management. Donors scrutinize public financial management especially closely when providing budget support, since they have little control over resources once they have been disbursed to the government and must rely on the government's own mechanisms to distribute and manage spending.[51] Even when donors provide sector-specific or project-based aid that allows them greater control, their assessment of public financial management institutions can inform their broader evaluation of the probity and reliability of the government. Where these institutions are weak, the donor may fear that alternative, nontraditional finance undermines the donor's development goals in the country, since the government is freer to engage in short-termist spending.

More broadly, donors' trust in the recipient government emerges out of the ongoing relationship between the two sides. A recipient governments builds up trust with a donor over time by being a reliable partner, implementing aid programs as agreed. By contrast, a government can undermine trust through public scandals or continuous poor performance on institutional criteria that donors care about.

---

[49] On the commitment problems of recipients, see especially Swedlund (2017b, pp. 78–81, 89–90, 95–96).

[50] Dietrich 2013.

[51] Koeberle and Stavreski 2006.

Repeated interactions with the government also lead donors to base their assessment of the recipient government on the prevailing political dynamics in the country. Since the 2010s, some donors have increasingly used the concept of a country's "political settlement" to guide their engagement with developing country governments.[52] One research center that received extensive funding from the UK's Foreign, Commonwealth & Development Office to research development effectiveness describes the approach as follows: "[D]evelopment practitioners can use political settlements analysis to better understand the context in which they work. Asking: who are the powerful groups in this society, how are they configured and what do they want? Doing so allows development work to be done with a state's political reality, rather than in spite of it."[53]

The core idea of political settlements is that the constellation of power in a developing country, including informal power, is important for understanding development outcomes.[54] When power is more concentrated in the leader and the coalition of interests around them, they need to dedicate fewer resources and energy to holding onto power. As a consequence, political settlements analysis suggests that governing coalitions with a greater concentration of power will have a longer time horizon, which allows them to invest in longer-term reforms and investments to pursue development.[55] By contrast, leaders in regimes with diffuse or dispersed power face recurrent threats to their hold on power and have much shorter time horizons, relying on clientelist distribution or force to secure their hold on power. These short time horizons can make it more difficult for leaders to undertake interventions that may take years to generate development gains, and they instead prioritize short-term measures that can satisfy those that would otherwise challenge their hold on power.

---

[52] Yanguas 2017.

[53] ESID 2022.

[54] Khan 2010.

[55] Scholars differ in their conceptualization of the political settlement but most consider the power of the leader relative to the opposition, as well as relative to other co-opted groups within the governing coalition (Kelsall et al. 2022; Khan 2010; Whitfield et al. 2015). Leaders can be vulnerable along two dimensions: They can be challenged from outside or from within their own group. For purposes of simplicity, I juxtapose leaders who hold concentrated power with those that do not.

In the context of the recipient–donor relationship, governments with more concentrated political power may be better able to make long-term commitments to abide by aid agreements and therefore enjoy greater trust from donors. It might be surprising to claim that governments with a stronger grasp on power are able to garner more trust from donors, since the foreign aid literature has found that donors prefer working with democracies and are more likely to offer favorable aid terms to democratic recipient countries.[56] However, donors have not prioritized democracy to the exclusion of other priorities in developing countries and have willingly continued to provide aid to autocratic regimes, as well as softening their democracy promotion to make it more palatable to autocratic governments.[57] Moreover and more importantly, a country's political settlement and the level of power concentration do not map neatly onto formal democratic institutions. There are liberal democracies where the governing regime enjoys security due to a concentration of political authority, just as there are autocracies where power is dispersed and the regime fears challenges to its power.

My focus on power concentration as a determining factor in the credibility of governments' commitments, and donors' trust in those commitments, diverges slightly from standard arguments about credible commitments. Research on the credibility of states' commitments to foreign counterparts, whether security allies or foreign investors, has often argued that democracies make more credible commitments than non-democracies, due to greater transparency and greater constraints on the executive.[58] Following the literature on political settlements, I suggest that while democratic institutions can enhance the confidence of outside observers, they are not the only determinant of government credibility. Beyond formal political institutions, the governing regime's concentration of power can also be an important clue for donors evaluating whether the government will abide by its aid agreements. Since donor agencies have shown considerable interest in political settlements research, funding scholarship in this area and using the concepts in their operational work, it is likely that donors will use the political settlement of a recipient country as an indication for

---

[56] Alesina and Dollar 2000; Dietrich 2013; Kersting and Kilby 2014.
[57] Bush 2015; Hagmann and Reyntjens 2016.
[58] Cowhey 1993; Jensen et al. 2012.

how reliably they can trust the government. The UK's Department for International Development (DFID), for example, stated a commitment to "inclusive political settlements" in a 2010 paper.[59] In their book on political settlements and development, Kelsall et al. conclude with advice for development practitioners, saying that most "standard bilateral and multilateral support" is only likely to work well in "broad-concentrated political settlements," while in "broad-dispersed political settlements ... the government's capacity to plan and implement effective long-term development policy is likely to be weak."[60] Donor agencies influenced by the political settlement approach and receiving such advice will look to the domestic political context and the concentration of political authority to inform their trust in the recipient government.

Multiple factors thus shape a donor's trust in recipient governments, including levels of corruption, the performance of public financial management institutions, past compliance with aid agreements, and the prevailing political settlement. Some of these, such as the prevalence of corruption or the autonomy of public financial management systems, can be seen as symptoms of the underlying political settlement. Where the governing coalition is weak, informal distribution may be a means of holding onto power. However, for some donors, the political settlement may be much less important than the observable performance of the borrowing country's institutions, which increases the donor's confidence that the aid agreement and development plans will be implemented as agreed. What is relevant for the argument about financial statecraft is that a borrowing government's ability to leverage alternative finance as a source of bargaining power will depend on a donor's trust. Donor distrust of the recipient government may outweigh the incentives to respond to the recipient's reduced dependence by offering greater discretion. Even when the recipient borrows from alternative sources, a donor may be unwilling to satisfy the recipient's preferences by offering greater flexibility if they fear that greater flexibility may lead to reputational costs for the donor agency.

In the bargaining context, when a donor distrusts the government, alternative finance may in fact *lower* the donor's reservation point, making them less willing to compromise and satisfy the recipient's

---

[59] DFID 2010.
[60] Kelsall et al. 2022, pp. 171, 172.

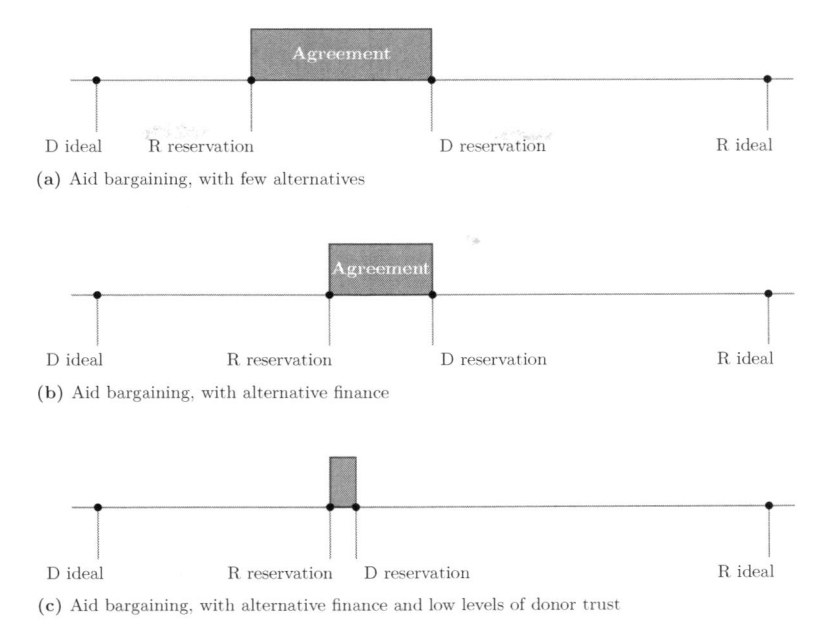

(a) Aid bargaining, with few alternatives

(b) Aid bargaining, with alternative finance

(c) Aid bargaining, with alternative finance and low levels of donor trust

Figure 2.4 Donor–recipient negotiations and donor trust.

preferences. Figure 2.4 shows this scenario. Panels (a) and (b) show the familiar step in which alternative finance increases the recipient government's reservation point, making them less likely to accept outcomes far from their preferences. Panel (c) shows what happens when the recipient government enjoys little trust. Although alternative finance raises the recipient's reservation point, making them less willing to accept unfavorable agreements, the government's use of alternative finance also raises the donor's suspicions and lowers the donor's reservation point. Fearful that the recipient may misuse alternative finance, the donor becomes less inclined to satisfy the government's preference for flexibility. As a consequence, the zone of possible agreement shrinks substantially, and an agreement may become impossible. Governments with lower levels of donor trust may therefore find it difficult to translate alternative finance into greater leverage.

This leads to my second expectation about variation in debt-based financial statecraft among recipient countries:

Recipient governments with higher levels of donor trust will experience a stronger positive relationship between borrowing from alternative creditors and the alignment of aid agreements with their preferences.

2.4 Situating Debt-Based Financial Statecraft

My argument that developing countries' use of alternative finance is a form of financial statecraft contributes to a broader literature on the uses of economic interdependence. Economic statecraft refers to a country using relationships of economic interdependence to achieve foreign policy goals,[61] while financial statecraft refers more narrowly to the use of financial tools. For instance, a country might extend favorable loans to a fellow member of an international organization to secure support or may restrict a specific country's firms from accessing its banking system as a sanction for violating a weapons treaty.

The starting point for analyses of economic or financial statecraft is the deep interdependence among states in the modern economy. Global relationships of trade, production, and credit lead to close connections between states, such that actions under the control of one state can have direct effects on another. It has long been recognized that this interdependence enables states to deliberately influence one another. Scholarship in the 1970s considered how interdependence affected the power and vulnerability of states and might, in the aggregate, sustain international cooperation.[62] More recently, there has been a renewed interest in the phenomenon and effects of economic interdependence, particularly how interdependence at the level of the international economic system creates opportunities and constraints for states and other actors.[63]

Most analyses of financial statecraft have focused on large states. The size and centrality of these economies in webs of economic interdependence provides them with the capabilities to exercise leverage over other states, restricting access to their sizable markets, withdrawing large loans, or exploiting the ubiquity of their currency in global transactions.[64] More recently, scholars have worked to broaden the concept of financial statecraft, emphasizing that emerging powers working individually and collectively have also begun to use "monetary or financial regulations, policies, or instruments to achieve foreign policy ends."[65] This research agenda has not only highlighted that

---

[61] Baldwin 1985.
[62] Keohane and Nye 2001.
[63] Farrell and Newman 2014, 2016; Newman and Posner 2011; Oatley 2019.
[64] Armijo 2019, p. 29.
[65] Armijo and Katada 2014, 2015; Katada et al. 2017; Roberts et al. 2018, p. 67.

actors beyond the United States engage in financial statecraft but also that financial statecraft may be used to influence a wider range of targets and serve different ends than previously thought. Beyond the classical conception of one state using financial relations to influence or coerce another, "powerful states employ financial and monetary levers to create, constitute, and govern interstate economic relations, as well as to shape global markets."[66] Moreover, empirical work on how emerging powers such as China or Brazil actually use financial statecraft suggests that the aims may be defensive, geared toward preserving autonomy from outside influence, rather than coercing other states.[67]

My concept of the financial statecraft of borrowers builds on the notion of financial statecraft as a "defensive search for autonomy," but moves beyond the focus on powerful states.[68] A developing country that borrows from new creditors uses a new financial relationship to reduce the country's reliance on traditional donors, thereby enhancing the government's bargaining leverage. This form of financial statecraft is fundamentally different from that exercised by creditors and major powers. Most importantly, the borrowers remain in relationships of asymmetric interdependence in which they are the weaker actor. Unlike the emerging powers that Roberts et al. describe as amassing greater economic power as the global "distribution of monetary and financial capabilities" shifts away from the United States,[69] the developing countries considered here are not internationalizing their currencies or becoming global lenders. Instead, these countries increase and diversify their borrowing relationships, using new asymmetric relationships to gain greater bargaining power in their existing ones.

Although the focus on borrowers extends the concept of financial statecraft to new sets of actors, I do not think that the departure is so extreme as to constitute "conceptual stretching."[70] The claim is that developing countries use financial policy – in this case, the choice of creditor – to achieve the broader foreign policy goal of greater autonomy in their aid relationship with donors. Most conceptions of

---

[66] Armijo 2019, p. 27.
[67] Armijo 2019, p. 30; Roberts et al. 2018, p. 68.
[68] Katada et al. 2017, p. 405.
[69] Roberts et al. 2018, p. 25.
[70] Collier and Mahon 1993.

financial statecraft require the state to deliberately use financial levers to achieve foreign policy aims.[71] For an action to qualify as financial statecraft, the foreign policy outcome must be an explicit motivation, rather than an unintended consequence. While the desire to achieve a certain foreign policy outcome is important to distinguish financial statecraft from unintended side effects of economic policy, the foreign policy goal need not be the *only* aim of a financial action for it to count as financial statecraft. In the case of debt-based financial statecraft, countries may contract a loan from China or issue an international bond for a variety of reasons, but as long as *one* of the aims is to reduce the dependence on traditional donors, the country is engaging in debt-based financial statecraft.

It is worth noting that debt-based financial statecraft does not upend the position of developing countries in the international financial system. By borrowing from alternative lenders, developing country governments do not overturn the asymmetry of their financial relationships. This modest and defensive application of financial statecraft distinguishes it from efforts by emerging powers to use financial levers to reshape global economic governance, increasing their structural power.[72]

My emphasis on how a recipient country can exercise newfound leverage due to additional borrowing relationships does not deny the uneven structural context in which these borrowing relationships are found. Much of the recent work on financial interdependence has emphasized that the global web of interdependence is not neutral. Instead, it gives some states – those at the central hubs of interconnected networks – power over others. For instance, one recent contribution on interdependence argues for "a structural explanation of interdependence in which network topography generates enduring power imbalances among states."[73] That uneven playing field of economic interdependence forms the backdrop to the negotiations I examine.

Even if developing countries are able to receive aid on terms that are more aligned with their preferences, they nevertheless remain reliant on foreign actors for external finance. However, the dynamic of the

---

[71] See, for instance, Armijo 2019, p. 28.
[72] Roberts et al. 2018, pp. 68–69.
[73] Farrell and Newman 2019, p. 45.

financial statecraft of borrowers does highlight how even an asymmetric context creates opportunities for developing countries to increase their autonomy and leverage. A distinction from a much earlier literature may be helpful here. In the 1970s, responding to an explosion of work on interdependence as well as dependency arguments about poor countries' underdevelopment, Caporaso distinguished between the concepts of "dependence" and "dependency." Dependence, in his understanding, is a "dyadic" and "net" concept "measured by looking at the differential between A's reliance on B and B's reliance on A."[74] By contrast, dependency is a structural concept based on a "a more complex set of relations" that considers the "unit in relation to all external influences."[75] Following this distinction between dyadic dependence and structural dependency, I want to stress that debt-based financial statecraft enables countries to reduce their dyadic dependence, even while the broader structural asymmetry remains in place.

2.5 Conclusion

Developing countries' borrowing choices can be the basis of strength in relations with donors and creditors. Access to new forms of finance provides borrowing governments with outside options that reduce their dependence on individual donors and creditors. Reduced reliance on donor funds increases borrowing governments' bargaining leverage and allows them to achieve negotiating outcomes that are more aligned with their preferences. However, not all countries are equally likely to be successful at debt-based financial statecraft. Differences in the importance of a recipient country to its donors and the extent of donor trust will shape whether a recipient can translate a diverse portfolio of external finance into greater bargaining leverage.

Debt-based financial statecraft differs from an alternative view grounded in dependency theory. A dependency perspective sees developing countries' unequal integration into the international financial system as self-reinforcing. In this view, developing countries have little capacity for agency, with exploitative and extractive relationships with rich countries inhibiting their autonomy. Seen in this light, new borrowing relationships with China or other emerging creditors are simply

---

[74] Caporaso 1978, p. 18.
[75] Caporaso 1978, pp. 13, 18.

"diversifying dependency."[76] As Taylor skeptically concludes, "with the arrival of emerging economies in Africa ... the historical process of underdevelopment is in danger of being further entrenched."[77] While I am cautious not to claim that new borrowing relationships allow developing countries to alter the fundamental structure of the international financial system, I nonetheless see possibilities for developing countries to exploit the greater diversity to their advantage.

The financial statecraft of borrowers also diverges from an alternative account that interprets the rise of emerging lenders primarily through the lens of geopolitical competition. Though I agree that donors are sensitive to policy influences that directly counter their influence, making them more reactive to lending by geopolitical rivals, geopolitical competition is only one part of a larger phenomenon. Donors are interested in their access to the recipient's policymaking process, which they receive in connection with their aid. As the recipient becomes less reliant on the donor's aid, whether though bilateral loans or private finance, the donor risks losing access to the recipient's policymaking process and must offer more attractive aid to remain influential.

The theoretical framework of the financial statecraft of borrowers makes a number of contributions to the literature in international political economy and International Relations. At its core, it specifies how borrowing governments can use relationships with creditors to their advantage. The existing literature on financial statecraft has demonstrated that lending relationships can be a tool for influence but has almost exclusively focused on creditors. By contrast, this framework argues that borrowing governments, despite being in a structurally weaker position, can use their relationships with particular creditors as a source of leverage vis-à-vis other creditors and donors. Moreover, it adds to research on multipolarity in the international economy, shedding light on how the financial clout of emerging economies affects smaller developing countries. Changes at the level of the international financial system create new opportunities and constraints for developing countries managing their relationships with donors and creditors.

---

[76] Taylor 2014.
[77] Taylor 2014, p. 40.

3 | *The Big Picture: Large-n Evidence*

In the year 2000, aid from Western bilateral donors made up almost 80 percent of external finance in Uganda. Most of the remaining 20 percent of foreign finance came from the World Bank and other multilateral lenders. At the time, Uganda was almost entirely reliant on traditional development actors for external funding. Fifteen years later, the picture had changed. Bilateral donors from the Development Assistance Committee (DAC) of the Organisation of Economic Cooperation and Development (OECD) now made up only 32 percent of external finance, with large commitments from Chinese lenders supplementing traditional sources of development finance. Though traditional donors still played an important role in Uganda's portfolio of external finance, they no longer held a monopoly.

During that same time, aid agreements between Uganda and its traditional donors also changed, becoming more flexible and more closely aligned with the government's priorities. In 2001, a World Bank loan to support poverty reduction had sixteen conditions for the government to fulfill, while the 2012 successor loan only had ten such requirements. In 2000, DAC donors committed only 12 percent of their projects to infrastructure-intensive sectors. By 2015, the share of DAC projects assigned to infrastructure intensive sectors increased to an average of 20 percent, coming closer to meeting the country's infrastructure funding needs. In part, these changes in donors' foreign aid in Uganda were shaped by global trends that had little to do with Uganda or its portfolio of external finance. However, the shifting composition of Uganda's external finance also altered the dynamic between the government and its traditional donors, reducing the government's reliance on traditional donors. The reduced reliance on traditional donors, in turn, made it easier for the Ugandan government to advocate for its own interests in aid negotiations with donors.

In this chapter, I systematically examine the relationship between developing countries' portfolios of external finance and their aid relationships with traditional donors. Throughout, I demonstrate that trends in sub-Saharan Africa are similar to those across developing countries as a whole, but that the shift from reliance on traditional donor aid to greater diversity of finance has been more pronounced for sub-Saharan African countries.

I compile data on the composition of developing countries' portfolios of external finance to show how governments have reduced their reliance on traditional DAC donors, turning to external finance from new sources. I then draw on a range of measures to capture how the relationship between traditional donors and recipient governments has changed in response to recipients' new borrowing relationships. Determining the extent to which donors or recipients have more influence over negotiations is challenging, since not all recipient governments want the same thing out of their relationship with donors. However, using a number of different measures – how much aid money recipient governments receive, which kinds of development projects donors are willing to fund, and how many conditions donors attach to development projects – I establish a picture of the balance of donor–recipient relations. The analysis reveals that as countries borrow from a wider range of creditors, borrowers are more likely to receive preferred aid terms from traditional donors.

3.1 Diversity in Portfolios of External Finance

The story of developing countries' increasingly diverse portfolios of external finance begins with a decline in the overall importance of foreign aid. Buoyed by several decades of economic growth, developing countries have increasingly reduced their reliance on traditional aid. Whereas the median level of official development assistance (ODA) in developing countries was 8.1 percent of gross national income (GNI) in 1990, median levels of ODA had declined to 2.8 percent of GNI in 2018.[1] In sub-Saharan Africa, levels of aid have come down from

---

[1] OECD DAC donors use a strict definition of ODA to distinguish foreign aid from other bilateral flows such as military aid or export credits. The OECD DAC definition requires ODA to (1) be allocated to countries on the DAC List of ODA Recipients or multilateral development institutions, (2) be extended

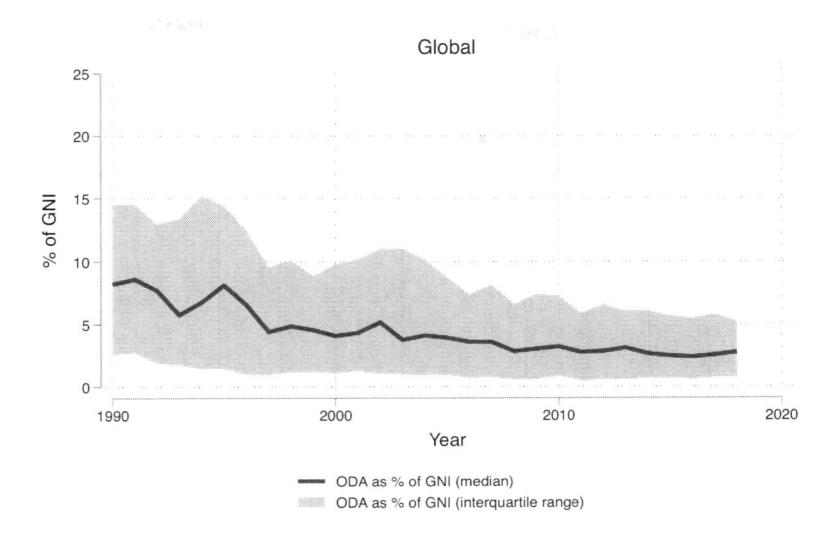

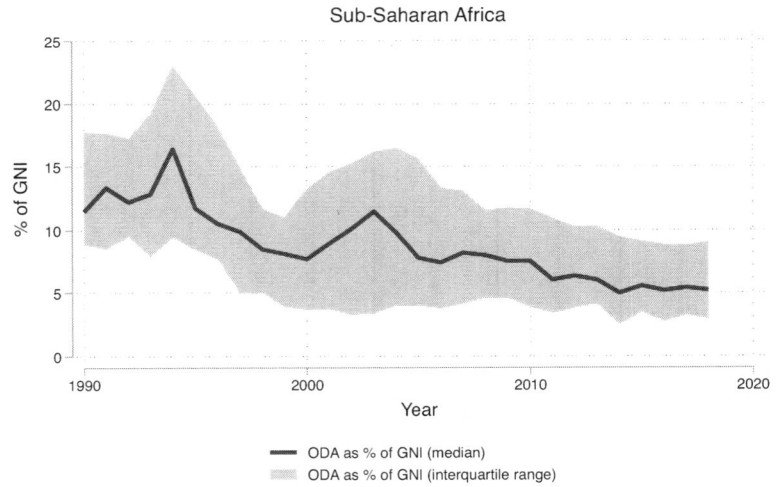

Figure 3.1 Official development assistance as share of GNI, 1990–2018. Source: World Bank International Development Statistics.

a higher level, declining from a median of 11.6 percent of GNI in 1990 to 5.5 percent of GNI in 2018 (see Figure 3.1). This broad trend

by public agencies, (3) be concessional (i.e., grants or soft loans), and (4) have the "main objective" of "the promotion of the economic development and welfare of developing countries" (OECD 2021).

masks considerable heterogeneity among countries. For some developing countries, especially very poor and fragile states, aid remains very important. In the Central African Republic, for instance, ODA amounted to 17.5 percent of GNI in 1990 and increased to 27.5 percent of GNI in 2018. For the majority of developing countries, however, rapid growth in the 2000s and 2010s led to a diminished reliance on traditional donor aid.

Developing countries not only reduced their reliance on ODA through economic growth but also expanded and diversified their portfolios of external finance by turning to new creditors. To track these changes in countries' portfolios of external finance, I assemble a dataset covering the full extent of outside finance, ranging from foreign aid to bilateral loans and debt owed to private creditors. Measuring the different components of developing countries' portfolios of external finance can be challenging, since not all donors and creditors are equally transparent about their lending and lenders use different definitions of financial flows, making it difficult to compare like with like. In particular, Chinese lenders have been reluctant to provide systematic data on their overseas financing, emphasizing confidentiality and discretion in their development finance.

In response to the opacity of Chinese finance, numerous independent data collection efforts have attempted to identify and measure Chinese overseas aid and loans. Strange et al. (2017) use a "tracking under-reported financial flows" methodology that combines official records from Chinese lenders and recipient governments with third-party data and media reports to identify Chinese financing commitments. This dataset, assembled by AidData, provides the most comprehensive project-level global database of Chinese lending. In a separate data collection effort focusing specifically on African borrowers, Brautigam and Hwang (2016) compiled a dataset of Chinese lending by analyzing official reports in recipient countries and verifying individual projects through in-country interviews. These data collection efforts have cast light on Chinese overseas finance, allowing scholars and policymakers to better understand the patterns in Chinese development finance.

However, it is difficult to compare data on Chinese financing commitments compiled through triangulation of third-party sources with data on the financing commitments of other lenders provided by those lenders themselves. To understand how Chinese finance compares to other source of finance, including private loans and more traditional sources of external finance, it helps to use a data source that tracks commitments across different lenders. For this reason, I follow Bunte (2019) in using data from the World Bank's Debtor Reporting System to analyze which governments borrow from which creditors. This data is compiled from borrowing governments' own accounts of the loans they receive. Since 1951, the World Bank has collected data from all low- and middle-income countries on each of the public or publicly guaranteed loans they take on. This loan-by-loan data is quite sensitive, as it gives an insight into the terms of both private and official financing. Until recently, the World Bank released this data only in highly aggregated form or in response to specific requests. In 2020, however, in light of global concerns about how the COVID-19 crisis had impacted developing countries' debt sustainability, the World Bank released data on annual loan commitments broken down by lender. This data makes it possible to identify how much a country received in loan commitments from private lenders, official bilateral lenders from different countries, and multilateral creditors. A further benefit of data from the Debtor Reporting System compared to the various data collection efforts on Chinese finance is the length of the time series. Data is available annually from the 1950s to the present, which allows me to focus my analysis on the period 1990 to 2018, comparing a time of greater dominance by traditional donors to the period of greater diversification.

The data in the Debtor Reporting System relies on borrowers disclosing the loans they receive. If governments fail to provide information on certain loans, especially Chinese loans, the data may be incomplete. Recent research by Horn et al. (2021) combined the AidData dataset with other data sources to establish a "consensus" database of Chinese lending and found that a large share of Chinese loans, up to 50 percent, were not found in the World Bank's Debtor Reporting System. A large portion of this "hidden" Chinese debt comes from loans to state-owned enterprises or special-purpose vehicles in the borrowing country, occasionally without the active participation of the central government.[2] Such off-balance-sheet lending is worrying from a debt sustainability perspective, especially since the

---

[2] Horn et al. 2021, p. 16.

central government will likely be called upon to assume the debts of state-owned enterprises if the latter become unable to pay.

Nevertheless, for my analysis of developing countries' portfolios of external finance, I prefer to use data from the Debtor Reporting System, even if some portion of Chinese loans are undercounted in the data. For one, I prefer to use a single data source for the vast majority of countries' external finance, so that measurement error across different lenders is likely to be somewhat similar. If governments fail to disclose Chinese loans to state-owned enterprises because they want to lower their seeming debt burden, then they will likely also not disclose private loans to these businesses, increasing the validity of a comparison between these two lenders. Moreover, since my analysis focuses on how alternative finance affects borrowing governments' negotiations with traditional donors, data in the Debtor Reporting System offers a reasonable approximation of the information donors have available about the borrowing country's relative autonomy from traditional donor funds. Finally, any undercounting of Chinese loans as alternative finance should bias against my findings. If I find that countries that report higher levels of Chinese inflows receive better terms on their finance from traditional donors, the overall impact of Chinese lending, including "hidden" debt, may be larger than this estimated effect. In robustness tests, I do find broadly similar results when using alternate data sources.[3]

Even the comprehensive data on external debt from the Debtor Reporting System does not give a complete picture of developing countries' portfolios of external finance, however. Foreign aid or ODA, which is a crucial component of developing countries' external finance, is largely absent from the Debtor Reporting System data. ODA includes both grants, which are transfers with no expectation of repayment, and concessional loans, which are loans priced more cheaply than commercial finance would be.[4] While concessional loans

---

[3] In earlier work, using the AidData data, I find that Chinese loans are associated with the World Bank providing more infrastructure-focused projects (Zeitz 2021a).

[4] The OECD's standards on concessionality have changed over time. Until 2017, loans needed to have a "grant element" of 25 percent to qualify as ODA. This means that the difference between the repayment of the donor's concessional loan and a comparable market loan – the portion that the donor "grants" to the recipient – needs to be 25 percent of the total value of the

are included in the Debtor Reporting System data, grant aid is absent, since grants do not entail liabilities that require payment by the debtor government in the future. On its own, the Debtor Reporting System cannot give a complete picture of developing countries' changing portfolios of external finance.

To establish a more complete picture of developing countries' external finance, I therefore include data on foreign aid commitments reported by donors themselves. Members of the OECD DAC report their annual ODA commitments to the OECD, disaggregated by recipient country and project. This data on foreign aid fills the gaps in the debt data, showing DAC donors' commitments of ODA, including grant aid that is not included in the Debtor Reporting System. Combining the debt and aid data reveals how much developing countries have shifted their funding sources from aid to other, more expensive, financing sources.

The combined data on developing countries' portfolios of external finance shows that nontraditional financing sources became increasingly important from the 2010s onward, while aid from traditional donors remained an important flow. This pattern was first introduced in the Introduction in Figure 1.4. While there is an overall trend of reduced reliance on traditional donors, there is considerable variation among developing countries, with some shifting away from the finance of traditional donors much more dramatically than others. Figure 3.2 plots the median share of external finance from traditional sources, as well as the twenty-fifth and seventy-fifth percentiles. This figure shows that while traditional finance made up virtually the entirety of African countries' external finance in the 1990s, this share began to drop in the mid 2000s. Moreover, the figure shows that the importance of traditional finance varies across African countries, increasingly so over time. While traditional finance from DAC donors and multilateral creditors still makes up more than 80 percent of external finance for half of African governments, that share has reduced to below 60 percent for a substantial minority of countries. Among the global sample of developing countries, including many middle-income countries, there was

loan. Since 2018, the OECD has applied stricter standards for loans to count as ODA, requiring loans to low-income countries to have a 45 percent grant equivalent, while those to lower- and upper-middle-income countries can have a 15 percent and 10 percent grant equivalent, respectively (OECD 2021).

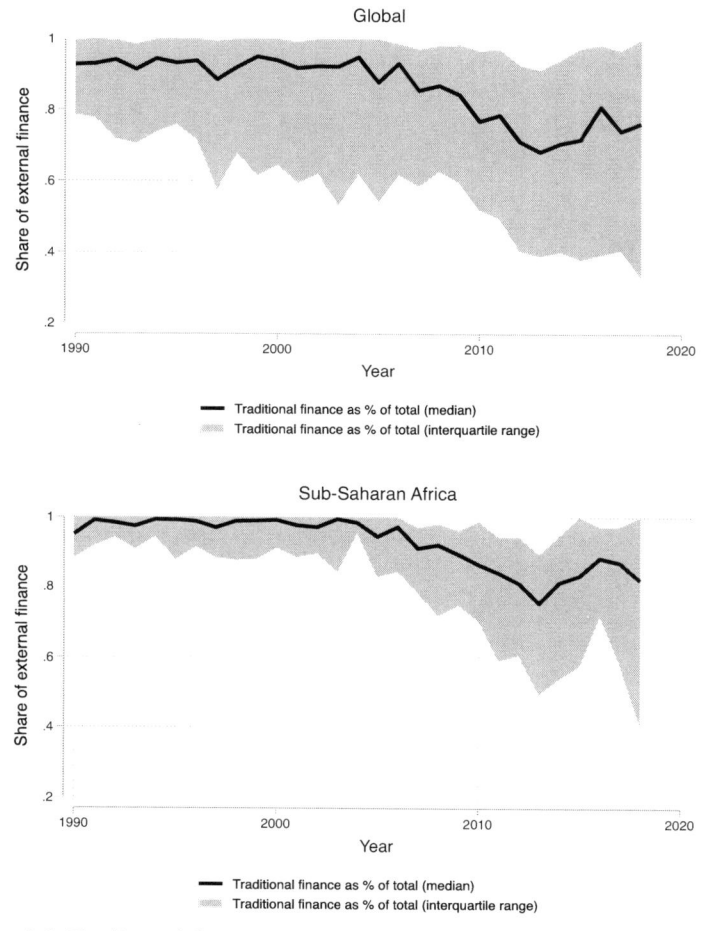

Figure 3.2 Traditional finance as a share of total external finance, 1990–2018. Note: Traditional finance includes DAC ODA, DAC loans, World Bank, and other multilateral finance.

always a considerable range in the importance of traditional finance. For African countries, this variation increased in the 2010s, as some African governments moved away from their reliance on traditional donor funds.

To illustrate the differences among African countries in the extent of their diversification of external finance, Figure 3.3 shows the

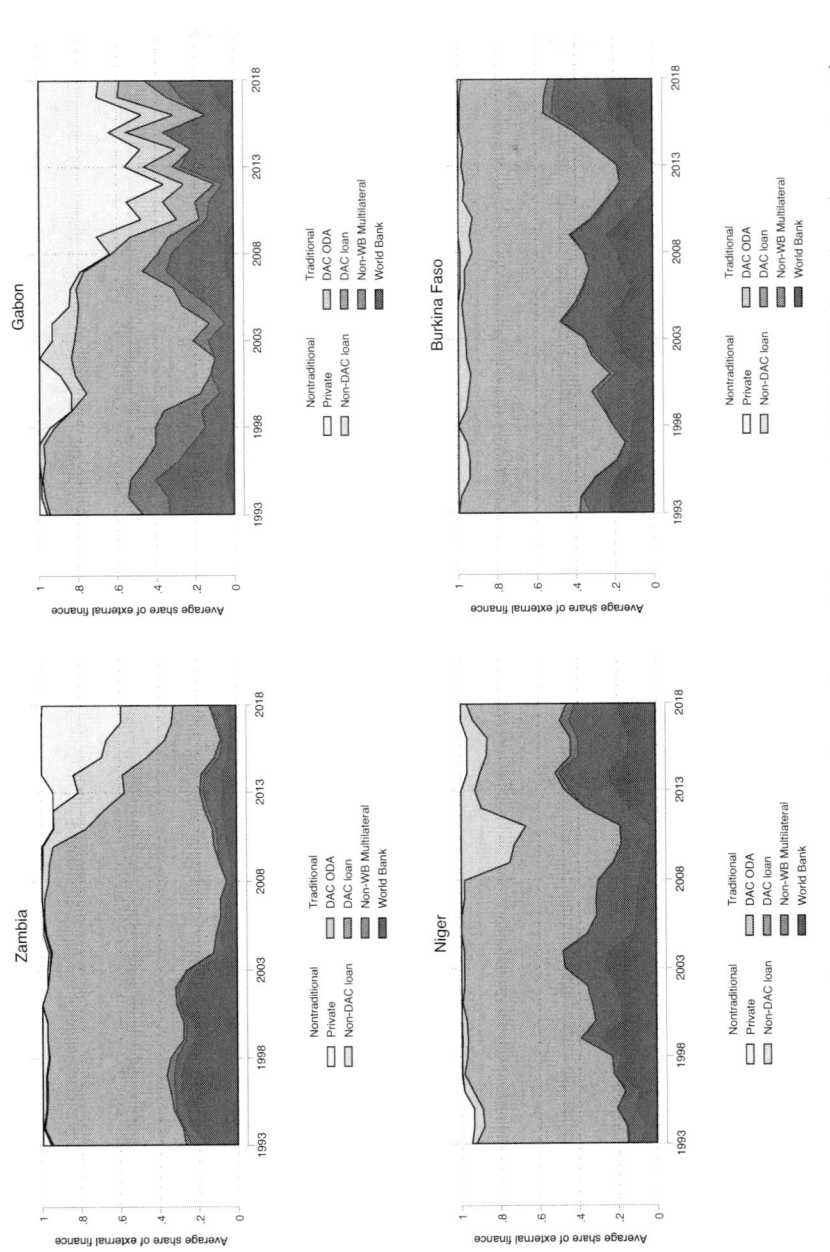

Figure 3.3 Shares of external finance commitments by creditor and donor type in 1990–2018 for selected countries (three-year moving averages).

composition of four African countries' portfolios of external finance over time. All four began with traditional finance, especially DAC ODA, making up the vast majority of their external finance in the 1990s and early 2000s. But then, from the late 2000s onward, the countries' experiences diverged. In Zambia and Gabon, nontraditional finance became an important part of the government's portfolio of external finance. For Zambia, the change to nontraditional finance was more gradual, driven largely by non-DAC loans, especially from China. For Gabon, large private inflows in the 2010s, together with expanding Chinese lending, reshaped the country's portfolio of external finance. By contrast, in Niger and Burkina Faso, the portfolio of external finance remained more oriented toward traditional sources of external finance. While Niger received some Chinese loans in the late 2000s, both Niger and Burkina Faso continued to receive the vast majority of external funding in the form of ODA from DAC donors. The variation over time and across countries in access to and uptake of alternative finance allows me to investigate the effects of reduced reliance on traditional donors on aid negotiations and the aid relationship.

The shifting composition of external finance has led to a decline in the share of countries' external finance coming from traditional donors, but traditional finance has not declined in absolute terms. Total commitments from traditional donors and creditors are considerably higher in the 2010s than they were in the 1990s (see Figure 3.4). New sources of finance have been added to the external finance from traditional donors and creditors. Developing country governments that shifted some share of their external finance to alternative sources in the 2010s still continue to access large amounts of finance from traditional donors and creditors. Negotiations with traditional donors over the terms of aid therefore remain important.

In the analysis, I use three measures from this data to capture the extent to which a borrowing government has reduced its reliance on traditional sources of development finance. *Nontraditional finance (% of external)* includes the total loan commitments from private sources, whether banks or bond markets, as well as all bilateral loans from countries that are not members of the OECD DAC. The denominator includes all loan commitments that borrowing governments received

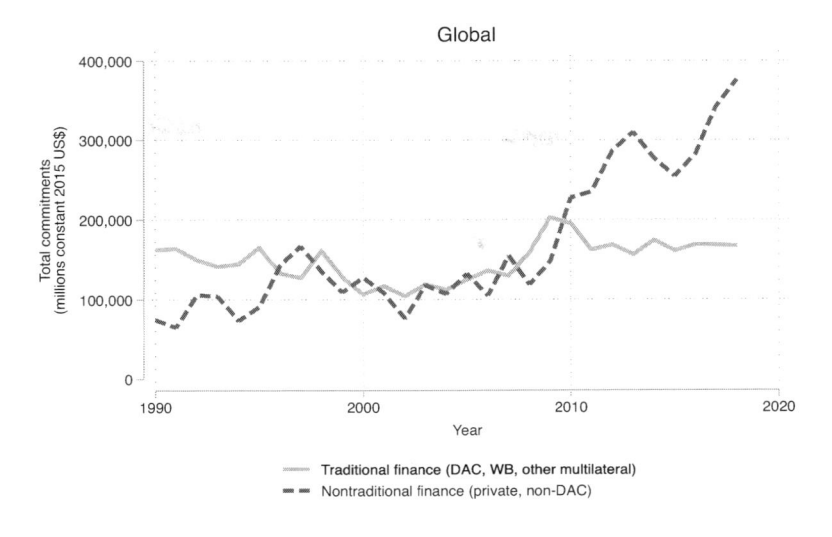

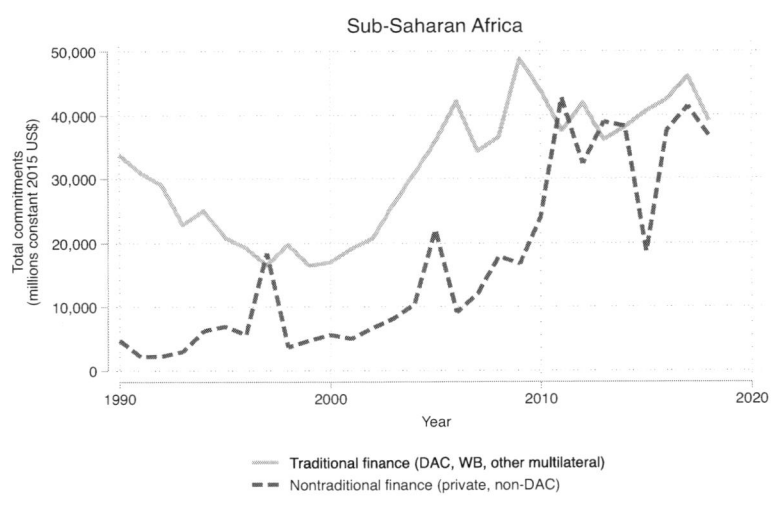

Figure 3.4 Total external finance commitments, 1990–2018

from any sources, including multilateral development banks and DAC bilateral lenders, as well as ODA from DAC donors.[5]

---

[5] The results are largely robust to using the logged volumes of borrowing from China, private lenders, or all nontraditional lenders, rather than the shares of total external finance.

To isolate the specific effects of Chinese loans, since China has been the most significant non-DAC bilateral lender, I use the measure *Chinese finance (% of external)*, which sets annual Chinese finance commitments relative to the remainder of a country's portfolio of external finance, including private loans and other non-DAC loans. To distinguish the effects of private finance, I use the measure *private finance (% of external)*, which sets annual private finance commitments relative to the remainder of a country's portfolio of external finance, including all non-DAC loans, as well as multilateral loans and DAC loans and ODA. For the summary statistics of these measures of alternative finance, as well as other variables used in the analyses, please see Table 3.13 in the appendix to this chapter. Table 3.14 lists the data sources for all indicators used in the analysis.

3.2 Measuring Negotiating Outcomes in the Aid Relationship

To test my expectation that a more diverse portfolio of external finance allows developing countries to increase their bargaining power in negotiations with donors, I measure the extent to which aid negotiations align with the preferences of recipient countries. Measuring the alignment of aid agreements with recipient preferences in a systematic way across developing countries is difficult, since recipient governments differ in their aid preferences. I focus on three observable features of the aid relationship that reflect widely shared preferences among recipient countries, specifically those that have become salient in the comparison between traditional and nontraditional donors. Examining this specific set of outcomes makes it more plausible to pick up changes in the extent to which aid agreements reflect developing countries' preferences. The first outcome measure is the amount of aid that donors extend to a recipient country, since most recipient governments would prefer to receive more aid than less. The second indicator is the share of a donor's projects that are in infrastructure-intensive sectors, since many recipient governments would prefer for aid to help close the infrastructure investment gap. The third variable is the number of conditions attached to development finance, since most borrowers would prefer more flexible aid with fewer conditions. I briefly describe each of these outcome measures in turn.

Beginning with the most basic, recipient governments usually prefer receiving more aid to receiving less. Research on the relationship between donors and recipient governments often uses the volume of donor aid as an indicator of favorable treatment toward a particular recipient.[6] Even if developing country governments have diversified their external finance by shifting to new sources of funding, they are likely to continue to want to receive low-cost concessional or grant finance from traditional donors. In the analysis that follows, I use (logged) total amounts of ODA commitments a donor extends to a recipient country as a measure of generosity toward the recipient.[7]

The measure is taken from the DAC's Creditor Reporting System (CRS), which records project-level data from more than 55 bilateral and multilateral donors to more than 160 recipient countries. I aggregate project-level commitments into annual commitments from each donor to each recipient; in the analysis, I restrict the sample to all bilateral donors that are members of the OECD DAC and to major multilateral donors.

Figure 3.5 reports the average annual commitments of leading traditional donors to recipient countries. Top traditional donors include bilateral DAC donors such as the US, Japan, France, and the UK, as well as multilateral donors such as the European Union and the World Bank agencies, the International Development Agency (IDA) and the International Bank for Reconstruction and Development (IBRD). The figure shows that average aid commitments increased over time and that average levels of ODA commitments are higher for sub-Saharan Africa than for developing countries as a whole. I expect that as borrowing countries decrease their reliance on traditional donors and draw on nontraditional finance, traditional donors will respond by providing more aid.

Second, I capture the extent to which donors' aid aligns with recipient countries' substantive development priorities by measuring the share of donor aid projects that are in infrastructure-intensive sectors. Over the course of the 1990s and 2000s, most traditional donors reduced funding for infrastructure. Several donors' budgets had stagnated, the Millennium Development Goals (MDGs) shifted the focus to achieving social sector goals, and development policy

---

[6] See, for example, Alesina and Dollar 2000; Berthélemy 2006; Dreher et al. 2011; Hoeffler and Outram 2011.

[7] The variable is measured as ODA commitments, rather than disbursements, since commitments are directly under the control of the donor.

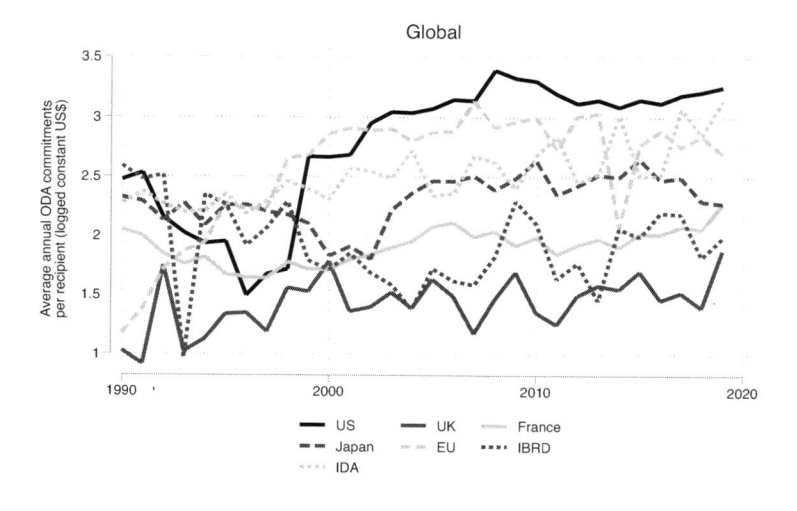

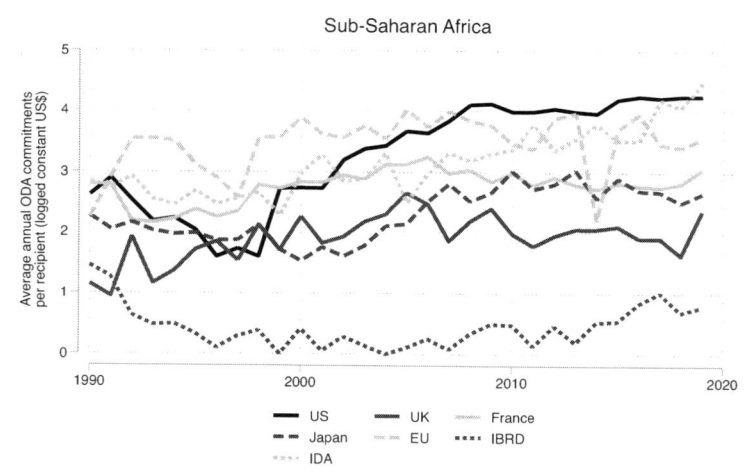

Figure 3.5 Average annual ODA commitments per recipient (logged constant US$), leading donors, 1990–2019.

emphasized the importance of strengthening institutions and governance. By the 2010s, infrastructure projects made up a much smaller share of traditional donors' aid projects, while governance projects were an increasingly important part of donors' aid spending (see Figure 3.6). Meanwhile, China's growing loan portfolio was heavily oriented toward infrastructure. Many developing countries lamented the decline of infrastructure funding and explained their turn toward Chinese loans with reference to their infrastructure funding needs.

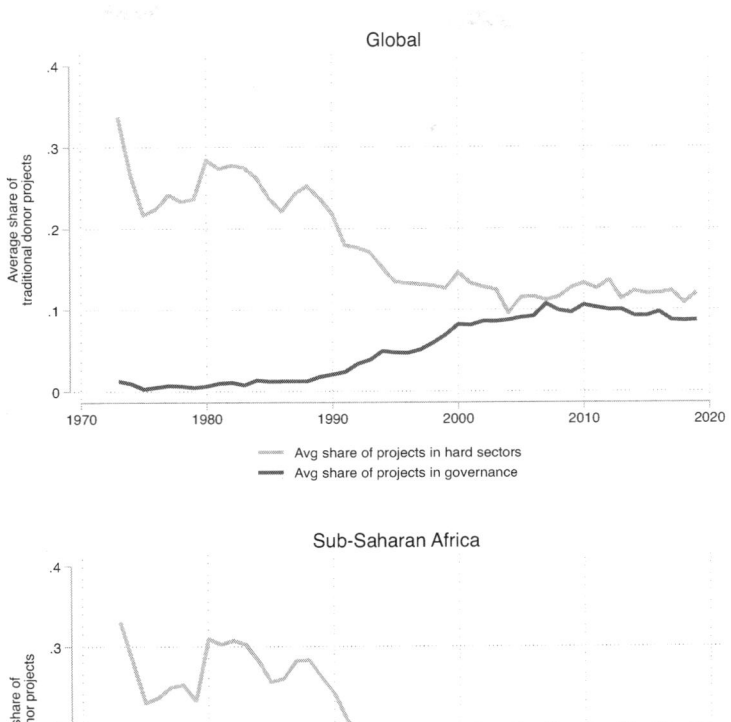

Figure 3.6 Average sectoral allocation of traditional donor projects, 1973–2019.
Note: Traditional donors include all DAC donors, plus the World Bank, Inter-American Development Bank, African Development Bank, Asian Development Bank, European Bank for Reconstruction and Development, and EU institutions.

While not all developing country governments are equally interested in funding for infrastructure projects, it is still reasonable to expect that many developing country governments would prefer more infrastructure funding from traditional donors to fill the funding gap.

Humphrey and Michaelowa (2019, p. 22) report from their case studies of Ethiopia, Tanzania, and Malawi that recipient governments had a strong preference for infrastructure finance, second only to fully flexible budget support. Governments may use greater bargaining leverage to push donors to allocate a greater share of their projects to infrastructure. In the following analysis, I therefore use a measure of the percentage of donor projects in a given year that are in infrastructure-intensive sectors. I refer to these infrastructure-intensive sectors as "hard" sectors as a short-hand to distinguish them from "soft" sectors such as health and education. The data for the sectoral allocation of donors again comes from the OECD CRS database. When donors enter their projects into the database, they assign each project to one of fifty-four sub-sectors. I classify projects as being in "hard sectors" if they fall into one of the following six categories: (1) water supply and sanitation; (2) transport and storage; (3) communications; (4) energy; (5) agriculture, forestry, and fishing; and (6) industry, mining, and construction, since these are sectors that are most likely to have some sort of infrastructure component.[8]

The data shows that hard-sector projects compose less than 20 percent of traditional donors' projects in the 2000–2019 period (see Figure 3.6). One exception among the traditional bilateral donors is Japan, which allocated 30 percent of its projects in recipient countries to hard sectors in 2000–2019. For multilateral donors such as the World Bank, African Development Bank, and Asian Development Bank, with more resources, expertise, and the ability to raise funds in private markets, hard-sector projects compose between 20 percent and 50 percent of all projects, with the percentage increasing in the latter half of the 2010s. I expect that borrowing countries that increase their autonomy from traditional donor aid and thereby increase their bargaining power subsequently receive a higher share of donor projects in infrastructure-intensive sectors.

Finally, I measure negotiation outcomes using data on the policy requirements that donors attach to their aid. All else equal, recipient governments would usually prefer the flexibility of fewer conditions attached to aid, while donors would prefer the control, oversight, and accountability of attaching more conditions to aid. For this reason, previous studies have used the number and stringency of conditions

[8] Zeitz 2021a.

as an indicator of donor favoritism toward particular countries, with the interpretation that countries that receive fewer conditions are receiving special treatment.[9] The World Bank first released data on the conditionality of its development policy loans in the late 2010s, enabling scholars to study patterns and partiality in World Bank conditionality.[10]

Unlike the World Bank and IMF, most bilateral donors do not release systematic data on the conditions they attach to their aid. I therefore use World Bank data to examine whether countries receive fewer conditions when they diversify their portfolio of external finance. In particular, I use two measures of the conditionality of World Bank lending. The first is the total count of "prior actions," which are the most binding conditions, since they must be satisfied before governments receive funds from the World Bank. The second is a more specific count of prior actions pertaining to governance issues, since borrowing governments often perceive these to be the most intrusive. The World Bank's data classifies conditions as belonging to different sectors, and for this governance conditionality indicator I count the number of conditions per project that are classified as focusing on the "public administration" sector.

In the analysis, I investigate whether countries receive fewer conditions on their World Bank loans when they diversify their external finance away from traditional sources. This analysis builds on the work of Hernandez (2017), who shows that the World Bank reduces its conditionality in African countries when those countries borrow in larger amounts from nontraditional donors, including China, though he does not consider private credit as an alternative form of finance, nor whether countries' overall reliance on traditional donors declines when they borrow from new creditors. I expect that countries that reduce their reliance on traditional sources of finance will receive fewer conditions attached to their World Bank projects, reflecting their increased bargaining power.

3.3 Differences among Borrowing Governments

To fully test my argument about the financial statecraft of borrowers, I examine differences among borrowing governments in translating

---

[9] Clark and Dolan 2020; Kilby 2009; Nelson 2014; Stone 2008.
[10] Clark and Dolan 2020; Hernandez 2017.

a diverse portfolio of external finance into preferred aid terms. As outlined in Chapter 2, I expect greater autonomy from traditional donor funds to be more likely to translate into negotiating leverage when the recipient country is especially important to traditional donors and when donors have greater trust in the borrowing government. I test for these differences among borrowing governments using several indicators of borrower strategic significance and donor trust.

To measure which developing countries are especially important to donors, I rely on indicators that have been validated in previous studies of foreign aid. The first is a binary indicator for whether a country hosts US military bases on its territory.[11] Countries that host US bases are close allies of the US, key to the US' broader foreign policy goals and often considered important anchors within their subregion by other Western countries besides the US. While the US' foreign policy does not completely overlap with that of other DAC donors, developing countries that are close allies of the US are likely to also be important to DAC donors. I therefore investigate whether there is a stronger effect of alternative finance on aid terms among those countries that host US military bases.

The other measure of recipient importance is a binary indicator for whether the recipient country currently holds a temporary seat on the United Nations (UN) Security Council.[12] Countries that hold the rotating temporary seats vote on important resolutions on matters of international peace and security. Research has shown that in the years a country holds a temporary Security Council seat, it tends to receive higher amounts of aid, likely because donors want to maintain a good relationship with countries that can cast influential votes.[13] I test whether a positive relationship between alternative finance and aid agreements is stronger when a recipient country holds a temporary UN Security Council seat.

I use a number of measures to capture donor trust in the recipient government, since the sources of donor trust (and distrust) are

---

[11] Vine 2019. Note that Vine's data provides snapshots of countries hosting US military bases in 1776–1903, 1939, 1945, 1989, 2015, and 2019. For my purposes, I use data from 1989, 2015, and 2019 and carry data forward in the years between snapshots, presuming that most bases remain open until the next year with available data.

[12] Dreher et al. 2009a.

[13] Vreeland and Dreher 2014.

varied. As a first step, I use an indicator that captures behavior consistent with donor trust, namely, a donor's use of recipient country institutions for executing development programs. In surveys monitoring the implementation of the Paris Declaration on Aid Effectiveness in 2005, 2007, and 2010, donor staff in recipient countries reported what share of their aid to the government sector used recipient country public financial management systems, providing data at the dyad-survey level. Following Knack (2013), I treat the donor's reported share of aid using government systems as a measure of donor trust and expect that in dyads with higher levels of trust, an increase in borrowing from alternative creditors will have a bigger impact. Unfortunately, however, the data is only available from three survey waves and a limited number of recipient countries.[14] I carry the data forward by three years to fill missing observations between 2005 and 2013, which still only covers a small share of the dyad-years in the dataset. I therefore complement this survey-based measure of donor trust with indicators at the recipient level that are likely associated with donor trust.

To capture donors' likely trust in the country's public financial management systems, I use data from the World Bank's Country Policy and Institutional Assessment (CPIA), which annually measures the quality of a country's public sector management and institutions in countries that borrow from the World Bank. One CPIA subcomponent assesses countries' "quality of budgetary and financial management," evaluating the "the extent to which there is a comprehensive and credible budget, linked to policy priorities."[15] I expect that if the World Bank assesses a country to have higher quality budgeting and financial management institutions, donors are more likely to trust the government and respond to a diverse portfolio of external finance by accommodating the recipient government's preferences. As a more general indicator of the institutional context that is likely to shape donor trust, I use a measure of perceptions of corruption from Transparency International. This measure is widely available for recipient countries in the sample and uses the assessments of country experts and private sector participants to score the level of public sector corruption in a country. I expect that countries with higher levels of perceived corruption will benefit less from diversifying their portfolio of external finance.

---

[14] Thirty-four countries in 2005, fifty-four in 2007, and seventy-eight in 2010.
[15] World Bank 2017a, p. 35.

Finally, I use two measures to get at the political roots of donors' trust in the government. To measure the recipient country's political settlement, I draw on the PolSett dataset, which relies on the coding of country experts to classify the political settlement in forty-two developing countries from 1945 to 2019.[16] Governments are classified along two dimensions over time: the breadth of the social foundation and the power configuration. Regimes with broader social foundations are more inclusive, integrating a greater number of social groups. Regimes with a concentrated power configuration have clear authority resting with one group within the regime, while those with dispersed power have "no such coherence, often reflecting active social cleavages among powerful groups that foment conflicts among insider factions."[17] The combination of broad-narrow social foundation and concentrated-dispersed power configuration leads to a four-part typology of broad-dispersed, narrow-dispersed, broad-concentrated, and narrow-concentrated. I expect that regimes with a concentrated power configuration, and especially a broad-concentrated political settlement, will be best placed to use borrowing from alternative creditors to their advantage, since donors likely see them as more reliable and credible. Given the limited number of countries in the PolSett dataset, I also use data from the Varieties of Democracy dataset on the size of groups supporting the governing regime, which is available for a much wider set of countries.[18] This indicator reflects the assessment of country experts on what proportion of the population support the regime, with support drawn from population groups such as the urban middle classes, specific ethnic or racial groups, or the military. Governments with a larger support base are likely to enjoy greater stability and therefore greater trust from donors, putting them in a better position to use alternative finance to their advantage.

3.4 Estimation

To estimate the relationship between a country's portfolio of external finance and the terms of its aid agreements with traditional donors, I rely mostly on dyadic data at the donor–recipient–year level. The data

---

[16] Kelsall et al. 2022.
[17] Kelsall et al. 2022, p. 53.
[18] Coppedge et al. 2021, p. 137.

on volumes of traditional donor aid and the infrastructure focus of aid are both in this structure. The dyadic format of the data allows me to control for factors specific to the donor–recipient relationship that might bias estimates of the relationship between alternative finance and aid terms. Moreover, in robustness tests, I can probe which individual donors or multilateral lenders are driving the results. Since the data on the number of conditions is only available in a systematic fashion from the World Bank and since countries may receive multiple loans in the same year, this data is at the project-year level.

Across models, there are temporal patterns in the data that might induce spurious correlations. At the same time that developing countries increased their access to alternative finance, driven by debt forgiveness and global liquidity, donors reduced conditionality and increased infrastructure financing in response to pressure from activists and scholars, and to changing thinking within aid bureaucracies. A positive relationship between diverse external finance and preferred aid terms might simply be a function of concurrent trends. To account for these temporal trends in the data, all dyadic models include year-fixed effects. The dyadic models also include donor-fixed effects to account for unobserved heterogeneity at the donor level. I do not include recipient-fixed effects since the aim of the models is to understand how donors respond to variation in reliance on alternative finance *across* recipients.

To account for factors that vary across recipient countries and correlate with their access to alternative finance and relationship with traditional donors, I include a battery of controls drawn from the literature on aid relationships, Chinese development finance, and developing countries' market access. While many attributes of recipient countries are likely to affect the aid package they receive from donors or how much alternative finance they are able to access, I only include variables as controls if they affect both alternative finance and the outcome, thereby acting as confounders in the relationship of interest.

The first cluster of controls are those that are likely to affect both Chinese finance and private market finance, as well as the aid agreements with traditional donors. These include a country's level of development, measured as *GDP per capita (log)*; its level of indebtedness, measured as *government debt (% of GDP)*; and *natural resource rents (% of GDP)*. Furthermore, research has shown that the domestic political environment affects donor generosity, market access, and Chinese finance.[19] I therefore control for democracy, using the V-Dem measure of *electoral democracy* (or "polyarchy").

The second cluster of control variables are those that are more specific to a country's access to Chinese finance, rather than private market finance, yet are also likely to affect the terms of a country's traditional aid. These concern a borrowing country's geopolitical importance, ideological alignment, and economic relationship with China and traditional donors. I control for whether a recipient country holds a temporary seat on the *UN Security Council*, which boosts a country's geopolitical appeal for DAC donors in those years. At the dyadic level, the models include *ideological proximity* between the recipient country and the bilateral donor, using Bailey et al. 2016's measure of ideal point distance estimated using UN General Assembly votes. To capture whether aid from either China or traditional donors is deployed in line with trade competition, the models include a measure of the difference between total trade with the donor and total trade with China. Higher values of *dyadic trade vs China* indicate that the recipient is a more important trading partner for the donor than for China.

The models of aid commitments and sectoral allocation are both estimated using a simple linear model for ease of interpretation. As a robustness check, I also estimate the models of hard sector aid using a fractional probit estimator as a robustness check, to account for the fact that the dependent variable is constrained to range between 0 and 1. The results obtained using the fractional probit estimator are very similar, and I report the results from the linear models for ease of interpretation. The dyadic data on aid allocation includes many zeros, since not all donors extend aid to all recipients in all years. However, models that are frequently used to account for a high incidence of zeros, such as hurdle models, are not appropriate for this data. Hurdle models assume there are separate data-generating processes for zero and nonzero observations, such that they can be modeled in separate equations, with the residuals from the hurdle equation separating zeros and nonzeros uncorrelated to the residuals of the outcome equation that models nonzero outcomes. However, in the dyadic aid allocation data, very few of the zeros come from dyads where the donor extended

---

[19] Alesina and Dollar 2000; Ballard-Rosa et al. 2019; Bermeo 2017; Dreher and Fuchs 2015.

no aid to the recipient in any of the years.[20] The vast majority of zeros come from dyads where the donor does extend aid to that recipient in other years, suggesting that the zeros should be modeled together with nonzero outcomes.

For the sake of simplicity, these models are estimated using ordinary least squares, as depicted in Eq. 3.1. β_1 is the coefficient of interest on *Alternative finance$_{it-1}$*, lagged by a year and measured as the share of external finance from all nontraditional sources, the share of external finance from Chinese lending, or the share of external finance from private lenders. δ is a vector of coefficients on a matrix of controls x_{it-1} measured at the level of the recipient country and lagged by a year, while μ is a vector of coefficients on a matrix of controls x_{ijt-1} measured at the dyadic level and lagged by a year. All dyadic models include α_j, donor-fixed effects, and σ_t, year-fixed effects. Standard errors are clustered at the dyad level.

$$Aid\ terms_{ijt} = \beta_1 Alternative\ finance_{it-1} + \delta x_{it-1} + \mu x_{ijt-1}$$
$$+ \alpha_j + \sigma_t + \epsilon_{ijt}. \tag{3.1}$$

The World Bank's data on "prior actions" is available at the project level. Recipients can receive multiple development policy loans in a given year and receive none in other years. I therefore follow Clark and Dolan (2020) in analyzing the data at the project-year level, where the year is the year a project was approved. The dependent variables are the total count of conditions attached to a development policy loan and the count of public administration-specific conditions. The models include recipient country-fixed effects to account for unobserved factors that determine why some countries receive more conditions than others. An internal policy shift within the World Bank led to a reduction in the conditions attached to programs from 2012 onward.[21] I therefore include a binary variable for whether the project is in the post-2012 period. Unlike in the dyadic models of donor aid, the measure of alternative finance is not lagged by a year, since the planning and negotiating period for development policy loans is short, so alternative finance is measured in the same year as the year of

---

[20] Among the ca. 36,000 observations used in the main model, less than 1 percent come from dyads where there was no aid in any of the years.
[21] Clark and Dolan 2020.

approval.[22] These models are estimated as depicted in Eq. 3.2, where β_1 is the coefficient of interest on *Alternative finance*$_{it}$, α_i is a recipient country-fixed effect, and $\sigma_{Post-2012}$ is a binary measure for years after 2012. In extensions, I include the same matrix of control variables from the models above. Since the dependent variable in these models is a count measure, the models are estimated using the Poisson pseudo-maximum likelihood (PPML) estimator, which allows for the inclusion of fixed effects even in smaller samples. Standard errors are clustered at the recipient country level.

$$Conditions_{it} = e^{\beta_1 \, Alternative \, finance_{it} + \alpha_i + \sigma_{Post-2012} + \epsilon_{it}}. \qquad (3.2)$$

Finally, to test whether alternative finance has different effects on aid agreements depending on the significance of the recipient country and donor trust, I estimate a series of models with interaction terms. As in the models above, the main measure of alternative finance is the share of external finance from nontraditional sources. In turn, I estimate models that interact this measure of alternative finance with two measures of recipient significance (US military bases and UN Security Council seat) and five measures of donor trust (use of country systems, CPIA budgetary management score, corruption perception, political settlement type, and regime support). These models are estimated as depicted in Eq. 3.3, with other controls, donor-, and year-fixed effects remaining the same as in the dyadic models above.[23]

$$\begin{aligned} Aid \, terms_{ijt} = {} & \beta_1 Alternative \, finance_{it-1} \times Moderator_{it-1} \\ & + \beta_2 Alternative \, finance_{it-1} + \beta_3 Moderator_{it-1} \quad (3.3) \\ & + \delta x_{it-1} + \mu x_{ijt-1} + \alpha_j + \sigma_t + \epsilon_{ijt}. \end{aligned}$$

3.5 Results

Across the board, I find that developing countries' access to alternative finance is associated with preferred aid agreements with traditional donors. When developing countries diversify their sources of external

---

[22] In 92 percent of cases in the dataset, projects are negotiated in the same year that they are approved.

[23] Note that one of these moderators, use of country systems, is measured at the dyad-year level, varying both by donor and recipient over time, but the rest are measured only at the recipient-year level.

finance, both by borrowing from China and from private lenders, they tend to receive terms on traditional aid that are more aligned with their preferences. This pattern holds across different features of aid agreements, including the volumes, sectoral focus, and conditionality of aid. The dynamic holds among both bilateral donors and multilateral donors, although bilateral donors appear more responsive to a recipient's changing portfolio of external finance, especially when recipients increase their reliance on Chinese bilateral loans. I report results for both the global sample of low- and middle-income countries, as well as only recipient countries in sub-Saharan Africa. These disaggregated results show that the relationship between alternative finance and preferred aid agreements is stronger among sub-Saharan African countries.

3.5.1 Volumes of Aid

Beginning with results on the volume of traditional donor aid allocation, I find evidence that traditional donors provide more aid to recipient countries when the latter receive a higher share of external finance from nontraditional sources. Table 3.1 reports findings on the total aid allocations of bilateral DAC donors disaggregated by the region of the recipient and the form of alternative finance. Column 1 reports results for all DAC donors and all aid recipients for which there is data in the period 1991–2019. It shows a positive and statistically significant relationship between the share of a country's external finance that comes from either private or non-DAC lenders and the volume of aid that DAC donors subsequently extend. When the sample of recipients is restricted in column 2 to only include countries in sub-Saharan Africa, the effect of alternative finance on the volume of donors' subsequent aid allocation is even stronger.

Substantively, the results in column 1 mean that a recipient country in the tenth percentile is expected to receive $4.17 million in aid, while a country in the ninetieth percentile of nontraditional finance would receive $5.24 million. For sub-Saharan African countries, the prediction for a country at the tenth percentile of nontraditional finance is $4.12 million in bilateral aid, while a country at the ninetieth percentile would expect $6.52 million. At first glance, these effect sizes may seem small. After all, countries in sub-Saharan Africa received an average of $422 million in annual aid commitments from DAC

Table 3.1 *Nontraditional finance as a share of recipient external finance and aid allocation volumes by DAC donors, 1991–2019*

	(1) Global	(2) Africa	(3) Global	(4) Africa	(5) Global	(6) Africa
Nontraditional finance share	0.276***	0.779***				
	(0.059)	(0.103)				
Chinese finance share			−0.106	0.379***		
			(0.085)	(0.102)		
Private finance share					0.627***	1.132***
					(0.071)	(0.130)
GDP per capita	−0.348***	−0.306***	−0.301***	−0.203***	−0.400***	−0.329***
	(0.027)	(0.048)	(0.026)	(0.047)	(0.028)	(0.048)
Central government debt (% of GDP)	−0.002***	−0.003***	−0.002***	−0.003***	−0.002***	−0.003***
	(0.000)	(0.001)	(0.000)	(0.001)	(0.000)	(0.001)
Natural resource rents (% of GDP)	−0.010***	−0.002	−0.010***	0.000	−0.010***	−0.003
	(0.002)	(0.003)	(0.002)	(0.003)	(0.002)	(0.003)
Polyarchy	0.639***	0.583***	0.624***	0.591***	0.550***	0.428**
	(0.116)	(0.190)	(0.117)	(0.197)	(0.114)	(0.189)
UNSC	0.274***	0.174***	0.292***	0.234***	0.236***	0.121***
	(0.031)	(0.044)	(0.032)	(0.045)	(0.030)	(0.044)
UNGA distance	0.349***	0.248***	0.362***	0.229***	0.352***	0.302***
	(0.039)	(0.075)	(0.039)	(0.075)	(0.038)	(0.075)
Dyadic trade vs. China	0.199***	0.167***	0.197***	0.158***	0.195***	0.161***
	(0.015)	(0.021)	(0.015)	(0.022)	(0.015)	(0.021)
Observations	42,022	17,049	42,022	17,049	42,022	17,049

Standard errors in parentheses.

All models include donor- and year-fixed effects.

* $p < 0.10$, ** $p < 0.05$, *** $p < 0.01$.

donors in the 1990–2019 period. However, it is important to bear in mind that these models are estimated at the dyadic level and include donor-fixed effects. The models therefore estimate the amount that a single DAC donor increases their funding allocation to recipient countries in response to higher levels of nontraditional finance. On average, individual DAC donors annually committed $28.48 million in aid to each country in sub-Saharan Africa in the period 1990–2019. Given these dyad-level averages in aid commitments, the effect of nontraditional finance on individual DAC donors' commitments is substantive. Moreover, since recipient countries receive aid from many different DAC donors, the cumulative effect on total aid, aggregated across all donors, can be substantively large.

Breaking down alternative finance into Chinese bilateral lending and private finance reveals that both are associated with higher levels of subsequent DAC aid commitments, though more so for recipient countries in sub-Saharan Africa. Columns 3 and 4 report results for the share of external finance coming from Chinese loans. For the global sample of developing countries, the association between the share of external finance from China and subsequent traditional aid commitments is statistically indistinguishable from zero. For African recipient countries, however, the share of external finance from China has a positive and statistically significant relationship with DAC donors' aid commitments. When it comes to private loans as a share of external finance, there is a positive and statistically significant relationship both among the global and the sub-Saharan African samples, though the effect is larger among African recipients.

Across the results in Table 3.1, the coefficients on controls are largely in the direction expected. Recipient countries that are wealthier, more indebted, and richer in natural resources receive lower volumes of aid from DAC donors. Meanwhile, recipient countries that are more democratic, hold a temporary UN Security Council seat, and are more important trading partners for a given donor receive more aid. The only coefficient on a control variable that is contrary to expectation is for the measure of ideological alignment, where the results suggest that donors allocate more aid to countries with diverging, rather than similar, UN voting records.

The models in Table 3.1 include donor-fixed effects, to account for differences in donors' aid allocation that might bias the results, such as if Germany is more likely to extend aid to countries that also happen to borrow in large volumes from China. Separating out the data on individual donor countries reveals differences among the donors in their responsiveness to recipients' portfolios of external finance. Table 3.2 reports results for a recipient's overall nontraditional finance share, combining private and non-DAC bilateral lending, and the subsequent volume of aid commitments to African countries, disaggregated by individual donor. The results in Table 3.2 show that the headline results in Table 3.1 are driven by the US, the UK, Nordic donors, and other Western European donor countries. These traditional donors are most likely to respond to a recipient's increased autonomy from donor funds by increasing their own aid commitments. By contrast, for Canada, France, and Germany, a recipient country's share of external finance from nontraditional sources appears to have little bearing on the volume of aid allocated.

To further distinguish among donors, Table 3.3 reports results using data on the aid allocation of major multilateral donors, including the World Bank's agencies and the leading regional development banks, such as the Inter-American Development Bank or the African Development Bank. I find that for the global pool of recipients, multilateral donors allocate increased amounts of aid when recipient countries receive a larger share of their external finance from nontraditional sources; see column 1 of Table 3.3. This result is driven by recipient countries' expansion of private borrowing, rather than Chinese finance. The results for African recipients replicate this pattern. These findings show that multilateral donors are also responsive to recipient countries' degree of autonomy from traditional donor funds, though they are less responsive to Chinese lending than bilateral donors are, which may be because bilateral donors are more likely to respond to Chinese lending in the context of geopolitical competition.

Next, I break the results for donors' aid commitments up into distinct time periods. Table 3.4 shows results for models estimating the relationship between alternative finance and subsequent donor commitments to African countries in the 1990s, 2000s, and 2010s. Columns 1–3 show results from the 1990s for the share of a country's external finance coming from all nontraditional finance, Chinese finance, and private finance. In this early period, when Chinese finance made up only 1 percent of recipient countries' portfolios of external finance on average, the relationship between the Chinese finance

Table 3.2 *Nontraditional finance as a share of recipient external finance and aid allocation volumes to sub-Saharan African countries, by donor country or grouping, 1991–2019*

	(1) US	(2) UK	(3) Canada	(4) France	(5) Germany	(6) Nordics	(7) W. Europe	(8) E. Europe	(9) Asia	(10) Antipodes
Non-traditional finance share	1.688*** (0.519)	1.709** (0.660)	0.556 (0.349)	0.846 (0.515)	0.789 (0.502)	0.344** (0.150)	0.170* (0.101)	0.099 (0.070)	0.196 (0.283)	0.202 (0.163)
GDP per capita	−0.525** (0.252)	−0.532* (0.305)	−0.338** (0.166)	0.166 (0.290)	−0.516** (0.206)	−0.483*** (0.066)	−0.265*** (0.044)	0.028 (0.027)	−0.367*** (0.114)	−0.058 (0.048)
Central government debt (% of GDP)	−0.008** (0.003)	−0.002 (0.003)	−0.005** (0.002)	−0.004 (0.004)	−0.008** (0.003)	−0.002** (0.001)	−0.001* (0.001)	0.000 (0.001)	−0.007*** (0.002)	−0.002*** (0.001)
Natural resource rents (% of GDP)	−0.013 (0.015)	−0.003 (0.016)	−0.011 (0.010)	0.006 (0.019)	0.001 (0.015)	−0.012*** (0.004)	−0.004 (0.003)	−0.003 (0.004)	−0.032*** (0.009)	−0.002 (0.005)
Polyarchy	0.929 (0.962)	−0.524 (1.199)	1.150 (0.812)	0.924 (1.277)	1.360 (1.074)	0.544** (0.259)	0.815*** (0.182)	−0.369*** (0.116)	0.806 (0.600)	−0.159 (0.291)
UNSC	0.472*** (0.167)	0.373 (0.285)	0.312* (0.184)	0.511** (0.219)	0.279 (0.171)	0.142** (0.069)	0.165*** (0.051)	0.071 (0.068)	0.646*** (0.168)	−0.016 (0.064)

Table 3.2 *(cont.)*

	(1) US	(2) UK	(3) Canada	(4) France	(5) Germany	(6) Nordics	(7) W. Europe	(8) E. Europe	(9) Asia	(10) Antipodes
UNGA distance	0.307	0.514	0.196	0.075	−0.227	0.326***	0.274***	−0.136***	0.797***	0.094
	(0.441)	(0.563)	(0.404)	(0.477)	(0.487)	(0.093)	(0.064)	(0.047)	(0.253)	(0.148)
Dyadic trade vs. China	0.006	0.582***	0.166*	0.623***	0.131	0.114***	0.184***	0.023	0.164**	0.117***
	(0.144)	(0.152)	(0.084)	(0.104)	(0.126)	(0.029)	(0.024)	(0.017)	(0.070)	(0.031)
Observations	865	849	848	865	840	6,657	13,193	1,266	2,441	1,908

Standard errors in parentheses.
All models include year-fixed effects.
* $p < 0.10$, ** $p < 0.05$, *** $p < 0.01$.

Table 3.3 *Nontraditional finance and aid allocation volumes by multilateral donors, 1991–2019*

	(1) Global	(2) Africa	(3) Global	(4) Africa	(5) Global	(6) Africa
Nontraditional finance share	0.801***	0.557*				
	(0.282)	(0.296)				
Chinese finance share			−0.723*	0.149		
			(0.372)	(0.359)		
Private finance share					1.596***	1.138***
					(0.339)	(0.362)
GDP per capita	−0.352***	−0.281**	−0.238**	−0.224*	−0.449***	−0.315**
	(0.120)	(0.137)	(0.117)	(0.131)	(0.116)	(0.134)
Central government debt (% of GDP)	−0.003**	−0.004***	−0.003**	−0.004***	−0.003**	−0.004***
	(0.001)	(0.001)	(0.001)	(0.001)	(0.001)	(0.001)
Natural resource rents (% of GDP)	−0.012*	−0.002	−0.011*	−0.000	−0.012*	−0.003
	(0.006)	(0.007)	(0.006)	(0.007)	(0.006)	(0.006)
Polyarchy	0.970**	1.018**	0.868*	0.983**	0.793*	0.920**
	(0.453)	(0.447)	(0.459)	(0.457)	(0.434)	(0.433)
UNSC	0.842***	0.559***	0.892***	0.589***	0.759***	0.503***
	(0.125)	(0.145)	(0.128)	(0.148)	(0.123)	(0.142)
Observations	8,731	4,287	8,731	4,287	8,731	4,287

Standard errors in parentheses.

All models include donor- and year-fixed effects.

* $p < 0.10$, ** $p < 0.05$, *** $p < 0.01$.

Table 3.4 *Nontraditional finance as a share of recipient external finance and aid allocation volumes from bilateral DAC donors to sub-Saharan Africa, by decade*

	(1) 1990s	(2) 1990s	(3) 1990s	(4) 2000s	(5) 2000s	(6) 2000s	(7) 2010s	(8) 2010s	(9) 2010s
Nontraditional finance share	1.214*** (0.272)			0.979*** (0.152)			0.580*** (0.099)		
Chinese finance share		−1.403 (0.991)			0.257 (0.156)			0.497*** (0.121)	
Private finance share			1.311*** (0.277)			1.269*** (0.176)			0.945*** (0.131)
GDP per capita	−0.039 (0.088)	0.114 (0.078)	−0.057 (0.088)	−0.384*** (0.059)	−0.251*** (0.057)	−0.388*** (0.058)	−0.357*** (0.046)	−0.284*** (0.044)	−0.382*** (0.046)
Central government debt (% of GDP)	−0.006*** (0.001)	−0.007*** (0.001)	−0.006*** (0.001)	−0.003*** (0.001)	−0.002*** (0.001)	−0.002*** (0.001)	−0.006*** (0.001)	−0.005*** (0.001)	−0.006*** (0.001)
Natural resource rents (% of GDP)	−0.005 (0.006)	−0.002 (0.006)	−0.006 (0.006)	0.004 (0.003)	0.006* (0.003)	0.003 (0.003)	−0.008** (0.003)	−0.006* (0.003)	−0.009*** (0.003)
Polyarchy	0.456* (0.266)	0.443 (0.270)	0.439* (0.264)	0.701*** (0.226)	0.711*** (0.238)	0.583** (0.228)	0.661*** (0.198)	0.686*** (0.202)	0.478** (0.197)

UNSC	−0.055	−0.173	−0.045	0.245***	0.301***	0.209***	0.142**	0.234***	0.052
	(0.117)	(0.123)	(0.117)	(0.074)	(0.077)	(0.072)	(0.071)	(0.070)	(0.073)
UNGA distance	0.165	0.102	0.187	−0.029	−0.073	0.077	0.582***	0.568***	0.617***
	(0.130)	(0.130)	(0.131)	(0.116)	(0.117)	(0.120)	(0.081)	(0.081)	(0.081)
Dyadic trade vs. China	0.231***	0.222***	0.228***	0.146***	0.131***	0.137***	0.166***	0.159***	0.163***
	(0.029)	(0.031)	(0.029)	(0.027)	(0.027)	(0.027)	(0.026)	(0.026)	(0.026)
Observations	2,940	2,940	2,940	6,095	6,095	6,095	8,014	8,014	8,014

Standard errors in parentheses.
All models include donor- and year-fixed effects.
* $p < 0.10$, ** $p < 0.05$, *** $p < 0.01$.

share and donors' aid allocations was negative, though not statistically significant. This pattern changed in later periods, as columns 5 and 8 report. As the share of Chinese finance went from an average of 1 percent of countries' external finance in the 1990s to 4 percent in the 2000s and 9 percent in the 2010s, the association with traditional donors' aid became positive and significant over time. Private finance, by contrast, had a stronger positive association with traditional donors' aid commitments in the early period, waning somewhat over time, though remaining statistically significant, as columns 3, 6, and 9 report.

Finally, as an extension of the main results, I consider the possibility that the relationship between alternative finance and donors' aid commitments is nonlinear, with the relationship becoming weaker at very high levels of alternative finance. If donors are responding to recipient's increasing use of alternative finance in order to retain their relationship with the recipient government, they may conclude that a close relationship is no longer possible once the recipient draws extensively on alternative finance. In Table 3.5, I report results of models including the squared term of each nontraditional finance share. The results show that the overall linear relationship remains robust to including the squared term. In general, recipients that draw a greater share of their finance from nontraditional creditors receive higher aid commitments. Nevertheless, Table 3.5 shows that there is a curvilinear relationship, especially for Chinese finance. At very high levels of reliance on Chinese finance, traditional donors become less likely to commit additional aid funds. This nuances the main finding above, while confirming the overall relationship between a country's use of alternative finance and the volumes of aid they receive from traditional donors.

3.5.2 Infrastructure-Intensive Aid

I next turn to evidence for whether traditional donors shift their aid projects to respond to recipient preferences when recipients draw a greater share of their finance from nontraditional sources. Table 3.6 reports results from models that estimate the relationship between a recipient country's portfolio of external finance and the sectoral allocation of traditional donor projects. The dependent variable measures the percentage of donor projects in a recipient country in a given year

Table 3.5 *Nonlinear relationship between nontraditional finance as a share of recipient external finance and aid allocation volumes, 1991–2019*

	(1) Global	(2) Africa	(3) Global	(4) Africa	(5) Global	(6) Africa
Nontraditional finance share	0.551*** (0.141)	0.479** (0.223)				
Chinese finance share			0.490** (0.227)	1.725*** (0.282)		
Private finance share					1.194*** (0.185)	1.443*** (0.330)
Nontraditional finance share (squared)	−0.346** (0.174)	0.396 (0.304)				
Chinese finance share (squared)			−1.116*** (0.330)	−2.653*** (0.450)		
Private finance share (squared)					−0.754*** (0.226)	−0.419 (0.434)
GDP per capita	−0.348*** (0.027)	−0.308*** (0.048)	−0.299*** (0.026)	−0.207*** (0.047)	−0.406*** (0.028)	−0.330*** (0.048)
Central government debt (% of GDP)	−0.002*** (0.000)	−0.003*** (0.001)	−0.002*** (0.000)	−0.003*** (0.001)	−0.002*** (0.000)	−0.003*** (0.001)

Table 3.5 *(cont.)*

	(1) Global	(2) Africa	(3) Global	(4) Africa	(5) Global	(6) Africa
Natural resource rents (% of GDP)	−0.010***	−0.002	−0.010***	0.000	−0.010***	−0.003
	(0.002)	(0.003)	(0.002)	(0.003)	(0.002)	(0.003)
Polyarchy	0.638***	0.574***	0.624***	0.605***	0.548***	0.428**
	(0.116)	(0.190)	(0.117)	(0.197)	(0.114)	(0.189)
UNSC	0.266***	0.180***	0.291***	0.230***	0.223***	0.118***
	(0.031)	(0.044)	(0.032)	(0.045)	(0.030)	(0.044)
UNGA distance	0.345***	0.257***	0.360***	0.229***	0.348***	0.300***
	(0.038)	(0.074)	(0.039)	(0.074)	(0.038)	(0.075)
Dyadic trade vs. China	0.198***	0.167***	0.197***	0.157***	0.193***	0.160***
	(0.015)	(0.021)	(0.015)	(0.022)	(0.014)	(0.021)
Observations	42,022	17,049	42,022	17,049	42,022	17,049

Standard errors in parentheses.

All models include donor- and year-fixed effects.

* $p < 0.10$, ** $p < 0.05$, *** $p < 0.01$.

that are in any of the six sectors that may involve infrastructure investment, such as transport or communications. The models reported in Tables 3.6–3.8 are estimated using OLS for ease of interpretation, but the results are robust to using a fractional probit estimator to more precisely model the dependent variable, which is constrained to range from 0 to 100.

The results in Table 3.6 indicate that donors do increase the share of projects in infrastructure-intensive sectors when a recipient borrows more from nontraditional sources, but this relationship is largely confined to countries in sub-Saharan Africa. Comparing the results in columns 1 and 2 of Table 3.6 reveals that while there is no statistically significant relationship between a country's portfolio of external finance and the sectoral focus of donor projects in the global sample of donor–recipient dyads, there is a positive and statistically significant relationship for African recipient countries. For the subset of African recipients, increasing the share of external finance from nontraditional sources is associated with a higher share of donor projects in infrastructure-intensive sectors. Substantively, the difference between an African recipient country with none of its external finance from nontraditional sources and one with 50 percent of its finance from nontraditional sources, which is the difference between the tenth and ninetieth percentile, is associated with a move from 12.9 percent to 15.1 percent of a traditional donor's projects being allocated to infrastructure-intensive sectors. Though this is a small effect, recall that these results are estimated with donor-fixed effects and thus only capture variation within donors, and many DAC donors allocate only a small share of their aid projects to these infrastructure-intensive sectors. On average, DAC donors allocated 12.5 percent of their aid projects in African countries to these six sectors in the period 1990–2019.

As an illustration, take the example of one DAC donor, Canada. In 2014, in the nine African countries in the lowest quartile of nontraditional finance, Canada's aid agencies allocated 15 percent of projects to infrastructure-intensive sectors, on average. Meanwhile, 18.4 percent of Canadian aid projects in the ten African countries in the top quartile of nontraditional finance were in those same sectors. In Angola and Ethiopia, some of the leading African borrowers from China, 50 percent and 40 percent of Canadian aid projects in 2014 were in infrastructure-intensive sectors.

Table 3.6 *Nontraditional finance as a share of recipient external finance and the share of donor projects in infrastructure-intensive "hard" sectors, 1991–2019*

	(1) Global	(2) Africa	(3) Global	(4) Africa	(5) Global	(6) Africa
Non-traditional finance share	−0.005	0.040***				
	(0.006)	(0.010)				
Chinese finance share			−0.006	0.033***		
			(0.009)	(0.012)		
Private finance share					0.009	0.049***
					(0.006)	(0.013)
GDP per capita	−0.017***	−0.020***	−0.018***	−0.015***	−0.019***	−0.020***
	(0.002)	(0.004)	(0.002)	(0.003)	(0.002)	(0.004)
Central government debt (% of GDP)	−0.000***	−0.000***	−0.000***	−0.000***	−0.000***	−0.000***
	(0.000)	(0.000)	(0.000)	(0.000)	(0.000)	(0.000)
Natural resource rents (% of GDP)	−0.001***	−0.001***	−0.001***	−0.001**	−0.001***	−0.001***
	(0.000)	(0.000)	(0.000)	(0.000)	(0.000)	(0.000)
Polyarchy	0.076***	0.083***	0.076***	0.085***	0.075***	0.076***
	(0.010)	(0.015)	(0.010)	(0.016)	(0.010)	(0.016)
UNSC	0.017***	0.014**	0.017***	0.017**	0.016***	0.012*
	(0.004)	(0.007)	(0.004)	(0.007)	(0.004)	(0.007)
UNGA distance	0.027***	0.025***	0.026***	0.024***	0.026***	0.027***
	(0.003)	(0.006)	(0.003)	(0.006)	(0.003)	(0.006)
Dyadic trade vs. China	0.009***	0.007***	0.009***	0.006***	0.009***	0.006***
	(0.001)	(0.002)	(0.001)	(0.002)	(0.001)	(0.002)
Observations	42,005	17,044	42,005	17,044	42,005	17,044

Standard errors in parentheses.
All models include donor- and year-fixed effects.
* $p < 0.10$, ** $p < 0.05$, *** $p < 0.01$.

The positive and statistically significant relationship between alternative finance and the share of donor projects in infrastructure-intensive sectors in African countries is driven by both Chinese and private finance, though the relationship is stronger for private finance, as shown in columns 3–6 of Table 3.6. For both measures, there is no statistically significant association in the global sample, but for African countries, diversification of the portfolio of finance is significantly associated with an increase in donor projects in infrastructure intensive sectors.

The headline results for sectoral allocation are not as strong and consistent as those for the total amount of aid that donors commit. This difference in results between the two outcome measures may reflect the fact that it is more difficult for donors to adjust their aid programming and shift projects to sectors that are more attractive to recipient governments than to increase their aid. It may take time for donor agencies to adjust their aid programming to satisfy the recipient government's preferences, even as the recipient government reduces its dependence on traditional donor finance and increases its bargaining power. Results broken up by time period appear to confirm this dynamic. Table 3.7 reports results for the sectoral allocation of DAC donor aid in African recipient countries, broken down by decade. While there is no significant association between a country's nontraditional finance share and donors' allocations to infrastructure-intensive sectors in the 1990s and 2000s, by the 2010s, there is a positive and significant association across the board. In the 2010s, when developing countries most extensively diversified their portfolios of external finance, higher levels of Chinese and private finance are both associated with traditional donors committing to more projects in infrastructure-intensive sectors. Since all of the models include year-fixed effects, this result is not an artifact of temporal trends in infrastructure finance and recipients' portfolios of external finance. Instead, it shows that DAC donors became more likely to extend infrastructure-intensive projects to those countries with higher levels of finance from alternative sources, but only once alternative finance expanded sufficiently that developing countries could plausibly reduce their reliance on traditional donor funds.

I examine whether the relationship between recipients' portfolios of external finance and donors' focus on infrastructure-intensive sectors also extends to multilateral donors. Table 3.8 reports results for

Table 3.7 *Nontraditional finance as a share of recipient external finance and share of projects in infrastructure-intensive "hard" sectors, by decade*

	(1) 1990s	(2) 1990s	(3) 1990s	(4) 2000s	(5) 2000s	(6) 2000s	(7) 2010s	(8) 2010s	(9) 2010s
Nontraditional finance share	0.027 (0.031)			0.017 (0.015)			0.057*** (0.011)		
Chinese finance share		−0.109 (0.204)			0.006 (0.020)			0.046*** (0.014)	
Private finance share			0.032 (0.031)			0.018 (0.019)			0.076*** (0.015)
GDP per capita	−0.013 (0.010)	−0.010 (0.008)	−0.014 (0.010)	−0.013*** (0.005)	−0.011** (0.004)	−0.013*** (0.005)	−0.024*** (0.004)	−0.017*** (0.004)	−0.024*** (0.004)
Central government debt (% of GDP)	−0.001*** (0.000)	−0.001*** (0.000)	−0.001*** (0.000)	−0.000*** (0.000)	−0.000*** (0.000)	−0.000*** (0.000)	−0.000*** (0.000)	−0.000*** (0.000)	−0.000*** (0.000)
Natural resource rents (% of GDP)	−0.001* (0.001)	−0.001 (0.001)	−0.001* (0.001)	−0.001** (0.000)	−0.001* (0.000)	−0.001** (0.000)	−0.001** (0.000)	−0.001* (0.000)	−0.001** (0.000)
Polyarchy	0.098** (0.039)	0.098** (0.039)	0.097** (0.039)	0.074*** (0.020)	0.074*** (0.020)	0.072*** (0.020)	0.084*** (0.019)	0.086*** (0.019)	0.069*** (0.019)

UNSC	0.022	0.019	0.022	0.026**	0.027**	0.026**	−0.001	0.008	−0.007
	(0.022)	(0.022)	(0.022)	(0.011)	(0.011)	(0.011)	(0.008)	(0.008)	(0.008)
UNGA distance	0.058***	0.057***	0.059***	0.004	0.004	0.006	0.024***	0.023***	0.027***
	(0.016)	(0.016)	(0.016)	(0.008)	(0.008)	(0.008)	(0.007)	(0.007)	(0.007)
Dyadic trade vs. China	0.010**	0.010**	0.010**	0.006***	0.006***	0.006***	0.007***	0.006***	0.006***
	(0.004)	(0.004)	(0.004)	(0.002)	(0.002)	(0.002)	(0.002)	(0.002)	(0.002)
Observations	2,939	2,939	2,939	6,091	6,091	6,091	8,014	8,014	8,014

Standard errors in parentheses.

All models include donor- and year-fixed effects.

* $p < 0.10$, ** $p < 0.05$, *** $p < 0.01$.

Table 3.8 *Nontraditional finance as a share of recipient external finance and share of projects in infrastructure-intensive "hard" sectors, multilateral donors, 1991–2019*

	(1) Global	(2) Africa	(3) Global	(4) Africa	(5) Global	(6) Africa
Nontraditional finance share	0.001	−0.014				
	(0.021)	(0.032)				
Chinese finance share			−0.036	−0.004		
			(0.038)	(0.041)		
Private finance share					0.037*	0.014
					(0.022)	(0.043)
GDP per capita	−0.005	0.008	−0.005	0.007	−0.010	0.006
	(0.009)	(0.013)	(0.009)	(0.013)	(0.009)	(0.013)
Central government debt (% of GDP)	−0.000***	−0.000***	−0.000***	−0.000***	−0.000***	−0.000***
	(0.000)	(0.000)	(0.000)	(0.000)	(0.000)	(0.000)
Natural resource rents (% of GDP)	0.000	−0.000	0.000	−0.000	0.000	−0.000
	(0.001)	(0.001)	(0.001)	(0.001)	(0.001)	(0.001)
Polyarchy	0.037	0.043	0.034	0.044	0.034	0.044
	(0.033)	(0.043)	(0.033)	(0.042)	(0.033)	(0.042)
UNSC	0.009	0.009	0.010	0.008	0.006	0.007
	(0.013)	(0.019)	(0.013)	(0.019)	(0.013)	(0.019)
Observations	8,730	4,286	8,730	4,286	8,730	4,286

Standard errors in parentheses.

All models include donor- and year-fixed effects.

* $p < 0.10$, ** $p < 0.05$, *** $p < 0.01$.

the allocations of major multilateral donors in both the global and African sample of recipient countries. The results indicate that an increase in private finance is associated with higher levels of infrastructure finance for multilateral donors. However, multilateral donors are less likely to respond to increased Chinese finance by allocating more aid projects to infrastructure-intensive hard sectors. In earlier work, I found that the World Bank responds to Chinese competition by offering recipient countries more infrastructure-intensive aid projects without a governance component.[24] However, data on a wider population of multilateral donors suggests that multilateral donors as a whole are less likely to respond to Chinese finance by increasing their focus on infrastructure finance. Nevertheless, developing countries that diversify their portfolio of external finance by borrowing from private lenders can expect their multilateral donors to offer a greater share of projects in infrastructure-intensive sectors, rather than other, softer sectors.

As with aid commitments above, I consider whether the relationship between alternative finance and the infrastructure focus of traditional donor aid is nonlinear, with the impact of alternative finance decreasing at higher levels. Table 3.9 reports the results of models including a squared term of each of the share measures. The linear relationship is largely robust, with a positive linear association between nontraditional finance and the share of projects in infrastructure sectors, which is largely driven by private finance. The results for private finance also indicate a curvilinear relationship, as reported in columns 5 and 6 of Table 3.9. At very high levels of private finance in a recipient's portfolio of external finance, the positive association with infrastructure projects dissipates. This may suggest that donors are prioritizing these projects for countries that lack market access and are less able to finance these projects themselves. The evidence is also consistent with donors prioritizing attractive infrastructure finance for those countries where they believe they can still feasibly maintain a close relationship.

A potential concern in interpreting the overall results is that donors may simply be more likely to offer infrastructure-intensive projects to larger and more advanced economies, which also are more likely to diversify their portfolios of external finance. There is no wholly

---

[24] Zeitz 2021a.

Table 3.9 *Nonlinear relationship between nontraditional finance as a share of recipient external finance and share of projects in "hard" sectors, 1991–2019*

	(1) Global	(2) Africa	(3) Global	(4) Africa	(5) Global	(6) Africa
Nontraditional finance share	0.045***	0.061***				
	(0.014)	(0.023)				
Chinese finance share			0.018	0.053*		
			(0.022)	(0.030)		
Private finance share					0.101***	0.237***
					(0.017)	(0.032)
Nontraditional finance share (squared)	−0.063***	−0.027				
	(0.017)	(0.030)				
Chinese finance share (squared)			−0.045	−0.038		
			(0.032)	(0.050)		
Private finance share (squared)					−0.123***	−0.253***
					(0.020)	(0.041)
GDP per capita	−0.017***	−0.020***	−0.018***	−0.015***	−0.021***	−0.021***
	(0.002)	(0.004)	(0.002)	(0.003)	(0.002)	(0.004)
Central government debt (% of GDP)	−0.000***	−0.000***	−0.000***	−0.000***	−0.000***	−0.000***
	(0.000)	(0.000)	(0.000)	(0.000)	(0.000)	(0.000)
Natural resource rents (% of GDP)	−0.001***	−0.001***	−0.001***	−0.001**	−0.001***	−0.001***
	(0.000)	(0.000)	(0.000)	(0.000)	(0.000)	(0.000)

Polyarchy	0.076***	0.084***	0.076***	0.085***	0.075***	0.076***
	(0.010)	(0.015)	(0.010)	(0.016)	(0.010)	(0.015)
UNSC	0.015***	0.014**	0.017***	0.017**	0.014***	0.010
	(0.004)	(0.007)	(0.004)	(0.007)	(0.004)	(0.007)
UNGA distance	0.026***	0.024***	0.026***	0.024***	0.026***	0.026***
	(0.003)	(0.006)	(0.003)	(0.006)	(0.003)	(0.006)
Dyadic trade vs. China	0.008***	0.007***	0.009***	0.006***	0.008***	0.006***
	(0.001)	(0.002)	(0.001)	(0.002)	(0.001)	(0.002)
Observations	42,005	17,044	42,005	17,044	42,005	17,044

Standard errors in parentheses.
All models include donor- and year-fixed effects.
* $p < 0.10$, ** $p < 0.05$, *** $p < 0.01$.

satisfying way to address this endogeneity concern. In a modest way, the main models seek to account for these underlying attributes of recipient countries by controlling for the recipient's level of income and resource endowments. The results in Tables 3.10 further probe how income levels impact the relationship between nontraditional finance and donors' infrastructure commitments by breaking the sample of African countries into different categories. I report results for donors' volumes of aid commitments and the share of projects in infrastructure-intensive sectors, disaggregated by the recipient's income classification. The results in columns 1–3 show that higher shares of nontraditional finance are associated with higher aid commitments from DAC donors lower-middle-income and upper-middle-income countries. This is broadly consistent with the finding of Humphrey and Michaelowa (2019) that multilateral donors are responding to Chinese competition in countries that receive nonconcessional finance, which are likely to be higher-income countries. When it comes to the proportion of donor projects in infrastructure-intensive sectors, the results in columns 4–6 show that the positive relationship between nontraditional finance and donor commitments to hard sectors is driven by low- and lower-middle-income countries. These results somewhat assuage the concern that the headline results are simply associated with the most economically advanced developing countries. Instead, it appears that lower-income developing countries receive different types of aid from traditional donors when they draw a larger share of their external finance from nontraditional sources.

3.5.3 Conditionality

Third, I test whether countries that diversify their portfolio of external finance receive more flexible development finance, with fewer conditions attached. The analysis is at the project-year level and focuses on the number of conditions, known as prior actions, attached to World Bank Development Policy Financing in the period 2005–2018. The results reveal that in many cases when developing countries reduce their reliance on traditional donor funds, they subsequently receive development finance from the World Bank with fewer conditions attached. I report results for the total number of conditions per loan in Table 3.11 and for the number of public administration-specific conditions in Table 3.12.

Table 3.10 *Nontraditional finance as a share of recipient external finance and volumes and sectoral focus of traditional aid, by income category, 1991–2019*

	(1) Commitments LICs	(2) Commitments LMICs	(3) Commitments UMICs	(4) Hard LICs	(5) Hard LMICs	(6) Hard UMICs
Nontraditional finance share	0.186	1.404***	0.823***	0.024*	0.066***	−0.005
	(0.129)	(0.151)	(0.154)	(0.013)	(0.014)	(0.018)
GDP per capita	0.084	−0.704***	−1.597***	0.004	−0.022*	−0.115**
	(0.073)	(0.135)	(0.410)	(0.006)	(0.013)	(0.052)
Central government debt (% of GDP)	−0.004***	−0.001	0.024***	−0.000***	−0.001***	0.002***
	(0.001)	(0.002)	(0.004)	(0.000)	(0.000)	(0.001)
Natural resource rents (% of GDP)	0.005	−0.003	0.022**	−0.001***	−0.000	0.001
	(0.004)	(0.004)	(0.009)	(0.000)	(0.000)	(0.001)
Polyarchy	0.629***	0.115	4.259***	0.106***	0.099***	0.147*
	(0.221)	(0.303)	(0.857)	(0.019)	(0.026)	(0.080)
UNSC	0.110*	0.368***	0.283***	0.015	−0.002	0.032**
	(0.060)	(0.111)	(0.100)	(0.010)	(0.012)	(0.015)
UNGA distance	0.054	0.567***	−0.407**	0.022***	0.016	0.027
	(0.074)	(0.132)	(0.192)	(0.007)	(0.010)	(0.040)
Dyadic trade vs. China	0.211***	0.186***	0.041	0.007***	0.006**	0.013***
	(0.023)	(0.041)	(0.069)	(0.002)	(0.003)	(0.005)
Observations	11,757	4,080	1,212	11,753	4,079	1,212

Standard errors in parentheses.
All models include donor- and year-fixed effects.
$*p < 0.10$, $**p < 0.05$, $***p < 0.01$.

When it comes to the overall number of conditions, the results reported in Table 3.11 show that developing countries with a more diverse portfolio of external finance receive more flexible loans. However, the results are somewhat inconsistent across different sources of finance and different subsets of recipient countries. As reported in column 1, among the global sample of developing countries, when a recipient country receives a higher share of external finance from nontraditional sources, World Bank loans have fewer prior actions attached. And yet, this same association with the overall share of non-traditional finance does not hold in the African sub-sample of recipient countries in column 2. Instead, among the African sample of recipient countries, the conditionality of World Bank projects is more responsive to the share of a recipient country's external finance coming from Chinese lenders. This finding is in line with Hernandez's (2017) earlier finding about nontraditional lenders and the conditionality of World Bank lending to African countries. Column 4 reports a negative and statistically significant effect of Chinese finance on the number of prior actions attached to World Bank development finance loans. Substantively, the results in column 1 mean that a borrowing country that goes from receiving none of its external finance from nontraditional sources to receiving 66.7 percent, moving from the tenth to ninetieth percentile, can expect to go from 9.96 prior actions to 8.9 prior actions per World Bank loan. Similarly, the results in column 4 mean that an African country that goes from the tenth to ninetieth percentile of Chinese finance, can expect to go from 9.7 prior actions to 8.9 prior actions per loan. Even the reduction of a single prior action can be substantively meaningful, since each individual condition can entail significant reform efforts for the government.

The results for governance-specific conditionality reported in Table 3.12 indicate that African countries are more likely to see a reduction in governance conditions when they diversify their portfolios of external finance. Column 2 reports a negative and statistically significant association between the share of a country's external finance that comes from nontraditional lenders and the number of governance conditions attached to World Bank development finance loans. This overall effect appears to be equally driven by Chinese and private finance, which are both negatively associated with governance conditions attached to World Bank loans in sub-Saharan Africa. These results are consistent with the argument that African governments

Table 3.11 *Nontraditional finance and the number of prior actions attached to World Bank loans*

	(1) Global	(2) Africa	(3) Global	(4) Africa	(5) Global	(6) Africa
Nontraditional finance share	−0.168** (0.066)	−0.118 (0.131)				
Chinese finance share			−0.168 (0.147)	−0.526** (0.225)		
Private finance share					−0.120 (0.099)	0.170* (0.101)
Post-2012	−0.183*** (0.031)	−0.196*** (0.044)	−0.196*** (0.035)	−0.200*** (0.043)	−0.189*** (0.030)	−0.215*** (0.046)
Observations	665	238	665	238	665	238
Recipient FE	Yes	Yes	Yes	Yes	Yes	Yes

Standard errors in parentheses.
*$p < 0.10$, **$p < 0.05$, ***$p < 0.01$.

Table 3.12 *Nontraditional finance and the number of governance-specific prior actions attached to World Bank loans*

	(1) Global	(2) Africa	(3) Global	(4) Africa	(5) Global	(6) Africa
Nontraditional finance share	−0.215 (0.168)	−0.634** (0.284)				
Chinese finance share			−0.240 (0.278)	−0.858* (0.465)		
Private finance share					−0.241 (0.204)	−0.423* (0.232)
Post-2012	−0.380*** (0.071)	−0.355*** (0.102)	−0.397*** (0.072)	−0.394*** (0.093)	−0.381*** (0.068)	−0.380*** (0.098)
Observations	665	238	665	238	665	238
Recipient FE	Yes	Yes	Yes	Yes	Yes	Yes

Standard errors in parentheses.

* $p < 0.10$, ** $p < 0.05$, *** $p < 0.01$.

that experienced the greatest reduction in their reliance on traditional donors were able to translate their greater autonomy from traditional donor funds into negotiating leverage to bring aid agreements more in line with their preferences. The reduction in governance conditionality is particularly meaningful, since these are the conditions that recipient governments often find the most intrusive.

3.5.4 Differences among Borrowers

I test whether the relationship between alternative finance and traditional donors' aid agreements differs by attributes of the recipient country, in line with my argument. In keeping with the theory, I find alternative finance has a stronger association with the terms of aid agreements when recipient countries are strategically important to donors and when donors have greater trust in the recipient government, though the evidence for strategic significance is more mixed than for donor trust. The plots in Figures 3.7–3.9 report the coefficients on the interaction of alternative finance and recipient-level (or dyad-level) attributes associated with importance to the donor and donor trust. For consistency with the analysis in Sections 3.5.1 and 3.5.2, I organize these results by outcome variable and present results separately for the global sample of developing countries and the subsample of countries in sub-Saharan Africa. These models only use data on bilateral DAC donors, but the patterns are broadly similar for multilateral donors.

Results for the models predicting annual volume of aid commitments are reported in Figure 3.7. There is some evidence that strategically important borrowers see a greater boost from alternative finance, and greater evidence that recipients that are more trusted by donors see a stronger positive relationship between alternative finance and traditional aid commitments. A recipient government hosting a US military base sees a stronger association between alternative finance and traditional donor commitments only for Chinese finance, and only among African recipient countries.[25] This result suggests that traditional donors may be especially sensitive to a shifting reliance on China

---

[25] Note that 4.4 percent of observations in the sample include sub-Saharan African countries that hosted a US base according to the data from Vine (2019), including Kenya, Liberia, and Niger.

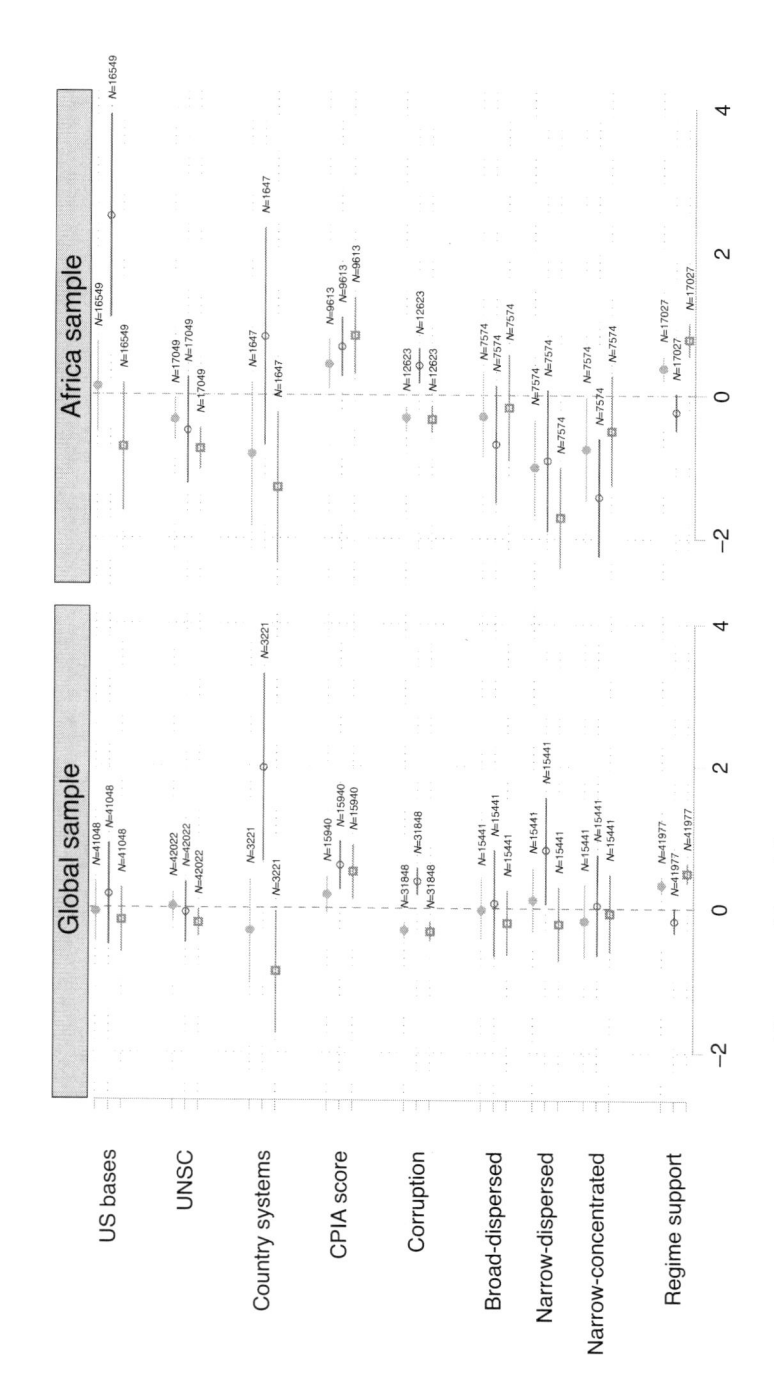

Figure 3.7 Coefficients on interaction terms in models predicting annual **volume of donor aid commitments** for DAC bilateral donors. 95 percent confidence intervals.

● All nontraditional finance   ○ Chinese finance   □ Private finance

in recipient countries where security interests are paramount. Surprisingly, however, a greater share of private finance is associated with lower aid commitments in countries holding a temporary seat on the UN Security Council, both globally and in the Africa sample.[26] The evidence on strategic significance as a moderator for alternative finance and donors' commitments is thus mixed.

For interactions with donor trust, the results are more consistent. Beginning with donors' use of country systems, which is the most direct measure of trust but is only available for a smaller number of dyad-years, the results indicate that when donors use recipient country public financial management systems, a borrower's turn to Chinese finance is more strongly associated with greater aid commitments. Notably, the same pattern does not hold for private finance, where there is a negative and significant coefficient on the interaction between the share of private finance and the use of country systems. This difference between Chinese and private finance may be because use of country systems is also a sign of donor commitment to institution-building, and greater private market access may signal that the borrower is less in need of such institution building. When trust is measured using the World Bank's appraisal of country budget systems there is a clear positive relationship: Countries with better CPIA scores see a stronger positive relationship between alternative finance and traditional donor commitments. Broadening out to a general measure of perceived corruption, the pattern mostly holds. Countries that are perceived as more corrupt receive less traditional donor aid when they draw a larger share of their external finance from nontraditional sources, especially private sources. The relationship is reversed with Chinese finance, perhaps suggesting that donors are more sensitive to corruption with private finance, which usually flows directly into the recipient country's budget, rather than Chinese finance, which is ringfenced into specific projects.

When it comes to the political roots of donors' trust, the results are broadly consistent with the theory. Using the political settlements categories, I expect that donors will consider broad-concentrated regimes, which are inclusive but have clear consolidation of political

---

[26] Note that 5.6 percent of observations in the sample include twenty different sub-Saharan African countries that held a temporary UN Security Council seat.

power, to be more credible than other regimes, enabling these governments to benefit from alternative finance. The results, especially in the Africa sample, are consistent with this expectation. Compared to the broad-concentrated reference category, countries with other political settlements see a negative relationship between alternative finance and traditional donor commitments, especially between Chinese finance and commitments. This pattern is largely confirmed with the more widely available data on regime support, which shows that governments enjoying wider domestic support see a positive relationship between the share of alternative finance and traditional donor commitments, especially private finance.

Broadly similar results obtain when the outcome variable is the share of donor projects allocated to infrastructure-intensive sectors, as reported in Figure 3.8, though the patterns are somewhat attenuated for sectoral allocation compared to aid commitments. In African countries that host US bases, the relationship between private finance and hard sector projects is stronger. However, there is no statistically significant interaction between holding a temporary UN Security Council seat and borrowing from nontraditional sources. When it comes to measures of donor trust, neither use of country systems nor evaluations of budgetary institutions or corruption are associated with differences in the association between alternative finance and the sectoral allocation of traditional donor aid. Yet, there is a pattern of relationships when it comes to the political roots of donor trust. Compared to the broad-concentrated reference category, countries with narrow-dispersed regimes see a negative association between alternative, especially Chinese, finance and infrastructure projects. Regimes that are narrow-concentrated, where there is high consolidation of political power, see a positive relationship between alternative finance and the share of projects in infrastructure-intensive sectors. This result on the political basis of donor trust is largely supported by the data on regime support, where governments with higher levels of regime support see a positive association between alternative, especially private, finance and the share of projects in hard sectors.

Turning to the governance conditionality of World Bank projects, similar patterns appear. Since recipient countries would prefer to receive loans with fewer governance conditions, here the expectation is that significance and trust will have a negative interaction with alternative finance. Since this data is at the project level, there are far fewer

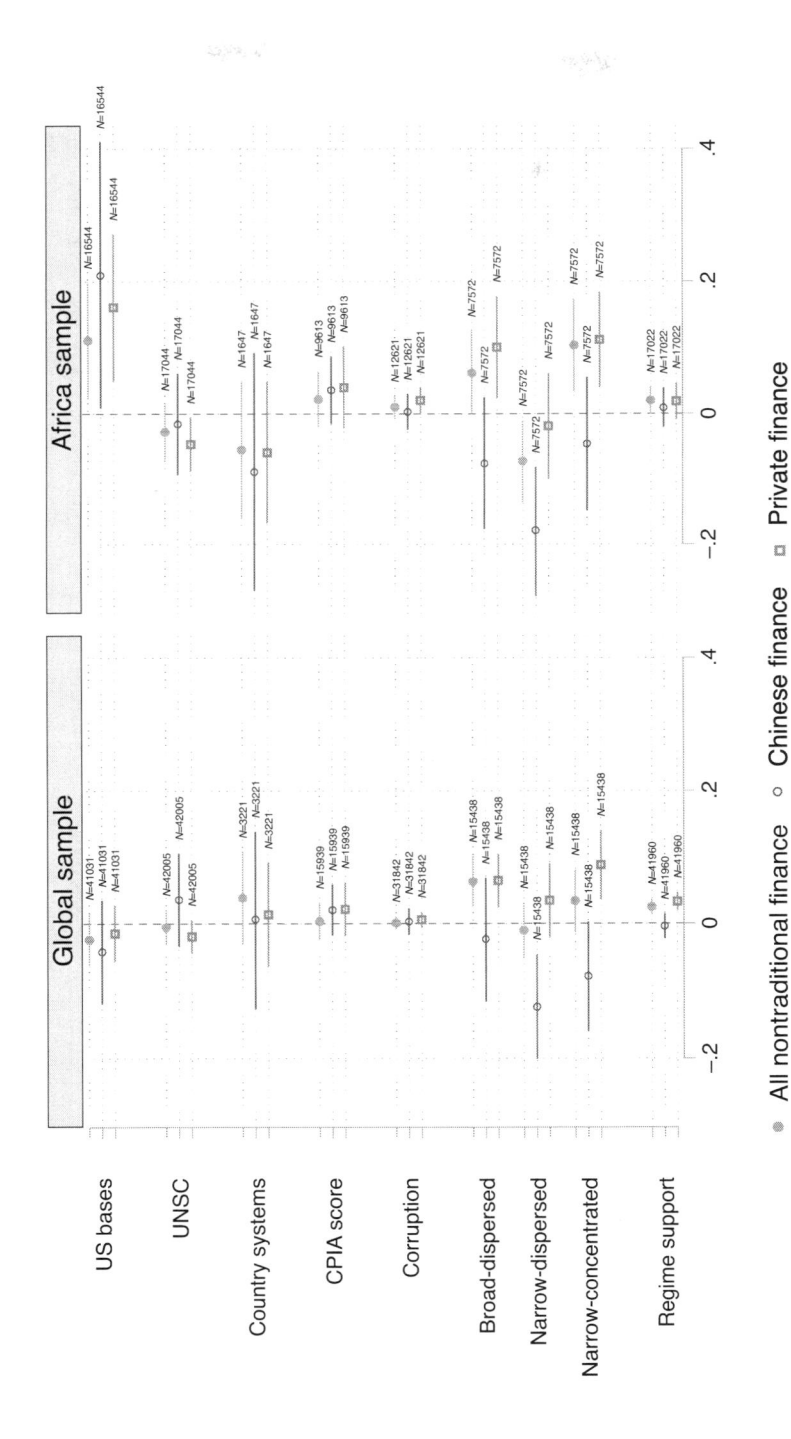

Figure 3.8 Coefficients on interaction terms in models predicting share of projects in infrastructure-intensive sectors for DAC bilateral donors. 95 percent confidence intervals.

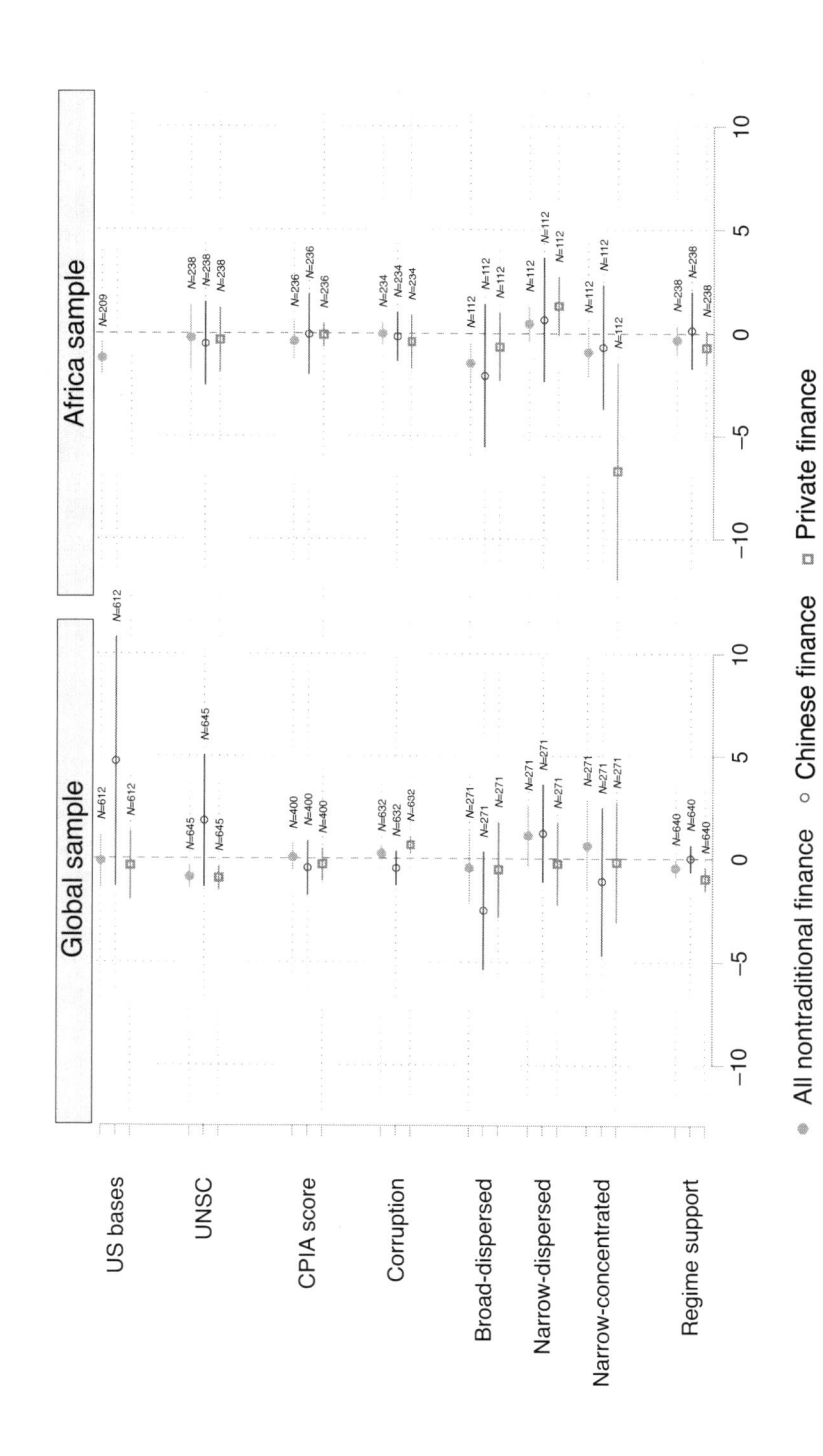

Figure 3.9 Coefficients on interaction terms in models predicting **number of governance conditions** attached to World Bank projects. 95 percent confidence intervals.

observations in these models than in the dyadic models of DAC donor aid allocation. Nonetheless, we observe relationships in the expected direction. African countries that host US bases see a negative association between nontraditional finance and the number of governance conditions. Globally, countries that are on the UN Security Council see a negative relationship between receiving a larger share of their external finance from nontraditional sources, especially private lenders, and the number of governance conditions attached to World Bank programs. This result suggests that countries that are significant to major shareholders see a stronger association between shifting their portfolio to alternative creditors and receiving more flexible projects from the World Bank. For the World Bank, it is not possible to use the same data as above on the use of country systems for implementing aid projects, since the data comes from surveys of only bilateral donors. However, the World Bank's own CPIA assessment of the quality of borrower budgetary institutions does not lead to differential associations with alternative finance. For the broader measures of corruption, the results indicate that in the global sample, countries that are perceived as more corrupt will receive projects with more governance conditions after taking on more private finance, suggesting that the World Bank responds to alternative finance with some suspicion in the context of corruption. Turning to the political context for recipient governments, there is some evidence that narrow-concentrated regimes receive fewer governance conditions when taking on more private finance, though this finding comes from a very small sample. Where there is slightly more data available, with measures of regime support, results from the global sample suggest that governments with higher regime support will receive fewer governance conditions as they shift to nontraditional finance, especially private finance.

Overall, these results are broadly consistent with the argument. Countries that are strategically important to donors see a stronger relationship between alternative finance and their preferred aid outcomes. Similarly, countries where donors likely have greater trust in the recipient government also see a stronger association between alternative finance and preferred aid terms, whether larger quantities of traditional aid, more infrastructure-focused aid, or fewer conditions. However, it is important to acknowledge that the results are not wholly clear-cut, with weaker results for strategic significance. This uneven pattern of results may be because strategic significance and donor trust are difficult to measure, especially because they vary from donor to donor and recipient to recipient. The case studies allow importance to donors and trust of donors to be calibrated to the country context, as well as allowing for a more fine-grained assessment of recipient country's preferences, more directly evaluating whether alternative finance enabled governments to achieve their particular preferences.

3.6 Conclusion

Developing countries have expanded and diversified their portfolios of external finance. Whereas these governments largely relied on DAC donors and international financial institutions for external finance into the early 2000s, from the mid 2000s onward they increasingly borrowed from private lenders and non-DAC countries, especially China. The data in this chapter brought together information on aid and loans to provide a comprehensive picture of developing countries' portfolios of external finance, showing how countries have shifted from relying largely on traditional foreign aid to borrowing from a wider set of creditors.

When countries diversify their portfolios of external finance, they also see improvements in the terms of their aid agreements with traditional donors. Countries that received higher shares of their external finance from private lenders and from China subsequently saw an increase in the amount of traditional donor aid, an increase in the share of aid projects in infrastructure-intensive sectors, and a reduction in the conditions attached to World Bank loans. The data shows that African countries experienced a greater reduction in their reliance on traditional development finance than other developing countries, on average, and that African countries reaped slightly larger benefits than the average developing country. The data also shows that the relationship between alternative finance and aid negotiations is affected by key attributes of the recipient country. When recipients are more strategically significant to donor countries, as measured by the presence of US military bases, the relationship between alternative finance and donors' willingness to reduce conditionality and allocate projects to infrastructure-intensive sectors is stronger. Moreover, where governments enjoy greater political support and more respected budgeting institutions, the relationship between nontraditional finance and donors' overall commitments is stronger.

These findings provide an important first validation of the arguments in this book. On average, developing countries see preferred terms from traditional donors when they borrow from alternative creditors. I interpret these results as evidence that alternative finance reduces borrowing countries' reliance on traditional donors, thereby enhancing their bargaining power. However, the results in this chapter cannot speak to the mechanism by which alternative finance is associated with preferred negotiating outcomes for recipient governments. Furthermore, the statistical tests in this chapter rely on the assumption that all recipient governments have preferences in the same direction, such that a positive relationship between alternative finance and infrastructure-focused aid projects, for example, is evidence that recipient governments have secured a "win." But countries have different preferences over foreign aid. The case studies in the following chapters therefore complement the evidence provided by this statistical analysis, directly evaluating negotiating outcomes against government preferences and tracing the mechanisms by which alternative finance does – or does not – enhance governments' bargaining power.

Appendix

Table 3.13 *Summary statistics*

Variable	Mean	Std. Dev.	Min.	Max.	N
Dyadic data – global sample					
Donor ODA commitments (logged)	1.501	1.654	0	8.791	42022
Share projects in hard sectors	0.133	0.192	0	1	42005
Nontraditional finance share	0.264	0.29	0	1	42022
Chinese finance share	0.048	0.124	0	0.916	42022
Private finance share	0.177	0.269	0	0.988	42022
One or more US military bases	0.085	0.278	0	1	41048
Temporary UNSC seat	0.061	0.24	0	1	42022
Aid using recipient systems	0.341	0.358	0	2.727	3221
CPIA budget score	3.261	0.543	1.5	4.5	15940
Corruption perception	6.917	0.931	3.2	9.6	31848
Political settlement (ESID)	2.437	1.068	1	4	15441
Regime support	3.129	0.745	0.463	3.964	41977
GDP per capita	7.563	0.935	5.214	9.561	42022
Central government debt (% of GDP)	53.527	37.915	2.263	441.752	42022
Natural resource rents (% of GDP)	8.193	9.913	0.001	87.577	42022
Polyarchy	0.456	0.202	0.06	0.912	42022
UNGA distance	1.692	0.693	0	5.048	42022
Dyadic trade vs. China	−2.299	2.455	−12.352	7.551	42022

Table 3.13 *(cont.)*

Variable	Mean	Std. Dev.	Min.	Max.	N
Dyadic data – Africa sample					
Donor ODA commitments (logged)	1.552	1.635	0	7.978	17049
Share projects in hard sectors	0.136	0.189	0	1	17044
Nontraditional finance share	0.175	0.245	0	0.983	17049
Chinese finance share	0.057	0.126	0	0.861	17049
Private finance share	0.084	0.204	0	0.969	17049
One or more US military bases	0.044	0.205	0	1	16549
Temporary UNSC seat	0.056	0.229	0	1	17049
Aid using recipient systems	0.368	0.351	0	1	1647
CPIA budget score	3.145	0.560	1.5	4.5	9613
Corruption perception	6.999	0.999	3.5	9	12623
Political settlement (ESID)	2.233	1.037	1	4	7574
Regime support	3.082	0.799	0.742	3.962	17027
GDP per capita	6.939	0.784	5.473	9.134	17049
Central government debt (% of GDP)	58.571	43.671	2.263	441.752	17049
Natural resource rents (% of GDP)	11.501	10.164	0.633	59.433	17049
Polyarchy	0.426	0.18	0.067	0.792	17049
UNGA distance	1.788	0.577	0.014	4.635	17049
Dyadic trade vs. China	−2.396	2.486	−12.352	7.551	17049

Table 3.13 *(cont.)*

Variable	Mean	Std. Dev.	Min.	Max.	N
World Bank data – *global sample*					
Prior actions	9.513	3.707	1	37	665
Governance prior actions	4.373	3.314	0	29	665
Nontraditional finance share	0.272	0.267	0	0.972	665
Chinese finance share	0.046	0.11	0	0.794	665
Private finance share	0.191	0.261	0	0.969	665
One or more US military bases	0.095	0.293	0	1	612
Temporary UNSC seat	0.098	0.297	0	1	645
CPIA budget score	3.481	0.491	2	4.5	403
Corruption perception	6.757	0.829	3.3	8.6	637
Political settlement (ESID)	2.399	0.968	1	4	271
Regime support	3.284	0.618	1.062	3.964	640

Table 3.14 *Data sources and variable descriptions*

Name	Variable	Units	Level	Source
Explanatory variables				
Nontraditional finance share	Commitments from non-traditional sources (private finance + non-DAC loans) as % of total external portfolio	Share (0-1)	Recipient-year	For all three: OECD DAC Creditor Reporting System and World Bank International Debt Statistics. IDS series: DT.COM.BLAT.CD, DT.COM.MLAT.CD, DT.COM.PRVT.CD, DT.COM.DPPG.CD
Chinese finance share	Commitments from Chinese lenders as % of total external portfolio	Share (0-1)	Recipient-year	
Private finance share	Commitments from private lenders as % of total external portfolio	Share (0-1)	Recipient-year	

Table 3.14 (*cont.*)

Name	Variable	Units	Level	Source
Dependent variables				
Commitments	Logged sum of ODA commitments	Logged constant US$	Donor–recipient-year	OECD DAC Creditor Reporting System
Share hard projects	Share of donor projects in infrastructure-intensive "hard" sectors. (Hard sectors = (1) water supply and sanitation; (2) transport and storage; (3) communications; (4) energy; (5) agriculture, forestry, and fishing; and (6) industry, mining, and construction)	Share (0-1)	Donor–recipient-year	OECD DAC Creditor Reporting System. Sector codes for hard sectors: 140 210 220 230 232 233 234 235 236 310 311 312 313 320 321 322 323
World Bank prior actions	Number of prior actions per World Bank project	Count	Project	For both: World Bank Development Policy Financing Policy Action Database
World Bank governance prior actions	Number of prior actions related to public administration and governance per World Bank project	Count	Project	

Interaction terms				
US military base	Dummy: Country hosts any US base or "lilypad"	0/1	Recipient-year	Vine (2019)
UNSC	Dummy: Country has temporary UNSC seat	0/1	Recipient-year	Dreher et al. (2009b)
Country systems	Average share of donor aid using recipient budget execution, financial reporting, and auditing procedures	Share (0-1)	Donor–recipient-year	Survey on Monitoring the Paris Declaration. Calculated as average of QD8, QD9, and QD10 over QD3.
CPIA budget score	CPIA quality of budgetary and financial management rating	Interval (1 = low to 6 = high)	Recipient-year	World Bank Group, CPIA database (IQ.CPA.FINQ.XQ)
Corruption perception	Perception of corruption in the recipient country	Interval (0 = low corruption to 10 = high corruption)	Recipient-year	Transparency International

Table 3.14 *(cont.)*

Name	Variable	Units	Level	Source
Political settlement	Recipient political settlement, classified according to the ESID political settlement categories	Categorical (1 = Broad-concentrated, 2 = Broad-dispersed, 3 = Narrow-dispersed, 4 = Narrow-concentrated)	Recipient-year	PolSett Dataset, Schulz and Kelsall 2021 (x_esidsettlementtype)
Regime support	Estimate of size of the groups supporting the political regime	Interval (0 = small to 4 = large)	Recipient-year	VDem V11.1 Coppedge et al. (2021) (v2regsupgroupssize_osp)
Controls				
GDP per capita	Logged GDP per capita (constant 2015 US$)	Logged constant US$	Recipient-year	World Development Indicators (NY.GDP.PCAP.KD)
Central government debt (% of GDP)	Central government debt as % of GDP	% of GDP	Recipient-year	IMF Global Debt Database (CG_DEBT_GDP)
Natural resource rents (% of GDP)	Total natural resources rents (% of GDP)	% of GDP	Recipient-year	World Development Indicators (NY.GDP.TOTL.RT.ZS)

Polyarchy	VDem measure of electoral democracy / polyarchy	Index (0-1)	Recipient-year	VDem V11.1 Coppedge et al. (2021) (v2x_polyarchy)
UNGA distance	Absolute distance between donor and recipient's ideal points, estimated using UN voting records	Interval	Donor–recipient-year	Bailey et al. (2016)
Dyadic trade vs. China	Total volume of dyadic trade minus total volume of recipient trade with China	Logged constant US$	Donor–recipient-year	CEPII BACI Gaulier and Zignago (2010) (tradeflow_baci)

4 | *Probing the Financial Statecraft of Borrowers through Comparative Cases*

Chapter 3 used data on borrowing patterns and the terms of traditional donor aid to show that developing countries with more diverse portfolios of external finance receive aid from traditional donors on terms more likely to satisfy the government's preferences. This finding is consistent with the theoretical expectations introduced in Chapter 2. Moreover, alternative finance has a stronger association with the terms of aid agreements for some recipients (and for some donors), giving credence to the mechanism I propose. That recipient countries receive aid terms more aligned with their preferences when they borrow from private creditors as well as when they borrow from China, for instance, gives support to the idea that alternative finance affects aid negotiations through the recipient's reduced dependence on traditional donors, rather than simply competition between rival donors.

However, the statistical analysis alone cannot test the mechanism I put forward for debt-based financial statecraft, namely that recipients' reduced dependence allows them to push for their preferred terms, with donors accommodating them because they want to preserve their relationship with the recipient government. On their own, the statistical results could be consistent with alternative mechanisms. For example, the positive relationship between alternative finance and the terms of donors' aid agreements could be the result of positive spillovers from alternative creditors' finance for traditional donors' aid. As the recipient country uses alternative finance to construct roads, it may simply become easier for traditional donors to execute their own infrastructure projects, leading to the positive relationship between alternative finance and the share of projects in infrastructure-intensive sectors. Whether alternative finance affects donor–recipient negotiations through the debt-based financial statecraft mechanism I suggest depends on *how* and *why* the terms of aid agreements change when the government gains (or loses) access to alternative creditors.

In Chapters 5–7, I trace and analyze the relationship between a changing portfolio of external finance and the terms of the relationship with traditional donors in three countries: Ethiopia, Kenya, and Ghana. I draw on intensive fieldwork research, including more than 170 interviews with, among others, high-ranking government and donor officials with first-hand experience of aid negotiations. My argument that borrowing from new creditors changes the relationship between the government and donors rests on the assumption that donors want to maintain their relationship and influence with the recipient government. To know whether donors approach the relationship with the recipient government in the way I theorize, and whether donors' interest in maintaining influence explains the changes in the terms of aid agreements after a recipient borrows from alternative creditors, I need to hear from the officials actively negotiating and implementing aid agreements. After all, my argument relies on recipients' and donors' *motivations*, which are difficult to ascertain from observing the terms of aid alone.

The case studies offer a number of different empirical tests of the theory. First, analysis *within* each case offers a test of the mechanism of debt-based financial statecraft. Tracing the changes in the aid relationship alongside changes in the recipient's portfolio of external finance reveals whether borrowing from alternative creditors altered the donor–recipient relationship because the government reduced its reliance on traditional donors and donors were willing to accommodate the government's preferences in order to retain the relationship. Second, comparison *across* the cases tests the expectations about enabling and constraining conditions that respectively enhance or inhibit debt-based financial statecraft. As I explain further below, I selected the case study countries based on their variation in the two features of the donor–government relationship that I expect to affect the financial statecraft of borrowers. During the period in which they diversified their portfolios of external finance, Ethiopia, Kenya, and Ghana differed in their value to donors and donors' trust in the country's government. Moreover, each of the countries experienced changes in their importance and donor trust over time, allowing me to examine different permutations of enabling and constraining conditions to test expectations about variation in the financial statecraft of borrowers.

The case studies complement the statistical analysis in one further respect, allowing for a more nuanced and context-specific measure of the outcome variable. The theory predicts that developing countries that borrow from alternative creditors will receive aid agreements more aligned with their preferences. In the statistical analysis in Chapter 3, I used a range of different measures to broadly capture which kind of aid is more attractive to developing countries. However, given differences in preferences among governments, the exact terms that recipient governments seek to improve are necessarily idiosyncratic. In the case studies, I use interview evidence and secondary sources to identify the most contentious topics in negotiations between the government and donors, providing a more fine-grained measure of the outcome variable.

In this chapter, I set the scene for the case study analysis, explaining the rationale for case selection, my process of analysis within each case, and how I collected the data that I use. I provide some brief background on each of the cases, highlighting salient attributes of the politics and aid relationships in each of the countries, which will enable the reader to better follow the analysis in Chapters 5–7. I conclude with a short comparative overview of the case study findings with respect to the theory.

4.1 Rationale for Case Selection

Each of the three case study countries diversified their portfolios of external finance during the 2000s and 2010s, allowing for comparison of aid negotiations before and after each country's government reduced its reliance on traditional donors. Ethiopia, Kenya, and Ghana all borrowed from China and international bond markets, but at different times and to different extents.

I focus on three countries that all *did* borrow from alternative sources, rather than comparing countries that borrowed from alternative creditors to those that did not. I make this choice because countries that did not borrow at all from China or private markets differ systematically from countries that did borrow from these alternative creditors. In the statistical analysis in Chapter 3, I accounted for differences between diversifiers and nondiversifiers in a number of ways, by controlling for factors that affect countries' access to alternative finance or using borrower-fixed effects. In the case studies, I hold these factors constant by focusing on countries that all borrowed from alternative creditors and then exploiting within-case variation in the

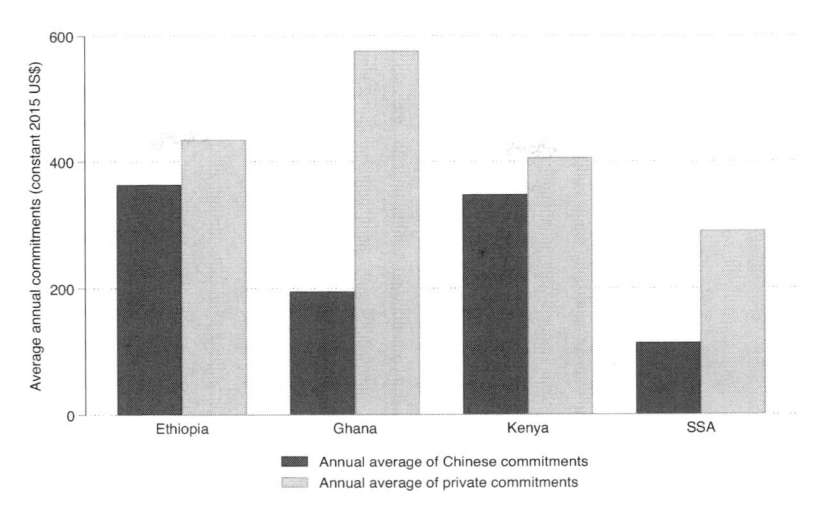

Figure 4.1 Annual commitments from alternative creditors to case study countries (constant 2015 US$), compared to average across sub-Saharan African countries, 1990–2018.

timing of the government's borrowing to see how negotiations with traditional donors changed once the government diversified its portfolio of external finance.

Of all the African countries that borrowed from alternative creditors in this period, why choose these three? For one, the three countries reflect the broad trends in the expansion of credit to African governments. Figure 4.1 shows how Ethiopia, Ghana, and Kenya compare to average annual amounts of credit from Chinese bilateral lenders and private creditors to sub-Saharan African governments in the years 1990–2018. All three countries received somewhat above average commitments from alternative creditors, but the patterns are broadly in line with the continental averages. Across African countries and in the cases studies, annual commitments from private lenders – whether international bond markets or private banks – were higher than those from Chinese bilateral creditors. At the same time as borrowing from new sources, traditional donors and creditors remain important in the case study countries, as panels (c) and (d) in Figure 4.2 show. Whether concessional foreign aid or loans, the case study countries continue to receive substantial volumes from traditional donors and creditors.

Despite all drawing on development finance from the same major sources, the case study countries differ in the timing and volume of

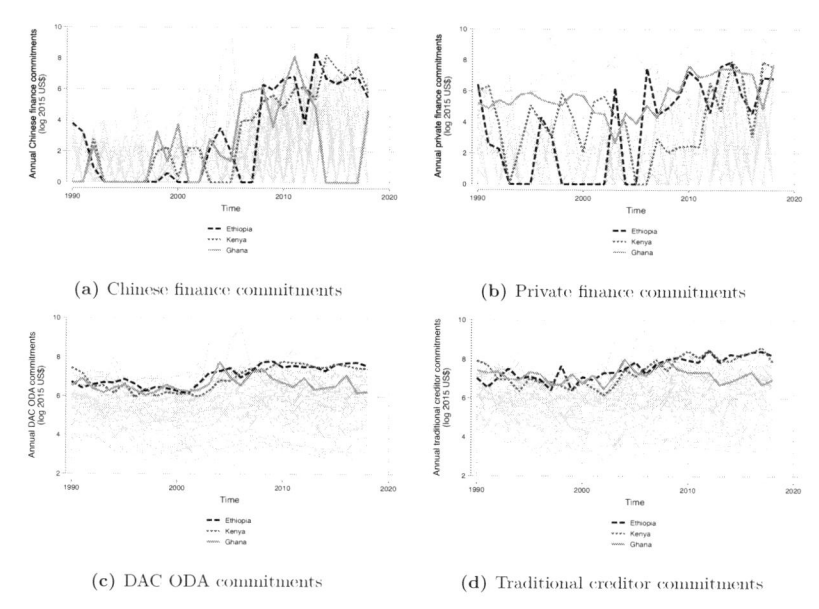

Figure 4.2 Trends in case study countries' portfolios of external finance, compared to other sub-Saharan African countries, 1990–2018 (log 2015 US$).

their borrowing from alternative creditors, allowing me to trace the impacts of this borrowing. Panels (a) and (b) in Figure 4.2 show the timing of Chinese and private finance, respectively. Figure 4.2(a) shows that Ghana was among the earlier borrowers from Chinese lenders but that it sharply reduced its borrowing from China in the late 2010s, when Ethiopia and Kenya expanded their borrowing from China. By contrast, Ghana has a longer history of borrowing from private creditors, which it further expanded in the late 2000s. Kenya and Ethiopia were slower to borrow from private creditors but did so increasingly in the 2010s, as Figure 4.2(b) shows. These temporal patterns allow me to trace the effects of alternative finance on aid negotiations.

In addition to being emblematic of trends in African countries' borrowing during this time, I selected these cases for variation in the factors that enable and constrain debt-based financial statecraft, namely the importance donors attach to the relationship with the government and their trust in the government. Comparing across the cases allows me to test whether recipient governments obtain greater leverage when donors place greater value on the relationship with the government and have greater faith that aid agreements will be upheld.

Tracing within the cases over time allows me to show that the moderating variables operate as I expect, amplifying or dampening donors' reactions to a country's diversified portfolio of finance.

The theory predicts that recipient countries that are particularly valuable to donors will extract greater benefits from the turn to alternative creditors, since donors will be more willing to accommodate these governments when they become less reliant on traditional aid. To test this expectation I chose two countries that are valuable to donors for geopolitical reasons, Ethiopia and Kenya, and compare them to Ghana, a country that was historically important to donors for its development performance, but that faded in its significance for donors over the period examined here. The theory also expects that when donors have greater trust that the government will uphold aid agreements, they will be more accommodating in the face of the recipient's declining dependence on them. This greater trust can come about through institutional probity or political circumstances in the recipient country. The three countries also vary in this respect. In Ethiopia, the government's track record of poverty reduction and development, as well as the strength of institutions for overseeing development projects, gave donors greater confidence in the government. Moreover, the government's substantial centralization of political authority during the period under study provided it with long time horizons that made the government's commitments more credible to donors, even as donors criticized the government's authoritarianism. By contrast, in Kenya and Ghana, donors worried about corruption and financial management, especially concerned that public resources, including alternative finance, were misused for political competition, making them less trusting of the government's commitments.

Across the three cases, the levels of importance to donors and donor trust vary over time and across donors within each of the cases, leading to more observed combinations. While none of the three countries falls solidly in the quadrant of high donor trust and low value to donors, there are times and particular donors where this combination is observed, as with donors who found Ethiopia less geopolitically important for their priorities or donors who had greater trust in the Ghanaian government even in the face of electoral budget cycles. Within the cases, I thus rely on variation over time and across donors to trace how these attributes enabled or impeded debt-based financial statecraft.

4.2 Within-Case Analysis: Process Tracing

For each of the cases, my analysis proceeds the same way. First, I build a timeline of changes in the country's portfolio of external finance over the period 2000 to 2018, including turning points that signal a step change in the government's external finance. These events might be a major Chinese loan package, announced with great diplomatic fanfare, or the country's debut international bond, involving international "roadshows" in which government representatives meet with potential bond investors. These highly publicized events were usually salient to traditional donors as indications of the recipient country's shifting portfolios of external finance. I focus on the period 2000–2018, when alternative sources of finance became available to African governments and compare the government's changing reliance on traditional donors in this later period to the 1990s, when there were fewer sources of external finance available to African governments.

Second, for each country, I identify which issue areas have historically been the most contentious in the donor–government relationship, where I would expect to observe variation in outcomes if the recipient has increased its bargaining leverage. To determine these sensitive issue areas, I look at aid agreements from before the government diversified its portfolio of external fiance, and use media reporting, interviews, and donor commentary to identify which issues were most contentious and where donors were best able to align aid agreements with their preferences. Identifying those issue areas where donors' and the recipient's preferences are furthest apart allows for a more precise measure of the recipient's ability to achieve their preferred outcomes in negotiations.

In the third and final step, I trace whether changes in a recipient's portfolio of external finance led to any changes in donor–recipient agreements in these most sensitive areas of negotiation. The point here is not simply to observe a coincidence in time between a government's borrowing from China or private creditors and more attractive aid agreements but also to find evidence that the proposed mechanism accounts for the effects of borrowing from alternative creditors on aid agreements. I look for evidence that the recipient government became less willing to accept unattractive aid, and that donor officials observed the recipient government's turn to alternative finance, subsequently worried about losing influence with the government, and were willing to accommodate the government's preferences to retain the relationship. When a government borrowed from alternative creditors but *did not* experience an improvement in their aid agreements, I examine whether this lack of influence was because donors did not sufficiently value their access to the recipient government or that they did not trust the government's uses of alternative finance.

My method for within-case analysis is guided by a process-tracing approach, which is a tool for qualitative analysis well suited to "measuring and testing hypothesized causal mechanisms."[1] To test hypotheses, process tracing analyzes the "unfolding of events or situations over time," linking changes in the explanatory variable to those in the outcome variable.[2] Process tracing requires thorough and careful descriptions of the explanatory and outcome variable at different points in time, allowing the scholar to "characterize key steps in the process, which in turn permits good analysis of change and sequence."[3] In particular, process tracing relies on identifying pieces of diagnostic evidence (sometimes referred to as "causal process observations") that are consistent with the proposed mechanism, rather than with alternative mechanisms that could lead to the same outcome.[4] This approach allows one to conclude more confidently that co-occurrences of the explanatory and outcome variable are linked through the proposed mechanism.

4.3 Data Collection for the Cases: Fieldwork and Elite Interviews

To collect evidence for process tracing, I conducted six months of fieldwork in the capital cities of the case study countries, the bulk of which took place in 2017, together with a shorter trip to Ghana in 2013. While in Addis Ababa, Nairobi, and Accra, I met with high-level donor and government officials with first-hand experience of donor-government negotiations, as well as journalists, researchers, and civil society and private sector observers. In total, I interviewed more than 170 individuals who either directly participated in donor–government

[1] Bennett and Checkel 2015, pp. 3–4.
[2] Collier 2011, p. 824.
[3] Collier 2011, p. 824.
[4] Checkel 2008.

negotiations or followed these relationships as part of their job. I triangulated this interview material with media coverage, government documents, and donor reports, many of which are publicly available, but some of which are internal materials that informants shared with me.

My main objective in fieldwork was to speak with individuals who could reconstruct the government's and donors' interests during negotiations, which would allow me to test whether these interests, and the interaction among them, changed when the government borrowed from alternative creditors.[5] On the government's side, I interviewed officials in the finance ministry, which in each country had the mandate of negotiating with donors. Specifically, I interviewed senior officials in external resource mobilization and debt management departments. Across developing countries, finance ministries have departments responsible for donor relations, which are usually subdivided into donor-specific "desks," such as the World Bank desk, North America desk, or Europe desk. The officials in these offices handle the day-to-day relationships with donors, reporting to donors on the implementation of existing aid agreements and laying the groundwork for future aid agreements, which might ultimately be agreed to and signed by more senior officials within the ministry. In each of the case study countries, I spoke with the official leading the donor relations or resource mobilization department, as well as with the desk officers responsible for most of the major donors.

To understand how relations with donors fit in the government's political priorities, I not only interviewed civil servants negotiating and implementing agreements with donors but also the politicians designing these policies. Relevant political actors included Deputy Finance Ministers, members of relevant Parliamentary committees, and staff in the President or Prime Minister's Office. In Ghana and Kenya, where there were important differences between political parties that had been in power at different points during this period, I also interviewed

---

[5] My focus on specific *categories* of interview respondents – government officials working in resource mobilization, bilateral donor representatives, and multilateral donor representatives, for instance – is referred to as a "purposive" sampling strategy. My aim was to speak to sufficient respondents in these different categories to be able to triangulate responses, rather than to reach representative interviewees (J. F. Lynch 2013; Tansey 2007).

individuals who held senior positions in the previous government and were now in the opposition. Interviews with senior officials in each country's central bank, including present and former governors and deputy governors, complemented the evidence from politicians and civil servants in the ministry of finance. Though the central bank is rarely directly involved in negotiations with creditors and donors, their assessments of debt sustainability play an important role in the government's decision to take on loans.

On the donors' side, I interviewed senior in-country staff for the major donors active in each country, both multilateral and bilateral. The official charged with managing the donor's relationship with the government is usually referred to as the "Head of Development Cooperation" or the "Resident Representative." In most cases, I was able to speak with this leading official, though in some cases, such as if they were new to the country, the head of cooperation referred me to a less senior staff member who was well versed in the relationship with the government, such as a sectoral specialist. For larger donors, I made an effort to speak with multiple representatives of the donor agency, to understand how negotiations played out in different issue areas and at different points in time. I complemented these interviews with in-country staff with further conversations with officials at the headquarters of major multilateral development institutions in Washington D.C. and New York in 2013 and 2017. Financial institutions vary in the amount of discretion they grant to in-country staff, and officials at headquarters could comment more broadly on the organization's strategy in response to the rise of alternative finance.

Since my argument focuses on the effect of alternative finance on the relationship between developing countries and their traditional donors, I focused on speaking with the representatives of these donors, defined as established multilateral donors and bilateral members of the DAC. I made an effort to speak with representatives of emerging donors, including Chinese lenders, though reaching these representatives was much more difficult, since the emerging bilateral donors only maintain small staff in their embassies, with most decisions made at headquarters. However, my more limited access to these individuals does not inhibit tests of my hypotheses, which focus on the relationship between the government and traditional donors.

Most respondents spoke to me only on the condition of anonymity, sometimes because they were not authorized to provide the official position of their employer or because donor–recipient relations were considered sensitive. I therefore cite interview material in the case studies by the broad category in which respondents fall ("Ministry of Finance official," "multilateral donor official," etc.).[6]

4.4 Introducing the Case Study Countries

The relationships between donors and the governments of each of the case study countries are shaped by the economic and political history of the country in question. To make it easier for the reader to follow the analysis in Chapters 5–7, I briefly introduce Ethiopia, Kenya, and Ghana in turn, providing some background on each country. These brief summaries necessarily gloss over much of the complexity of each country's history and contemporary political context, but they provide a sense of how donors see and approach the governments of each country, which helps to set up the subsequent analysis of aid negotiations. Readers who are already familiar with the case study countries may wish to skip these summaries and move ahead to the preview of the findings in Section 4.5.

4.4.1 Ethiopia

Ethiopia is a vast country, with a primarily agricultural economy and an immense cultural and linguistic diversity among its large population. The country ranks second in sub-Saharan Africa in population (112 million), surpassed only by Nigeria. Ethiopia remains relatively poor; in 2019 the country's GDP per capita stood at $602.2, compared to an average of $1,669.2 for all sub-Saharan African countries.[7] The population is overwhelmingly rural, and 66 percent of the population was employed in agriculture as of 2019.[8] Found in the Horn of Africa in the north-east of the African continent, Ethiopia borders a number of volatile countries in the subregion, including Somalia, Sudan, and South Sudan, and shares a fraught and disputed border with its neighbor Eritrea to the north.

---

[6] More details about the interviews are available in Appendix A.
[7] Figures in constant 2010 US dollars (World Bank 2020b).
[8] World Bank 2020b.

Accounts of Ethiopian politics usually emphasize the long continuity of centralized state control, as well as the country's autonomy. Ethiopia was never colonized, and a brief occupation by Italy in the 1930s was the country's only experience of control by a foreign power. A single hereditary line held the throne of the Ethiopian Empire from the thirteenth century until the 1970s, when Ethiopia was ruled by Emperor Haile Selassie, the last successor to the Solomonic dynasty.[9] After an uprising against Haile Selassie, a military regime, the *Derg*, seized power in 1974. The *Derg*'s brutal and autocratic rule spawned resistance from armed movements across the country, triggering a civil war that combined with famine in the mid 1980s to claim the lives of more than one million Ethiopians. The group that emerged victorious against the *Derg* in 1991 after more than fifteen years of civil war was the Tigray People's Liberation Front (TPLF), stemming from a small region in Ethiopia's north. The TPLF established a governing coalition with national movements from other regions of the country, forming the Ethiopian People's Revolutionary Democratic Front (EPRDF), which went on to govern Ethiopia for the next three decades.

The EPRDF justified its hold on power and suppression of opposition with reference to a political model of "revolutionary democracy," which emerged out of the TPLF's origins as a revolutionary peasant movement and was premised on strong leadership by a "vanguard party," rather than liberal principles of individual representation.[10] In practice, these ideas were used to justify increasing authoritarianism during the EPRDF's time in power. With respect to economic policy, the EPRDF expressed a commitment to a "developmental state."[11] The idea that Ethiopia should pursue a developmental state was most strongly associated with Meles Zenawi, who was a leader in the TPLF during the civil war, a founding figure of the EPRDF, and Prime Minister of Ethiopia from 1995 until his death in 2012. As expressed by Meles and the EPRDF, pursuing a developmental state entailed a focus on infrastructure, industrialization, and commercialization of agriculture, with activist state involvement to overcome the risk of private actors becoming rent-seeking.[12] Observers point out

[9] Keller 1988.
[10] Bach 2011; Vaughan 2011.
[11] Clapham 2017; Dejene and Cochrane 2019.
[12] Lavers 2023.

that the developmental state was never expressed as a single coherent policy,[13] but instead was used as a shorthand to describe Ethiopia's statist approach to development, with widespread state ownership in key sectors, financial repression in order to direct credit to strategic projects, and restrictions on foreign investment.[14]

Importantly for Ethiopian politics, Meles' notion of the developmental state combined economic policy with a claim about the political requirements for such a plan to succeed.[15] To avoid the rent-seeking pressures from special interests, political elites were expected to be unified in their support for the economic project of the developmental state. As critics highlight, this political model resulted in the EPRDF centralizing authority in the hands of a small number of party elites.[16]

Until the mid 2010s, consensus among the EPRDF leadership on the goals of the developmental state underpinned elite political cohesion. However, the uneven balance of regional influence within the EPRDF ultimately destabilized this cohesion. The TPLF had much greater influence over the EPRDF than the parties representing Ethiopia's largest ethnic groups, the Oromo and Amhara. Public dissatisfaction with this political compromise and the repressive nature of the regime found its outlet in widespread protests in 2015 and 2016 in the Oromia and Amhara regions.[17] By late 2017, the enduring unrest had activated existing fractures in the governing coalition, and Amhara and Oromo representatives openly challenged the TPLF's dominance of the EPRDF.[18] In the final years of the period under study, ethnic fractures and instability became much more prominent and apparent in Ethiopian politics. In 2018, under growing public pressure, the EPRDF for the first time selected as Chairman and Prime Minister a non-Tigrayan, Abiy Ahmed, who is Oromo. Abiy's ascendance to the top of the party appeared to redress the ethnic imbalance of the coalition and his first moves as Prime Minister – pursuing rapprochement with neighboring Eritrea, freeing political prisoners, and privatizing

[13] S. Brown and Fisher 2020.
[14] Weis 2015, 2017.
[15] Lavers 2023.
[16] Lefort 2013.
[17] The protests were initially triggered by a proposed urban development plan for Addis Ababa that would have seen the city's borders expand into the neighboring region of Oromia.
[18] Fisher and Gebrewahd 2018.

key firms – drew accolades from the opposition, foreign observers, and the Ethiopian diaspora, even earning him the Nobel Peace Prize in 2019.[19] However, Abiy's tenure was also marked by repression and by redistribution of political control that provoked conflict, especially with the TPLF, which had been sidelined in Abiy's administration. These tensions broke out into armed hostilities between the federal government and the TPLF in 2020.

Despite this more recent conflict, in preceding decades Ethiopia was an important counterpart for donors precisely because of its stability in the broader security context of the Horn of Africa. Even more so, the Ethiopian government's willingness to directly respond to terrorist threats in Somalia, including invading the country in 2006–07, made it an important partner especially for the US.[20] Ethiopia's support for US policies associated with the global war on terror was decisive in increasing US assistance to the EPRDF government over the course of the 2000s.[21] For European donors, the focus on Ethiopia as an anchor of stability and bulwark against terrorism is augmented by Ethiopia's role as host country to refugees in the region. Given the politicization of inflows of refugees and irregular migrants to Europe since 2015, stability in Ethiopia was part of a larger strategy for the EU and European donors to limit the arrival of refugees in Europe. In addition to these security and geopolitical concerns, donors' relationship with the Ethiopian government has been shaped by donors' perception of the government's ability to translate development plans into concrete outcomes, achieving economic growth and poverty reduction.[22] Poverty in Ethiopia fell from 44 percent in 2000 to 30 percent in 2011, and the country's economy grew at an average of 8.5 percent during 2000–2010 and 9.6 percent during 2011–2018.[23]

4.4.2 Kenya

Kenya is a large, economically dynamic, and ethnically diverse country in East Africa. For a sense of scale, Kenya's population of over fifty

---

[19] Verhoeven and Woldemariam 2022.
[20] Verhoeven 2009.
[21] Borchgrevink 2008, p. 214.
[22] Abegaz 2015; Feyissa 2011.
[23] World Bank 2015b.

million is similar in size to the population of South Korea, while
the area of the country is comparable to France. Despite not having
any significant natural resource wealth, the country ranks among the
wealthier countries on the continent. In 2019, GDP per capita in Kenya
stood at $1,237.5, compared to a continental average of $1,669.2.[24]
Though Kenya's economy is still largely agricultural – its main exports
are tea, cut flowers, and coffee – the economy is diversifying, with particular growth in the services sector. Numerous foreign investors have
chosen Kenya's capital Nairobi as their hub for the subregion and the
rapid growth of Kenya-based IT and software firms has earned the
country the moniker of "Silicon Savannah."

Since independence from British rule in 1963, Kenyan politics have
largely been shaped by divisions along ethnic lines. The country is ethnically and linguistically diverse, and no single ethic group accounts
for a majority of the population.[25] Ethnic groups are strongly associated with different regions of the country and an enduring tension in
Kenyan politics has been between the autonomy of individual regions
and the centralization of state control. Patterns of ethnic politics
and clientelist distribution were first established in Kenyan politics
in the immediate postindependence years and have continued to the
present day.

In the early 1990s, Kenya reintroduced multiparty competition in
response to civil society demands and donor pressure after several
decades of single-party rule.[26] The return of multiparty competition
exacerbated both ethnic politics and patronage distribution, since
political elites needed to offer inducements to secure election victories and governed in the knowledge that their time in power – and
therefore their time to satisfy clientelist demands – could be cut short
by the next election. Since none of the ethnic groups is large enough
to win an election on their own, the era of democratic governance
has involved various multiethnic coalitions.[27] However, these coalitions tend to be fractious and loosely held together, based on alliances
between politicians that act as regional and ethnic power brokers. To

---

[24] Figures in constant 2010 US dollars (World Bank 2020b).
[25] Ethnic identity and belonging in Kenya have been subject to dispute and
change. For example, on the Kalenjin, see G. Lynch 2011.
[26] S. Brown 2001; Roessler 2005.
[27] Arriola 2013.

secure and maintain the coalitions that bring them to power, politicians have relied on strategies of clientelist distribution, creating a pattern in which personal and community wealth becomes a spoil of political power, as well as a requirement to acquire and retain political power.

These mounting tensions made Kenyan elections increasingly fraught, with numerous instances of intercommunity violence. In 2007, after a very close presidential election won by the incumbent Mwai Kibaki, there was widespread violence, especially in "ethnic homelands," where minorities were targeted for their presumed support for the opposing political candidate.[28] An estimated 1,400 people were killed and more than 600,000 internally displaced in the two months after the election.[29] The International Criminal Court (ICC) indicted Uhuru Kenyatta and William Ruto in 2010 for their roles on opposite sides of the postelection violence.[30] Although they each played role in voter intimidation and violence for opposing parties, the two politicians joined forces to create the Jubilee Alliance to contest the 2013 election, going on to win, with Kenyatta becoming President and Ruto Deputy President. This "alliance of the accused" is just one example of the fragmenting and forming of electoral alliances in Kenya, sometimes bringing together unlikely partners.[31]

Despite the fraught stakes of Kenyan electoral politics, political conflict in Kenya has never reached the level of civil war or enduring hostilities, and repeated elite compromises have maintained a relative stability that makes the country appealing to foreign investors, outside observers, and donors. The 2017 election and its aftermath are a case in point. Raila Odinga, the perennial opposition challenger whose (predominantly Luo) supporters believe they were robbed of the presidency in the 2007 and 2013 elections, again faced off against the Kenyatta–Ruto alliance. Despite widespread and suspicious irregularities in the tallying of results and the unsolved murder of a high-ranking election official in the week before the election, the electoral commission declared Kenyatta the winner. The Supreme Court nullified

---

[28] Cheeseman et al. 2014; G. Lynch 2011.

[29] Brownsell 2013.

[30] The charges against both were confirmed in 2012, though the ICC case against Kenyatta was withdrawn in 2014 and the case against Ruto was withdrawn in 2016.

[31] G. Lynch 2013.

the results and required a rerun, but Odinga boycotted the election and with a turnout of just 39 percent, Kenyatta won 98.3 percent of the votes in the rerun and was inaugurated as President. Opposition frustration spilled into the streets and Odinga appeared to fan the flames, holding a parallel inauguration ceremony. However, just a few months later, Kenyatta and Odinga struck an opaque deal, known as the "handshake," that involved Odinga calling off his challenge and instead joining the government. The established patterns of Kenyan politics had repeated themselves: With an eye toward the prize of the 2022 election and the greater share of resources to be commanded from within the government, Odinga formed a temporary pact with Kenyatta.[32]

Kenya's reputation for relative stability also extends to the role it plays in its immediate neighborhood. The country has been a key counterpart for the US in the African arena of the global war on terror, playing a prominent role in combating violent extremism within Kenya as well as in neighboring countries. In the post-9/11 period, Kenya became a substantial recipient of US military assistance, also participating in the US-funded Combined Joint Task Force for the Horn of Africa.[33] The US military still maintains a base on the Kenyan coast, close to the Somali border, from which it conducts training missions for the Kenyan military and reportedly operates reconnaissance and drone flights into Somalia.[34] In 2011, Kenya invaded neighboring Somalia with the stated goal of pushing the Islamist militant group al-Shabaab back from the Somali–Kenyan border.[35] Kenya's willingness to use force to confront sources of instability in its neighborhood have thus given it the status of an "anchor" in the region. As a 2009 US diplomatic cable noted, "no country between Cairo and Capetown is more important [to the US] than Kenya."[36]

As in the case of Ethiopia, Kenya's strategic importance for European donors has further increased with the politicization of refugee arrivals in the EU since 2015. As a host to over 400,000 refugees, especially from South Sudan and Somalia, Kenya plays a crucial role in

---

[32] Cheeseman et al. 2019.
[33] Fisher 2013, p. 6.
[34] Turse 2018.
[35] Anderson and McKnight 2014.
[36] Cited in Fisher 2013, pp. 12–13.

curtailing the numbers of refugees departing Kenya for Europe. More than 200,000 refugees live in the Dadaab complex of refugee camps close to the Somali border alone. The Kenyan government has since 2016 repeatedly announced plans to close the refugee camp, citing security concerns, provoking rebukes from human rights organizations, and prompting commitments of more assistance from European donors.[37]

4.4.3 Ghana

A medium-sized country in West Africa, Ghana's history has been closely intertwined with the history of the African continent as a whole. In 1957, Ghana was the first sub-Saharan African country to regain independence after colonialism and Ghana's first president Kwame Nkrumah shaped anti-colonial and pan-African movements across the continent.[38] More recently, Ghana has been regarded as a symbol of the third wave of democratization in Africa. Since the country returned to multiparty competition in 1992, the two main parties have alternated in power multiple times in calm and peaceful elections. Ghana is roughly the size of the United Kingdom or the US states of Minnesota or Utah, while its population of 30.4 million is comparable to that of Peru or Saudi Arabia. In 2019, Ghana's GDP per capita stood at $1,844.3, above the sub-Saharan African average of $1,669.2.[39]

Ghana's economy is heavily concentrated in natural resource extraction and agriculture, with gold and cocoa the country's leading exports over the last two decades, and offshore oil and natural gas deposits discovered in the late 2000s. While Ghana began exporting petroleum in the early 2010s, oil production has so far fallen short of the initial expectation that the discovery would catapult Ghana into the ranks of Africa's wealthy oil producers. Moreover, Ghana's economy remains heavily focused on a few sectors; the Observatory of Economic Complexity, which measures the diversification of countries' economies, ranked Ghana 125th out of 137 countries in 2018.

Ghana effectively has a two-party political system, with both major parties tracing their roots to the political groupings that emerged

[37] Lischer 2017.
[38] Apter 1968.
[39] Figures in constant 2010 US dollars (World Bank 2020b).

during decolonization.[40] The first of these historic groupings was a nationalist party led by Kwame Nkrumah, premised on mass appeal and supported by trade unionists, while the second was a more conservative coalition of newly educated urbanites, landed elites, and neo-traditional chiefs.[41] Today's contemporary heirs to these parties are the National Democratic Congress (NDC), which has acquired the mantle of Kwame Nkrumah's broadly left-leaning mass political tradition, and the New Patriotic Party (NPP) in the tradition of conservative elites, with its political identity broadly understood as "elitist, ethnically exclusive … liberal-democratic and right-wing."[42] Unlike in Kenya, where political parties have largely been temporary containers to combine ethnic voting blocs, often dismantled after elections, the party landscape in Ghana has been more stable and consistent.

Democratic competition between these two parties has been back in place since the early 1990s, when Ghana faced external pressure to restore multiparty competition after years of alternating political instability and military rule in the 1970s and 1980s.[43] While the first elections were of dubious integrity, democratic institutions strengthened considerably in subsequent years. For instance, by 2012, when the opposition challenged the outcome of an election, the authority and independence of the Supreme Court were sufficiently established that the Court's ruling that the election was valid was widely accepted, including by the opposition. This resilience of Ghana's democratic institutions made it an appealing partner for many traditional donors.

Ghana has long been considered a "donor darling." From the mid 1980s until the mid 2010s, Ghana received above-average levels of per capita overseas development assistance compared to the rest of sub-Saharan Africa,[44] and donors have often taken a flexible, accommodating stance toward the country. Unlike other developing countries whose privileged status with donors derives from their geopolitical

---

[40] The following account of Ghana's political system draws on Whitfield 2009a and Whitfield 2018.

[41] Osei 2015.

[42] Whitfield 2009a, p. 629.

[43] Green 1995.

[44] World Bank, World Development Indicators.

position or natural resources, Ghana's significance has largely derived from "soft" or symbolic features. Ghana's 1992 transition to democracy and subsequent consolidation of peaceful elections were attractive for donors for whom democratization is an important component of their aid. Ghanaian governments were also seen as reliable reformers, implementing donor-recommended policies and achieving development gains.

At the same time, the context of political competition has undermined donor trust in public institutions. The two parties compete in closely fought and narrowly won elections, drawing on regional bases of support that are rewarded and reinforced through clientelist distribution. Given the unpredictability of electoral competition, Ghana's politics have been characterized by short–time horizons, with projects that can be quickly delivered and easily pointed to during election seasons.[45] To gain an upper hand in the competition, politicians are inclined to redirect resources to their home regions.[46] Persistent electoral budget cycles undermined donors' trust and eroded some of Ghana's significance to traditional donors toward the end of the period under study.

4.5 Overview of the Case Study Findings

Among the three case studies, Ethiopia was the most successful with debt-based financial statecraft during the period under study, with Kenya achieving some negotiating successes and Ghana the fewest bargaining wins on the basis of its diversified portfolio of finance. These differences across the cases are visible across the outcome measures used in Chapter 3 to capture negotiating outcomes, as reported in Figure 4.3.

From the mid 2000s, Ethiopia and Kenya received higher annual commitments from traditional donors, while average commitments to Ghana dropped off (Figure 4.3(a)). Part of the decline in aid commitments to Ghana can be explained by Ghana's growth and transition to lower-middle-income status, but Kenya was also a lower-middle-income country during this time, with a GDP per capita very close

---

[45] Whitfield 2018, p. 116.
[46] Abdulai and Hickey 2016, p. 65.

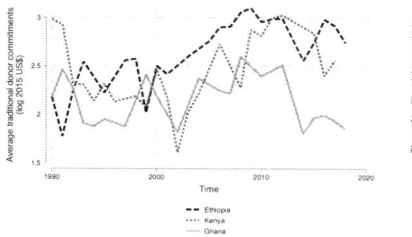 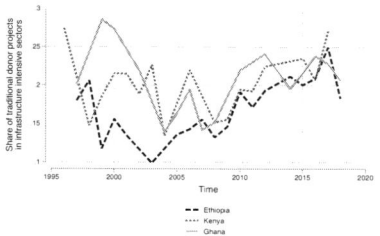

(a) Average annual commitments from traditional donors (log 2015 US$)

(b) Average annual share of traditional donor projects in infrastructure-intensive sectors

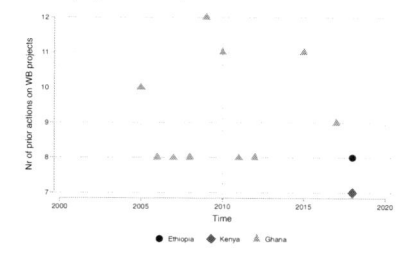

(c) Prior actions attached to World Bank projects

Figure 4.3 Variation in outcome measures in case study countries.

to Ghana's.[47] The difference between those two countries is in large part attributable to how donors appraised their relationship with the respective governments, especially in light of alternative finance. There is less of a sharp separation in donors' focus on infrastructure projects across the three countries, as Figure 4.3(b) shows. In Ghana, the average share of donor projects in infrastructure increased in the late 2000s and then plateaued at around 25 percent, while Ethiopia and Kenya had more of a steady increase from the mid 2000s to the late 2010s to reach a similar level. There does appear to be a difference in the conditionality of World Bank projects, though this divergence is in part a function of Ghana having received far more of the Development Policy Financing loans for which data on conditionality is available, with Kenya and Ethiopia perhaps eschewing these loans. In interviews, government officials in Ethiopia explained that they sought to avoid the World Bank programs with the greatest conditionality or reporting

---

[47] Ghana transitioned to lower-middle-income status in 2010, Kenya in 2014.

requirements.[48] Comparing the number of conditions attached to World Bank Development Policy Financing Loans in Ethiopia, Ghana, and Kenya shows that the few loans to Ethiopia and Kenya received seven or eight conditions, while Ghana received loans with up to twelve conditions, especially in the later years in the period. The pattern in conditionality speaks to donor's decreasing flexibility with Ghana during this time, despite Ghana's diversified portfolio of external finance.

The differences across the three countries become even clearer in the case studies, where I trace negotiating outcomes on issues of particular importance to the government, demonstrating whether the government was able to benefit from the leverage of alternative finance in areas it prioritized. In Ethiopia, donors had geopolitical and development reasons for wanting a close relationship with the government and considerable trust in the government's commitment to its development plans. These combined to lead to effective debt-based financial statecraft. Specifically, donors modified their criticism of the governing regime's clampdown on opposition freedoms, largely because continued access to the government was so important and donors were aware that other creditors did not condition their finance on domestic politics. This donor leeway becomes particularly clear when the apex of diversified finance in the early 2010s is compared to 2016 onward. In later years, the government made concessions it previously would not have considered, since its growing indebtedness reduced the number of willing lenders, limiting its portfolio of external finance.

In Kenya, the government had a more uneven track record of debt-based financial statecraft. The Kenyan case highlights how governments with less credibility with donors may struggle to translate alternative finance into preferred aid terms. While the government secured some wins in negotiations with donors, most notably a dampening of donor criticism of governance and human rights outcomes, in other areas it was much less successful. Donors' concern about government spending enabled by alternative finance led them to adopt a much stronger stance on issues important to the government, especially financial management.

---

[48] Interview 148. Ethiopian Investment Commission official. Addis Ababa, Ethiopia. August 3, 2017.

In Ghana, the government was the least successful at using new sources of external finance as a basis for greater leverage with traditional donors. Since Ghana's importance to its donors has historically rested on the country's success story of democratization and market-oriented reforms, Ghana's worsening debt situation decreased its significance to donors, who were more inclined to harden their terms as a form of insurance. On issues of macroeconomic policy and public financial management, the government was largely unable to use alternative finance as a means of achieving its preferred outcomes in negotiations with donors.

5 | *Ethiopia: Successful Financial Statecraft*

In Addis Ababa, the embassies of the United States, United Kingdom, Russia, and Germany are located on vast grounds on the outskirts of the city. At the end of the nineteenth century, the Ethiopian Emperor Menelik II gifted the ample swaths of land to those countries that the Emperor saw as the Ethiopian Empire's natural peers, with the select group of countries indicating where the Ethiopian Empire saw its rank in the world in the late 1800s. Closer to the focus of this book, the embassies are also evidence of Ethiopia's long-standing practice of using its foreign relations to its own advantage. The German embassy is reached by crossing a squat stone bridge adorned with Gothic lettering that stands out in its surroundings and reveals the bridge's provenance. When Menelik II granted Germany the tract of land that today makes up Germany's largest embassy grounds in the world, he requested that the German Empire fund and construct a bridge to connect the area surrounding the embassy to the core of the city. Recounting this story more than a century later, a German diplomat joked it revealed Ethiopia's long history of savvy engagement with external partners and the country's enduring appetite for infrastructure investment.

In the twenty-first century, Ethiopia's management of its foreign relations has similarly involved securing external funding, often for infrastructure investments. The country has juggled relationships with diverse sets of lenders, giving it more choice and greater strength in negotiations with individual donors and creditors. As a result, the government in power until 2019 was able to attract donor support for its developmental state agenda, among other priorities.[1] Ethiopia was

---

[1] As described in the introduction to the Ethiopian case in Chapter 4, the developmental state refers to the state-led development approach adopted by the Ethiopian government, emphasizing infrastructure investment and industrialization.

the most successful among the three case studies in this book, deploying alternative finance to achieve preferred outcomes across numerous dimensions of donor–recipient negotiations. These outcomes include some donors muting their criticisms of the government's political repression, while others avoided harshly penalizing the government for its debt accumulation. Further, the Ethiopian government persuaded traditional donors to fund key parts of its state-led development agenda. When it became more difficult for the government to borrow from expensive alternative creditors after 2016, given the country's growing debt burden, the government again had to make greater compromises in negotiations with traditional donors. This over-time variation in the Ethiopian government's reliance on traditional donors and the associated shifts in aid agreements, fluctuating from greater alignment with donor preferences relative to recipient preferences, and back again, provides support for the proposed mechanism of debt-based financial statecraft.

The Ethiopian experience demonstrates how both significance to donors and donor trust affect debt-based financial statecraft. Traditional bilateral and multilateral donors had a particular interest in their relationship and influence with the Ethiopian government, which made them more responsive to the government's independence when it turned to alternative creditors. Moreover, donor trust in the Ethiopian government reinforced the negotiating benefits of alternative finance. Donors trusted the government would uphold its commitments in aid agreements, due to several years of accomplishments in poverty reduction and domestic political conditions that for a long time gave the government considerable autonomy in implementing development plans. The coalition in power from the 1990s until 2019, the Ethiopian People's Revolutionary Democratic Front (EPRDF), had largely insulated itself from political competition. Though donors worried about its autocratic tendencies, they also saw the government as a reliable partner in implementing development policy. My argument in this chapter builds on research that has shown how both donors' security interests in Ethiopia and confidence in the government's technocratic ability to deliver development outcomes led them to extend greater flexibility and avoid censuring the government on its authoritarianism and human rights violations.[2] I add to this work a consideration of how the Ethiopian government deployed a diverse portfolio of external finance to its advantage.

As in the other cases in the book, the analysis of Ethiopia's relations with donors runs until 2018, when global conditions for external finance started to worsen. In Ethiopia, 2018 also marked a shift in domestic politics that makes this year an appropriate end point for the analysis. Cohesion among Ethiopia's political elite increasingly eroded from the mid 2010s onward, and by 2018 it had fragmented, as struggle among various factions broke into the open, culminating in the appointment of a new Prime Minister, Abiy Ahmed, from a historically marginalized ethnic group. In the years that followed, conflict in Ethiopia intensified, ultimately resulting in 2020 in the outbreak of civil war. The instability in Ethiopia in more recent years casts into sharper relief donors' earlier perception of the country's stability and the government's reliability as a credible counterpart in the period under study.

The evidence for this case comes from more than fifty interviews conducted in July and August 2017 in Addis Ababa with Ethiopian civil servants, policymakers, academics, journalists, and experts, as well as donor representatives based in Addis Ababa and Washington D.C.[3] This chapter first outlines in Section 5.1 what the theory indicates we should observe in the Ethiopian case. In Section 5.2, I describe the variation over time in Ethiopia's portfolio of external finance, highlighting key turning points when the government reduced or increased its reliance on traditional donors. I then map these changes in the government's access to alternative finance onto changes in the relationship between the Ethiopian government and traditional donors in Section 5.3, identifying which issues were most salient in the relationship and describing outcomes in these issue areas. Finally, in Section 5.4, I analyze how Ethiopia's significance to donors and the government's political control shaped the country's success with debt-based financial statecraft. Section 5.5 concludes the chapter.

---

[2] Abegaz 2015; S. Brown and Fisher 2020; Feyissa 2011; Furtado and W. J. Smith 2009.
[3] For more details, see Table A.1.

5.1 Theoretical Expectations in the Ethiopian Case

The framework introduced in Chapter 2 suggests that the Ethiopian government should have experienced an improvement in its relationship with traditional donors, with aid agreements more aligned with the government's preferences as Ethiopia diversified its portfolio of external finance. Despite being a low-income country that continued to receive substantial amounts of aid from traditional donors, Ethiopia considerably diversified its portfolio of external finance from the late 2000s into the 2010s. As I further describe later in this chapter, the country drew on large quantities of finance from China and also turned to private creditors. These alternative creditors reduced the Ethiopian government's reliance on traditional donor aid. Moreover, the government largely expanded its portfolio of external finance by borrowing from China. The theoretical framework indicates that donors are especially responsive to alternative creditors when they perceive the latter as a source of geopolitical competition, in addition to their effect of reducing the recipient's reliance on traditional donors. In Ethiopia's case, the government's close relationship with China likely raised competitive concerns for traditional donors, who feared losing their own access to the government.

As a case, Ethiopia scores highly on the two dimensions that increase the likelihood of successful financial statecraft. First, the country enjoyed a high level of strategic significance with donors. Ethiopia's geographic position in the Horn of Africa made it an important counterpart for donors concerned with stability in the subregion, as well as the flows of migration originating in neighboring countries such as Eritrea, Somalia, or Sudan.[4] The value that donors attach to their relationship with the Ethiopian government leads to the expectation that donors will be especially motivated to retain their access to the government. I will elaborate on the sources of Ethiopia's strategic importance and its impact on negotiations later in this chapter.

Second, traditional donors operating in Ethiopia had fairly high levels of trust in the government due to their assessment of the government's development track record, which led to poverty reduction and encouraged stability in a country that had experienced conflict and disaster in decades prior. Moreover, donors saw the government

---

[4] Feyissa 2011; Verhoeven and Woldemariam 2022.

as a counterpart capable of making credible commitments, with elite consensus on aligning development policy with the goals of a "developmental state." This donor confidence leads to the expectation that the government should extract greater negotiating benefits from its access to alternative finance.

Altogether, the theoretical framework suggests that when the Ethiopian government diversified its portfolio of external finance, the government should shift its relationship with traditional donors to align more closely with its preferences. This greater alignment with the government's preferences could manifest as more flexible aid agreements, with more funding for the government's preferred projects, and more discretion and leeway for the government's policies. In the analysis, I refer to negotiations between various traditional donors and the Ethiopian government, though agencies and ministries within Ethiopia maintain their own distinct relationships with donors. However, the priorities for and approach to relations with donors were established centrally and implemented through the Ministry of Finance or Prime Minister's office, and these are generally the institutions I mean when referring to the Ethiopian government.

5.2 Variation in Ethiopia's Portfolio of External Finance

In the three decades after the end of Ethiopia's civil war in 1991, the country experienced significant changes in its portfolio of external finance. Long dependent on traditional donor aid, especially humanitarian aid during the postwar reconstruction, the Ethiopian government gradually expanded its sources of finance in the 2000s. From a number of smaller Chinese-financed projects in the mid 2000s, Ethiopia grew to become one of the largest borrowers from China in sub-Saharan Africa by the 2010s, also adding private finance to the mix. Though traditional donors also increased their aid and loans to the country during this time (see Table 5.1), the expansion of alternative credit meant that Ethiopia substantially reduced its reliance on traditional donors during the 2010s. In 2014, funds from traditional donors and lenders made up only 50 percent of the country's total external finance, down from 96 percent in 1994 and 97 percent in 2004.[5]

---

[5] Data taken from World Bank Debtor Reporting System and OECD Creditor Reporting System, as described in Chapter 3.

Table 5.1 *Average annual ODA commitments of top DAC-reporting donors to Ethiopia, 1990–2019 (millions 2015 US$)*

1990–1999		2000–2009		2010–2019	
IDA	211	IDA	646	IDA	1,501
EU	161	US	609	US	888
US	85	EU	271	EU	231
AfDF	79	UK	154	UK	211
Italy	67	AfDF	104	AfDF	192
Netherlands	51	Germany	79	Germany	144
Germany	51	Canada	76	Korea	112
Sweden	41	Italy	69	Canada	105
Canada	33	Netherlands	63	Netherlands	94
Japan	31	Ireland	44	Japan	82
Norway	29	Japan	41	France	73
UK	19	Norway	41	Norway	65
AfDB	16	Sweden	37	Ireland	45
UNDP	11	France	22	AfDB	41
Finland	10	AfDB	21	Sweden	40

For the analysis of the donor–government relationship in the Ethiopian case, there are three important turning points. In 2004, Ethiopia received substantial debt forgiveness. Its lower debt burden enabled it to borrow from alternative creditors at exactly the time when China was expanding its lending. Ethiopia borrowed in increasing amounts from Chinese lenders, reaching new heights in the 2010s (see Figure 5.1). Second, in 2014, Ethiopia issued its first international sovereign bond. Though Ethiopia had already borrowed in substantial amounts from private creditors, especially private banks, the debut bond issuance was a public signal of the country's access to private alternative finance. Finally, after 2016, with worsening debt sustainability indicators, Ethiopia's options narrowed yet again.

Before Ethiopia diversified its portfolio of external finance, in the years immediately after the EPRDF came to power in 1991, Ethiopia was highly aid dependent, drawing on funds from traditional multilateral and OECD DAC donors. Most aid programs at the time focused on postwar rehabilitation and building up Ethiopia's fragile social sectors, with projects in health and education. In addition, the World Bank provided structural adjustment loans to support economic

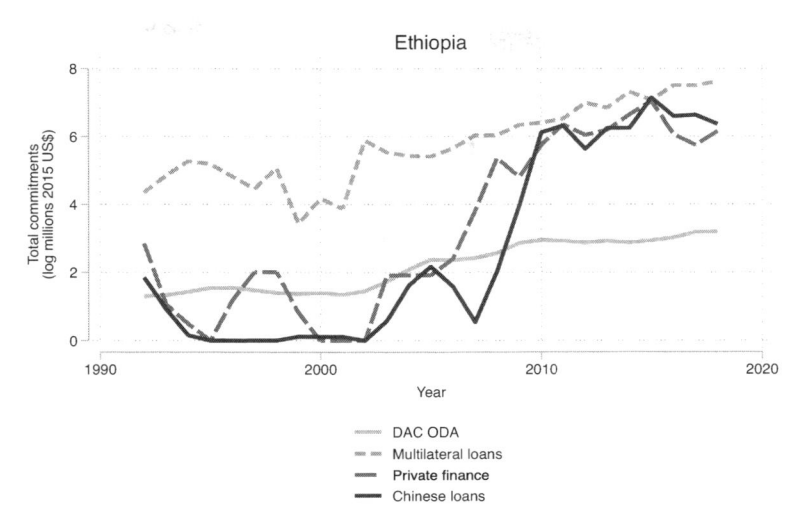

Figure 5.1 Ethiopia's portfolio of external finance, 1992–2018.
Three-year rolling average of total commitments (log millions 2015 US$).

reforms. Most traditional donors suspended aid in the late 1990s during the war with Eritrea, in an attempt to bring the conflict to an end.[6] By the early 2000s, after the conclusion of hostilities with Eritrea, the emergence of the global war on terror led the US to take an increasing interest in Ethiopia's role as an anchor of stability in the Horn of Africa, and it became the leading bilateral donor in Ethiopia during the 2000s.[7]

The first turning point in Ethiopia's ability to diversify external finance came in 2004, when the country reached the completion point of the debt relief process through the Highly Indebted Poor Countries (HIPC) Initiative and was granted substantial debt forgiveness from traditional donors. In the following years, as China became a more active lender across sub-Saharan Africa, Ethiopia was in a position to take on new loans. In 2006, Ethiopia signed its first large loan agreements with the Export-Import Bank of China, including a $500 million loan for the construction of a hydroelectric power plant and expansion of a cement factory and an $822 million loan for China's ZTE

---

[6] Lavers 2023, p. 99.
[7] Borchgrevink 2008; Verhoeven and Woldemariam 2022.

corporation to develop Ethiopia's telecommunications infrastructure.[8] These projects were only the beginning of what came to be an enormous flow of Chinese finance over the following decade (see Figure 5.1). Over the 2000–2018 period, Ethiopia was the second largest borrower from China of any country in sub-Saharan Africa, after Angola.

The Ethiopian government was particularly eager to borrow from China because of China's willingness to support large infrastructure projects, as well as its hands-off approach to governance and domestic political issues. Ethiopian political elites crafting plans for the Ethiopian developmental state were impressed by China's own development experience, especially the use of public infrastructure investment to support export-led growth.[9] The EPRDF government borrowed from Chinese lenders for large infrastructure projects at the core of the country's developmental state agenda, including a railway link connecting landlocked Ethiopia to a port in neighboring Djibouti. As an official from the Ethiopian Ministry of Finance put it, "Chinese financing is changing everything. The railway, the tram, this is all unthinkable from the others, from the Western world."[10] The Ethiopian government not only appreciated that Chinese loans enabled major infrastructure projects but also that China's no-questions-asked approach to governance and domestic political issues left Ethiopia relatively free from scrutiny. For instance, one Ministry of Finance official explained the difference between funding projects with a Chinese loan or with American aid,

Sometimes if there is conditionality, that is a problem. Some from America are always saying, 'You give preference to the Chinese!' But that's not the case. The Chinese never asked us, for example, for good governance changes. For America, it is a part [of aid].[11]

This greater flexibility, together with the close alignment between the EPRDF's infrastructure ambitions and Chinese lenders' willingness to

---

[8] Strange et al. 2013.
[9] Fourie 2015.
[10] Interview 129. Ministry of Finance official. Addis Ababa, Ethiopia. July 17, 2017.
[11] Interview 134. Ministry of Finance official. Addis Ababa, Ethiopia. July 19, 2017.

finance large infrastructure projects, led Ethiopia to become a major borrower from China over the course of the 2010s.

In addition to China, other nontraditional bilateral lenders joined Ethiopia's portfolio of external finance during this time. India's Exim Bank opened an office in Addis Ababa in 2010 to cover the entire East African region, and over the next years approved more than $300 million in loans for the development of Ethiopia's sugar industry.[12] In 2015, the Saudi Arabian central bank made a deposit of $1 billion with the Ethiopian central bank, helping to ease the country's foreign exchange constraints.[13] Traditional donors observed the rise of these other donors, noting that they operated outside of coordinating mechanisms and did not have the same objectives of shaping the government's development policy. As one donor official put it, "It's not just the Chinese, it's the Saudis, Turkish, India, Qatar ... But all these partners don't care about coordination. It's the Western donors who care about coordination and influencing the government in some way. Sometimes the government feels it isn't comfortable to listen to the West, then they prefer other financing."[14]

The second turning point in Ethiopia's portfolio of external finance came as the Ethiopian government drew on private credit. In December 2014, Ethiopia debuted in international bond markets, issuing its first-ever international bond.[15] Considering the government's heterodox development approach, the choice to borrow in international markets and open itself up to foreign investors' scrutiny might appear surprising.[16] However, the government was motivated to issue the bond by the appeal of flexible and unconditional funds with which to implement key public investments faster than would be possible with traditional lenders and donors. One Ministry of Finance representative explained the appeal of the sovereign bond by saying, "Of course, it's not cheap,

---

[12] India Exim Bank 2023.

[13] Interview 49. Multilateral donor official. Washington D.C. February 27, 2017; Interview 131. Multilateral donor official. Addis Ababa, Ethiopia. July 17, 2017.

[14] Interview 132. Bilateral donor official. Addis Ababa, Ethiopia. July 18, 2017.

[15] Ethiopia's $1 billion bond was priced at an interest rate of 6.625 percent for a maturity of ten years, an interest rate below the average for sub-Saharan African issuers that year (excluding South Africa).

[16] Zeitz 2021a.

but nevertheless it's very good. It's more flexible, it's not project tied, it's not tied to conditions."[17]

By the mid 2010s, the Ethiopian government was less reliant on traditional donor aid than it had been in the 1990s or even 2000s. Although the annual commitments of all the major traditional donors increased from the 2000s to the 2010s (see Table 5.1), the relative importance of each of those donors declined. With the growth of Ethiopia's economy, official development assistance declined from an average of 14.16 percent of GDP in 2000–2009 to 7.33 percent of GDP in 2010–2018. Further, traditional donor aid shrank as a share of Ethiopia's overall external finance. As Ethiopia took on more loans from nontraditional lenders and private sources, concessional aid from OECD DAC donors declined from 66 percent of Ethiopia's external finance in the 1990s to 56 percent in the 2000s and 35 percent in the 2010s.[18] Though the EPRDF government continued to draw on traditional donor funds, these resources became less important, giving the government greater autonomy when negotiating with traditional donors.

A final turning point in Ethiopia's portfolio of external finance came when the country's options narrowed in the late 2010s. Over the course of the 2010s, as Ethiopia borrowed from new creditors, the country's debt burden grew (see Figure 5.2). While an increase in a government's overall debt does not immediately spell a debt crisis, a country becomes less able to borrow as the expense of maintaining its outstanding debt increases. Since much of the debt Ethiopia contracted in the 2010s was commercial finance at high interest rates, the costs of debt service rapidly increased. Moreover, Ethiopia's poor export performance in the late 2010s meant the country struggled to earn sufficient foreign currency to meet its debt obligations. While the government initially ignored warnings to cut back on its non-concessional borrowing, by 2016 the government became increasingly cautious about non-concessional debt.

[17] Interview 126. National Bank of Ethiopia official. Addis Ababa, Ethiopia. July 14, 2017.
[18] World Bank International Debt Statistics. Total traditional development finance (including loans from multilaterals) also declined during this period, though less dramatically, from 93 percent in the 1990s to 86 percent in the 2000s, and 66 percent in the 2010s.

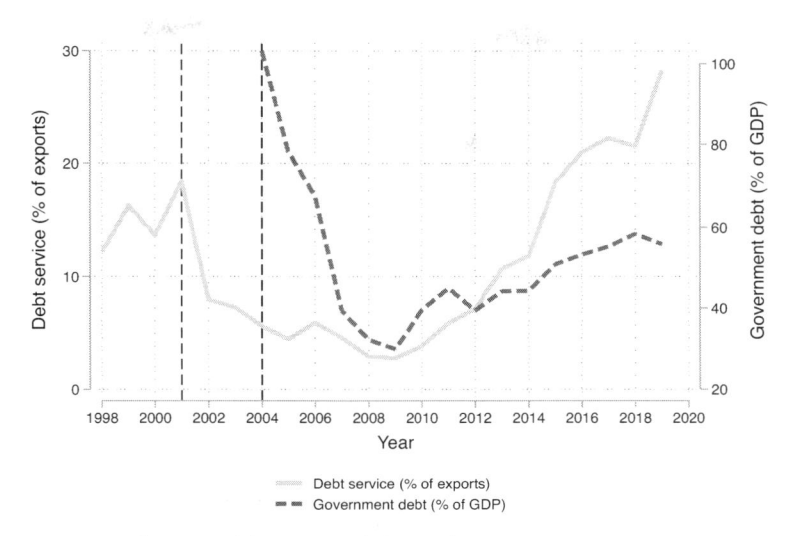

Figure 5.2 Ethiopia's debt sustainability indicators, 1998–2018.
The decision and completion points for debt relief under the HIPC initiative
were 2001 and 2004, respectively.

At the same time, responding to Ethiopia's worsening debt sustainability indicators, alternative lenders became more cautious about lending, with some Chinese creditors becoming less willing to lend to the Ethiopian government. An official from the Chinese Economic and Commercial Counsellor's Office in Addis Ababa confirmed that China's Export-Import Bank was taking greater precautions in its lending to Ethiopia and had turned down projects in 2017.[19] Such precautions did not preclude all Chinese finance, but did narrow the range of finance available to the government.[20] As the options for market-rate borrowing narrowed, Ethiopia became slightly more reliant again on traditional donors' concessional finance. Figure 5.1 shows the slight downward trend in private finance and Chinese loans toward the end of the 2010s.

---

[19] Interview 151. Bilateral donor official. Addis Ababa, Ethiopia. August 7, 2017.

[20] Data from the World Bank's International Debt Statistics indicates that Chinese bilateral commitments to Ethiopia declined from $815 million in 2016 and $851 million in 2017 to $230 million in 2018.

5.3 Preferred Outcomes with Donors

The Ethiopian government substantially increased its influence in the relationship with donors when it borrowed from China, international bond markets, and other alternative sources. No longer as reliant on traditional donor aid as it had been in the 1990s and 2000s, the government could push for a relationship with donors that was more to its liking. From the late 2000s to the late 2010s, the Ethiopian government strategically pursued new sources of finance, and deliberately played lenders off against each other to enhance its bargaining leverage.

Since Ethiopia is sometimes described as exceptional in sub-Saharan Africa for the strength of its government and capacity of its bureaucracy, it might appear that donors' willingness to fund the government's preferred projects in the 2010s was simply a function of the government's negotiating skill. Indeed, it is true that the EPRDF government was already more influential than many other African countries in negotiations with donors in the 1990s and 2000s,[21] and some scholars suggest this is an even more enduring feature of Ethiopia's relations with foreign funders, reaching back to imperial rule in the mid twentieth century.[22] Nonetheless, the access to alternative finance was decisive. Compared to earlier decades when the EPRDF government was more reliant on traditional sources of development finance, the 2010s stand out for how much the government–donor relationship aligned with the EPRDF's preferences. Moreover, the subtle shift in the donor–government relationship when the government lost some of its access to alternative finance in the late 2010s, with the pendulum swinging back to greater donor influence, highlights the importance of the government's relative autonomy from donor resources for the government–donor relationship.

In tracing the changes in Ethiopia's relationship with traditional donors as a result of the government's reduced dependence on traditional donor funds, I focus on outcomes of particular importance in this relationship. First, a comparison of donors' responses to crackdowns on anti-government protests in 2005 and 2015–16 reveals how donors muted their criticism of the government's authoritarianism

---

[21] Clapham 2009; Furtado and W. J. Smith 2009.
[22] Fantini and Puddu 2016.

once the government borrowed from alternative lenders. Second, the World Bank chose to be lenient when the government violated agreements about debt and financial stability, demonstrating the Bank's interest in maintaining a close relationship with the government. Finally, traditional donors supported the government's state-led development agenda, including funding key infrastructure projects. However, as access to alternative finance waned, the government again made some concessions on economic policy in their negotiations with traditional donors.

5.3.1 Governance and Democratization

Governance and democratization are often fraught areas of the government–donor relationship, hence my examination of the relationship between the number of governance-specific conditions and the diversification of external finance portfolios in the large-n analysis in Chapter 3. Donors may directly support democratization by funding programs that strengthen political institutions, may fund the governance-oriented work of local NGOs, or they may simply use their prominent position in the recipient country to publicly encourage democratization and respect for human and political rights. Depending on the orientation of the government, these donor efforts may be more or less contentious. In Ethiopia, political rights and democratization were especially sensitive points in the relationship between the government and donors, given the government's authoritarianism. The changes in government–donor relationship on these issues are therefore a good indicator of the relative influence of each side. A comparison of donors' responses to crises in 2005 and 2015–16 illustrates how much more bargaining leverage the government had acquired by the mid 2010s.

In the postwar period of the 1990s, most donors believed the EPRDF's reforms to domestic governance were steps in the right direction.[23] After the authoritarianism of the previous *Derg* regime, the new EPRDF government appeared to pursue political liberalization, including introducing a new constitution in 1995 that created a legislature and introduced regular elections.

---

[23] Feyissa 2011, pp. 791–792.

Donors' confidence in the government's commitment to political liberalization was rudely shaken in 2005 when the government responded
with harsh repression to an unfavorable electoral result. In the May
2005 parliamentary elections, which were first openly contested elections in Ethiopia's history, the EPRDF lost many more seats to the
opposition than it had anticipated, with the opposition gaining 174
out of 546 seats in the House of People's Representatives, especially
in cities and larger towns, as well as all the seats on the Addis Ababa
city council. The EPRDF government delayed recognizing opposition
victories and used complaints procedures to nullify results and rerun
elections in thirty-one jurisdictions, all of which the government won
in the rerun. When students and opposition supporters demonstrated
against the government's efforts to secure its hold on power, the government banned public demonstrations; arrested opposition leaders,
students, and journalists; and sent troops into the streets that shot
and killed protesters.[24] Independent reports suggest 19,000 opposition supporters were detained and 193 protesters died at the hands of
the police.[25]

In response, donors publicly criticized both the irregularities in the
conduct of the election and the government's crackdown on opposition protests in the following months. The EU, the US, and individual
European bilateral donors condemned the violence by the authorities and urged the government to exercise restraint toward opposition
leaders. In November 2005, the EU and the United States called on
the government to release "political detainees," directly challenging
the government's claim that opposition leaders had been arrested for
criminal activity.[26] Deeds followed words, and as the government's
repression of protests worsened, many donors halted their aid flows.
In December 2005, after security forces killed dozens of protesters,
donors including the World Bank, the EU, and the African Development Bank, as well as the UK, Canada, Ireland, Germany, and Sweden
announced plans to withhold $275 million in budget support.[27]

Ten years later, donors responded differently to similar levels of
government repression. In 2015 and 2016, protesters in the Oromo

---

[24] Clapham 2005.
[25] Amnesty International 2006; BBC 2006.
[26] Lyons 2006.
[27] Gilmore 2006.

and Amhara regions took to the streets to challenge a new development plan for the capital of Addis Ababa, which would see the city encroaching land in the neighboring regions. This development plan was seen by opponents as emblematic of the government's disregard for the interests of underrepresented ethnicities and overreach in favor of centralized authority in the capital.[28] The protests grew into a wider movement that criticized the government's exclusion of Oromos and Amharans from key political decision-making processes. Though the Oromo and Amhara are the largest ethnic groups in Ethiopia, they were underrepresented in decision-making under the EPRDF, which remained heavily controlled by the Tigray People's Liberation Front (TPLF). The protest movement attracted international attention when Ethiopian marathon runner Feyisa Lilesa crossed his wrists in an Oromo protest gesture while crossing the finish line as silver medalist in the 2016 Rio Olympics. The authorities responded fiercely to the protests; estimates suggest 11,000 people were arrested and at least 500 people were killed.[29]

This time, the response from donors was more muted, with fewer actions to back up the words of criticism.[30] On a visit to Addis Ababa in October 2016 just days after a national state of emergency was introduced that gave the government sweeping powers, German Chancellor Angela Merkel encouraged the government to develop a dialogue with the opposition, rather than directly denouncing the government's role in the violence. More importantly, donors' statements were not accompanied by cuts to foreign aid as they were in the mid 2000s. As the NGO Human Rights Watch noted in its 2016 report on Ethiopia, while individual legislatures such as the EU Parliament or the US Senate had condemned the violence, donor agencies, "including the World Bank, have continued business as usual without publicly raising concerns."[31] Nor did donors make sustained efforts to address the protests in private dialogue with the government. In fact, donor officials who regularly interacted with the government were wary of raising the government's repression. One donor representative noted

[28] Terrefe 2020.
[29] Brechenmacher 2017.
[30] S. Brown and Fisher 2020, p. 189.
[31] Human Rights Watch 2016.

she "ha[d] never been in a country before where donors are so afraid of the government."[32]

The comparison between 2005–06 and 2015–16 highlights that the balance of influence between the government and donors had shifted in this sensitive area. The government's reduced dependence on traditional donor funds and access to financing with fewer political expectations played a considerable role in dampening donors' criticism of the government. One donor official explained how his government had contemplated cutting aid to the government, but the Ethiopian government's access to outside options affected donors' reactions to the crackdown. He said,

In the context of the current state of emergency, there were donors who indicated they would reduce their programs in-country and the government responded by saying they were *welcome to leave if they wanted to*. That's only really possible because there are others standing at the ready, able to provide financing.[33]

As outside options reduced the government's dependence on traditional donor funds, the government was in a stronger position to push back against donors' critiques, leading to a more muted outcome.

As the theoretical framework suggests, concern about the influence of alternative donors, especially China, further enhanced the government's bargaining leverage, even on sensitive issues around respect for human rights. As one donor representative bluntly put it, "The reason, to some extent, the Western partners are all here, is because if they weren't, they know the big bogeyman China is here."[34] A 2017 Carnegie Endowment report echoed this appraisal, noting that "Donor governments also worry that isolating the Ethiopian government could further increase China's influence in the country – particularly since the EPRDF already views Chinese investment as an important alternative to Western support."[35] The combination of Ethiopia's importance to traditional donors and the government's access to

---

[32] Interview 149. Bilateral donor official. Addis Ababa, Ethiopia. August 4, 2017.
[33] Interview 142. Bilateral donor official. Addis Ababa, Ethiopia. July 26, 2017. Emphasis added.
[34] Interview 141. Bilateral donor official. Addis Ababa, Ethiopia. July 26, 2017.
[35] Brechenmacher 2017.

alternative finance, particularly Chinese loans, thus dampened donors' criticism of governance shortcomings in line with government preferences.

When comparing donors' responses to the 2005–06 and 2015–16 crises, skeptics might note that donors' responses to the government's repression in 2005–06 proved short-lived. After the 2005 protests, the donors who withheld aid mostly cut their budget support programs that flowed directly into the government's coffers. In the following year, many of these donors restored funding but avoided budget support and instead routed their aid into programs earmarked for specific sectors, where the government would have less direct control over the resources, or to development initiatives at the regional and subregional woreda level.[36] International human rights organizations criticized the rerouting as insufficient to censure the ruling party for their role in the violence, as most local governments were controlled by the EPRDF.[37] Further, since donors shifted their aid out of budget support programs under direct control of the national government to sectoral and regional programs, donors no longer had direct budgetary support they could withdraw in response to the 2015–16 crisis. The difference between 2005–06 and 2015–16 might simply appear to be path dependence: As donors lost trust in the government, they withdrew aid that directly supported the national government and therefore had no need to withdraw aid from the national government in the later crisis.

This explanation ignores the depth of donors' support for the government's development policies, which continued throughout the 2015–16 crisis. As an example, donors played a crucial role in the government's Productive Safety Net Program, one of the world's largest cash and food transfers programs, which is designed to help rural farmers bounce back from the ravages of regular droughts. Collectively, ten donors, including the World Bank, the US, and the UK, provided $2.3 billion for the program in the years 2011 to 2015.[38] The program not only provided direct humanitarian support to rural Ethiopians but was also an important part of the government's appeal in rural areas. Nevertheless, donors did not curtail their support for this program

---

[36] Borchgrevink 2008.
[37] Human Rights Watch 2007.
[38] World Bank 2013, p. 2.

during the crisis and, in fact, in its midst the World Bank approved an extension of the program, agreeing in December 2015 to provide $300 million of the $450 million cost for an urban version of the program.[39] There are compelling humanitarian reasons for donors not to withdraw funding from a social safety net program in response to government policies, but the same was true when donors chose to withhold aid in 2005. That donors chose not to respond to the 2015–16 crisis by cutting aid is an indication of donors' motivation to retain close relations with the Ethiopian government.

5.3.2 Economic Monitoring

Ethiopia's reduced reliance on traditional development finance also led donors to be less strict when monitoring the government's borrowing and spending. An important role that international financial institutions play in developing countries is to provide an outside assessment of the government's finances. Most often, this role is played by the IMF, which provides regular assessments of a country's economy that are useful for investors, trading partners, or other donors to evaluate the stability of a country's economy. In some cases, the World Bank plays a similar role, evaluating and reporting on the macroeconomic conditions in recipient countries. In particular, the World Bank monitors the finances of those developing countries that have received multilateral debt relief to ensure these countries do not take on unsustainable levels of non-concessional debt thereafter.[40]

As a low-income country that received debt write-offs through the Multilateral Debt Relief Initiative (MDRI) in 2004, Ethiopia falls under the World Bank's economic monitoring remit. The World Bank monitored Ethiopian government debt for its overall level of sustainability during the period under consideration, setting limits on the amount of non-concessional finance the country could take on. In the years in which Ethiopia diversified its portfolio of external debt, the country borrowed extensively, breaching the limits on non-concessional borrowing that it had agreed on with the World Bank. And yet, in the mid-2010s, the World Bank chose not to discipline or

---

[39] World Bank 2015d.
[40] World Bank 2006b, This is known as the non-concessional borrowing policy (NCBP).

sanction the Ethiopian government for its accumulation of debt. The evidence suggests that the World Bank's flexibility was at least partly motivated by its wish to continue providing loans to Ethiopia, to retain its relationship with the government as other lenders were increasing in importance and influence. Though borrowing from other creditors directly led to Ethiopia's violation of the non-concessional borrowing limits, it also risked undermining the World Bank's influence with the government. Given Ethiopia's development track record and importance for achieving the World Bank's goals, the Bank appears to have been reluctant to reduce its own access to the government.

Beginning in the early 2010s, the Ethiopian government repeatedly violated the limits the World Bank imposed on non-concessional borrowing. In 2013 and 2014, for instance, the World Bank set the government's non-concessional borrowing ceiling at $1 billion per year. The Ethiopian government far exceeded these limits each year, borrowing $5.8 billion on non-concessional terms in 2013 and $2.9 billion in 2014. This debt consisted mostly of loans from Chinese lenders, as well as $300 million from Turkey's Eximbank and roughly $900 million in a loan from the private Swiss bank Credite Suisse.[41]

When developing countries breach the agreed-upon limits on non-concessional borrowing, the World Bank has two sets of responses. It can either charge higher interest rates on its own loans or reduce the total amount of funding it allocates to a recipient country. The Bank's internal policy indicates that cuts of 20–40 percent to a country's allocation are appropriate responses for extensive violations of agreed-upon borrowing limits.[42] When faced with Ethiopia's breach of the agreed-upon debt cap in 2014, the World Bank considered the full range of possible responses. A confidential, internal World Bank document shows that staff considered increasing the cost of financing to an intermediate "blend" level or increasing the costs of borrowing even further toward market terms.[43] According to the World Bank's policy, both the fact that Ethiopia had demonstrated an ability to borrow in private markets and the scale of its violation of the debt ceiling made it a candidate for the World Bank to raise interest rates on its loans.

[41] World Bank 2014.
[42] World Bank 2006b, p. 22.
[43] World Bank 2014.

However, in 2015 the World Bank chose to simply impose a 5 percent cut to the country's funding allocation.[44] This was a mild response, given that the World Bank's commitments to Ethiopia increased, on average, 40 percent year-on-year during the period between 2000 and 2014. Of the range of options the Bank considered, it opted for the most lenient response to Ethiopia's violation of the debt agreement, short of granting the country a waiver.

Ethiopia was under review for failures to comply with the World Bank's non-concessional borrowing policy for six of the thirteen years that the policy was in effect.[45] Only once did the World Bank choose to cut its funding and then only by 5 percent. Certainly, the World Bank's non-concessional borrowing policy is designed to give the Bank flexibility in how it responds to countries' borrowing, since the implications of non-concessional debt depend on a country's context. Nevertheless, in Ethiopia, the World Bank did not impose measures such as substantial cuts to their funding or significantly increasing the cost of their loans. Explaining its choices in a number of countries in a 2019 review, the World Bank notes that the reluctance to cut its funding in response to violations "... may have been out of a concern that affected countries might further turn to non-concessional sources to compensate for reduced IDA allocations."[46] The concern that withheld World Bank funds would simply be replaced with expensive alternate financing may have been a concern about debt sustainability, but it is also connected to the World Bank's desire to retain a relationship with the Ethiopian government.

If the World Bank were to withdraw large volumes of funding as a disciplining mechanism, it would risk losing influence with the government. As one donor representative who had observed the discussions over Ethiopia's debt burden put it, "... the World Bank is somewhat

---

[44] The World Bank also chose to provide the entirety of Ethiopia's funding allocation as low-cost credits, rather than providing any grants. However, this was not a significant imposition, since Ethiopia had received its World Bank funds as credits in all preceding years and only became eligible to receive grants in 2015 when it went from being assessed at low/"green light" risk of debt distress to medium/"yellow light" risk of debt distress. The decision to provide all credits rather than a half–half mix of credits and grants was thus technically a hardening of terms but in fact simply continued the earlier pattern of funding (World Bank 2014).

[45] World Bank 2019a, p. 33.

[46] World Bank 2019b, p. 13.

shaped by the fact that they want to maintain a relationship [with the government]."[47] Despite the World Bank's relative leniency, a representative from a different donor expressed concern that adhering to debt sustainability standards could compromise donors' relationships with the government if these rules allowed other creditors to make inroads, saying

Who is cautious about lending? China? No. India? No. Turkey? No. But the [World] Bank? Yes. The IMF? Yes. When we designed these principles [on debt sustainability] we were a bit stupid. We didn't think about the competition. And now we have these principles and we are losing.[48]

Even if only in part, the concern about "losing" to "the competition" helps explain why the World Bank took a moderate stance when Ethiopia exceeded the agreed-upon debt ceiling by 480 percent in 2013 and 190 percent in 2014. The Ethiopian government was able to achieve its preferred outcome – retaining access to cheap World Bank financing – because it had demonstrated the diversity of its portfolio of external finance.

5.3.3 Donor Support for the Developmental State

The EPRDF built much of its political legitimacy, both domestically and internationally, on the achievements of its state-led development strategy. The proportion of population living on less than $2.15 per day more than halved from 69 percent in 1995 to 27 percent in 2015, while GDP per capita doubled from $241.78 to $630.31 during this time.[49] Development policy was not only central to the EPRDF's hold on power but also an important area of donor technical advice and conditionality. Given strong views on both sides, development policy was a sensitive area of the donor–government relationship. As in other areas, the government was largely successful in aligning donors with its preferences once it diversified its portfolio of external finance, garnering donor support for its economic approach and receiving

---

[47] Interview 125. Bilateral donor official. Addis Ababa, Ethiopia. July 13, 2017.

[48] Interview 138. Multilateral donor official. Addis Ababa, Ethiopia. July 25, 2017.

[49] Data from the World Bank's World Development Indicators, series SI.POV.DDAY and NY.GDP.PCAP.KD.

large volumes of traditional donor finance for projects at the heart of its developmental state model. I agree with the analysis of Abegaz (2015), S. Brown and Fisher (2020), and Feyissa (2011) that donors extended considerable flexibility to the Ethiopian government in its developmental state policies because of aligned security interests and shared development and poverty reduction objectives, adding to this the impact of Ethiopia's reduced reliance on traditional donor funds, which gave the government greater bargaining leverage.

In the first decade the EPRDF government was in power (1991–2001), the government frequently clashed with donors over economic policy. Molded by heterodox economics, the government's economic strategy diverged especially from the recommendations of the IMF for restoring Ethiopia's postwar economy.[50] Nevertheless, the government was reliant on donor funds to restore its financial balance and rebuild the country's war-torn economy. The EPRDF government and the IMF thus went through a series of tough negotiations, in which the government conceded to opening most of the economy to domestic private firms, allowing foreign investors in a few sectors of the economy, and removing price and distribution controls. However, the government refused to allow foreign participation in the banking sector, to liberalize the exchange rate, or to open the country's capital account. Relations between the EPRDF government and the IMF worsened over the course of the 1990s. Disagreements over capital controls led to a dramatic showdown in 1997, when the Fund suspended its program, withdrawing $125 million in financing.

At the time, the IMF insisted that developing countries should move quickly to liberalizing their capital accounts, allowing free movement of capital in and out of their economies. Prime Minister Meles Zenawi resisted, arguing that removing capital controls would expose Ethiopia to the instabilities experienced by East Asian economies in the Asian financial crisis at the time.[51] The dispute between Ethiopia and the IMF caught the attention of Joseph Stiglitz, then chief economist of the World Bank, who traveled to Addis Ababa to meet with Meles Zenawi and advocated on Ethiopia's behalf with the IMF.[52] Despite Stiglitz's protestations, the IMF continued to withhold funds, labeling

[50] Weis 2015.
[51] Wade 2001.
[52] Stiglitz 2001.

Ethiopia a "reluctant reformer."[53] Observers suggest Stiglitz's forceful defense of Ethiopia, which fell afoul not only of the IMF's view but also the US's position on Ethiopia's economic policy, contributed to his departure from the World Bank in 2000 after only three years as chief economist.[54]

The IMF was not the only lender with whom Ethiopia engaged in disputes over economic policy. For the World Bank, African Development Bank, and other donors, liberalization and privatization were central to the structural adjustment loans they provided in the 1990s. The overall goal of these loans was to "facilitate the transformation of the country from central planning to a market economy."[55] Though the government may have been in broad agreement with this goal, it delayed and hedged on planned privatizations. In response, donors paused their aid for almost two years. For these large multilateral donors, much as for the IMF, negotiations with the government revolved around economic issues and tensions arose when the government appeared to veer from the agreed-upon path of liberalization.

Two decades later, as the government diversified its sources of finance in the mid 2010s, several traditional donors were more willing to support the government's state-led development agenda. In part, donors were more open to Ethiopia's approach to development policy because the government's track record with poverty reduction gave its development plans greater credibility. Moreover, changes in donors' approaches to development assistance over the course of the late 2000s emphasized the importance of government ownership of development projects and donor alignment with government plans.[56] And yet, donors were also persuaded to take the government's economic policy seriously because the government signaled it would pursue this agenda regardless of traditional donor support, given its access to alternative sources of finance. In particular, the EPRDF government funded many key projects in its developmental state agenda using Chinese loans, which were a good fit since the EPRDF's development policy is partly modeled on the Chinese

---

[53] Wade 2001.
[54] Wade 2001.
[55] African Development Bank 2000, p. ii.
[56] Booth 2012.

experience with public investment-led growth.[57] This close alignment on economic policy between the EPRDF government and China risked displacing traditional donors' access to the government. Several traditional donors, especially larger donors with the resources to support large infrastructure projects, were motivated to provide development finance aligned with the government's development strategy to remain relevant.

While not all traditional donors wholesale embraced the government's state-led development model by the 2010s, key donors with large aid portfolios chose to fund and support landmark projects in the government's development agenda. Chief among these were the World Bank, the African Development Bank, the European Union, and the UK.[58] Using the indicator from Chapter 3 that measures the infrastructure-intensity of donors' development finance, the share of World Bank projects in infrastructure-intensive sectors in Ethiopia increased from an average of 27 percent in the 1990s to an average of 38 percent in the 2000s and 43 percent in the 2010s.

Traditional donor funding for industrial parks vividly illustrates donor support for the government's development strategy. These industrial parks were a key part of the government's industrialization agenda, especially its ambitions to establish a light manufacturing hub in Ethiopia. Based on the East Asian model of export-led growth, the industrial parks were intended to attract foreign investment in priority sectors, including textiles and leather.[59] Though the aim was to encourage private firms to invest, the development plan relied on public investment to encourage the growth of manufacturing, including by building factory infrastructure that private investors could use. Traditional donors were initially skeptical of these plans, seeing the government as overreaching and recommending that industrial development be left to private actors. A joint World Bank and IMF assessment of Ethiopia's 2010–2014 development plan notes, "Ethiopia's approach to industrial development is largely ineffective given the extremely low level of manufacturing and industrial development, low productivity levels, and persistent trade deficit. Staff advise rethinking industrial policy as a process of collaboration and problem-solving with the

---

[57] Fourie 2015.
[58] Abegaz 2015.
[59] Oqubay 2015.

private sector."[60] Finding little support from donors, the EPRDF government instead paid for its first large industrial park using money raised from the its 2014 international bond. This industrial park, built very rapidly by a Chinese contractor near the city of Hawassa, became the government's showcase for the possibilities of using public investment to foster manufacturing growth.[61]

After the success of the Hawassa industrial park, the government redoubled its efforts to use public funding to boost manufacturing, and over the course of the 2010s it increasingly found donor support for these efforts. The government's 2015–2019 development plan placed industrial parks at the center of its development strategy, emphasizing that "speeding up industrial parks development at both federal and regional levels ... needs to be given utmost emphasis."[62] Increasingly, donors agreed. In 2014, the World Bank committed $250 million to develop industrial zones in Addis Ababa. In 2015, the UK's aid agency DFID agreed to provide direct support to the Ethiopian government to assist with public investment, noting that it supported the government as it "actively pursued a 'development state' model with a strong pro-growth and pro-poor focus and a highly interventionist industrial policy."[63] In 2018, Ethiopia received a sizable boost to its funding for industrial parks when the World Bank, European Union, European Investment Bank, and DFID collectively provided more than $550 million to support the government's improvement of its industrial parks. Far from its criticism seven years earlier, the World Bank's 2018 project proposal noted the success of Ethiopia's industrial park strategy, writing, "the country is being perceived as an attractive investment destination and major investors have seized the opportunity to set up production facilities in the industrial parks."[64]

In part, donors aligned with the government's strategy of public investment-led development because the performance of earlier initiatives persuaded these donors of the feasibility and effectiveness of this development approach in Ethiopia. As one World Bank official put it when describing the negotiations over funding industrial parks, "When

---

[60] IDA-IMF 2011, p. 5.
[61] Mihretu and Llobet 2017.
[62] Government of Ethiopia 2014, p. 72.
[63] DFID 2017, p. 4.
[64] World Bank 2018, p. 5.

you go to negotiate with them [the government], they can say 'We did it already.' They know more than anyone in the World Bank."[65] In his analysis of the relationship between the EPRDF and aid donors up to the end of the 2000s, Feyissa notes that "most of the donors ... have come to terms with the EPRDF's model of development and appreciate the steady economic growth it has generated."[66]

However, it is not only that donors were persuaded by the government's argument for public investment in industrialization. Traditional donors also realized the EPRDF government would pursue its plans with other creditors if traditional donors would not support the strategy, potentially undercutting donors' relationships and influence with the government. As the representative of one European donor put it, "This was the Europeans' mistake, that now China and Turkey come in here more and more. We didn't think enough about financing for infrastructure, and that's what governments need ... If we continue this way, then we will become irrelevant."[67] Another donor observed that the government turned to alternative creditors for public investment projects since the rapid and flexible financing offered by these lenders was particularly useful for politically salient projects, "If the government wants to go quickly, if they don't want to be slowed down by environmental or social safeguards, they will go for expensive money from China, where you don't even need to do a project feasibility study."[68]

Donors framed their efforts to design more attractive infrastructure projects in part as a response to the government's increasing reliance on alternative creditors. One donor official explicitly referenced their "market share" relative to alternative creditors, saying "We need to be on the right track to keep our market share ... we need to think differently, need to act differently to keep up. China, India, Brazil, the BRICS are coming. We need to come up with new financial products

---

[65] Interview 122. Multilateral donor representative, Addis Ababa, Ethiopia. July 11, 2017.

[66] Feyissa 2011, p. 799.

[67] Interview 169. Bilateral donor official. Addis Ababa, Ethiopia. August 18, 2017.

[68] Interview 119. Multilateral donor official. Addis Ababa, Ethiopia. July 10, 2017.

to compete with China."[69] Another multilateral donor representative described their efforts to design new financing arrangements combining private finance and development assistance, "blending," to be able to compete with Ethiopia's alternative creditors. He explained, "We have an envelope for infrastructure and we have not been able to get projects off the ground, because though we have very attractive financing terms, they [the government] have other sources that are more flexible ... With blending we could maybe get the big projects the government wants. So we're considering blending."[70]

Donors funded the government's preferred projects at least partly to remain relevant in a period in which the EPRDF government could also turn to alternative creditors. By financing initiatives at the heart of the government's agenda, donors could secure greater access and influence with the government. An internal review of DFID's public investment program comments specifically on the effectiveness of this program in improving the agency's access to and influence with the government, noting that where the program "has exceeded DFID's expectation more than anywhere else is in the strength of the relationship. No other DFID programmes have the same strength of relationship and *level of access at the highest levels of government.*"[71]

The theory of debt-based financial statecraft begins from the assumption that donors want to maintain or expand their access to the recipient government, which allows them to have some influence over development policy. When recipient governments borrow from alternative creditors, donor aid is less valuable in securing access, and donors must offer more attractive aid to retain their relationship with the government. Donors' willingness to support Ethiopia's public investment program aligns with these expectations. As the government borrowed from alternative lenders and reduced its dependence on traditional donors, some of these traditional donors chose to provide aid more closely aligned with the government's preferences, which they found allowed them to maintain a close relationship with the government.

---

[69] Interview 138. Multilateral donor official. Addis Ababa, Ethiopia. July 25, 2017.

[70] Interview 160. Multilateral donor official. Addis Ababa, Ethiopia. August 15, 2017.

[71] DFID 2017, 19, emphasis added.

However, when the government's access to alternative finance narrowed in the late 2010s, the pendulum of influence on issues of development policy swung slightly back toward traditional donors, and donors advocated for reforms and development policies that the government had previously kept off the agenda of aid negotiations. These reforms included privatization of state-owned enterprises, foreign investment in private–public partnerships, and refugee employment. Representatives of different donors spoke similarly about the contrast between the government's attitude toward negotiations during different periods. One donor official recalled, "A couple of years ago, it was 'we don't need you'."[72] A different donor representative described how reduced access to private finance had changed the government's stance, saying,

They said to us 'Well, we can always go back to the market.' They like to play with us, they like to signal they have alternatives, but this 'threat' will only be valid as long as the [debt sustainability analysis] remains good. Everyone knows this is an empty threat now [in 2017, with debt conditions worsening], but in 2014 this was more credible.[73]

In this way, the waning of Ethiopia's access to alternative finance further illustrates the logic of debt-based financial statecraft. Not only did Ethiopia achieve preferred outcomes when financing was abundant, but the government also faced more pushback from traditional donors when it was yet again more reliant on traditional donor funds.

The narrowing of financing options in the late 2010s set the stage for a number of donor–government negotiations in which donors advanced issues that had so far been too sensitive. One of these areas of negotiation was government policy on state-owned enterprises (SOEs). Though Ethiopia underwent a wave of privatizations in the 1990s, state- and party-owned enterprises remained central to the EPRDF's economic model, and were dominant in most sectors.[74] Because of their centrality in the economy, SOEs have also been at the core of Ethiopia's expanding public debt burden. Almost all non-concessional debt the government has taken on, such as for the Addis–Djibouti

---

[72] Interview 125. Bilateral donor representative, Addis Ababa, Ethiopia. July 13, 2017.
[73] Interview 52. Multilateral donor official. Washington D.C. February 27, 2017.
[74] Weis 2015.

railway, has been borrowed by SOEs such as the Ethiopian Railway Corporation, with a guarantee from the federal government. Donors were therefore interested in increasing the transparency of SOEs to improve Ethiopia's debt management but also saw opportunities to encourage further SOE privatization and liberalization of sectors of the economy that had remained government-controlled after the reforms of the 1990s.[75]

In the late 2010s, spurred by donor initiatives, the government introduced a number of SOE governance reforms, making modest changes to its economic model that relied on state- and party-owned enterprises. In early 2017, the Ministry of Finance announced a new mandate on SOE debt, which outlined that all SOE borrowing would have to be approved by the Ministry of Finance, curtailing the autonomy of SOEs. More significantly, in 2017, the Prime Minister appointed a group of advisers to advise on restructuring the governance of SOEs. Donors were a key part of this process, and one donor representative explained that the advisory council was a good context in which to advocate for SOE privatization.[76] Another donor representative explained that the government's debt constraints offered a crucial window of opportunity in negotiations, "They [the government] will hit a constraint very shortly with the debt. You need to be an opportunist in a good way, *to push them in a direction in this situation.*"[77] Though reforms were only small steps, donor representatives described a rebalancing in the relationship due to the government's greater need for concessional finance and narrowing of alternatives. That several donors saw this moment as a key window of opportunity for influencing government policy further confirms the leverage the government previously enjoyed when it borrowed from a wider portfolio of creditors.

A further area of economic policy where donors advocated for reforms that had long been considered too sensitive was in the area of public–private partnerships (PPPs). The EPRDF government had long avoided PPPs, particularly in what it saw as strategic sectors, including telecommunications and transportation. However, as borrowing

---

[75] See, for example, IMF 2015.
[76] Interview 143. Bilateral donor official. Addis Ababa, Ethiopia. July 27, 2017.
[77] Interview 153. Bilateral donor official. Addis Ababa, Ethiopia. August 7, 2017, emphasis added.

space narrowed, the government agreed to private participation in key infrastructure projects, and donors seized the opportunity to advocate for reform, especially in the energy sector.[78] As one donor representative put it, "The government would have preferred this hadn't happened so quickly, that they hadn't had to slam the brakes [on public investment]."[79] Given fewer funds available for public investment, the government sought out alternative funding arrangements, which allowed donors to advocate for private participation. DFID, the World Bank, and the African Development Bank provided assistance to research and draw up a law, and in June 2017, the Ministry of Finance and Economic Cooperation introduced its draft bill to govern PPPs.[80] An official at the Ministry of Finance explained, "Because of our capacity to borrow, and lenders' capacity to lend, there are limitations to debt … so we considered private financing."[81] In the Ethiopian context, this new openness to private investment and PPPs was a noteworthy development.

Finally, donors' greater influence in aid negotiations in the late 2010s can also be observed in the structure and priorities attached to donor funding of public investment projects. Whereas donors began supporting the Ethiopian government's industrial park agenda from the mid 2010s, their later funding in this area also sought to achieve donor priorities. Specifically, donors wanted to encourage Ethiopia's industrialization efforts to provide benefits for refugees.

In 2017, when the EU, European Investment Bank, World Bank, and DFID agreed to contribute financing for the government's industrial parks, they did so on the condition that the government commit to employing 30,000 refugees in the industrial parks, under the heading of a "Jobs Compact." A donor representative involved in the negotiations suggested that such a deal would not have been possible if the government had still had access to commercial financing to fund the project on its own.[82] Another donor official pointed out that

---

[78] Interview 123. Multilateral donor official. Addis Ababa, Ethiopia. July 12, 2017; Interview 132. Bilateral donor official. Addis Ababa, Ethiopia. July 18, 2017.

[79] Interview 125. Bilateral donor official. Addis Ababa, Ethiopia. July 23, 2017.

[80] Abdu 2017.

[81] Interview 159. Ministry of Finance official. Addis Ababa, Ethiopia. August 15, 2017.

[82] Interview 125. Bilateral donor official. Addis Ababa, Ethiopia. July 13, 2017.

since industrial parks are so central to the government's developmental agenda and its access to commercial finance was narrowing, "they were willing to do anything to get the financing."[83] One government official from the Ethiopian Investment Commission corroborated this perspective, saying, "When the Jobs Compact came, we said 'Of course we'll do out-of-camp programming for refugees, but only if it supports industrialization. Only if it funds industrial parks, because we are short on funds'."[84] Given the EPRDF's insistence on closely controlling projects at the core of its developmental agenda, the "Jobs Compact" project is a telling indication of how the regime's need for concessional finance readjusted the balance of bargaining influence between donors and the government.

5.4 What Was behind Ethiopia's Success?

Across a number of important and sensitive areas of the government–donor relationship, the Ethiopian government achieved outcomes with donors closer to its preferences once it borrowed from alternative sources of finance. Notably, the Ethiopian government was more successful than either the Kenyan or Ghanaian governments. The comparison with Kenya and Ghana suggests that donors were motivated both by the importance they attached to the relationship with the Ethiopian government and their trust in how the Ethiopian government deployed resources. Both Ethiopia's significance to donors and perceived reliability played in its favor, with donors eager to retain their relationship with the government and fairly trusting of the government's uses of donor funds.

5.4.1 Ethiopia's Significance to Donors

The EPRDF government's success in translating its greater autonomy from traditional donors into preferred aid agreements was aided by the fact that donors were especially motivated to retain their relationships with the Ethiopian government, seeing the relationship as

---

[83] Interview 122. Multilateral donor representative, Addis Ababa, Ethiopia. July 11, 2017.
[84] Interview 148. Ethiopian Investment Commission official. Addis Ababa, Ethiopia. August 3, 2017.

valuable to achieve both security and development aims. The value that donors placed on their relationships with the Ethiopian government is closely related to the broader security context in the Horn of Africa. Ethiopia's relative stability until the outbreak of hostilities in 2020 made it an attractive partner in the region. For the US in particular, Ethiopia's support for policies associated with the global war on terror in the 2000s was decisive in increasing assistance to the EPRDF government.[85] Its partial reliance on Ethiopia to maintain stability in the Horn of Africa led the US to be more flexible on governance issues, as Borchgrevink notes, "Western – and in particular US – interests in containing the spread of radical Islamism in the Horn of Africa, a recognition of Ethiopia's legitimate security concerns towards Somalia, and the concern for regional stability were important reasons for toning down criticism of the EPRDF regime."[86]

The security concerns surrounding instability in the Horn of Africa persisted into the 2010s, leading Western donors to be especially preoccupied with the possibility that alternative creditors could undercut their relationship and influence with the Ethiopian government. These strategic interests enhanced the bargaining leverage the EPRDF was able to extract from its greater autonomy from traditional donor funds. One donor official described the government directly benefiting from its strategic significance to donors, especially larger donors such as the US, as well as its importance to donors' development aims, saying

They [the government] leverage the hell out of the fact that there are two main reasons [donor] countries are here. Number one is geopolitical. There are 100 million people here in one of the most fragile regions in the world . . . the US needs to be here. You have Eritrea, you have the Chinese [building a support base] in Djibouti. The second reason everyone is here is the extreme poverty, so you feel you need to be here.[87]

For many European donors, the focus on Ethiopia as an anchor of stability and bulwark against extremism was augmented by Ethiopia's role as host country to refugees in the region. Since European donors had an interest in reducing migration from Africa to Europe, and

---

[85] Verhoeven and Woldemariam 2022.
[86] Borchgrevink 2008, p. 214.
[87] Interview 141. Bilateral donor official. Addis Ababa, Ethiopia. July 26, 2017.

they relied on cooperation with the Ethiopian government to help achieve that aim, these donors were more likely to worry about preserving their relationship with the government. A donor official put this very bluntly, claiming "You can justify almost anything by reducing migration to Europe."[88] The combination of Ethiopia's importance in regional security issues and donors' migration interests gave the government considerable leverage in negotiations, enhancing the impact of the government's reduced dependence on traditional donors. This leverage was described by one donor official as follows, "Geopolitically, this country is perhaps the most important in Africa. You have the war on terror on the one side, and migration on the other. No one wants Ethiopia to go down ... If you look at the geopolitical picture you see why the strings attached don't work. You can't tell the government what to do."[89] Ethiopia's strategic significance to donors thus helps to explain the limited donor censuring of the EPRDF's political repression. Donors' interest in Ethiopia appears to have increased the effects of the government's greater autonomy, since donors were especially worried about losing their access to the government.

In addition to security and geopolitical concerns, donors placed value on their relationship with the Ethiopian government because of the perception that it could reliably deliver development outcomes.[90] Both for multilateral donors such as the World Bank or the African Development Bank and for bilateral donor agencies needing to demonstrate the impact of their aid spending to domestic audiences, the Ethiopian government's effectiveness in implementing development programs made it an important recipient in their overall aid portfolio.

Though the heterodox orientation of the EPRDF's economic policy split the preferences of donors, even those who were critical of the regime's state-led approach appreciated the government's ability to translate development plans into concrete outcomes, achieving economic growth and poverty reduction.[91] One donor representative explained, "Success attracts friends, and we all want to be part of that

---

[88] Interview 143. Bilateral donor official. Addis Ababa, Ethiopia. July 27, 2017.
[89] Interview 170. Bilateral donor official. Addis Ababa, Ethiopia. August 19, 2017.
[90] Abegaz 2015.
[91] Feyissa 2011.

glow."[92] Another donor representative noted that the government's "progress leads to credibility, and everybody wants to be partners with you when you have results."[93] Government officials recognized this appeal for donors. As one Ministry of Finance official noted, commenting on donors' decision to withdraw from other developing countries, "If you have a situation [like in Ethiopia], where aid is working, you [the donor] will not discontinue."[94]

The "glow" of the government's effectiveness attracted donors, who were eager to retain a relationship with the government and to continue playing a role in the country's development. This dynamic was already in place in in the 2000s, when donors provided aid even when disagreeing with the government's policy.[95] These same qualities reappeared a decade later when donors explained their reasons for valuing a relationship with Ethiopia, with one representative describing the country as having "lots of needs, with a government that knows what it wants, where it is possible to get things done."[96]

The government's ability to demonstrate the impact of some of its policies further enhanced its stature with donors, putting it in a position to benefit from its greater autonomy. As one donor representative put it, speaking of the government, "If you don't follow their rules, you'll just have to leave, and they don't care ... they [the government] engage in partnership with very strict conditions, probably the strictest you'll see."[97] Aware that donors wanted to maintain the relationship, the government could push for its preferred negotiating outcomes, especially when the government had alternative lenders it could fall back on.

5.4.2 Donor Trust in Ethiopia's Government

In the period under study, most donors had a high level of trust in the Ethiopian government, which encouraged donors to be

---

[92] Interview 122. Multilateral donor representative, Addis Ababa, Ethiopia. July 11, 2017.

[93] Interview 131. Multilateral donor official. Addis Ababa, Ethiopia. July 17, 2017.

[94] Interview 128. Ministry of Finance official. Addis Ababa, Ethiopia. July 17, 2017.

[95] Furtado and W. J. Smith 2009, p. 153.

[96] Interview 52. Multilateral donor official. Washington D.C. February 27, 2017.

[97] Interview 141. Bilateral donor official. Addis Ababa, Ethiopia. July 26, 2017.

accommodating of the government's preferences when the government diversified its portfolio of external finance. Donors' confidence that the government would adhere to aid agreements was based on the government's development track record, as well as donors' assessment of political conditions in Ethiopia. The EPRDF's centralization of political power allowed it to implement its "developmental state" policies without significant pushback from the opposition or the broader public, making the government's commitments to related aid agreements more credible. For many donors, their trust in the government was begrudging or only partial, since the ruling party's authoritarianism conflicted with their commitments to democracy and human rights. However, they nonetheless acknowledged that development and financial management institutions worked well and that they were less concerned about corruption than in many other countries where they provided aid. They were thus more willing to be flexible on financial management and the government's developmental state policies, particularly once the government diversified its portfolio of external finance and could exercise greater bargaining leverage. My analysis here builds on the work of scholars that have identified that many donors in Ethiopia accepted an implicit trade-off between democracy and development in Ethiopia, putting considerable faith in the government, despite its authoritarianism.[98]

For donors, the fact that the EPRDF oversaw considerable poverty reduction and economic growth provided an important basis of trust. Donors had the sense that resources allocated to Ethiopia would be spent as agreed and that these resources would generate development outcomes. Poverty in Ethiopia declined from 44 percent to 30 percent in the years 2000 to 2011 and further declined to 24 percent by 2016.[99] This substantial reduction in poverty coincided with the EPRDF's implementation of its developmental state agenda, beginning in the early 2000s.[100] When these policies began achieving demonstrable outcomes with respect to poverty reduction and growth, donors gradually developed greater confidence in the government's development plans and their ability to implement them.

In particular, donors had confidence that government officials and public institutions were oriented toward development, including

---

[98] Abegaz 2015; S. Brown and Fisher 2020.
[99] Bundervoet et al. 2020; World Bank 2015e.
[100] Lavers 2023.

pro-poor development. This alignment between the government's objectives and donors' goals made it easier for donors to trust the government. As one staff member at a multilateral donor described it, "They [the government] own that responsibility, they see themselves as the custodians of national development."[101] Another donor official underscored the government's clear articulation of development priorities, saying "The development focus here is not unimpressive. There are clear strategies and plans. It's very positive that the government so clearly knows what it wants."[102] A bilateral donor representative contrasted Ethiopia to other aid recipient countries, saying "Ethiopia is one of the countries where the development strategy is very good, where the government commitment is very high."[103] Another donor official explained that this development performance overrode other governance concerns that donors may have, explaining "It's an authoritarian regime and it will stay that way. But because of their strong developmental orientation we stay here."[104]

Not only were most donors fairly confident in the government's prioritization of development, but they also had considerable trust in the institutions for overseeing and implementing development projects. This confidence is reflected in the scores and assessments of Ethiopia's public financial management institutions. In the World Bank's Country Policy and Institutional Assessment, Ethiopia scored above the sub-Saharan average for its debt policy and its budgetary and financial management in the 2010–2019 period.[105] Similarly, the African Development Bank's overall assessment ranked Ethiopia above the average for sub-Saharan Africa, with especially strong scores for transparency, accountability, and control of corruption in the public sector, as well as quality of budgetary and financial management, where Ethiopia had the third highest average score in the 2010–2018 period.[106]

[101] Interview 122. Multilateral donor representative, Addis Ababa, Ethiopia. July 11, 2017.
[102] Interview 142. Bilateral donor official. Addis Ababa, Ethiopia. July 26, 2017.
[103] Interview 153. Bilateral donor official. Addis Ababa, Ethiopia. August 7, 2017.
[104] Interview 166. Bilateral donor official. Addis Ababa, Ethiopia. August 17, 2017.
[105] World Bank 2020c.
[106] African Development Bank Group 2022.

Donor officials working in Addis Ababa shared this view of the reliability of public finance institutions, and it gave them confidence that the government would implement aid programs as agreed and use both donor and alternative finance in support of development plans. Many donor officials highlighted the relative lack of corruption in Ethiopia, with one donor representative saying, "The government is very strong in implementing [projects], corruption is very low."[107] Compared to other recipient countries, donors had greater confidence in the government's use of public funds; as one multilateral donor official described it, "We know this government is good in how they use borrowed money. They are very smart, they borrow for projects that repay … It's a very tough, very prudent government. Their PFM [public financial management] is very good, very tough."[108] Similarly, a UN staffer is quoted in S. Brown and Fisher (2020) as saying, "you can trust Ethiopia more than Kenya."[109] Officials in the Ethiopian government recognized the benefits of this donor trust and sought to deploy it in order to enhance their negotiating position. As one official explained,

Ethiopia is one of the countries that give DPs [development partners, i.e. donors] the assurance that public resources are being used for their intended purpose. The control and monitoring of resources are highly centralized. We are very meticulous to look into the engagement [with donors], but once we reach an agreement, our engagement is intact until the end of the project.[110]

Given donors' faith in the probity of uses of public funds, they responded to the government's diversified portfolio of external finance with more attractive aid offers, rather than increasing their scrutiny to prevent misuses of finance.

Some donors explicitly connected Ethiopia's political context to the credibility of the government's development plans and adherence to aid agreements. One donor representative suggested that the government's commitment and lack of corruption was attributable to the fact that EPRDF justified its hold on power by promising to deliver growth,

[107] Interview 132. Bilateral donor official. Addis Ababa, Ethiopia. July 18, 2017.
[108] Interview 138. Multilateral donor official. Addis Ababa, Ethiopia. July 25, 2017.
[109] S. Brown and Fisher 2020, p. 194.
[110] Interview 135. Ministry of Finance official. Addis Ababa, Ethiopia. July 19, 2017.

saying "The government really feels the imperative from the political settlement and the need to deliver growth ... There's not a huge amount of corruption in Ethiopia."[111] This particular donor official's use of the term "political settlement" is indicative of how widespread this concept is in the development community, with donors interpreting the government's development plans in light of the distribution of political power.

For the government, the justification for its centralization of political authority was that this gave it sufficient autonomy to implement decisive and long-term development policy. Donors differed in their assessment of this claim. Those donor agencies that worked most closely with the government often tacitly endorsed this view, as when one donor official said, "This is a government that plans to be in power in a generation. So there is a degree of long-term thinking that might be absent elsewhere."[112] Another donor invoked the ruling party's ideology in explaining why the government had such a strong negotiating stance, suggesting that centralized political authority allowed the government to "own" development plans as envisioned in the aid effectiveness agenda, "It's part of the ideology of democratic centralism. It's a very attractive feature for donors, it's basically what we all hoped for with the aid effectiveness agenda."[113] Others were more skeptical, with one representative of a smaller bilateral donor suggesting that large donors had bought into the government's own account of its development policy because they had funded key projects, saying "The biggest donors have bet on the developmental state here, and so they need to sell the success story."[114]

While donors differed in their stance on Ethiopia's domestic politics, they emphasized that their trust in the government's planning and institutions gave them greater confidence in extending flexibility. One donor official expressed this directly, saying "The government has a strong commitment, so we can provide our assistance comfortably."[115] A donor representative explained that the strength of government at

[111] Interview 125. Bilateral donor official. Addis Ababa, Ethiopia. July 13, 2017.
[112] Interview 125. Bilateral donor official. Addis Ababa, Ethiopia. July 13, 2017.
[113] Interview 160. Multilateral donor official. Addis Ababa, Ethiopia. August 15, 2017.
[114] Interview 169. Bilateral donor official. Addis Ababa, Ethiopia. August 18, 2017.
[115] Interview 127. Bilateral donor official. Addis Ababa, Ethiopia. July 14, 2017.

different levels further enhanced donor confidence, noting "They [the government] deliver on development programs, because of the strong government framework that exists. We [donors] work through the government and get results. They have strong institutions all the way down to the woreda [district] level."[116] That confidence was an important condition for donors to be more flexible on financial management issues and supporting the developmental state, as they did when the government diversified its portfolio of finance. For Ethiopia, translating alternative finance into greater bargaining leverage was made easier by the high level of trust of donors in government development plans and institutions.

5.5 Conclusion

In Ethiopia, the government was able to extract considerable leverage from its turn to alternative sources of finance. During the high point of diversity in its portfolio of external finance, up until 2016, the government was helped by its strategic significance to traditional donors and the extent of donor trust. Their confidence in Ethiopia's development plans and public finance institutions meant traditional donors were more trusting and were thus willing to accommodate the government's preference for flexibility. Moreover, the country's strategic significance shaped how donors responded to the country's reduced dependence. Ethiopia's geopolitical importance increased the salience of the government's closer relationship with China and its ability to "deliver" development heightened the value of a close relationship. Under these conditions, the government was able to translate its access to into greater influence over negotiations.

The EPRDF government pursued a deliberate strategy of diversifying its financing options, signaling its reduced dependence, and playing potential lenders off each other to secure more favorable negotiating outcomes. Specifically, the government benefited from more muted donor criticism of political rights violations, greater leniency in the application of formal rules over the debt ceiling, and support for its public investments in the developmental state. However, when

---

[116] Interview 144. Bilateral donor official. Addis Ababa, Ethiopia. July 28, 2017.

access to alternative finance narrowed as the country faced increasing debt constraints, the balance in negotiations appeared to shift yet again. As the government became more reliant on concessional finance, traditional donors were more successful in securing government commitment to economic reforms for which they had long advocated. The variation over time in the Ethiopian government's access to alternative finance shows how conditions need to align for successful financial statecraft. These conditions include not only a diversified portfolio of external finance but also favorable conditions with respect to strategic significance and donor trust.

Donors' trust in the Ethiopian government's commitments to aid agreements and development plans was a feature of a specific period in Ethiopia's political history. Given the instability and conflict that unfolded in Ethiopia after 2018, this time period appears, in retrospect, to have been temporary, ultimately rendered unsustainable by the political exclusion of large groups of society. However, it is important to note that the extent of earlier donor trust in the Ethiopian government was not due to the regime's repressive nature, but rather the commitment to development plans and strength of implementing institutions. Governments in much more inclusive political systems can similarly cultivate and sustain donor confidence, perhaps in "pockets of effectiveness" in particular sectors,[117] allowing them to extract greater flexibility when they diversify their external finance. As the comparison to Kenya and Ghana in Chapters 6 and 7 makes clear, donor confidence in the government's credibility is crucial for using alternative finance as a source of negotiating leverage.

---

[117] Hickey 2019.

6 | Kenya: Uneven Financial Statecraft

In gleaming office towers in downtown Nairobi and extensive compounds in the city's suburbs, diplomats and donor officials plan, negotiate, and oversee development programs not only for Kenya but also for countries across the East African subregion. The choice of Kenya as a seat for many donors' regional offices and the African headquarters of the United Nations is no coincidence. Many donors and foreign partners see Kenya as an African hub, a commercial gateway to East Africa, and an important ally in the region. This importance of Kenya to outside actors has long shaped relations between the country and its donors and has, as I show in this chapter, amplified the effects of Kenya's more recent diversification in external finance, leading to moderate successes in financial statecraft. However, while the Kenyan government gained some flexibility from donors on governance issues, the government struggled to fully bring its relationship with donors in line with its interests, especially on matters of economic management and financial accountability.

Like other sub-Saharan African countries, Kenya's access to alternative finance expanded in the mid to late 2000s. Private lenders were attracted by the country's open and diversified economy, allowing Kenya to borrow in large sums from international bond investors and private banks. Moreover, the Kenyan government borrowed extensively from Chinese lenders, especially for large infrastructure projects such as the railway linking Nairobi to the port city of Mombasa. This expansion of finance, coming at the same time that the country was recategorized from a low-income country to a lower-middle-income country, altered the balance of Kenya's relationship with donors. Traditional donors' aid funds were no longer as important to the country, though Kenya continued to maintain relationships with traditional donors and receive large sums of development aid and loans from them.

The theory suggests that as Kenya reduced its reliance on traditional donors, it should be able to extract bargaining benefits, so long as donors remained interested in maintaining the relationship. To evaluate this, I focus on two areas of the aid relationship that were particularly sensitive for both the government and donors: governance and financial management. I find that some traditional donors moderated their criticism of the government on issues of human and political rights. Faced with the government's reduced reliance on traditional donor funds, and given donors' interest in maintaining a close relationship, donors chose not to emphasize politically sensitive governance issues.

However, there were limits to Kenya's debt-based financial statecraft. On issues of economic management and financial accountability, the outcomes of donor–government negotiations remained broadly in line with donors' interests. Donors made few changes to the procedures for disbursing and evaluating their aid to bring them in line with government preferences. Donors' reluctance to offer the government its preferred level of flexibility was partly shaped by their lack of trust in Kenya's institutions of public financial management. Donors worried about the credibility of Kenya's commitments to aid agreements, given Kenya's highly fractious domestic political context, and the associated patterns of borrowing and spending. Concerned that the government's spending could put their own aid programs at risk, traditional donors tightened their scrutiny of financial management, rather than loosening it to meet government preferences. By contrast to Ethiopia, where the government benefited from donor confidence in development plans and institutions for financial management, the success of financial statecraft in Kenya was diminished by donor distrust. Furthermore, as in Ghana, a vocal opposition foreclosed certain financing options, limiting the breadth and attractiveness of outside options available to the government.

This chapter draws on evidence from more than fifty interviews conducted in January and February 2017 with government officials in the National Treasury and the Central Bank of Kenya, donor representatives in Nairobi and Washington D.C., and journalists and civil society representatives in Nairobi.[1] I first outline in Section 6.1 what the

---

[1] For more details about the interviews and response rates of interviewees see Table A.2.

theoretical framework suggests we should expect in the Kenyan case. Next, I describe the expansion and diversification of Kenya's portfolio of external finance in Section 6.2, highlighting the turning points where substantial changes in Kenya's access to alternative finance are likely to have changed the relationship between the government and donors. In Section 6.3, I trace negotiation outcomes, describing how donors granted the government greater flexibility on governance issues but neglected to do so on financial management. I show in Section 6.4 that the uneven track record of Kenya's debt-based financial statecraft is likely attributable to the country's strategic significance to donors and donor distrust.

6.1 Theoretical Expectations in the Kenyan Case

In Kenya, the theory suggests the government may have extracted leverage from alternative finance. The government reduced its dependence on traditional donors as it borrowed from China from the late 2000s onward and from private lenders with its 2014 debut bond issuance and later bank borrowing. Together with economic growth, these new sources of finance reduced the government's reliance on traditional aid funds, even while the government continued to maintain relationships with traditional donors and to receive traditional development finance. This combination of external finance set the Kenyan government up to use its borrowing relationships as a basis for financial statecraft.

And yet, the theory also suggests that the Kenyan government might only be moderately successful in using new borrowing to bring aid agreements in line with its preferences. This is because in Kenya, the enabling conditions for debt-based financial statecraft cut in opposite directions. Many donors saw the relationship with the Kenyan government as strategically important, which ought to increase the likelihood that donors accommodate the government's demands. Most donors placed a high value on their relationship with the Kenyan government, which ought to increase the government's leverage with traditional donors. Kenya shares an border with Ethiopia, and like Ethiopia, Kenya's relationship with donors has been shaped by its role as an "anchor of stability" in the region. For the relationship with the US, Kenya's 2011 invasion of Somalia to counter the threat posed by the terrorist group al-Shabaab cemented Kenya's reputation as a crucial counterpart for counterterrorism and regional security. Moreover, as in Ethiopia, European donors value the relationship with the Kenyan government because of their desire to manage global migration flows, since Kenya is host to refugees and migrants from neighboring Somalia, Sudan, and South Sudan. Finally, the growing size of Kenya's economy and its increasing prominence as a commercial hub in East Africa increased the country's value for donors, since the aid relationship helps sustain a broader diplomatic relationship in support of commercial objectives. Altogether, these factors made their relationships with the Kenyan government more valuable to traditional donors, likely increasing their motivation to retain that relationship as Kenya reduced its reliance on foreign aid.

Despite this advantage, Kenya also had a weakness on the second dimension that shapes debt-based financial statecraft. The theory expects that borrowing countries with high levels of donor trust will do particularly well at financial statecraft, because the credibility of their commitments in aid agreements and uses of alternative finance will encourage donors to be more accommodating in response to the government's greater bargaining leverage. By contrast, governments with lower levels of donor confidence may find it challenging to extract better agreements from traditional donors even when they diversify their portfolios of external finance, since donors may distrust their uses of alternative finance. In Kenya, the lack of donor trust in the government's public financial management likely made it more difficult for the government to effectively exercise debt-based financial statecraft. Donors observed that Kenya's political context, with loose and fractious governing coalitions often relying on public spending as a means of political survival, meant that the government's commitments to public spending were not always credible. This increased donors' distrust of the government's spending, causing donors to be less willing to accommodate the government's preferences.

6.2 Variation in Kenya's Portfolio of External Finance

During the period between 2000 and 2018, Kenya's portfolio of external finance expanded and diversified considerably, changing Kenya's relationship with foreign aid donors and the international economy and bringing the country into closer contact with new lenders and private investors. Though Kenya did not have a history of civil war or acute humanitarian crisis the way Ethiopia did, it was nonetheless reliant on foreign aid from traditional donors in the 1990s. Official development assistance to Kenya in the 1990s averaged 8.67 percent of gross national income (GNI), reaching well above 10 percent of GNI in the early years of the 1990s. Economic growth substantially reduced Kenya's dependence on foreign aid over time, and aid declined to an average of 3.89 percent of GNI in the 2000s and 4.18 percent of GNI in the 2010s. However, the diversification of Kenya's external finance did not come until the 2010s, with traditional donors and multilateral development banks still making up the vast majority of Kenya's external finance into the 2000s. These donors and lenders made up an average of 89 percent of Kenya's external finance in the 1990s and 90 percent of Kenya's external finance in the 2000s. By the 2010s, the share of traditional finance had reduced to an average of 70 percent, with a low of 29 percent in 2014, the year Kenya first borrowed in international bond markets and signed a loan for more than $3 billion from the Export-Import Bank of China for a major railway project.

In tracing Kenya's relationship with its donors and lenders, there are a number of important turning points. The first came in 2013, when the incoming Kenyatta administration declared its intention to pursue closer relationships with emerging lenders. Within a year, the country had signed an agreement for an enormous loan from China's Export-Import bank and debuted in international bond markets. A second turning point in Kenya's relations with external creditors in the last decade came during the 2016 election campaign, in which the government's accountability came under scrutiny due to a shift to borrowing from private lenders. Below, I describe these turning points in Kenya's portfolio of external finance in the 2010s, contrasting them especially to the country's greater aid reliance in the 1990s.

Economic crisis and weak export performance put the Kenyan economy under pressure in the late 1980s and early 1990s. In this context, aid from traditional donors was extremely important for the administration of President Daniel arap Moi (1978–2002). Aid was equivalent to 38 percent of imports of goods, services, and primary income in Kenya in 1990, compared to a 20 percent average for sub-Saharan Africa that year.[2] The reliance of the Kenyan government on

---

[2] World Bank 2020b.

Table 6.1 *Average annual ODA commitments of top DAC-reporting donors to Kenya, 1990–2019 (millions 2015 US$)*

1990–1999		2000–2009		2010–2019	
IDA	194	US	396	US	905
Germany	99	IDA	252	IDA	851
Japan	87	EU	131	Japan	296
EU	62	UK	119	France	218
UK	62	France	94	AfDB	204
Netherlands	59	Japan	92	EU	185
US	39	Germany	68	Germany	164
AfDF	35	AfDF	66	AfDF	160
Canada	30	Denmark	43	UK	112
Sweden	29	Sweden	37	Sweden	54
France	22	Netherlands	24	Denmark	53
Italy	20	Canada	20	Korea	47
Denmark	19	Finland	17	Canada	42
Norway	13	Belgium	16	Norway	40
Finland	13	Spain	14	Finland	28

donor aid allowed donors to exercise considerable pressure in favor of democratizing reforms. The US, in particular, placed democratization at the center of its engagement with the Kenyan government, making aid disbursement in 1991 contingent on governance and human rights reforms.[3] Following the lead of the US and in response to highly publicized human rights violations, traditional donors collectively suspended all aid in 1991.[4] Responding to donor pressure, Moi legalized opposition parties and in 1992 held the first multiparty elections in two decades.

In the following decade, Kenya maintained a close relationship with traditional donors, even as the economy grew and the country became gradually less reliant on aid. In the 2000s, Kenya's relationship with traditional donors, especially the US, was heavily shaped by the global war on terror, and the US became Kenya's leading donor (see Table 6.1). Kenya had few other sources of external finance during this time and relied on traditional donors both for access to external

[3] Roessler 2005.
[4] Cohen 2003.

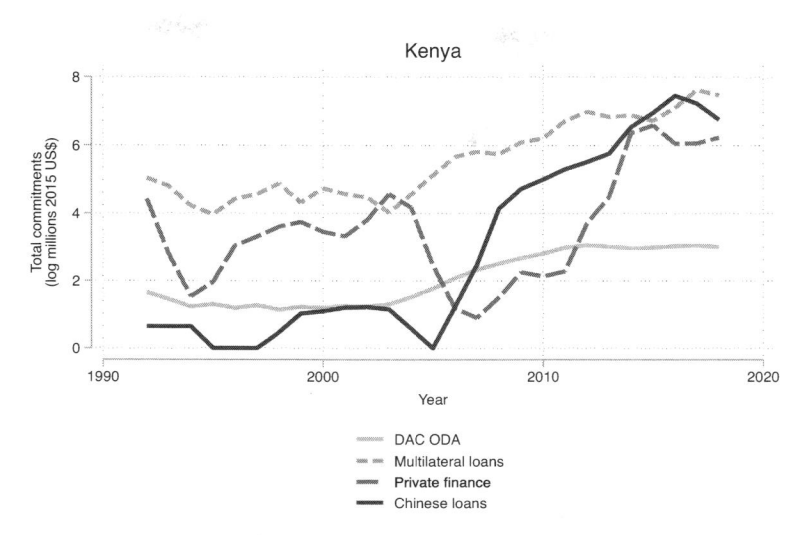

Figure 6.1 Kenya's portfolio of external finance, 1992–2018.
Three-year rolling average of total commitments (log millions 2015 US$).

finance and for international validation of its counterterrorism strategy. These donors, in turn, relied on the Kenyan government as a cooperative counterpart for their regional security objectives. Among the traditional donors active in Kenya, the US, the World Bank, Japan, France, and the African Development Bank have consistently been the largest, as Table 6.1 shows. Under President Mwai Kibaki (2002–2013), multilateral and DAC ODA increased, while the amount of private borrowing declined (see Figure 6.1).

A distinct turning point in Kenya's relationship with donors and creditors came in 2013, when incoming President Uhuru Kenyatta (2013–2022) announced a pivot in Kenya's foreign policy, declaring a "Look East" approach. Kenyatta's efforts to attract alternative finance and deepen Kenya's relationship with non-Western partners accelerated a trend that had already begun under his predecessor President Kibaki, when Kenya first contracted large loans from China (see Figure 6.1). For its relationship with traditional donors, Kenyatta's "Look East" policy marked a step change, in line with broader shifts in Kenya's foreign policy. Kenyatta's rhetorical distancing from the West had begun during his campaign, when he and his running mate William Ruto adopted a defiant posture toward their indictment by the International Criminal Court (ICC) for their roles on opposing sides of the communal violence after the 2007 election. Kenyatta and Ruto framed the prosecutions as neocolonial interference and overreach by Western powers, and the government declared it would strengthen alternative international relationships premised on greater mutual respect.[5] A closer relationship with China and a growing number of Chinese loans were the outcomes of this strategy.

Kenya's pursuit of new borrowing relationships thus accelerated in the 2010s. A 2014 government policy on external finance clearly identified new sources of finance as a priority, stating, "With the advent of rapid globalization and increased competition among states for scarce resources, a re-orientation of Kenya's foreign policy has become necessary ... Kenya has sought to strengthen traditional ties while deepening cooperation with new emerging economies."[6] China's Export-Import Bank had funded several large road construction projects in Kenya in 2008 and 2009, and Kenya pursued additional Chinese infrastructure funding from 2013 onward. The most prominent of these loans was a financing agreement for more than $3 billion agreed to in May 2014 to fund a railway connecting the capital Nairobi to the port city of Mombasa, known as the Standard Gauge Railway (SGR). These new loans fundamentally reduced Kenya's reliance on traditional donors. A Kenyan journalist summarized the change in the country's borrowing options, saying, "The problem for Kenya is not that it doesn't have options; it has money knocking at the door, unlike other countries."[7]

As in other borrowing countries, the Kenyan government saw in Chinese loans a means to fund politically and economically important infrastructure projects. One official explained that "even if the interest rates on the loans are commercial and thus higher, the fact that the project is delivered on time means that benefits manifest in the economy more quickly and can thus flow into repayment of the loan."[8] Another senior official at the National Treasury described the approach of Chinese lenders as follows, saying, "China is about results. If they deliver roads, they want to see roads, and not more meetings."[9]

[5] G. Lynch 2013, p. 105.
[6] Government of Kenya 2014, pp. 1.3.1–1.3.2.
[7] Interview 9. Kenyan journalist. Nairobi, Kenya. January 23, 2017.
[8] Interview 16. National Treasury official. Nairobi, Kenya. January 25, 2017.
[9] Interview 28. National Treasury official. Nairobi, Kenya. February 1, 2017.

This trend toward diversifying external finance was further compounded by Kenya's borrowing in private markets. In June 2014, Kenya entered international bond markets with its $2 billion debut bond, the largest ever debut offering by an African government.[10] Kenya was able to borrow at low, attractive rates, lower than what Ghana and Zambia paid for their twelve- and ten-year bonds that same year. Investors eagerly purchased the Kenyan bond, which was four times oversubscribed, and Kenya returned to the markets later in 2014 to "re-open" the bond and raise a further $750 million.[11] Government officials and observers noted the government could access financing on attractive terms because bond market investors were searching for lucrative investments in light of low global interest rates.[12] As one Kenyan commentator put it: "Investors are not that worried about details, they see enough figures to know they'll get the money … In Europe and America there is glut of savings, so there is a search for yield."[13]

The government was interested in bond financing because it offered large sums of flexible funding that could be rapidly disbursed to achieve political priorities.[14] A senior former Central Bank official explained, "There's political pressure to complete projects, which makes rapid financing attractive."[15] A lawyer in the Attorney-General's office involved with the preparation of the Eurobond similarly emphasized the speed and availability of finance, saying it was "clear that the money was there in the markets, to feed an immediate need."[16]

A final turning point in Kenya's relations with creditors and donors in the period under study came during the campaign period ahead of the 2017 election. The opposition, led by perennial opposition candidate Raila Odinga, picked up and amplified swirling allegations that the government had misappropriated the funds from Kenya's

---

[10] Manson and Blas 2014.
[11] Reuters 2014b.
[12] Zeitz 2021b.
[13] Interview 9. Kenyan journalist. Nairobi, Kenya. January 23, 2017.
[14] Prizzon and Hart 2016, p. 14.
[15] Interview 40. Former Central Bank of Kenya official. Nairobi, Kenya. February 13, 2017.
[16] Interview 21. Official in the Attorney-General's Office. Nairobi, Kenya. January 30, 2017.

2014 sovereign bond issuance. In the years after Kenya's debut in sovereign bond markets, critics had challenged the government to explain how it had spent money raised through the Eurobond issuance, alleging that leading politicians had stolen the proceeds, failing to transfer funds from the New York bank underwriting the bond to the Kenyan National Treasury. Given the explosive claim that a US bank might have assisted in the misappropriation of public funds, both the IMF and New York Federal Reserve investigated the allegations and publicly stated that the bond proceeds had in fact been transferred to Kenya.[17] The opposition continued to question how the funds had been used once they arrived in Kenya, and the government struggled to provide evidence of individual projects paid for with the Eurobond.[18] The Kenyan Auditor-General initiated a lengthy investigation, ultimately concluding that there had been an increase in off-budget expenditure by key ministries in 2014, meaning that Eurobond proceeds flowed into projects unaccounted for in the public budget.[19] The election campaign intensified these debates over the accountability of the government in its uses of private finance. Raila Odinga took the unusual step of addressing international investors directly in October 2016, warning that any further bonds issued by the Kenyatta government would be declared "odious debt" and not be honored if Odinga won the 2017 election.[20]

For the relationship with donors and creditors, these debates led to a growth in donor skepticism about the government's probity and reliability in its choice of external finance. Borrowing in private markets had become politicized domestically, and the opposition appeared to have hit a nerve in accusing the government of using borrowed funds irresponsibly. The government's reaction to opposition critiques further stoked donors' concerns. To avoid returning to international bond markets and attracting more scrutiny, the government instead increasingly borrowed from private banks. Syndicated bank loans, which bring together a number of banks to jointly lend to the government, are less public that bond issues, since they do not require

---

[17] Irungu 2016.

[18] As in Ghana, a significant portion of the Eurobond was used to retire existing debt, with $600 million allocated to repaying earlier syndicated loans.

[19] Ngirachu 2018; Wafula 2019.

[20] Sammy 2016.

governments to issue a public prospectus and advertise the bond to potential investors. Scholars have found that across developing countries, governments that are less transparent are more likely to borrow from banks than in international bond markets.[21] In late 2015, the government borrowed $750 million in syndicated bank loans, following this up in early 2017 with a further loan of $800 million. Unlike with the Eurobond, the terms of these loans were not made public, with the National Treasury simply stating that the rates were "quite favorable."[22] A Kenyan journalist commented on the government's borrowing strategy, explaining that relatively smaller syndicated loans were less likely to attract media or opposition scrutiny, saying "The trick with the syndicated loans are the amounts. Syndicated loans are smaller amounts, while a Eurobond is one big amount."[23] A donor official echoed the assessment that the government's choice of financing reflected political calculations, saying, "The only reason they chose to go for the syndicated loan rather than a Eurobond is because of the opposition attention to the Eurobond."[24]

After this turning point, while the composition of Kenya's portfolio of external finance remained largely as it had been, perceptions of the country's borrowing choices shifted, with donors becoming more skeptical. The domestic debates about the uses of the Eurobond and the government's turn to more opaque bank loans raised doubts about the government's accountability in its use of external finance. Given the history of large-scale corruption scandals in Kenya, donors already held baseline concerns about the government's financial management, which the politicization of government borrowing in the election campaign further amplified. Even as the government was becoming less reliant on traditional donors, donors also had greater reason to worry about the government's use of funds.

6.3 Uneven Debt-Based Financial Statecraft

Kenya's increasingly diverse portfolio of external finance made it much less reliant on traditional donors. As one donor official described it,

---

[21] L. Mosley and Rosendorff 2023.
[22] Reuters 2015.
[23] Interview 9. Kenyan journalist. Nairobi, Kenya. January 23, 2017.
[24] Interview 50. Multilateral donor official. Washington D.C. February 27, 2018.

"Kenya is an interesting case, because they are well courted. Somehow they have a choice [of lenders]. That is not the case everywhere. So they can indicate their preferences ... there is a degree of competition."[25] In this section, I examine whether that "degree of competition" among donors and creditors altered aid negotiations, bringing outcomes more in line with the government's preferences.

Overall, government officials and donors indicated that the diversification of Kenya's portfolio of finance changed negotiation dynamics. One National Treasury official explained, "we now look at concessional financing in a new light, we have realized that in some cases, cheap is expensive ... What the traditional development partners will see is a pushback from the government in terms of what it will accept."[26] A donor official corroborated this, saying the government had been more careful about what it agreed upon with traditional donors, and suggesting this caution was due to the greater number of financing options available to the government, "Today, maybe because they have more options, maybe also because they have more capacity, they are more keen on the terms, scrutinizing them closely."[27]

To capture the extent to which the government's stronger negotiating position altered the its influence in the donor–recipient relationship, I focus on two areas of the aid relationship that were particularly sensitive for both the government and donors: governance and financial management. First, issues of governance and democratization have been important to traditional donors in their cooperation with Kenya since the early 1990s, when donors played a key role in Kenya's transition to multiparty democracy. Kenya's postindependence politics have been fraught, characterized by winner-takes-all patterns along ethnic lines that make it hard for those in power to cede ground to the opposition, a feature that became even more pronounced after the transition to multiparty elections. This history makes negotiations over donor-proposed governance reforms particularly sensitive in Kenya.

Second, donors and the government have disagreed over Kenya's institutions of financial management. Worried about the misuse of funds and the corrosive effects of corruption, donors have attempted to strengthen financial management institutions to uphold greater

---

[25] Interview 54. Multilateral donor official. Nairobi, Kenya. April 5, 2017.
[26] Interview 16. National Treasury official. Nairobi, Kenya. January 25, 2017.
[27] Interview 25. Bilateral donor official. Nairobi, Kenya. February 1, 2017.

standards of accountability. Government officials can have more or less principled reasons to oppose donors' suggestions of financial management reforms, seeing them as simply intrusive or even as a direct challenge to officials' ability to derive personal benefits. Negotiations over financial management are therefore sensitive.

Tracing how negotiation outcomes in these two areas changed when the government diversified its portfolio of finance reveals a mixed track record of debt-based financial statecraft. On issues of governance and democratization, the government's reduced reliance on traditional donors was associated with donors muting their criticism of the government. However, the government was less successful converting its greater autonomy into changed donor behavior on financial management issues. In fact, donors' concerns about how the government spent funds from Chinese loans and private sources led them to take a stricter approach in negotiations with the government on financial management.

6.3.1 Governance and Democratization

Democratization and political reforms have been core to negotiations between the Kenyan government and traditional donors. Historically, donors have exercised considerable leverage to achieve their preferred outcomes on governance issues in the face of government reluctance. When the Kenyan government was especially reliant on traditional donors for access to external finance, donors were able to persuade the government to pursue liberalizing reforms to enable multiparty competition. Donors' interventions in the early 1990s to encourage Kenya's transition to multiparty competition illustrates donors' influence at this time of considerable government reliance on donor funds.

Fifteen years later, donors were again able to use their status to influence the Kenyan government's course in resolving conflict in the aftermath of the 2007 election. At the time, though Kenya's economy had grown considerably, the government still had few alternatives to traditional donor funds. The government's reliance on aid funds gave donors considerable influence in a moment of political crisis. The 2007 elections laid bare the dangerous consequences of a fraught winner-takes-all electoral system in which political mobilization was organized primarily along ethnic lines. Violence spread around the country as groups targeted ethnicities presumed to have voted for the "wrong" candidate. Leader of the opposition Raila Odinga and his supporters alleged that the incumbent Mwai Kibaki had benefited from a fraudulent election. Amid credible evidence of election malfeasance and opposition allegations that the election had been stolen, the tense and bloody stalemate appeared unlikely to be resolved. Traditional donors, this time led by the UK, coordinated to withhold portions of their aid and directly push for a power-sharing agreement between the winning and losing sides.[28] Donors' involvement was instrumental in creating the "Government of National Unity" that took office in 2008 and brought an end to the crisis that had engulfed the country.

This balance of influence between the government and donors on democratization and governance began to shift as the government diversified its sources of external finance in the late 2000s and early 2010s and became increasingly independent from traditional donor funds. As S. Brown noted on the limits of political conditionality, already in 2009, "Many donors also feel that ... their leverage is not as strong as it used to be, especially since the Kenyan government increasingly enjoys access to other sources of funds, notably financial markets and China."[29]

Kenya's active pursuit of Chinese finance directly played into these competitive dynamics among donors. After his election in 2013, Uhuru Kenyatta's first official state visits outside of Africa were to Russia and China, a move widely regarded as a signal of Kenyatta's intention to realign Kenya's foreign relations to new partners. This view was reinforced when, during an official visit by China's Premier Li Keqiang to Kenya in May 2014, Kenya signed a large loan agreement with the Export-Import Bank of China for the SGR railway project. Kenyatta strategically deployed "Look East" as a means of signaling the government's reduced dependence on traditional donors.

For the Kenyan government, Chinese loans were attractive on their own terms, as well as for the potential bargaining leverage they offered. One National Treasury official explained it was easier to negotiate without disagreeing over "governance issues ... [or] demands on areas that insinuate things about the government."[30] That flexibility was particularly welcomed by the Kenyatta administration, which

---

[28] S. Brown 2009.
[29] S. Brown 2009, p. 399.
[30] Interview 28. National Treasury official. Nairobi, Kenya. February 1, 2017.

wanted to push back against the perceived intrusion of the ongoing ICC investigations. As a Kenyan commentator noted,

There were people for whom "looking East" was convenient, because the President and the Deputy faced trials in the Hague. So, that kind of sharp rhetoric was used for political functions ... they argued it because there was a political problem that needed to be solved, and one way of addressing it was to say: "look, we are turning East because ... they are picking on us because we are Africans."[31]

The Kenyan government's public pursuit of alternative finance had the effect of not only reducing the government's reliance on traditional donors but also expressing the government's preference for financing without explicit or implicit governance conditionality.

As expected, the closer relationship between Kenya and China raised traditional donors' concerns that their own influence and access to the government was being undercut. However, donors rarely directly criticized the government for pursuing relations with new creditors. As one donor official put it, "I don't fault the Kenyan government for taking advantage of attractive financing in the short term."[32] Another said, "I get the question very often, if this [China's growing presence] is bothering us, and it is not ... It is only in infrastructure and energy that we come into contact with the Chinese, but there is so much to do [that there is room for both of us]."[33]

Instead, rather than publicly critiquing the government's pursuit of alternative external finance, donors worried about their reduced access and influence with the government. One senior donor representative noted that "All the donors feel the quality of the relationship is not as good as it should be."[34] Several donor officials complained they were left waiting for meetings, the government communicating its diminished interest – and reliance – by allocating less time to traditional donors. One donor representative commented that "... maybe that waiting time is also a sign that they [Kenya] have too many donors, that there's too much interest."[35] Several donors expressed the concern

---

[31] Interview 7. Think tank researcher. Nairobi, Kenya. January 20, 2017.
[32] Interview 34. Bilateral donor official. Nairobi, Kenya. February 8, 2017.
[33] Interview 32. Donor official. Nairobi, Kenya. February 6, 2017.
[34] Interview 29. Donor official. Nairobi, Kenya. February 2, 2017.
[35] Interview 54. Donor official. Nairobi, Kenya. April 5, 2017.

that their ability to influence or advise the government was undercut by the government's ability to turn to other creditors. One donor official bluntly summarized this stance on the part of government counterparts as "screw you, we will go elsewhere."[36]

Donors worried about the relative prestige of their development projects and their access to the Kenyan government. A multilateral donor representative described the reaction of the donor community as follows, "of course [there is competition], it's for the government to decide how to handle this. China is funding the SGR, which none of the traditional donors would have funded. That relegates traditional donors to building schools and clinics."[37] The reference to "relegating" traditional donors to less attention-grabbing projects reflects donors' concern that they would lose status and access as the government increasingly drew on alternative creditors. To traditional donors, the government's pursuit of alternative finance was also a deliberate strategy to signal its greater independence from traditional donor funds. Others reported that the government deliberately withheld information about Chinese projects to improve their negotiating position: "Sometimes we hear of this in newspaper articles, but in real life we don't hear much from the Chinese projects ... The government is keeping us a bit apart, they discuss different projects with different donors."[38]

Donors were cautious not to put their relationship with the government further at risk. They widely understood that the Kenyan government was interested in Chinese loans because this financing involved fewer negotiations over governance conditions. As one donor representative put it, "Now, China is coming in as a donor, with terms that are more expensive, but they maybe close their eyes on issues like governance or the environment."[39] The government's increased autonomy from donor funds led donors to be more cautious in their approach, with one donor official saying, "In Kenya, it's important for donors to be humble, because donors are a small part of financing in Kenya ... Sometimes the donors act as though the country

[36] Interview 2. Donor official. Nairobi, Kenya. January 18, 2017.
[37] Interview 30. Multilateral donor official. Nairobi, Kenya. February 2, 2017.
[38] Interview 32. Donor official. Nairobi, Kenya. February 6, 2017.
[39] Interview 25. Donor official. Nairobi, Kenya. February 1, 2017.

would fall apart without them, when that's not true."[40] Another donor representative described the government's negotiating position, explaining, "Kenya is not very donor dependent, so they can play very hard; even if they don't explicitly play hard, they can just ignore [donors]."[41] In response to the government's greater access to more flexible finance, several traditional donors chose to deemphasize governance concerns in their engagement with the government.

While most traditional donors did not broadcast their accommodating stance as a policy position, observers noticed that as the government announced its increased autonomy with the "Look East" policy, donors were far less critical of the government's governance shortcomings. One Nairobi-based analyst described how donors' stances had changed,

I think to start with, the UK and other partners didn't know how to interpret it [the "Look East" rhetoric]. I don't know if they panicked ... but there was a softening of the approach. And I think that's one of the reasons that you could consider the rhetoric succeeded. They were too careful after that not to look like they are following a political agenda. So even issues that domestically the West has always had as irreducibles [requirements], suddenly were happening [in Kenya], but people were watching [and letting them happen].[42]

Government officials confirmed that donors' approach had changed, with negotiations over governance criteria increasingly sidelined. One official who regularly participated in negotiations with donors described how the relationship had shifted, "It works better when we separate politics from development, which we did after 2006–7. Here, at this level, we don't discuss politics with development partners [donors]. If they need to discuss politics, they go higher."[43] Already from 2007 onward, when donors withdrew the budget support programs that had involved deep reform commitments, sensitive governance issues had been removed from the agenda. The government's growing autonomy from traditional donor funds further

---

[40] Interview 30. Multilateral donor official. Nairobi, Kenya. February 2, 2017.
[41] Interview 46. Donor official. Nairobi, Kenya. February 14, 2017.
[42] Interview 7. Think tank researcher. Nairobi, Kenya. January 20, 2017.
[43] Interview 38. National Treasury official. Nairobi, Kenya. February 10, 2017.

encouraged donors to avoid this sensitive topic that risked worsening their relationship.

Relegating governance issues allowed donors to satisfy one of the government's preferences and thereby retain their access and influence with the government to achieve their own priorities in the relationship. In one example, an IMF official explained that removing governance issues from their negotiations with the Kenyan government had preserved the quality of the relationship so that the IMF could continue to engage Kenyan policymakers on other issues, specifically public financial management. He described the evolution of the relationship as follows, "In 2000–2010, the focus of the Fund in Kenya was on governance and this put us on shaky ground with the government, this poisoned the relationship with no clear pay-off. So, we've moved away from direct governance issues towards PFM [public financial management], so the relationship has improved, even though the indicators on governance issues haven't changed much."[44]

Donors that satisfied the Kenyatta government's preference for a more hands-off attitude to governance enjoyed better access to the government and ability to shape government policy in other areas. Critics of the Kenyatta government alleged that donors were failing to hold the government accountable because donors prioritized their ability to continue to carry out development programs in the country. A Kenyan columnist who had been a vocal critic of the Kenyatta administration offered this critique of the donors' relationship with the government, saying

It [the government's relationship with China] has really eroded what they [traditional donors] used to consider their leverage. So you will find that they [traditional donors] are now becoming poodles of the government ... people from the IMF and World Bank used to make objective statements about the economy, policy, and so on, now they don't ... They're being poodles because they want to lend.[45]

This analysis of donors as "poodles of the government" is shaped by this journalist's opposition to the Jubilee administration. Nonetheless, it is indicative of how dynamics changed when the government

---

[44] Interview 50. Multilateral donor official. Washington D.C. February 27, 2017.
[45] Interview 10. Kenyan journalist. Nairobi, Kenya. January 23, 2017.

borrowed from alternative sources and reduced its reliance on traditional donors. In response to the government's growing autonomy, donors were willing to meet the government's preference for a diminished focus on governance issues.

6.3.2 Financial Management

The government was much less successful exploiting new sources of finance for greater negotiating leverage in the area of financial management. In essence, donors want assurance that public funds – including aid resources – are spent transparently and responsibly, while the government resists intrusion into domestic processes, wanting autonomy and flexibility in the reporting and spending of public funds. When Kenya borrowed from alternative sources in the 2010s, especially private creditors, the government found funding options that posed fewer reporting requirements, offering them greater flexibility. Despite this access to attractive alternatives and the government's demonstrated preference for greater flexibility, donors were unwilling to deprioritize financial management issues in line with the government's preferences. Instead, financial management remained central in government–donor negotiations and donors insisted on a range of economic reforms to address Kenya's shortcomings in this domain.

Disputes over the accountability and transparency of financial management have been central to the relationship between the Kenyan government and traditional donors since before to the transition to multiparty democracy in the early 1990s. With the country's gradual political liberalization, donors increasingly turned their focus to weak institutions for financial management, which were being further hollowed out by the Moi administration in its final years in power.[46] During this time, the importance of traditional donor aid to Kenya's economy gave donors considerable influence in negotiations over institutions of financial accountability. Kenya had an active IMF program in all but four years between 1975 and 2003, and donors often aligned their evaluations of the country's reform progress with the IMF's assessments. As in most countries, the number of reform conditions attached to IMF programs in Kenya increased over time.

---

[46] Mueller 2008.

While IMF programs in the 1980s had 10–20 conditions attached, programs in the 1990s and 2000s had upward of thirty conditions, of which an increasing number focused on the privatization of state-owned enterprises and fiscal reforms intended to increase transparency and discipline.[47]

In this earlier period, when the Kenyan government proved evasive and slow to implement economic reforms, donors were willing to apply considerable pressure. In the run-up to the 1997 election, for instance, substantial financial irregularities led the IMF to halt their program. The World Bank, the EU, and a number of bilateral donors followed suit, freezing a cumulative $400 million in financing to encourage the government to reform economic governance and address persistent corruption.[48] The IMF returned to lending only in 2000, with a program so strict that *The Economist*, hardly an outspoken critic of the IMF, described it as "a virtual surrender of the country's sovereignty."[49] In disputes over the quality and institutions of financial management, Kenya's reliance on traditional donors prior to the 2010s gave donors the upper hand, leading to aid agreements that were premised on increasing transparency through institutional reforms.

Donors remained focused on corruption and financial management throughout the 2000s, when Kenya's economic growth had diminished the overall importance of foreign aid, but traditional donors still remained the main source of external finance. In the mid 2000s, a large and complex corruption scandal came to light, undermining the good governance credentials of the recently elected Kibaki administration.[50] What came to be known as the "Anglo-Leasing" scandal involved high-ranking government members being linked to fraudulent procurement contracts worth more than $750 million. In a long-running scheme, contracts for passport readers and forensic laboratory equipment were awarded to foreign firms without tender, overinvoiced by tens of millions of euros. As the scale of ongoing corruption became clear, donors responded by attaching further reform conditions and reporting requirements to their development assistance. In particular,

---

[47] Kentikelenis et al. 2016.
[48] S. Brown 2001, p. 734.
[49] The Economist 2000.
[50] Wrong 2009.

donors were frustrated that the government was misusing donor funds, implicating them in the government's corruption. The British High Commissioner vehemently expressed donors' frustration, saying "Evidently the practitioners now in government have the arrogance, greed and perhaps a desperate sense of panic to lead them to eat like gluttons. But they can hardly expect us not to care when their gluttony causes them to vomit all over our shoes."[51] Donors responded to the persistent shortcomings in financial management by increasingly shifting their resources from budget support into ring-fenced projects with individualized reporting requirements.[52] This move protected donors from some of the reputational risks of extending aid to an unreliable government. Moreover, donors prioritized financial management issues in their engagement with the government, placing anti-corruption reforms at the center of negotiations.

A key turning point in the negotiations between the government and donors over financial management came when the government expanded its borrowing from Chinese and private lenders, which offered financing with a more flexible approach, with very little scrutiny of the government's internal financial processes and fewer administrative hurdles governing the use of funds. Government representatives indicated that more flexible finance made them more critical of the terms attached to traditional donor funds, particularly requirements intended to increase accountability that also had the effect of slowing down the disbursement of funds. One government official highlighted that private borrowing had allowed the government to signal to donors its preference for rapid and flexible funds, saying "Now, donors have realized that predictability is major concern. Even with a signed agreement with donors, conditions precedent[53] will affect the release of funds."[54] Another official at the National Treasury described how the government's access to private market finance had reduced the appeal of traditional donor funds, saying "In a way, the Eurobond affects the relationship with donors ... if I borrow and I get friendly terms, then I prefer that."[55]

---

[51] Munnion 2004.
[52] Prizzon and Hart 2016, p. 22.
[53] These are ex ante requirements that must be fulfilled before disbursement, also known as "prior actions."
[54] Interview 28. National Treasury official. Nairobi, Kenya. February 1, 2017.
[55] Interview 6. National Treasury official. Nairobi, Kenya. January 20, 2017.

Since the government made its interest in flexible financing clear by actively pursuing alternative creditors, it was conceivable that donors might relax some of their requirements in response. Indeed, both government and donor representatives reported that during this time, the government pushed back on donors' conditions over financial management and reporting, and that donors were aware that the government had outside options that offered them different terms. A government official responsible for the relationship with the World Bank explained the impact of Chinese loans on negotiations, noting "with the East, the way the money is spent is up to the government, that's why the Bank feels a bit threatened."[56] Donor officials recognized that the government's new sources of financing made negotiations in this issue area more difficult. One donor official described the impression that if donors "twist the arm too tightly, then the country will go look elsewhere, perhaps go to China."[57] Another donor representative perceived the government's borrowing patterns as a deliberate strategy to increase bargaining leverage with donors, saying that although National Treasury officials "will never tell you, it [borrowing from China] is a way for them to put pressure on us."[58]

However, the outcome of negotiations over financial management was that donors instead intensified their focus on this issue, doubling down on a dimension of the government–donor relationship where the government had signaled its interest in flexibility. The key to understanding donors' reactions is the 2016 turning point, when allegations that the government had misappropriated private external finance became more prominent. Concerned that the government's use or misuse of alternative finance put their own projects and repayment at risk, donors were reluctant to give the government greater flexibility on financial oversight.

In particular, donors pushed for reforms to address institutional weaknesses that were enabling widespread corruption. In 2017, the World Bank announced a three-year project to improve public financial management in Kenya. The document justifying the project lays out the Bank's concerns:

---

[56] Interview 5. National Treasury official. Nairobi, Kenya. January 20, 2017.
[57] Interview 2. Multilateral donor official. Nairobi, Kenya. January 18, 2017.
[58] Interview 29. Bilateral donor official. Nairobi, Kenya. February 2, 2017.

Kenya still faces significant governance challenges that are symptomatic of institutional and systemic weakness ... public procurement and contracting reforms have not contributed significantly to reducing and/or preventing corruption in Kenya ... There remains no coherent system for making decisions on selection and prioritization of public investments on the basis of public policy objectives.[59]

The French development agency joined the World Bank's efforts and provided additional funding for institutional reforms within the Kenyan National Treasury, including setting up a unit for public investment management. Various donors placed technical experts within the Kenyan National Treasury in an effort to improve financial management. The United States seconded a US Treasury official to Kenya's debt management department, while France sent a French expert to advise the public investment unit.

These donor-funded projects were in principle aligned with the government's own Strategy for Public Financial Management Reform, but government respondents made clear that there was little high-level government support for these projects, and they were primarily championed by donors. Since Kenya is not very aid dependent, it is not as though the government had no alternative but to accept these projects. However, the design and implementation of the projects reflected donor priorities, rather than government objectives. As a consequence, the projects struggled in the implementation phase. At the halfway mark of the World Bank's program, for instance, none of the components of the program were more than 30 percent complete, with no progress on "efficient and transparent procurement," one of the most politically sensitive areas of financial management.[60]

6.4 What Was behind Kenya's Mixed Record?

Kenya diversified its sources of finance and reduced its dependence on traditional donors during the 2010s. This reduced dependence should have given the Kenyan government greater leverage in negotiations with those donors, allowing the government to achieve aid programs more aligned with its core preferences. Indeed, the government

---

[59] World Bank 2017b, pp. 2–3, 94.
[60] World Bank 2020a.

succeeded in shifting the emphasis of the aid relationship away from governance and democratization issues that had been a persistent source of tension with donors. All the same, the government was less successful in shifting donors' attention away from economic and financial management issues, especially weaknesses in the institutions for public procurement, budgeting, public investment, and debt management. What accounts for this mixed track record?

Kenya benefited from its importance for traditional donors. Donors were reluctant to lose their access and influence with the government and were therefore willing to accommodate some of the government's preferences. Once the Kenyan government reduced its dependence on traditional donors, donors were even more concerned to preserve their access and ensure they continued to receive a hearing as Kenya developed closer relationships with China and other alternative lenders. And yet, donors also had little trust in the government's use of traditional and alternate funds. This combination of factors explains why the Kenyan government was only partially able to benefit from its new borrowing relationships, achieving uneven success in financial statecraft.

6.4.1 Kenya's significance to donors

A large part of donors' motivation to remain close to the Kenyan government comes from Kenya's geopolitical and strategic importance. As a largely predictable country in a volatile region, a counterpart in the global war on terror, and host to large populations of refugees, Kenya ranks high on most traditional donors' lists of important African recipients. One donor official expressed this view when describing Kenya as "the only sane, stable country in the region, given the fragility of Somalia and the threat of terrorism," spelling out that therefore donors "might be willing to look the other way" during negotiations over the terms of aid agreements.[61] Kenya's importance to its donors extends beyond the subregion; as Barkan explains, "Along with Nigeria and South Africa, Kenya is one of three 'anchor states' in sub-Saharan Africa – countries that are key to the stability of the region because of location and resources."[62]

[61] Interview 2. Multilateral donor official. Nairobi, Kenya. January 18, 2017.
[62] Barkan 2004.

Donors' stakes in their relationship with the Kenyan government led to a more accommodating position in aid negotiations. This was true independent of the Kenyan government's access to alternative finance. As one government official put it bluntly, highlighting how donors' security interests led them to adopt a more flexible stance on governance and human rights, "Some of them don't want to put us in a corner. They have put their soldiers here, so they don't want to threaten us … so they end up not questioning so much our human rights issues."[63] In the early 2000s, as Kenya was consolidating its democratic transition and the global war on terror was getting under way, observers noted that donors were often quick to move away from pushing the government on political rights to instead prioritize security and economic concerns.[64]

Given donors' strong interest in the government's policy choices, they were concerned about its greater autonomy from donor advice. The effect of Kenya's "Look East" policy, which led donors to take a more accommodating stance on governance conditionality, is an illustration of how the government's strategic importance allowed it to deploy debt-based financial statecraft more effectively. Kenya had been an important counterpart for donors long before the "Look East" policy. Kenya's importance to donors had given it some flexibility, but it was not until the government reduced its dependence on traditional donor funds that participants in the negotiations noticed a step change in the relationship.

Government representatives clearly recognized how the confluence of alternative finance and traditional donors' interest in the relationship worked in their favor. Explaining why Western donors remained active in the country, even in the face of corruption scandals and mounting alternatives to traditional development finance, one National Treasury official explained, "Even the donors have their own interests, so they want to stay involved."[65] In Kenya's case, donors were invested in the relationship for broader security reasons and concerns about regional stability. Valuing the relationship in this way made donors more sensitive to the government's receptiveness and how alternative finance increased the government's autonomy. Faced

[63] Interview 39. National Treasury official. Nairobi, Kenya. February 10, 2017.
[64] S. Brown 2001, 2009.
[65] Interview 20. National Treasury official. Nairobi, Kenya. January 30, 2017.

with competition from alternative creditors, donors were inclined to be more flexible; as a government official observed, "There is a competition between the emerging and the traditional [donors] ... the traditional want to keep their position."[66]

When donor officials explained their agencies' decision to maintain the relationship with the government and to extend flexibility on certain issues, especially governance and human rights issues, they pointed to the overall value of the relationship. For instance, one donor official explicitly connected Kenya's role in combating terrorism to the donor community's stance, saying, "We have to take into account other factors, for instance [Kenya's efforts to combat the terrorist group] al-Shabaab. We cannot put Kenya under too much stress."[67] Similarly, a US official explained how the US' interest in ongoing relations with the Kenyan government shaped its stance, noting, "USAID funding goes to countries where the US has a strategic interest, so USAID is sticky in ways that other funding isn't."[68] That "stickiness" refers to donors' reluctance to withdraw aid, which they must be willing to do if their conditionality is to be credible. With donors particularly attached to the relationship with the Kenyan government, they were inclined to be more flexible toward the government's governance shortcomings, even more so once donors' influence appeared to be under threat from other lenders.

6.4.2 Limited Donor Trust in Kenya's Government

Cutting against the importance that donors attached to their relationship with the Kenyan government were donors' concerns about the credibility of the government's commitments with respect to public spending and aid agreements. In Kenya, controversies surrounding the government's use of alternative finance and donors' long-standing concerns about the transparency and reliability of Kenya's spending undermined the leverage that outside options offered.

Donors' lack of trust in the Kenyan government's public spending and development policy commitments were shaped by high levels of corruption and recurrent electoral budget cycles. Kenya consistently

---

[66] Interview 42. National Treasury official. Nairobi, Kenya. February 13, 2017.
[67] Interview 29. Bilateral donor official. Nairobi, Kenya. February 2, 2017.
[68] Interview 34. Bilateral donor official. Nairobi, Kenya. February 8, 2017.

scores among the worst in the world on the corruption perception index, an indicator that measures experts' and business leaders' perception of corruption in the public sector. In 2017, Kenya was ranked 143rd out of 180 countries in Transparency International's global ranking; by 2019 it had marginally improved its ranking to 137th. In addition to elite-level corruption, donors also expressed concerns that the government was facing pressure to distribute public resources to regions that are home to key supporters in the coalition, leading to unpredictable spending in the run-up to elections. One observer explained the rush of public spending ahead of the 2017 election in these terms, saying the government was "engaging in a stampede to deliver projects from the 2013 manifesto ... Kikuyus have been saying to the government, 'you take our votes for granted,' so the government has promised new projects."[69] Civil servants also acknowledged these patterns, such as one National Treasury official in the debt management office who explained the importance of reassuring international investors during the lead-up to the election, saying "This is not our first election, so we know the cycle. The important thing is to engage the investors. We have monthly calls."[70]

These concerns were reflected in Kenya's performance on donors' institutional assessments. While Kenya performed fairly well in the World Bank's overall Country Policy and Institutional Assessment, with an average score of 3.4 out of 6 in the 2010–2018 period, compared to an average of 3.0 for all sub-Saharan African countries, on management of corruption it performed worse, scoring just a 3.0 during this time. In the African Development Bank's assessment, Kenya similarly did well overall, with an average of 4.23 out of 6 in the 2010–2018 period, but performing below the median on transparency, accountability, and corruption in the public sector, with an average score of 3.1 during that time.

The concerns about corruption and patterns of government spending directly shaped how traditional donors approached negotiations with the Kenyan government over aid. Donors were well aware of the political context and guarded against having their resources diverted to serve political ends. As one donor representative put it, "When

---

[69] Interview 26. Civil society representative. Nairobi, Kenya. February 1, 2017.
[70] Interview 43. National Treasury official. Nairobi, Kenya. February 13, 2017.

there is a need for funding, it is because of political concerns."[71] He elaborated, "it is also a challenge, because a Minister may deter you from supporting something in an opposition region ... There is no possibility for traditional donors to implement in a region where the Minister or President don't want it."[72] Another donor representative described the vigilance on the part of donors about the end uses of their resources, saying "... we also have to be careful about allocating funds, because they may push you to allocate funds to where votes are coming from, in specific geographic regions."[73] These concerns are corroborated by research that found World Bank and African Development Bank projects in Kenya from 1992 to 2010 were more likely to be allocated to constituencies supporting the incumbent.[74]

The flexibility of Chinese loans and private finance from bond markets and bank loans provided few restrictions on the government's use of funds. As one Kenyan journalist put it, "You need to understand the political economy context, which is that projects are started for rent-seeking, not for economic reasons. In this context, the Chinese have become very influential."[75] Observers suggested the Kenyatta administration, in power from 2013 to 2022, had especially benefited from the availability of Chinese and private market finance because of its broad and unlikely coalition, bringing together representatives of groups that had been on opposing sides of the postelection conflict in 2008. To maintain this wide-ranging coalition, the government pursued large projects to reach relevant regions and supporters. A civil society observer commented, "This government, more than previous governments, has a craving for large projects."[76]

This greater flexibility of alternative finance meant that traditional donors were not only skeptical of the government's commitments to their own aid agreements but also concerned about how alternative finance impacted the government's development commitments. One donor official described the donor community's wariness, saying, "... the National Treasury has been big on debt financing, because the Jubilee government is under political pressure to look like a

---

[71] Interview 29. Bilateral donor official. Nairobi, Kenya. February 2, 2017.
[72] Interview 29. Bilateral donor official. Nairobi, Kenya. February 2, 2017.
[73] Interview 32. Multilateral donor official. Nairobi, Kenya. February 6, 2017.
[74] Jablonski 2014.
[75] Interview 14. Kenyan journalist. Nairobi, Kenya. January 25, 2017.
[76] Interview 26. Civil society representative. Nairobi, Kenya. February 1, 2017.

growing economy."[77] The SGR project, financed mostly by a large Chinese loan, typified donors' concerns about the government's use of alternative finance, with donors suggesting it was overpriced, poorly managed, and rushed for electoral purposes. As one donor official put it, "the SGR financing was on bad terms ... [and] the SGR is a terrible boondoggle."[78] Donors' skepticism was not specific to the SGR, nor to Chinese loans. Other donors worried that the flexibility of market finance enabled unsustainable spending. As one donor official put it, "... market financing should make corruption harder ... private funding should introduce more discipline. But that hasn't been the case in Kenya. It seemingly hasn't prevented corruption."[79]

The government's uses of alternative finance raised donors' concerns that this spending could put their development projects in Kenya at risk, or even make it difficult for the Kenyan government to repay them. Donors questioned the sustainability of alternative finance, with one donor representative explaining, "Of course there is, can I call it fear? Or at least some apprehension, that there is some alternative finance ... development partners are concerned, deeply concerned about the return on investment."[80] For donors whose development finance in Kenya included loans, such as the US, Japan, or France, an unsustainable buildup of debt could put their own repayment at risk. One donor representative explained their strategy when approaching the government, in light of concerns about repayment,

> ... what we need to do is make clear to Kenya that there can be disasters from Chinese-financed projects ... We have some concerns ... about the quality of debt management, because *we also have an interest in being repaid.*[81]

Although alternative finance reduced the government's dependence on traditional donors, it also potentially put donors' own programs at risk.

Ultimately, most donors were unwilling to compromise on economic management reforms they saw as a guarantee of their own financial

---

[77] Interview 34. Bilateral donor official. Nairobi, Kenya. February 8, 2017.

[78] Interview 34. Bilateral donor official. Nairobi, Kenya. February 8, 2017.

[79] Interview 2. Multilateral donor official. Nairobi, Kenya. January 18, 2017.

[80] Interview 1. Bilateral donor official. Nairobi, Kenya. January 18, 2017.

[81] Interview 29. Bilateral donor official. Nairobi, Kenya. February 2, 2017. Emphasis added.

exposure. Though the government would have preferred donors to take a more flexible approach to financial management issues, donors regarded financial management conditions as insurance against unsustainable and unpredictable government spending. In this way, donors' lack of trust in the Kenyan government undercut some of Kenya's efforts at debt-based financial statecraft.

6.5 Conclusion

In Kenya, the government had a mixed record in translating its access to alternative finance into negotiation outcomes aligned with its preferences. The government's reduced dependence did appear to have some effect on the outcomes of negotiations with traditional donors. On issues related to governance and human rights, donors became more circumspect in their public criticism of the government after 2013, despite the noncompliance of the Kenyan President and Deputy President with the ICC's international investigation. This muting of governance criticism appeared to be in large part due to donors' reluctance to endanger their relationship with the government, especially as the government reduced its dependence on traditional donor funds.

However, the government was not entirely successful in influencing negotiation outcomes in line with its preferences. In the domain of financial management, donors increased their pressure on the government despite Kenya's access to alternative finance. Here, donors' distrust in the government's public financial management systems played a substantial role. Fearful that the government's spending patterns and use of alternative finance could put Kenya in financial difficulty and imperil the success of their projects and repayment of their loans, donors insisted on reforms to strengthen oversight.

The difference between Kenya and Ethiopia illustrates how donor trust in the credibility of the government shapes debt-based financial statecraft. Donors' concerns about whether their aid agreements will be upheld and how alternative finance will be used inhibit their responsiveness to recipient preferences. When contrasted with the Ghanaian case in Chapter 7, the Kenyan case also highlights the benefits that governments can extract from their importance to donors. In Kenya, donors prized their relationship with the government, enabling the government to at least partly use its new borrowing relationships as a basis for leverage.

7 | *Ghana: Limited Financial Statecraft*

Throughout different phases of Ghana's recent history, the country has enjoyed a special relationship with aid donors as a "donor darling," granted flexibility by donors in return for its reforms, development track record, and good governance. In the 1980s, Ghana was a model student of the economic reforms advocated by international financial institutions, currying favor with donors. A decade later, with the transition to multiparty democracy, Ghana became one of the standard-bearers of the "third wave" of democratization in Africa, aligning with the priority donors attached to good governance. Given this history of close relations with donors, one might expect that Ghana did well out of the new constellation of available finance, using the strength of its existing ties to traditional donors while courting new sources. And yet, of the three case studies, Ghana saw the least impact of its diversified portfolio of external finance on its bargaining leverage with traditional lenders. In fact, in Ghana, the government's increasing reliance on alternative finance was associated with worsening relations with traditional donors. The surprising failure of this one-time donor darling to extract bargaining leverage from its diverse portfolio is a telling case, demonstrating the moderating effects of both strategic significance and donor trust.

As in both Kenya and Ethiopia, the Ghanaian government diversified its portfolio of external finance away from its reliance on traditional donors. In the late 2000s, Ghana borrowed in large volumes from Chinese lenders for infrastructure projects. From the 2010s, the country added international bond financing to the mix, becoming a repeat borrower in sovereign bond markets. Together, these new sources of finance reduced the government's dependence on aid from traditional donors.

And yet, in the most sensitive areas of donor–government negotiations, greater autonomy did not always translate into greater bargaining leverage. Unlike in Kenya and Ethiopia, where governance and democratization were fraught topics of negotiation, Ghana's governance institutions earned accolades from donors. Instead, the topics where donors and the government were furthest apart were on macroeconomic policy and financial management, including budgeting and procurement. Though the policy preferences and recommendations have changed over time, these are longstanding areas of negotiation between Ghana and its donors, from the structural adjustment period to the present. Whether in setting economic policy or financial oversight, the government sought greater flexibility from donors, wanting donors to match the approach of alternative creditors. However, donors proved largely unwilling to give the government greater flexibility, despite the government's increased autonomy from traditional donor funds.

In the time period covered by this book, from the early 2000s to 2018, the years that stand out as the high point of Ghana's borrowing from alternative creditors, 2012–2015, also stand out as the low point in relations with traditional donors. This low point was especially pronounced because of the close and supportive relationship that Ghana has historically enjoyed with traditional donors. Compared in absolute terms to other developing countries, Ghana's difficulties with its donors during this time may not appear so taxing, but compared in relative terms to the previous dynamics in the donor–recipient relationship, both donor and government representatives saw this as a breakdown. The policy tool that had been representative of donors' earlier trust in the government, the Multi-Donor Budget Support (MDBS) mechanism, instead became a site of fractious negotiations, with the government unable to bring donors around to their preferred outcomes on economic policy and financial management.

The reasons for Ghana's difficulties were twofold. First, as outlined in the theoretical framework, a government will have greater success translating its autonomy into preferred outcomes with donors if donors place great value on the relationship with the government. Having long enjoyed a close relationship with donors, Ghana would appear to be well suited to debt-based financial statecraft. However, Ghana's status with donors began to decline from 2012 onward, when donors worried about the government's mismanagement of recently discovered oil reserves. When an economic and currency crisis hit in 2013, donors became increasingly concerned about what they saw as the government's lack of fiscal discipline, undermining their sense of

Ghana's success story. As the value donors placed on their relationship with the government declined, so too did the bargaining leverage the government could derive from alternative borrowing relationships.

Second, in Ghana as in Kenya, a lack of donor trust that aid agreements would be upheld made it harder for the government to extract bargaining leverage from its new borrowing relationships. Donors observed the pressure on the government to satisfy political and regional demands for distribution and worried that the use of alternative credit to finance patronage spending could compromise debt sustainability. In response, donors hardened their negotiating positions, especially on financial management reforms that they saw as safeguards against unsustainable spending.

This chapter draws on interview evidence from over sixty interviews with Ghanaian government officials, donor representatives, and civil society observers, a third of which were conducted in September–October 2013, and the remainder of which stem from April–May 2017.[1] The two phases of data collection help illuminate how relations between the government and donors changed over time, particularly after the economic crisis Ghana experienced in 2013. I first describe in Section 7.1 what the theoretical expectations are in the Ghanaian case, then outline in Section 7.2 how Ghana's portfolio of external finance changed over time, highlighting key turning points in the country's access to external finance. In Section 7.3, I map these turning points onto outcomes in the negotiations between Ghana's government and its donors, demonstrating that the country struggled to secure its preferred level of flexibility, despite its greater autonomy from donor funds. Section 7.4 explains Ghana's difficulties with debt-based financial statecraft, and Section 7.5 concludes.

7.1 Theoretical Expectations in the Ghanaian Case

Applying the theoretical framework to the Ghanaian case leads to an expectation of limited success in using its new borrowing relationships for greater leverage in aid negotiations. The government certainly diversified its portfolio of external finance, borrowing in large quantities from China in the late 2000s and being among the first

---

[1] For more details about the interviews, see Table A.3.

sub-Saharan African countries to issue a bond in international markets. Despite this expansion of Ghana's portfolio of external finance, however, the theoretical framework suggests a number of factors that likely inhibited the government's leverage with traditional donors.

For one, at the same time that Ghana diversified its portfolio of external finance, the country's significance for traditional donors declined. For a recipient government to best exploit its greater autonomy for increased bargaining leverage, it helps if donors attach a high value to the relationship with the government and therefore are inclined to accommodate the government's requests to preserve the relationship. Though Ghana had historically been an important counterpart for donors, the relationship lost some of its luster as donors worried about the government's management of oil resources. The value that donors had for a long time attached to the relationship with Ghana was premised on the symbolic significance of Ghana's reform successes and development track record, rather than the geopolitical motivations that occupied donors in Kenya and Ethiopia. When the basis for Ghana's symbolic significance eroded, donors attached less value to maintaining the relationship.

Second, the theoretical framework highlights that donor trust in the government's credibility shapes the likely success of financial statecraft. For recipient governments to use alternative finance as a means to bargain for preferred aid from traditional donors, donors need to have confidence that the government will adhere to aid agreements. On this dimension, Ghana was not in an advantageous position for debt-based financial statecraft. Though elite-level corruption is not as pronounced as in Kenya, donors have long been concerned about the country's electoral budget cycles and the reliability of Ghana's financial planning. In this context, the theory suggests that the government may struggle to make credible commitments about their uses of alternative finance, which can undermine donors' willingness to accommodate the government in negotiations. As a case, Ghana provides a test of the extent to which alternative finance can increase a government's negotiating leverage under adverse conditions, when donors have a diminishing interest in the recipient government and when domestic politics make it harder for the government to credibly commit to its use of external finance.

Finally, the composition of the Ghanaian government's portfolio of external finance may have hampered the country's efforts at financial statecraft. The theory highlights that while various forms of finance reduce a government's dependence on traditional donors, thereby increasing their bargaining leverage, some forms of finance are likely to have a stronger effect on negotiating outcomes. Bilateral loans from political or geostrategic rivals can enhance the value of a recipient country, increasing donors' motivation to retain the relationship and some influence with the government. In Ghana's case, the government relied more heavily on private finance than Chinese loans to diversify its portfolio of external finance. Though borrowing from private creditors still reduced the government's reliance on traditional donor aid, it did not stoke donor competition or increase the government's value to donors in the same way that finance from Chinese lenders would have done.

7.2 Variation in Ghana's Portfolio of External Finance

Ghana began diversifying its portfolio of external finance earlier than most other African countries and experienced several distinct phases in its relationships with external creditors over the course of the 2000s and 2010s. After receiving substantial debt relief from the Highly Indebted Poor Country (HIPC) initiative in 2004, the country reached out to new creditors, and by the 2010s, Ghana's reliance on traditional donors had substantially decreased. Traditional development finance as a share of total external finance fell from an average of 83.4 percent in the 1990s and 82.6 percent in 2000s to 43 percent in the 2010s.[2]

In tracing Ghana's relations with external creditors from the 2000s to the end of the 2010s, there are three important turning points of expansion and contraction in the country's portfolio of external finance (see Figure 7.1). First, 2007, when the government signed a major loan agreement with a Chinese lender and issued the country's first ever international bond. Second, 2010, when a statistical revision of Ghana's GDP led to an abrupt transition to lower-middle-income status in the same year that the country began extracting oil in commercial quantities. Third, 2014, when Ghana canceled an enormous loan from a Chinese creditor, reducing the importance of Chinese loans and shifting Ghana's portfolio of external finance further toward private

---

[2] World Bank 2020b.

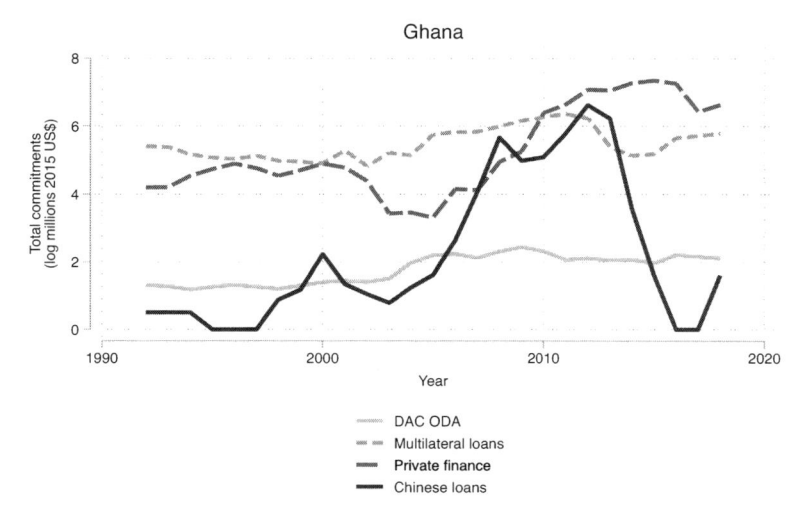

Figure 7.1 Ghana's portfolio of external finance, 1992–2018.
Three-year rolling average of total commitments (log millions 2015 US$).

credit, before difficulties in market access again increased the government's need for concessional finance. Finally, right at the end of the period under study, the government elected in 2016 announced a "Ghana Beyond Aid" policy that appeared to recalibrate the relationship with traditional donors, but in fact introduced very few concrete changes in Ghana's relationship with its creditors. I outline these twists and turns in Ghana's relationships with external creditors, describing how they changed the government's reliance on traditional donors' aid, setting up the analysis of government–donor negotiations that follows.

The expansion of external finance to Ghana in the 2010s stands in contrast to the country's earlier reliance on traditional donor funds. Total ODA from traditional donors amounted to 9.88 percent of GNI in the 1990s, remaining at an average of 9.81 percent in the 2000s, until declining to 3.22 percent in the 2010s. Aid from DAC donors and development finance from multilateral development banks were the country's main sources of external finance. The Ghanaian government's willingness to implement economic liberalization reforms and deepen democratization made Ghana an important counterpart for many traditional donors. Table 7.1 shows the leading traditional donors in these decades.

Table 7.1 *Average annual ODA commitments of top DAC-reporting donors to Ghana, 1990–2019 (millions 2015 US$)*

1990–1999		2000–2009		2010–2019	
IDA	295	IDA	329	IDA	379
UK	96	UK	184	US	257
Japan	84	US	177	AfDF	93
EU	82	Japan	140	Germany	80
US	54	Netherlands	126	EU	74
Germany	53	EU	115	France	70
Canada	42	Canada	77	Japan	62
AfDF	37	Germany	77	UK	56
Denmark	36	AfDF	74	Korea	55
France	35	Denmark	70	Canada	54
Netherlands	34	France	69	Denmark	43
AfDB	11	Spain	21	Netherlands	36
Spain	5	AfDB	16	AfDB	27
UNDP	4	Switzerland	12	Switzerland	20
Norway	4	Belgium	10	Belgium	9

Reflecting its close relationship with donors in the 1990s and 2000s, Ghana was one of the first countries to receive aid in the form of budget support.[3] From 2003 onward, eleven donors pooled their funds and contributed them directly to the Ghanaian budget in an arrangement known as the MDBS mechanism.[4] By directly supporting the government's budget, donors supported Ghana's institutions and reduced the transaction costs for the country's access to foreign aid. As in other developing countries, however, budget support also gave the donors considerable leverage over government policy. Funds from the MDBS were released twice annually, with the first tranche dependent on "satisfactory macroeconomic management" and the second consisting of a "performance payment" linked to the government's completion of

---

[3] A World Bank–EU evaluation of budget support refers to "Ghana's position as a pioneer in innovations related to development aid in the late 1990s/early 2000s" (EU and World Bank 2017, p. 25).

[4] These donors were the African Development Bank, Canada, Denmark, the EU, France, Germany, Japan, the Netherlands, Switzerland, the UK, and the World Bank.

pre-agreed policy measures.[5] Operating collectively, donors could exert greater leverage over government policy, potentially withholding many donors' funds at once. At a time when Ghana was largely reliant on traditional donor funds, coordinated action gave donors considerable influence in negotiations.

Ghana's relationships with traditional donors in this earlier phase of reliance were also shaped by the debt relief process. Like Ethiopia, and thirty-seven other developing countries, Ghana was eligible for debt relief under the HIPC initiative of the IMF and World Bank. The initiative offered debt forgiveness on multilateral and bilateral debt for low-income countries deemed to have an unsustainable debt burden, in exchange for reforms under World Bank and IMF programs, and for designing and implementing a poverty-reduction strategy. From 2000 to 2004, Ghana implemented various policies to satisfy the requirements for debt relief. Ghana received debt relief of 56 percent of total debt outstanding, an enormous respite for a country where government debt amounted to 135 percent of GDP by 2000.[6] The HIPC process underscored how reliant Ghana was on traditional donors, meeting their reform and policy expectations to secure much-needed relief.

After debt relief, the real expansion of Ghana's portfolio of external finance came in 2007, when the government received its first large loan from a Chinese lender and debuted in international bond markets. When Ghana issued its debut bond in 2007, it was the first country to have gone through the HIPC process to issue an international bond, signaling markets' willingness to lend to poorer developing countries.[7] After Ghana's initial bond, it did not return to international bond markets until 2013, when the governing National Democratic Congress (NDC) further expanded the country's borrowing in international markets. Sovereign bond finance appealed to governing officials in both parties for its flexibility and the large volume of funding made available. A later survey of Ministry of Finance officials found, "Despite the cost of Eurobonds ... vis-à-vis marginally less costly offers from official lenders, the government of Ghana favours this source of development finance given relative volumes, flexibility in use, and the absence of conditionality."[8]

---

[5] Killick and Lawson 2007.
[6] IMF 2002.
[7] Olabisi and Stein 2015.
[8] MacCarthy 2016, p. 24.

In addition to bond market finance, Chinese loans played an important role in diversifying Ghana's portfolio of external finance in the late 2000s. Though Ghana had received earlier, smaller Chinese aid projects, the big shift in Ghana's borrowing from Chinese lenders came in 2007, when the governing New Patriotic Party (NPP) negotiated a $562 million loan from China's Export-Import Bank for the Bui hydroelectric dam; the loan offered the government flexible funding for a project the World Bank had been wary of supporting. Ghana's diminished reliance on traditional donors and access to alternative finance was further underscored in 2009, when the newly elected NDC government announced an enormous $3 billion loan from the China Development Bank for a number of infrastructure and energy projects.

As in Kenya and Ethiopia, government officials arranging Chinese loans emphasized the potential for these loans to finance large, catalytic infrastructure projects. One official participating in negotiations on behalf of Ghana's National Development Planning Commission explained,

China was ready to make available ... an almost unlimited amount of resources with no conditions whatsoever. So, what has happened is that government attention has begun to shift from the traditional partners towards the Chinese, since the government recognized that the Chinese probably offered the best option for its infrastructure needs or investment needs at this time. From 2009 up until about 2012 most of the attention of government was on the Chinese.[9]

Traditional donor representatives observed and understood the government was drawn to the speed and flexibility of bilateral loans from China. One donor representative noted, "They want quick money. Going through the MDBS or through a regular loan with the [World] Bank they have to go through many processes ... So that takes time. With other people, there's no questions asked."[10]

The next turning point in Ghana's relationship with traditional donors came late in 2010. That year, a statistical adjustment exercise reestimated Ghana's GDP per capita as several hundred dollars higher than in the previous year. From one day to the next, Ghana's

[9] Interview 105. National Development Planning Commission official. Accra, Ghana. September 27, 2013.
[10] Interview 111. Multilateral donor official. Accra, Ghana. October 4, 2013.

classification was changed from low-income country to lower-middle-income country.[11] At the same time, Ghana first began producing oil in commercial quantities, after discoveries of significant oil deposits in the years prior. Suddenly, the country seemed poised to become a middle-income African petro-state.

These new economic circumstances altered Ghana's relationships with its donors and creditors. Traditional donors whose internal institutional guidelines prioritize low-income countries were likely to withdraw some of their resources, given the country's new income status.[12] Aware that donor aid might recede, the government sought to replace traditional donor funds, aided by the boost that promised oil revenue gave to its creditworthiness. The greater perceived creditworthiness enabled the government to tap deeper pools of private investment, including attracting foreign investors into the country's domestic bond market.

This turning point did not spell a decisive departure of traditional donors from Ghana, since many donors had reasons to maintain their aid programs, despite the country's new middle-income status. In fact, globally, foreign aid to middle-income countries makes up the largest share of foreign aid.[13] Nonetheless, this turning point did alter the terms of traditional donor aid. Most donors reserve their cheapest and most generous financing for low-income countries, offering development finance at higher interest rates and shorter maturities to wealthier middle-income countries. For the Ghanaian government, the higher costs on development finance in their new income category meant that traditional development finance became marginally less attractive, though still cheaper than loans at market rates.

Ghana's management of its newfound oil wealth also impacted relations with traditional donors, who were on guard for signs that oil discoveries could prove to be a "curse" that undermined Ghana's good governance track record. A 2010 dispute between the Ghanaian government and a US investor over the sale of a stake in one of Ghana's largest oil fields raised donors' concerns that Ghanaian institutions were weakening in the wake of oil discoveries.[14] Moreover, donors

---

[11] Jerven 2013.
[12] Moss and Majerowicz 2012.
[13] Dissanayake et al. 2020.
[14] Phillips et al. 2016.

worried about the government's management of oil income and sought to shape the design of Ghana's 2011 Petroleum Revenue Management Act. Oil extraction thus raised donors' concerns at the same time that it promised the Ghanaian government a revenue source that would make it less reliant on donors.

A final turning point in this time period came in 2014, when Ghana's portfolio of external finance narrowed yet again. First, the government turned down a major Chinese loan, due to disagreements over the projects to be funded and political tensions with China. Then, an enduring economic and currency crisis made it more difficult for Ghana to raise funds in international markets. Together, these developments led to Ghana becoming yet again more reliant on the concessional finance of traditional donors.

Domestic political disputes over Ghana's relationship with China made it difficult for the government to continue borrowing from Chinese lenders, leading to a steep decline in Chinese loans after the highpoint in the early 2010s (see Figure 7.1). As in Kenya, where opposition challenges prevented the government from quickly returning to Eurobond markets, so in Ghana the opposition's challenge dampened the appeal of further Chinese loans. In parliamentary debates and public commentary, the opposition NPP excoriated the government over the terms of the $3 billion China Development Bank loan, alleging the government had taken on expensive debt without planning how the funds would be used. In particular, the government came under fire for agreeing to pay commitment fees on the entirety of the loan, which meant that the government paid fees before accessing any of the loan.[15]

Even more challenging for the government, its borrowing from China became entangled with a heated controversy over Chinese migrants and illegal gold mining. Small-scale gold mining, known as "galamsey," in which miners use simple tools and chemicals to extract gold found near the surface, is widespread in Ghana. The practice drew increasing attention in the early 2010s, when the environmental impact of the mercury and cyanide used in these growing informal and illegal mining operations came under scrutiny. Moreover, Chinese firms

---

[15] CitiFM 2011. Commitment fees are a common feature of loans, including loans from the World Bank and other multilateral development banks. However, because the CDB loan was slow to be disbursed, the government paid commitment fees for an unusually extended period of time.

and individual Chinese migrants were increasingly active in galamsey mining. While exact numbers are uncertain, one Chinese newspaper estimated as many as 50,000 Chinese miners were engaging in galamsey mining in Ghana.[16] By 2013, Ghanaian public and media outcry over illegal Chinese mining had reached such a fever pitch that the government introduced a task force to address the issue and soon announced it had deported numerous Chinese miners who had been in the country illegally.

The Ghanaian government's relationship with China was severely strained by the galamsey controversy and the government sought to distance itself from reliance on Chinese resources. In July 2014, the government announced it would not be taking up the second half of its $3 billion loan from CDB, citing inability to reach an agreement with the Chinese creditor.[17] As one Ministry of Finance official put it when asked about different forms of finance, "I intentionally didn't mention China when you asked about new sources of financing ... no one is Father Christmas to be giving you money like that."[18]

As Chinese loans receded from Ghana's portfolio of external finance, private loans took on increasing importance. From 2013 to 2016, the government borrowed in international bond markets every year. In addition to pulling in international investment through dollar-denominated international bond issues, the Ghanaian government also attracted foreign investors into its domestic bond market. By 2017, foreign investors held 38.6 percent of Ghana's domestic currency debt.[19]

While officials stressed the appeal of large volumes of private finance for large-scale infrastructure investments, the flexibility of bond market finance also made it attractive for covering other gaps in the government's budget. As an advisor to the Ministry of Finance put it, "We're running a primary budget deficit, so it's not magic to see that Ghana is borrowing for consumption spending."[20] Government officials noted that bond market investors exercised little oversight of the exact uses of the money raised in sovereign bond issues, making these

---

[16] Crawford et al. 2015.
[17] Reuters 2014a.
[18] Interview 64. Ministry of Finance official. Accra, Ghana. April 21, 2017.
[19] Government of Ghana 2019b, p. 39.
[20] Interview 63. Ministry of Finance official. Accra, Ghana. April 20, 2017.

funds considerably more flexible than traditional donor resources. The advisor who assisted the Ministry of Finance with its bond issues commented, "You would think that investors care [about how funds are spent], wouldn't you? But they don't, they're just hunting yield. One of the nice things about the Eurobond markets is that no one polices your use of funds."[21]

Despite the Ghanaian government's preference for the flexibility of private finance, in the later years of this final period the government increasingly struggled to borrow in international markets at attractive interest rates, which in turn increased its dependence on traditional donors and lenders. The higher cost of borrowing in international markets was largely due to worsening global economic conditions. As an exporter of commodities, especially gold and cocoa, Ghana was hit hard by the decline in commodity prices in 2013 and 2014. Large budget deficits in 2013 exacerbated Ghana's economic woes, and in 2014 Ghana's cedi was the world's worst performing currency. Slumping commodity prices combined with global investor flight from emerging and frontier market debt after the 2013 "taper tantrum" to make borrowing in international markets increasingly expensive.

As the economic and currency crisis worsened and the cost of private finance increased, the Ghanaian government was again more reliant on traditional donors and development finance institutions. In 2015, Ghana issued a bond with a World Bank guarantee, relying on the World Bank's credibility to borrow in international markets, in exchange for commitments to a "fiscal and macroeconomic framework" approved by the World Bank.[22] Similarly, in 2015, the government agreed to an IMF program, concluding that it needed the resources of an IMF loan and the credibility of IMF-monitored reforms to regain market access. This episode highlights how Ghana's portfolio of external finance contracted once private finance became too expensive or unreliable.

At the tail end of the period under study, in 2017 and 2018, the NPP government elected in 2016 announced a policy that claimed to overturn the relationship with traditional donors. Under the heading of "Ghana Beyond Aid," Ghana's President Akufo-Addo announced

[21] Interview 63. Ministry of Finance official. Accra, Ghana. April 20, 2017.
[22] World Bank 2015a.

a vision to "build a Ghana that is prosperous enough to stand on its own two feet; a Ghana that is beyond dependence on the charity of others to cater for the needs of its people."[23] The stated aims of the policy were establishing a "national transformation agenda" and "reducing dependence on external aid, but not rejecting aid."[24] However, the initiative appeared to do little to change the relationship between the government and donors. For one, although "Ghana Beyond Aid" had been a campaign slogan in 2016, the main document explaining the policy was not released until 2019. More importantly, as Kumi explains, observers, donors among them, struggled to identify the concrete objectives of the policy, including how it would change relations with donors.[25] Donors shared the long-term vision of a prosperous and self-reliant Ghana and did not see Ghana Beyond Aid as a threat to their immediate influence in the country.

From the early 2000s to the late 2010s, there were four distinct phases in Ghana's access to external finance. First, a reliance on traditional donors for aid and debt relief. Then, after the turn to Chinese loans and international sovereign bonds, a greater diversity of lenders and reduced reliance on traditional donors. With income reclassification and newfound oil wealth, there was a moment when Ghana appeared to outgrow the need for traditional donor aid. Finally, beginning around 2013, Ghana moved into a period when economic difficulties and constraints on alternative finance increased Ghana's reliance on traditional donors yet again. These distinct phases invite consideration of how Ghana's negotiations with donors changed alongside the expansion and contraction of the country's portfolio of external finance.

7.3 Limited Debt-Based Financial Statecraft

Despite diversifying its portfolio of external finance, the Ghanaian government saw only limited increases in its negotiating leverage with traditional donors. When the government initially expanded its portfolio of external finance by borrowing from Chinese lenders, it managed to secure some early wins in negotiations with donors. However, as the

---

[23] Government of Ghana 2019a.
[24] Kumi 2020, p. 68.
[25] Kumi 2020.

government further increased its autonomy from traditional donors by borrowing repeatedly in international bond markets, relationships became more fraught and the government struggled to translate reduced dependence into greater leverage.

In analyzing the negotiations between the Ghanaian government and traditional donors, I focus on two issue areas that were particularly important for both sides. First, negotiations over the government's economic policy, including its approach to poverty reduction, economic development, and fiscal policy. Second, I trace government and donor negotiations over financial management, including the design of budgeting procedures and debt management. Though the two issue areas are closely related, the first covers substantive choices about the government's development policy while the second concerns the design of bureaucratic institutions that administer public funds.

Compared to aid negotiations in both Ethiopia and Kenya, governance and democratization were less contentious in Ghana. Since the transition to multiparty competition in the 1990s, Ghana's democratic institutions have shown themselves to be largely robust. Strengthening democratic institutions thus has not been a significant area of government–donor negotiation in Ghana, meaning that it is unlikely to shed much light on the relative influence of either party in negotiations. By contrast, bargaining over economic policy and financial management has involved greater disagreement between government and donors, therefore better revealing the extent to which the government was able to assert its preferences in negotiations.

7.3.1 Economic Policy

In negotiations over economic policy, the government and donors bargained over the design of poverty reduction and development programs, the speed and depth of liberalizing economic reforms, and where to prioritize public spending. Neither of the two major parties that have alternated in power since the 1990s, the NDC or the NPP, had fundamental disagreements with the overarching development approach underpinning donors' recommendations. Unlike in Ethiopia, disagreements over economic policy in Ghana were not foundational differences in economic orientation but rather struggles over the speed and scale of reforms or over the priorities of economic policy.

In the early 2000s, before Ghana received debt relief and first borrowed from alternative sources, the outcomes of negotiations over economic policy tended to reflect the policy proposals of donors. Negotiations were structured around the design of policies to satisfy World Bank and IMF requirements for debt forgiveness. As one official responsible for development planning explained, "the choices that were available to Ghana were limited at that time, because you are prescribed to respond to these things [the Highly Indebted Poor Countries (HIPC) Initiative]. In terms of negotiations, it tilted more towards donors, who were giving the relief."[26] Negotiations over Ghana's poverty reduction strategy, concluded in 2003, focused in large part on economic policy, including reforms to energy prices and government spending. The government and donors diverged on the pace of withdrawing fuel subsidies, with the government reluctant to commit to a rapid adjustment in the price of fuel, fearing the public response. The final agreement, however, included commitments to rapidly remove the subsidy.

Donors were able to exercise leverage in negotiations not only because of the importance of donor funds for the Ghanaian government's budget but also because of coordination among themselves. The MDBS mechanism, in which donors pool funds before contributing them to the government's budget, gave donors greater leverage over government policy. For instance, in 2005, the EU and bilateral donors decided to withhold a portion of their general budget support in response to the Ghanaian government's failure to meet targets on energy, payroll, and public sector reform.[27] The government's reliance on a small number of sources of finance thus increased donors' influence.

As Ghana diversified its portfolio of external finance in the late 2000s, the balance of influence in negotiations over economic policy began to shift. The development plans that formed the basis of donors' budget support and aid agreements during this period reflect the government's greater confidence in setting its own development priorities. For instance, Ghana's second poverty reduction strategy (GPRS II, 2006–2009) declares,

---

[26] Interview 105. National Development Planning Commission official. Accra, Ghana. September 27, 2013.
[27] Azeem et al. 2006.

> The nation must now aim for strategic objectives beyond the minimal goals of poverty reduction as envisaged under GPRS I ... It is essential for Ghana to dialogue freely with its development partners [donors] on these political/ideological issues so that the implementation of GPRS II is not obstructed by hidden political reservations.[28]

The development plan emphasizes infrastructure investment, the expansion of manufacturing, and moving beyond the "the economics of reconstruction and rehabilitation" that it associates with donors' focus on poverty reduction initiatives.[29] Reflecting on the negotiations, a government official explained, "our space to make choices on the policies was much stronger at the GPRS II than at the GPRS I, because we were not obliging to any specific [donor] requirements [for debt relief]."[30] Government officials involved in drafting the development plans of the late 2000s described how their negotiation tactics had changed. Rather than responding to drafts prepared by donors, as they had done in the debt relief negotiations, the government prepared its own policy proposals and reached internal agreement before presenting them to donors.

The greater alignment of economic policy with the government's preferences was at least partly a reflection of the government's greater choice of external finance and greater autonomy from traditional donor funds. In particular, Ghana's borrowing from alternative lenders raised donors' concerns about their access to and influence with the government. As one donor official explained, reflecting on the years in which Ghana borrowed from China, "I wouldn't say they [new creditors] were seen as a danger because there's enough potential here for projects to finance. What was concerning, of course, is that *we felt that we were no longer being taken as seriously as the new creditors*."[31] A government official described the government's deliberate efforts to signal greater autonomy and choice, saying, "Initially, in 2009 the posture of government was 'If we don't get what we want

---

[28] Government of Ghana 2005, p. iii.
[29] Government of Ghana 2005, p. iv.
[30] Interview 105. National Development Planning Commission official. Accra, Ghana. September 27, 2013.
[31] Interview 70. Bilateral donor official. Accra, Ghana. April 27, 2017. Emphasis added.

from you, we'll go to China' ... So, you could say that initially it was more threatening."[32]

Given the government's growing autonomy, donors were willing to be more flexible on aspects of economic policy to preserve their overall access to the government. Describing the late 2000s, a joint EU–World Bank evaluation notes,

> ... the tendency of the DPs [Development Partners, i.e. donors] has been to be *accommodating in the assessment of the scope and pace of country reform processes* largely due to their overall satisfaction with the open dialogue GoG [Government of Ghana] maintained with them during 2005–2010 and the positive evolutions Ghana experienced in a number of *areas particularly important for them* (e.g. democracy, freedom of expression, growth, poverty reduction).[33]

The donors' description of their flexibility on economic reform in exchange for "open dialogue" with the government on other important areas aligns with the expectation of the theoretical framework that donors will offer the government flexibility on some issues to preserve their access to and influence on other issues that matter to them.

The government's brief phase of greater negotiating leverage largely dissipated after the turning point in 2010 and 2011, when Ghana transitioned to lower-middle income status, began producing commercial quantities of oil, and increasingly relied on international bond market finance. The government began planning for the fact that the country's income reclassification would cause donors to withdraw their concessional development finance. One government official tasked with negotiations with multilateral donors explained how Ghana's access to concessional finance was reduced, saying, "Things changed in 2012, we went from grants to all loans, there was no blending phase. [Other c]ountries that are like Ghana in that they've transitioned [to lower-middle-income status], like Kenya and Uganda, they still get some grants, but we get only loans from the African Development Bank."[34] With financing from traditional donors becoming more expensive and less plentiful, the nonfinancial terms of traditional

[32] Interview 105. National Development Planning Commission official. Accra, Ghana. September 27, 2013.
[33] EU and World Bank 2017, 29, emphasis added.
[34] Interview 69. Ministry of Finance official. Accra, Ghana. April 25, 2017.

donors' aid also appeared less attractive. One government official contrasted the approach of traditional donors to that of private lenders, saying, "We are spoiled for choice now ... so the importance of the traditional donors has drastically decreased. They're no longer pleasing to us because of their paperwork and their small size."[35]

When Ghana experienced an economic crisis in 2013, negotiations over economic policy became more fraught. In these negotiations, donors were reluctant to satisfy the government's preferences, despite Ghana's diversified portfolio of external finance. In fact, donors' critical assessment of the government's uses of external finance made them less willing to meet the government's preferences. The government and donors each emphasized different causes of the crisis, leading to divergent proposals for recovery. The primary external driver of the crisis was a global downturn in commodity prices. Reliant on the export of gold, cocoa, and increasingly oil, Ghana was hit hard by the slowdown in the commodity boom that had fueled much of the country's growth in the preceding decade. At the same time, the government's spending decisions, especially increased public sector wages, placed further pressure on the economy. For several years before 2013, the government had planned to transition public sector workers to a new salary structure to harmonize civil servants' pay across ministries and departments. In the run-up to the 2012 election, the NDC government rushed to complete the change to salary structure. The recent oil discovery led public sector unions to bargain harder for salary increases during this process. After the reforms were completed, public sector wages ballooned to almost 10 percent of GDP and 72.3 percent of all tax revenues.[36]

While the government pointed to external shocks, such as the end of the commodity supercycle, the associated reduction in foreign exchange earnings, a drought and the related energy crisis, donors saw the economic crisis as arising from government mismanagement. Bolstered by its access to non-aid financing, the government hoped to weather the storm alone, and especially without an IMF program. The government developed what it called a "home-grown" fiscal consolidation program that emphasized increasing tax collection to narrow the

---

[35] Interview 65. Government official. Accra, Ghana. April 21, 2017.
[36] Public Finance Focus 2013; Younger 2016.

deficit.[37] Explaining the government's desire to avoid an IMF program, a former Deputy Finance Minister said, "The IMF doesn't say things we don't already know. We think we are better off without them ... I did my PhD in economics, do I need these young IMF staffers coming to tell me to lower the deficit, lower inflation? Everyone knows it's better to have lower deficits, lower inflation."[38]

By contrast, donors expected the government to enact sharper reforms to close the fiscal deficit under the guidance of an IMF program. Most donors maintained that since the crisis was born out of government mismanagement, the government did not have sufficient credibility to return the economy to macroeconomic stability. Donors attempted to use their influence to persuade the government to adjust its economic policies and adopt an IMF program. Those donors contributing to the MDBS arrangement withheld their aid funds in 2013, and again in 2014, refusing to disburse funds to the government until it agreed to an IMF program. Donors persisted, despite the government's resistance; as one donor official recollected, "... there was a lot of frustration from the government when the macroeconomic condition worsened, when they thought we [donors] were overly demanding."[39] Another donor official echoed this view, saying, "Relations were tough because they saw us as withdrawing when they needed us most."[40]

With donors encouraging the government to pursue an IMF program and the government preferring its "home-grown" policies, the two sides were at odds. In 2013 and 2014, the government issued almost $2 billion in international bonds and had not yet used the entirety of its $3 billion loan package from the China Development Bank. Nevertheless, donors held firm, and the MDBS withheld its disbursements.

Soon thereafter, the government's access to Chinese finance waned and worsening economic conditions made it harder for the government to tap international bond markets. After this turning point in late 2014, donors exercised greater influence in negotiations. In early 2015, the Ghanaian government agreed to an Extended Credit Facility with the IMF. For the government, the program not only carried

[37] Government of Ghana 2016, p. 5.
[38] Interview 59. Parliamentary official. Accra, Ghana. April 7, 2017.
[39] Interview 71. Bilateral donor official. Accra, Ghana. April 27, 2017.
[40] Interview 85. Multilateral donor official. Accra, Ghana. May 4, 2017.

the stigma of an agreement with the IMF that it had tried to avoid for two years but also the requirement to commit to fiscal consolidation beyond its "homegrown" program, especially on public sector employment. Donors aligned their aid with the IMF program, rewarding the government for satisfying the conditions of the loan.

The contraction in Ghana's portfolio of external finance was decisive in this shift to greater donor influence. The government's public cancellation of the second half of the $3 billion CDB loan in 2014 satisfied domestic constituencies worried about the government's relationship with China, but it also signaled that the government could no longer rely on large volumes of Chinese finance as an alternative funding source. In 2013, a government official described how the government's slow turn away from Chinese finance had affected the "balance of negotiations" with traditional donors, noting,

China coming on board … strengthened government's position … between 2009 and 2012 I would say that the balance of negotiations were stronger on the side of Ghana. However, what we have seen beginning to happen now in 2013 is the *balance turning a bit back to the middle*, in the sense that there have been some frustrations in terms of what is expected to come from China.[41]

Donor officials noticed the changes in the government's relationship with China, which they linked to an increase in their own importance to the government. A donor representative observed in 2013 that the viability of Chinese loans as an alternative funding source was waning, saying, "Their negotiating position looks a bit strong on the surface, yes [they can say] 'we have these alternatives,' but these alternatives don't seem always to be as solid as what they would like to convey to us."[42] A donor official cited in MacCarthy's 2016 study on development finance in Ghana uses the analogy of a straying lover to describe the government's renewed reliance on traditional donors after its "dalliance" with China, saying "GoG [Government of Ghana] was forced to go back to its old well-known boyfriend that it [had] deserted."[43] The use of this strange parallel to describe the donor–government

---

[41] Interview 105. National Development Planning Commission official. Accra, Ghana. September 27, 2013. Emphasis added.

[42] Interview 112. Donor official. Accra, Ghana. October 7, 2013.

[43] MacCarthy 2016, p. 51.

relationship highlights how Chinese finance had the potential to be
a competitor, but since the government did not further pursue Chinese
loans in response to domestic criticism, there was less pressure on traditional donors to accommodate government preferences or face losing
out to greater Chinese influence.

Ghana's bargaining position was worsened by its difficulties in tap-
ping private market funds, which further limited its outside options.
While the government had been able to borrow relatively cheaply in
2013 and 2014 even as donors sounded the alarm about the country's macroeconomic conditions, by 2015 indications from secondary
bond markets showed that Ghana would struggle to issue additional
sovereign debt. Ultimately, Ghana returned to bond markets in 2015,
but only with a partial guarantee from the World Bank. The World
Bank guaranteed up to $400 million of the $1 billion bond in exchange
for Ghana's commitment to policy measures intended to ensure fiscal
and macroeconomic stability. In this final phase, Ghana found itself
more reliant on traditional donors for access to concessional finance
and for the credibility and backing to return to international markets.

Even as bargaining influence over economic policy shifted toward
donors' interests from the mid 2010s onward, the Ghanaian government achieved some outcomes in aid agreements with donors that
were more closely aligned with their interests. These partial successes
appeared to be due to lingering effects from the high point in the
diversification of Ghana's portfolio of finance, with projects that were
initiated in the early 2010s being implemented several years later, as
well as the overall effects of Ghana's declining aid dependence.

One project that reflects Ghana's partial negotiating influence during
this time was the World Bank's support for a natural gas processing
plant in Sankofa. This project closely followed Ghana's 2010 loan
from the China Development Bank, which the government partly used
to fund a gas processing plant that opened in 2015. The government emphasized that domestically processing offshore gas deposits
was a strategic priority and promised that the project would minimize
the energy shortages that plunged Ghana into regular blackouts.[44] In
2015, the World Bank announced it would provide a $700 million
financing guarantee to support the construction of a separate natural
gas plant.

[44] Odoom 2017.

The guarantee structure meant that although the project still underwent environmental review, it would not be held up by gradual release of conditional funding tranches. The World Bank thus not only satisfied the government's interest in energy projects but also desire for rapid access to funds. An official from the World Bank explained that the Bank wanted to offer Ghana a creative solution to continue to play a role in conversations about the energy sector, "The Bank was also thinking, *how much do we really bring to the table? ...* The least we can do is help the country to access markets."[45] Reflecting on the Sankofa gas project, an advisor to the government noted that the project was a response to the rapidity and flexibility of market finance, "I think DPs realize they are at a competitive disadvantage with the speed that African countries are going to the market ... I sense that DPs are trying to streamline their operations."[46]

The outcome of debt-based financial statecraft on economic policy was uneven. The government secured some early wins, as one of the first countries in sub-Saharan Africa to substantially diversify its portfolio of external finance, borrowing from China and private markets. In later years, donors were less accommodating in response to the government's reduced dependence, becoming less flexible on issues of economic policy, even as some donors funded priority projects.

7.3.2 Financial Management

In government–donor negotiations over financial management, outcomes followed a similar arc as in the case of economic policy. Early aid agreements on financial management issues that were reached prior to Ghana's diversification of external finance reflected the priorities of donors, especially upgrading budgeting processes. While Ghana gained some flexibility to define financial management priorities when it gained access to alternative finance, especially in debt management, the government largely struggled to use its greater autonomy from donor funds to push for aid programs that aligned with its preferences on financial management. Ultimately, donors were successful

[45] Interview 81. Multilateral donor official. Accra, Ghana. May 3, 2017. Emphasis added.
[46] Interview 63. Ministry of Finance official. Accra, Ghana. April 20, 2017.

in encouraging financial management reforms they saw as preventing future crises like the one that beset the country in 2013.

Early phases of government–donor negotiations over financial management were heavily shaped by the Ghanaian government's reliance on traditional donor funds. From 1997 to 2003, the UK, Canada, the EU, and the World Bank supported the Public Financial Management Reform Program, a wide-ranging regulatory reform that planned to overhaul Ghana's budgeting, cashflow management, procurement, and payroll.

Donors not only hoped that improving government systems for managing funds would encourage fiscal discipline and support economic development but also that it would safeguard their own funds. By 2004, donors transferred more than a quarter of their aid to Ghana as budget support, directly into the government budget.[47] With so much of their aid passing directly into the control of the Ghanaian government, donors sought assurances that budgeting and payments systems were sound. Between 1998 and 2010, the UK, Canada, Germany, the World Bank, and the EU spent more than $50 million on public financial management reform efforts in Ghana.[48] Donors were willing to use their influence to insist the government follow through on its commitments to improve financial management processes. In 2006, donors in the MDBS withheld aid in part because of the government's delays in implementing public financial reforms.

Despite the large volumes of aid that donors allocated to financial management reforms, these programs did not meet their intended targets. Independent evaluations of the aid programs to reform Ghana's public finance systems found they had not been fully implemented, largely because the reforms did not really align with government preferences.[49] While the government was lukewarm about the financial management reforms, especially the speed at which new technology for overseeing government payments was rolled out to ministries and departments, the government's reliance on traditional donor funds made it difficult to influence the outcomes of negotiations. As a 2005 evaluation of donor-funded financial management reforms notes, "[t]here must be a temptation for government officials to accept

[47] Betley et al. 2012, p. 29.
[48] Betley et al. 2012, p. 28.
[49] Betley et al. 2012; Wynne 2005.

somewhat uncritically the recommendations provided by the international financial institutions, as a condition for receiving much needed international assistance and debt relief."[50]

A shift in negotiation outcomes came after the turning point at which Ghana increased its financing options. After Ghana diversified its portfolio of finance in 2007 and gained greater autonomy from traditional donors, negotiation outcomes on financial management and procedural conditions more closely reflected the government's interests. In the late 2000s, the government introduced an initiative to emphasize *donors' responsibility* for financial management, especially the predictability and consistency of donors' aid disbursements. In 2010, the government hired an external consultant to compile indicators to monitor donors' behavior, including the predictability of aid transfers.[51] Government officials saw this "Donor Performance Assessment Framework" as a way to push back against the policy conditions attached to donor aid, as one former Ministry of Finance official explained,

I think DPs, the last two years, I think that they are pushing less policy conditions because we made so much fuss about it. I think it's when we said 'Ok, we're going to come up with a Performance Assessment Framework (PAF) to assess you DPs and your performance'. ... [We said,] 'I'll give you the same amount of flexibility that you give me!'[52]

Government officials described that during this period, after the government increasingly borrowed from alternative creditors, donors reduced the number of policy conditions for disbursement of MDBS aid, giving the government greater flexibility in a number of areas, including financial management.

However, as donors attached less value to their relationship with the government and became more concerned about its credibility, negotiations over financial management again became more fraught. In particular, donors were concerned that alternative credit with few procedural requirements could undercut efforts to improve budgeting and procurement systems. One donor official noted, "External finance has played a direct role in the economic management flaws and slippage

---

[50] Wynne 2005, pp. 27–28.
[51] Gerster 2010.
[52] Interview 118. Former Ministry of Finance official. Accra, Ghana. October 9, 2013. Emphasis added.

... If the money is available, Ghana will find a way to spend it."[53] For their part, government officials saw donors' focus on financial management as a technical issue best left to the government. If anything, the aspect of financial management where government officials most wanted outside support was in developing the debt management office, increasing debt managers' sophistication in communicating with investors and in managing the maturity profile of outstanding debt. Even so, government officials often found technical assistance on financial management tedious to implement, coming in the form of small aid programs with many conditions to satisfy. One Ministry of Finance bureaucrat described the thinking of senior officials, recalling, "I was in a meeting with my Director recently and he asked how much the [donor-funded] project would be bringing in. It was 5 million euros, and he said, 'You want me to do what for those 5 million? Don't make me go through hoops when I can pull in $1 billion with a couple of investors'."[54]

After the final turning point in the mid 2010s, when Ghana's access to alternative finance dried up and the country became yet again more reliant on the concessional finance of traditional donors, the pendulum of influence swung back toward donors. In 2015, when the government finally agreed to an IMF program, it also signed an agreement with the World Bank for a Public Financial Management Reform project for improving "budget management, financial control and reporting."[55] Bureaucrats in Ghana's Ministry of Finance described the program as largely designed by the World Bank, reflecting the Bank's concerns about Ghana's budgeting and spending systems. In reflecting on the 2016 election, a World Bank official explained,

> The concern for everybody has been the cycle of debt accumulation before, during and after elections. There was hope that this wouldn't happen in 2016 because of the IMF program, but those of us who have been here for years knew it was going to happen and that's what happened ... that tells you the weakness of the systems in place. That's why the Bank is supporting PFM [public financial management].[56]

---

[53] Interview 61. Bilateral donor official. Accra, Ghana. April 20, 2017.
[54] Interview 78. Government official. Accra, Ghana. May 2, 2017.
[55] World Bank 2015c, p. 7.
[56] Interview 81. Multilateral donor official. Accra, Ghana. May 3, 2017.

Officials in the Ministry's debt management division commented that while the program had been useful for accessing funds from the World Bank, it did not reflect what the debt management division saw as the most important areas for improvement, such as managing the maturity and timelines of outstanding debt.

In the sphere of financial management, the government was unable to use its access to alternative finance to achieve its preferred outcome. Not only was the government unable to shift donors' attention away from public financial management to its own priorities, government respondents also described difficulties in negotiating aid programs for public financial management that aligned with the government's preferences.

7.4 What Was behind Ghana's Difficulties?

For a country that has long enjoyed favorable relations with traditional donors and that diversified its portfolio of external finance, Ghana's difficulty in using new external finance as a source of leverage might initially come as a surprise. The waxing and waning of Ghana's borrowing from external creditors partly explain the patterns of negotiation outcomes with traditional donors. When alternative finance was more plentiful, in the late 2000s, the government secured some wins in aid negotiations. As the range of alternative finance narrowed to largely private-market financing, and the latter became more expensive, donors faced less pressure to accommodate the government's preferences.

The explanation for Ghana's difficulties with financial statecraft also lies with donors' declining interest in their relationship with the government and donors' concerns about the government's credibility. The value donors attached to their relationship with the government diminished with the crisis, making them less willing to compromise in response to the government's greater autonomy. Moreover, donors' declining trust in the government hampered Ghana's efforts at debt-based financial statecraft. Donors feared that unsustainable, election-related borrowing would put their own repayment at risk and deepen the country's economic crisis. Their critical assessment of the government's borrowing in light of Ghana's political economy made donors more likely to harden their stance than to accommodate the government's preferences.

In Ghana's case, the two moderating factors of importance to donors and donor trust were more closely related than in the other two cases. Since donors have historically valued the relationship with the Ghanaian government in large part because of their faith in Ghana's institutions and policy reforms, their declining trust also led to a declining value of relationship. While donors still had faith in Ghana's democratic institutions, they worried about public financial management and the reliability of Ghana's budgeting commitments, in aid agreements and elsewhere. Kenya's significance to donors was separate from donors' trust in financial management, since that significance was largely driven by Kenya's importance geopolitical to donors, but for Ghana these two were linked. This made it harder for the Ghanaian government to leverage its diversified portfolio of external finance once donors hardened their assessment of the country's financial management.

7.4.1 Ghana's Waning Significance to Donors

For donors in Ghana, the value of their relationship with the government has rested on the country's robust governance institutions and credibility in implementing economic reforms. Historically, traditional donors have seen Ghana as a reliable reformer and a democratic exemplar. The quality of Ghana's governance institutions continued to earn donors' admiration, but in the 2010s, the transition to lower-middle-income status, the government's handling of its newfound oil wealth, and the economic crisis undermined donors' perception of the government's economic credibility. As this aspect of the government's value to donors faded, donors had less reason to accommodate the Ghanaian government's preferences to preserve the overall relationship. This waning of Ghana's significance to donors thus helps explain why Ghana struggled to translate alternative finance into greater negotiating leverage.

On matters of democracy and governance, Ghana's 1992 transition to democracy and subsequent consolidation of peaceful elections were attractive for donors for whom democratization is an important component of their aid. When asked to explain their interest in development cooperation in Ghana, almost all representatives of traditional donor agencies pointed to the country's democratic track record. One donor representative suggested that democracy is a "ticket" Ghana can use to its advantage, saying "DPs love Ghana, largely because of democracy. That's the big ticket Ghana has, democracy ... Also, their elections are not violent."[57] Another donor explained how democratic institutions impacted the relationship between the government and donors, saying, "Ghana is a country that people [in the donor community] look to, that they expect to do well, given its democracy. There is a sense that we need to make things go well in Ghana."[58]

Similarly, Ghana's approach to economic policy had long made it an attractive counterpart for donors that could be expected to "deliver" development policy. In the 1980s, Ghana's military government under Jerry Rawlings' Provisional National Defense Council (PNDC) surprised observers with its comprehensive embrace of IMF-recommended structural adjustment reforms, privatizing state-owned enterprises, liberalizing trade, and removing subsidies.[59] Ghana's reputation as a quick reformer gave the country access to considerable resources from the IMF and the World Bank. As Herbst notes about the Ghanaian experience, "The lesson for African countries is that it is important to be the second or third fastest reformer rather than the twentieth. In a world where countries increasingly compete on the basis of economic reform, those African countries that act quickest will naturally be better off."[60] This reputation persisted beyond the structural adjustment era and into the twenty-first century. One donor official explained how this dynamic had encouraged donors to be lenient with the government in the run-up to the 2013 crisis, saying, "Ghana has stood out in the region. DPs also need to hold someone up as a star, need to show someone as an example of success in the region, and who [else] are you going to pick as an example?"[61]

Nevertheless, by the 2010s, donors' perception of Ghana as a "star" of economic policy had been severely dampened by the country's handling of oil resources and the 2013 economic crisis. Traditional donors, especially the US, were concerned about Ghana's management of oil. In 2010, the Ghanaian government blocked a US company from selling its stake in an oil field to ExxonMobil, wanting Ghana's national oil

[57] Interview 55. Multilateral donor official. Accra, Ghana. April 4, 2017.
[58] Interview 57. Multilateral donor official. Accra, Ghana. April 6, 2017.
[59] Nugent 1996.
[60] Herbst 1993, p. 133.
[61] Interview 85. Multilateral donor official. Accra, Ghana. May 4, 2017.

company to have a right of first refusal in the sale, which was not guaranteed by the initial license. Though the dispute was resolved within a year, the uncertainty created by the conflict undermined "confidence in the continuity of stable and attractive investment environments" in Ghana.[62] Moreover, donors worried about the corrosive effects of the oil revenues on development policy, linking the government's expectation of incoming oil resources to worsening fiscal and monetary discipline.[63] The crisis of 2013 appeared to confirm donors' worst suspicions. In the 2012 election year, the government had a large number of unbudgeted and unplanned expenses, in part driven by rising expectations of the country's oil wealth.

The events undercut donors' confidence in the government, leading donors to see Ghana as a less reliable partner for implementation of economic policy. As one donor representative put it, "You have to distinguish between governance and economic management in making the judgment ... if Ghana is a 'high performer' ... The idea of Ghana as a rising star of West Africa has suffered a bit in the context of the economic crisis."[64] To make matters worse for the Ghanaian government, most donors saw the 2013 crisis not as an anomaly but rather as the culmination of a trend. Another donor official described the perceived weakening of economic management as follows: "... sliding down on the governance slope has been happening in Ghana for a while, but it has been much more felt recently."[65] Ghana's performance on the World Bank's Public Expenditure and Financial Accountability (PEFA) assessment worsened from 2006 to 2013. While in 2006, the country scored the lowest grade on only 16 percent of the budgeting indicators; by 2013, that percentage had increased to 25 percent.[66]

As Ghana's value as an exemplar of economic policy subsided, donors placed less of a priority on their overall relationship with the government. Government officials observed the change in donors' attitudes. An official from the Ministry of Finance noted a decline in the competence and seniority of World Bank staff posted to Ghana, which Ministry staff interpreted as a sign of the World Bank's diminished

---

[62] Phillips et al. 2016, p. 32.
[63] Bawumia and Halland 2017.
[64] Interview 70. Bilateral donor official. Accra, Ghana. April 27, 2017.
[65] Interview 60. Bilateral donor official. Accra, Ghana. April 19, 2017.
[66] Government of Ghana 2013; World Bank 2006a.

interest in the relationship with the government, "We can also see how important we are to the Bank by the quality of the staff they send here, who the TTLs [task team leaders] are. Under the last government [NDC, 2009–2017], the quality of the TTLs sent to Ghana has declined, as the importance of Ghana diminished and the quality of the relationship declined."[67]

Some donors were more affected by Ghana's economic performance than others. Those donors that had provided the largest volumes of aid and invested most directly in Ghana's development performance were most dissatisfied by what they saw as economic mismanagement. The UK, for instance, was one of the top three donors in Ghana throughout the 1990s to the 2010s, also channeling large portions of its assistance into budget support, in some years transferring 85 percent of its aid directly to the Ghanaian government's budget.[68] As such, the UK had been particularly committed to Ghana's economic performance and was among the most affected by the country's 2013 crisis, joining the pressure on the government to adopt an IMF program. One member of the donor community observed how the UK's engagement with the Ghanaian government changed over the course of the crisis, noting "The UK is very good at leveraging in international institutions, advancing the interests of these countries [including Ghana] ... But now, the UK is very rough, very hard on Ghana, more demanding than they used to be."[69] Compounded by Ghana's transition to middle-income status, the crisis weakened the relationship between the UK and the Ghanaian government. In 2016–2017, the UK reduced its in-country staff in Ghana and over the following years progressively cut its aid allocations to the country.[70]

Several bilateral donors justified the declining importance of Ghana in their aid portfolio with reference to Ghana's economic reclassification, explaining that aid resources were to be reserved for poorer developing countries. However, even those donors acknowledged that the selection of priority countries was rarely purely a function of recipient country income but reflected a broader set of donor interests. For instance, one donor official noted that though Ghana and Kenya are

---

[67] Interview 64. Government official. Accra, Ghana. April 21, 2017.
[68] EU and World Bank 2017.
[69] Interview 83. Bilateral donor official. Accra, Ghana. April 4, 2017.
[70] Independent Commission for Aid Impact 2020.

both lower-middle-income countries, his country had not reduced its footprint in Kenya.[71]

The demotion of Ghana's status with donors came from a confluence of factors. Many bilateral donor agencies faced budget cuts in the 2010s, as the aftermath of the global financial crisis led advanced economies to reduce spending on foreign aid. These agencies needed to prioritize among recipient countries, and Ghana's new income status and oil wealth made it less of a priority for donors seeking to target the least-developed countries. In his analysis of Ghana's relationship with the IMF and other external creditors, Gunu argues that Ghana had diminished in importance for traditional donors from 2010 onward, when its lower-middle-income classification made it harder for donors on tight budgets to justify prioritizing the relationship with the country.[72] Moreover, since Ghana's significance to donors had historically been driven partly by its development performance, the economic crisis and perceived weaknesses in development policy dampened donors' enthusiasm for maintaining a close relationship. While Ghana's democratic institutions continued to attract respect and donor approval, part of Ghana's symbolic appeal had been diminished.

Ghana's experience sheds some light on the limits of a country's "donor darling" status. While Kenya and Ethiopia's value to traditional donors was more closely tied to the geopolitical context – such as conflicts in neighboring states or hosting refugees – Ghana's status with donors was largely based on donors' perception of the country's commitment to reform. When the donor community's perception shifted, the government's negotiation leverage also ebbed.

7.4.2 Limited Donor Trust in Ghana's Government

In Ghana's case, more so than in Kenya or Ethiopia, donor trust and the value donors attached to the relationship with the government were more closely related, since Ghana's importance had largely come from its past development performance. Donors had considerable trust in Ghana's political institutions, confident that elections were credible and policy legitimate. For a long time, this faith in Ghana's political institutions and the relative performance of Ghana's

---

[71] Interview 60. Bilateral donor official. Accra, Ghana. April 19, 2017.
[72] Gunu 2023.

development policy encouraged donors to trust Ghana's institutions more broadly, which explains donors' willingness to pool their aid resources in the MDBS starting in the early 2000s. With the discovery of oil and increased private-market borrowing, however, donors became more concerned about the government's pattern of spending, worried that this would imperil debt sustainability and perhaps put their own projects at risk. Donors' doubts about the government's credibility were two-fold. First, donors distrusted the government's own budgeting. Second, donors distrusted that the government was committed to implementing aid agreements as negotiated.

When it came to Ghana's budgetary process, donors had long-standing concerns about the reliability of the government's spending plans. In 2005, a development think tank described Ghana's budgetary process as a "façade" and "so weak as to be essentially ritualistic."[73] Donors' worries about the financial management institutions had a greater impact on aid negotiations once the government gained access to alternative finance. Now, with the government able to tap into a wide range of funding, donors saw the weakness of the government's budgetary commitments as a greater risk. As one donor official put it, echoing the appraisal of the think tank a decade earlier, "The budget is a fiction. They [the government] will end up spending what they are able to raise."[74] What had changed by the mid 2010s was that the government was "spending what they are able to raise" and raising considerably more finance than they had been earlier.

Donor representatives emphasized that while Ghana performed better than many other countries in sub-Saharan Africa on financial management, it often failed to meet the expectations of the broader donor community. As one donor official explained, "Look, on the evidence we have, Ghana is not a catastrophe. But those indices are also about perception, and the perception is that corruption is a serious problem [in Ghana]."[75] Another donor official contrasted the assessments of staff working in-country with the prevailing views in the capital, saying

---

[73] Killick 2005.
[74] Interview 61. Bilateral donor official. Accra, Ghana. April 20, 2017.
[75] Interview 60. Bilateral donor official. Accra, Ghana. April 19, 2017.

I had come to Ghana with high expectations, but as soon as I looked into the figures [on economic management], it became clear that it's actually quite disappointing ... Our High Commissioner, he arrived around the same time as me, and he's quite vocal on Ghana: he tweets a lot, he's often in the press etc., and it took him about two weeks to change his opinion. But the perception of Ghana as donor darling has somewhat lingered at headquarters.[76]

These donor officials working in-country were the ones tasked with regular negotiations with the government, and their lack of trust led to the tense negotiations around the demise of the MDBS and donors' insistence on more stringent economic conditions during the crisis.

Donors understood the credibility issues of financial institutions primarily in terms of electoral budget cycles, which they attributed to the circumstances of political competition. Although donors often mentioned the need to improve bureaucratic institutions, they noted that the true drivers of cyclical spending were pressures for distribution. A donor official summarized the assessment of Ghana's spending as follows, "You can look at the patterns of slippages in election years and could say that there is something fundamental in the political economy of Ghana."[77] As another donor official put it, "Ghana has this cycle of significant overexpenditure coinciding with the political cycle ... Some will say this is because the elections in Ghana are very close, so the additional expenditure in the lead-up to the elections is in order to attract voters."[78] One multilateral donor official who had worked in Ghana for a long time explained how the regular cycle had seemed worse in 2013, because the incumbent had been reelected and had few incentives to course correct after the election:

There's a cycle related to the political cycle. You have stability and then in the fourth year you have a hike in the fiscal deficit, in borrowing and arrears. And then, after the election, the government cleans up. What had kept the [donors'] budget support going [in earlier years] was that after elections the government always said 'we want to clean up.' [But,] 2013 was different because it was the same situation in terms of an election year, but to add to

---

[76] Interview 61. Donor official. Accra, Ghana. April 20, 2017.
[77] Interview 56. Multilateral donor official. Washington D.C. March 16, 2017.
[78] Interview 80. Multilateral donor official. Accra, Ghana. May 2, 2017.

the political economy, it was the same administration and they didn't want to shoot themselves in the foot and admit there was a problem.[79]

Donors thus had long observed how political dynamics in Ghana had weakened the credibility of the government's spending commitments. In 2013 and 2014, negotiations between the government and donors became more fraught, with donors less willing to meet the government's preferences on economic management, because their trust in government institutions was steadily declining and alternative finance was seen as compounding the problem.

Donors' trust did not recover much with the change in government in 2016, though some donors appreciated the NPP's emphasis on fiscal discipline. Nevertheless, most donor officials suggested that the fundamental pattern was unlikely to change. Multiple donor officials commented on the number of ministers and deputy ministers in the cabinet, which they saw as evidence of continued political and regional pressures for distribution, which would undermine the credibility of the budget. One donor official described the process as follows:

The Minister of Finance has had a situation where the budget is set and then people will go directly to the President to ask for financing. Executive strength and executive discipline is missing ... This [NPP] government [elected in 2016] will also struggle with this because they have so many ministers and each of them promises something and then they will go to the Finance Minister and pressure.[80]

Another noted, "It's a winner takes all system. You win the election, and the Parliament, and then you've got people to pay off. There are 110 Ministers and Deputy Ministers in this parliament."[81] A third donor official explicitly connected the spending pressures to the breadth of the winning coalition that needed to be kept together, saying, "They've got 110 ministers in this administration ... it's obvious patronage, but they have no choice. The NPP are traditionally an Ashanti party, but the President isn't Ashanti, nor is the Minister of Finance or the Vice President, so they need to cover those bases from

---

[79] Interview 93. Multilateral donor official. Accra, Ghana. May 8, 2017.
[80] Interview 71. Bilateral donor official. Accra, Ghana. April 27, 2017.
[81] Interview 62. Bilateral donor official. Accra, Ghana. April 20, 2017.

the loyal heartland elsewhere."[82] For many donor officials, who were closely following Ghanaian electoral politics, distrust in the government's financial management came from their assessment of repeated cycles of election-related spending.

Donors' concerns about the credibility of the government's spending commitments made them less willing to meet the government's wishes for flexibility, even as the government diversified its sources of finance. A donor official explained the reasons for the donor community's responses to the 2013 crisis, saying, "They [the government] had to fund their election promises in 2012. The single spine salary structure was very expensive ... This then also *led donors to tighten their conditions and become more demanding.*"[83] Rather than enhancing the government's bargaining leverage, alternative finance instead combined with the domestic political context to raise donors' concerns about financial sustainability and the risks of indebtedness. A donor representative explained, "External finance has played a direct role in the economic management flaws and slippage."[84]

Donors not only worried about the credibility of the government's commitments to its own budget but also to aid agreements concluded with donors. Donors perceived the government, especially the NDC administration in power 2012–2016, to be less likely to follow through on their commitments in aid agreements. A donor official explained that the hardening of donors' negotiating positions on public financial management came from concerns about the government's dedication to policy reforms, saying "On PFM [public financial management], we all took a step back because we knew they weren't serious in their commitment."[85] Another donor official indicated that doubts about the government's commitments were even broader, saying, "Towards the end of the past administration [the NDC administration ending in 2017], it got to the time were there was very little engagement, if any."[86] One multilateral donor official explained the perception that the government's commitments in an agreement did not

[82] Interview 61. Donor official. Accra, Ghana. April 20, 2017.
[83] Interview 71. Bilateral donor official. Accra, Ghana. April 27, 2017. Emphasis added.
[84] Interview 61. Donor official. Accra, Ghana. April 20, 2017.
[85] Interview 85. Multilateral donor official. Accra, Ghana. May 4, 2017.
[86] Interview 71. Bilateral donor official. Accra, Ghana. April 27, 2017.

necessarily lead to implementation, saying, "in some cases this may happen because the government has other priorities ... there may be discontinuities between what they agree to and what they're actually willing to do six months down the line."[87]

Donors' concerns that aid agreements would not be upheld were compounded by their perception that the government did not to take ownership of development finance agreements but instead allowed donors to set the priorities. Many donors perceived that the political pressures the government was under to distribute resources meant that the government did not scrutinize aid agreements carefully or align them with government priorities. While this might appear to be to donors' advantage, giving them the space to pursue their own priorities in the agreement, it instead caused donors to worry whether projects would be fully implemented, if the government had not taken the lead on designing projects. One donor official described the discussions as follows, "Often we ask them 'which do you want?' and then they pick. We propose projects and they choose."[88] A multilateral donor representative explained that across developing countries, governments' development plans often seemed to be designed to attract donor funds, rather than representing a genuine government commitment. While he suggested this practice was less pronounced in Ghana than elsewhere, he indicated this dynamic also undermined donors' confidence in Ghana's plans, saying, "part of that is also reflective of demands from DPs ... you know, 'I'd like to give money for the health sector, but I don't see a plan' ... a lot of these [plans] are modalities for attracting funding. In a lot of these countries, I'm not necessarily saying that's the case in Ghana, it's polite mimicry, often this is not really owned by the government."[89]

This lack of clear priority projects corresponds to conclusions that other scholars have reached about Ghana's approach to development policy. Observers of Ghanaian politics have noted that the competitive political environment shortens politicians' time horizons and impedes long-term strategic planning in a range of policy areas. As Whitfield puts it, "Ghanaian governments prioritized the requirements of their political survival over economic growth, and because ruling political

---

[87] Interview 80. Multilateral donor official. Accra, Ghana. May 2, 2017.
[88] Interview 62. Bilateral donor official. Accra, Ghana. April 20, 2017.
[89] Interview 80. Multilateral donor official. Accra, Ghana. May 2, 2017.

elites had short time horizons, their political survival strategy included distributive, consumption-driven expenditures that ended up depleting the wealth of the country without reproducing it."[90] Ansu explains that the political cycles have undermined the capacity for strategic planning in the public sector, observing "State capacity in Ghana is generally weak. The main reason for this is not the lack of competent Ghanaians or poor remuneration. In large part, it is due to a partisan political environment that produces a large turnover of senior staff and technocrats whenever governments change."[91] Just as successive Ghanaian governments have found it difficult to implement investment or industrial policy plans, so they found it difficult to prioritize in negotiations with donors.

All in all, donors' distrust in the government's budgeting process and commitment to aid agreements undermined the bargaining leverage the Ghanaian government might otherwise have extracted from its diversified portfolio of external finance. Donors had observed electoral budget cycles for a long time, but during the crisis in 2013 and 2014, their distrust increased. Ghana's new oil revenues raised concerns about a "resource curse," and the country's access to alternative external finance actually heightened donors' worries that aid agreements would not be upheld. In particular, donors were apprehensive that they had provided debt relief just a decade earlier and now observed a renewed accumulation of debt, with one donor official commenting, "You imagine a country that has just been bailed out by HIPC and suddenly they're on a path where spending is increasing."[92] As I discuss in the conclusion of this book, those fears about a debt crisis would come to pass after the COVID-19 pandemic. In the negotiations during the time period covered by this analysis, the impact of those concerns was to make donors more wary of extending flexibility to the government, leading to negotiation outcomes that were less aligned with the government's preferences.

7.5 Conclusion

In a simple bargaining framework, Ghana's access to outside options should have led directly to a stronger negotiating position and

---

[90] Whitfield 2018, p. 10.
[91] Ansu 2013, p. 512.
[92] Interview 80. Multilateral donor official. Accra, Ghana. May 2, 2017.

increased the likelihood of negotiation outcomes aligned with the Ghanaian government's preferences. In practice, however, decreased dependence on traditional donors did not consistently increase the negotiating power of the Ghanaian government vis-à-vis traditional donors and did not always enable the government to achieve preferred negotiation outcomes.

In Ghana, the necessary conditions failed to align, and the government struggled to translate Chinese loans and bond market access into preferred aid agreements on economic policy or financial management. Ghana's importance to traditional donors had rested on the symbolic significance of the country as a "success story" of economic reforms. When the economic crisis of 2013 undermined this narrative of Ghana's success, some donors also reassessed the value of an accommodating stance toward the government, and introduced firmer conditions rather than meet the government's requests for flexibility. The crisis also undercut donors' trust in the credibility of the government's commitments. Donors had long worried that domestic political exigencies would lead the government to deviate from spending plans and aid agreements, but with the rise of alternative finance, donors became more concerned about debt sustainability and the viability of their own development programs. Concerned about the moral hazard of flexible commercial debt, traditional donors were unwilling to make accommodations and instead adopted a tougher stance on issues of economic policy and financial management.

The Ghanaian case demonstrates the conditional nature of the financial statecraft of borrowers. The effect of a diverse portfolio of external finance on aid negotiations depends on other dimensions of the donor–government relationship. For one, donors must attach enough value to their relationship with the government to be willing to compromise in order to retain their access to the government. For another, donors must have a certain level of trust in the government to satisfy the government's preferences in negotiations. Moreover, the Ghanaian case suggests that countries that have benefited from their symbolic significance to donors may be more vulnerable to shifts in donor opinion.

8 | Conclusion

This book has examined how greater choice in international finance affects developing countries' relations with the traditional donors that historically provided the majority of their external finance. It has found that governments can use borrowing relationships to their advantage, shifting some reliance for external finance onto alternative creditors, thereby increasing their autonomy from traditional donors and increasing their bargaining leverage. When donors place especially high value on their relationships with the recipient and when donors have greater faith in the recipient government's credibility, borrowing from alternative creditors is more likely to give recipient countries greater bargaining leverage with donors.

In this conclusion, I draw together evidence from the large-n analysis and case studies, present vignettes from other countries that further illustrate the argument, suggest implications for policymakers and researchers, and reflect on likely future developments in external finance for developing countries. The confluence of global conditions that allowed African governments to diversify their portfolios of external finance and bargain more assertively with donors may ultimately prove short-lived. In particular, the abundance of global liquidity that enabled first-time borrowers to enter international bond markets marked the high point of a cycle that was abruptly disrupted by the global economic contraction brought on by the COVID-19 pandemic. I close with some conjectures about how the greater diversity of external finance might affect the bargaining position of developing countries during periods of debt distress and financial scarcity.

8.1 Bringing the Evidence Together

Borrowing from alternative sources *can* enhance governments' leverage with their existing creditors and donors. Across different analyses, from the global large-n analysis to the Ethiopian, Kenyan, and

Ghanaian cases, the evidence all points in this direction. Yet, some countries do better at translating their diversified borrowing relationships into leverage with donors than others. Donors' perceptions of the credibility of government commitments affect governments' efforts to use a diversity of external finance sources as bargaining leverage with traditional donors. Recipient governments' strategic significance also plays a role. In Kenya and Ethiopia, where donors placed particular value on their relationships with the respective governments, the countries' greater autonomy did more to bring aid terms in line with government preferences than in Ghana, where the relationship with the government declined in importance for donors over time.

The outcome of interest in this book has been whether developing country governments, and African governments in particular, receive aid on terms more aligned with their preferences. To capture this outcome, I have used different measures of the aid agreements between governments and donors. Standardized measures allowed me to compare across a large number of developing countries in the large-n analysis in Chapter 3. Almost all countries would prefer more aid with fewer conditions, and many would prefer to receive more funding for infrastructure projects. Using these indicators, the analysis in Chapter 3 shows that, on average, countries that borrow from China and private creditors are more likely to receive aid in line with their preferences.

Using more contextualized and case-specific measures of the sensitive issue areas in donor–government negotiations reveals a pattern across the three cases. Table 8.1, first presented in the introduction, groups the various dimensions of negotiations into broad areas to compare outcomes across cases. Examining only the most contentious issues, where the government and donors had more sharply diverging preferences, shows that Ethiopia was most successful at achieving outcomes in line with its preferences. On governance issues as well as development policy, the government was able to secure donor support, or at the very least donor acquiescence. In Kenya, the government achieved some flexibility on sensitive issues of governance and democratization, while it had less success translating its greater autonomy into donor flexibility on issues of financial management. Finally, in Ghana, the government was ultimately not able to use alternative finance to secure flexibility from donors on either economic policy or financial management, despite borrowing from alternative sources.

Table 8.1 *Main negotiation areas and outcomes across the three cases*

Issue	Ethiopia	Kenya	Ghana
Governance and democratization	⇑	⇑	
Macroeconomics and development policy	⇑		⇓
Financial management	⇑	⇓	⇓

Outcomes are denoted as follows:
⇑ indicates an outcome aligned with recipient government preferences.
⇓ indicates an outcome diverging from recipient government preferences.

Not only did donors withhold aid until the government agreed to an IMF program that would require macroeconomic reforms, they also insisted on reforms to financial management procedures.

The results from the large-n analysis and the case studies indicate that debt-based financial statecraft can be effective with different kinds of donors. In Ethiopia, as in Kenya, alternative finance enhanced governments' negotiating leverage with both multilateral and bilateral donors. Multilateral donors including the World Bank and the African Development Bank were among the donors providing the greatest support to development projects aligned with Ethiopia's developmental state agenda. Multilateral donors' support for these projects is partly attributable to the resources these donors command but also because these donors wanted to preserve their relationship with the Ethiopian government. Bilateral donors, particularly the UK, also aligned their aid closely with the Ethiopian government's preferences. These findings mirror the results of the large-n analysis in Chapter 3, which show multilateral and bilateral donors increasing their volumes of aid when developing countries borrowed from alternative sources, with the World Bank reducing its conditionality in these countries, especially in sub-Saharan Africa.

By tracing the path to changed negotiation outcomes, the case studies provide support for the hypothesized mechanism underpinning debt-based financial statecraft, namely that a recipient's greater autonomy from aid funds causes donors to accommodate recipient preferences. In Kenya, the choice of lenders gave the government more room to assert its wishes in negotiations with donors. A donor official described the Kenyan government as "well-courted [by lenders]. Somehow, they have a choice … So they can indicate their preferences."[1] Similarly, in Ethiopia, donors' willingness to respond to the government's preferences was "shaped by the fact that they want to maintain a relationship," as one donor representative described it.[2] Moreover, once Ethiopia's debt levels rose and the country borrowed less from commercial sources, becoming again more reliant on traditional donors, the balance of negotiating leverage reverted, with one donor official noting that the government was "willing to do anything to get the financing."[3] This fluctuation in Ethiopia's negotiating leverage with donors illustrates the mechanism at work in debt-based financial statecraft, with bargaining leverage rising (and falling) with the government's access to alternative finance.

The case studies highlight that donors value their access to and influence with the recipient government and that alternative finance can impact negotiations by reducing donors' sway in the recipient country. While Ghana had only some success in translating alternative finance into preferred outcomes, here too donors were concerned that alternative finance could displace their influence with the government. As a donor official in Accra put it, "what was concerning, of course, is that we felt that we were no longer being taken as seriously as the new creditors."[4] The evidence from the case studies complements the findings from the large-n analysis, identifying and illustrating the mechanism that links alternative finance to changed negotiation outcomes.

The differences among the case study countries in terms of their success in aligning negotiation outcomes with government preferences (see Table 8.1) supports the argument that the effectiveness of debt-based financial statecraft is shaped by the recipient's significance and the extent of donor trust. Where donors worried more about preserving their relationship with the government, greater autonomy from donor funding led to greater negotiating leverage. In Kenya and Ethiopia, donors particularly valued their relationship with the respective governments and feared that they could be sidelined. The importance donors attached to their influence with the Kenyan and Ethiopian

---

[1] Interview 54. Multilateral donor representative. Nairobi, Kenya. April 5, 2017.
[2] Interview 125. Bilateral donor official. Addis Ababa, Ethiopia. July 13, 2017.
[3] Interview 122. Multilateral donor official. Addis Ababa, Ethiopia. July 11, 2017.
[4] Interview 70. Bilateral donor official. Accra, Ghana. April 27, 2017.

governments was partly driven by the geopolitics of the Horn of Africa, with donors keen to retain good lines of communication with countries that have supported Western policies in Somalia and Sudan. Significance was not only geopolitical, however, but also about commercial and developmental "success stories," with donors wanting to remain influential in countries that boasted good track records in terms of private sector development, in Kenya's case, and poverty reduction, in Ethiopia's case. By contrast, in Ghana, donors came to deprioritize their relationship with a one-time "donor darling" and were willing to accept a more distant relationship with the government as the price of insisting on economic and financial management reforms, even as the government increasingly turned to alternative sources of finance. The case studies thus provide greater support for this source of heterogeneity, where results in the statistical analysis in Chapter 3 were more uneven.

Differences in donor trust in the governments of Kenya, Ghana, and Ethiopia during the study period also affected the governments' abilities to use a diversified portfolio of external finance as a basis for leverage. In both Kenya and Ghana, the government's efforts to use alternative finance as a source of bargaining leverage were undermined by donors' lack of faith in the government's credibility. Due to a history of high-level corruption in Kenya and electoral budget cycles in Ghana, donors worried that these governments would not uphold key features of their stated development plans or agreements with donors. This concern made donors less trusting, more skeptical of both governments' uses of alternative finance, and less willing to accommodate each government's preferences. These dynamics played out especially in negotiations over financial management, where donors' concerns about weaknesses in institutions for monitoring spending led them to be more inflexible, despite the governments' greater autonomy from donor funds. By contrast, in Ethiopia donors had greater faith in the government's commitment to its development plans and aid agreements, leading donors to be more willing to meet demands for greater flexibility. Across the cases, donors often connected their trust in the government's commitments to spending plans and aid agreements to the domestic political context, seeing the Ghanaian and Kenyan governments as under greater pressure to meet short-term political goals than the Ethiopian government. These findings echo the results of the statistical analysis, which found that governments with higher institutional assessments and lower corruption, as well as those with a more concentrated political settlement, saw a stronger relationship between alternative finance and the terms of aid agreements.

8.1.1 Adding Nuance to the Theoretical Framework

The empirical analyses also generated some findings that nuance the theoretical framework, which I briefly discuss here. These include some donors' use of specialization to respond to recipient governments' greater autonomy, patterns in the issue areas where donors were more willing to extend concessions to governments, the role of recipient agency in debt-based financial statecraft, and borrowers' strategies toward alternative creditors.

The case studies showed some differences among donors in how they responded to recipients' reduced reliance that were not anticipated in the theoretical framework. I indicated in Chapter 2 that I expected heterogeneity among donors in the value they attached to the recipient and their trust in the government, leading to differences in how donors responded to the recipient's reduced reliance on traditional donor funds. I did observe behavior consistent with this expectation, with donors that were more sensitive to Ethiopia and Kenya's geopolitical significance being more willing to moderate their stances on governance issues, for instance. However, the case studies also revealed additional variation in donors' responsiveness to recipients' reduced autonomy. Across the cases, donors with smaller budgets and those primarily specialized in social sectors saw Chinese and private market finance as less of a threat to their influence, so long as they were confident that their aid programs secured them some level of access to the recipient government. An official from a Scandinavian donor in Kenya drew a contrast between their donor agency and the large multilaterals, saying, "In our area, we haven't felt that presence at all, because of the sectors that we work in. With the World Bank and IMF, I know there has been a response and commentary on Chinese lending."[5]

While this behavior indicates that some donors might not respond to recipients' greater autonomy by converging on the flexible infrastructure-focused finance provided by alternative creditors, it

---

[5] Interview 46. Bilateral donor official. Nairobi, Kenya. February 14, 2017.

nonetheless underscores the point that donors will make more of an effort to please the recipient government as that government becomes less reliant on donor funds. Donors often framed their choice to specialize in their niche of technical advice or social sector support as valuable to the recipient government, all the more so as the appeal of alternative finance risked displacing their access to the government. A donor official in Kenya explained, "China is definitely changing things, but for us it's not changing, because we're not in infrastructure. We need to think about our added value. What can I do here?"[6] In Ethiopia, too, a donor official explained specialization with reference to a close relationship with the government and the government's reliance on donor funds, saying, "We specialize ... we're very focused on dialogue with the government, we're investing in health, social, we're not competing with the Chinese in this ... You do get a better dialogue [in social sectors] because they [the government] are so much dependent on donors."[7]

Differences in donors' reactions to the recipient's greater autonomy were also a function of internal rules within donor agencies and multilateral development banks, especially when it came to governance, where several donors had internal red lines. In Kenya, some donors moderated their criticism of the government's governance shortcomings more than others, with the EU's representation holding fast to its more critical position, due to greater scrutiny from the EU Parliament. Among multilateral actors in Kenya, the IMF dropped governance issues to improve dialogue with the government, which was easier for the IMF than for other lenders because governance issues are not core to the Fund's mandate. When donors were unwilling or unable to accommodate some of the government's preferences due to internal rules or constraints, they sometimes chose to meet the government's preferences in other areas. In Ethiopia, some donors who withheld aid in response to the 2016–2017 state of emergency nonetheless continued discussions on how to support the government's industrialization agenda.[8] Further exploring the differences among donors in their

---

[6] Interview 41. Bilateral donor official. Nairobi, Kenya. February 13, 2017.

[7] Interview 160. Multilateral donor official. Addis Ababa, Ethiopia. August 15, 2017.

[8] Interview 169. Bilateral donor official. Addis Ababa, Ethiopia. August 18, 2017.

reactions to developing countries' portfolios of external finance is a promising area for future research. Future work in this vein could build on scholarship on the role of donors' domestic political economies in explaining their aid allocation strategies.[9]

Second, comparing negotiation outcomes in the three cases raises the question of whether donors simply have different standards for governance issues than for matters of economic and financial management. In both Ethiopia and Kenya, many donors muted their criticism of governance issues when confronted with governments' greater autonomy from donor funds, while in Kenya and Ghana, donors were stricter on financial management, despite those governments' diverse portfolios of finance (see Table 8.1). Skeptics might suggest these outcomes reflect donors' general willingness to compromise on matters of democratization and human rights, while taking a stricter approach to financial management issues that put their own repayment at risk. Critics have argued that donors are willing to sideline governance objectives to advance other priorities, including stability and economic development.[10] Even specifically within the realm of democracy promotion, research has found that democracy-promoting aid has been "tamed" to make it less threatening to autocrats.[11]

However, differences in donors' underlying preferences about these issue areas cannot fully explain the pattern of outcomes in the case study countries. In Ethiopia, donors responded to the government's greater autonomy by being more accommodating of the government's preferences around governance, as well as those around development policy and financial management. Moreover, when officials reflected on the donor community's flexibility on governance issues, they usually connected it to the government's reduced reliance on traditional donor funds. A donor representative in Ethiopia expressed this view, saying, "The recipient countries are no longer so dependent on the traditional donors. One consequence of this is that questions of the rule of law and democratization may be less stressed now … The reduction of development funds is, in general, no longer as much of a source of pressure. Our means of influence have been reduced."[12] Nevertheless,

---

[9] Dietrich 2016, 2021.
[10] S. Brown 2001, 2009.
[11] Bush 2015.
[12] Interview 142. Bilateral donor official. Addis Ababa, Ethiopia. July 26, 2017.

the findings across the three cases suggest that recipient governments may find it easier to shift negotiation outcomes in those areas where donors have been more willing to compromise in the past or where they see their own interests as less threatened. Certainly, donors' level of trust in the recipient government appears to have played a stronger role for outcomes related to economic and financial management. Where donors had more concerns about the credibility of the government's commitments to development plans and aid agreements, they were less likely to extend flexibility on financial management issues, despite the government's greater autonomy from aid funds.

The empirical analysis raises separate questions about the extent of recipient agency in triangulating among sources of external finance. This study was motivated in part by wanting to turn the focus of research on emerging creditors from those creditors to their borrowers, examining how recipient countries navigate diverse external financing options, and how they can use a diverse portfolio of external finance to their advantage with traditional donors. The case studies do show considerable variation in government approaches to alternative finance and traditional donors, as well as variation in the alignment of aid relationships with recipients' preferences. However, the variation in outcomes across the three cases is largely explicable with reference to *donors'* preferences and perceptions. Where donors saw the government as more important for their own objectives or where they had greater trust in the recipient's credibility, the government derived greater bargaining leverage from alternative finance. The Ghanaian case strikingly illustrates the role of donor perceptions, with donors' increasing frustration and skepticism making it more difficult for the government to use alternative finance to their advantage. What room does the role of donor concerns leave for recipient government *agency* in exercising debt-based financial statecraft?

Despite the crucial role of donor interests and perceptions in shaping the success of debt-based financial statecraft, the cases show that recipient governments do exercise control in how they present their reduced dependence to donors and use it to their advantage. In Kenya, for instance, the government's decision to present its relationship with Chinese creditors under the heading of "Look East" placed considerable pressure on traditional donors. Donor representatives similarly saw the Ethiopian government as especially skilled in signaling its closer relationship with alternative creditors and reduced reliance on traditional donors. Multiple donor officials, including ones working outside Ethiopia, described the layout of offices for meeting with donors, with one donor official in Kenya describing it as follows, "In Ethiopia, the head of resource mobilization has one door labeled 'China' and the other door simply labeled 'other'."[13] While my visits to the Ethiopian Ministry of Finance suggest this description was a slight exaggeration, the spread of this story attests to donors' sense of their waning importance in Ethiopia, heightened by the government's strategic approach to relations with different creditors. Across the cases, governments made strategic choices about when to borrow from different creditors and how to present this choice in their aid negotiations.

This element of recipient strategy points to a final insight from the cases that goes beyond the initial theoretical framework of debt-based financial statecraft, which is recipient governments' strategy toward nontraditional donors. The argument outlined in Chapter 2 did not seek to explain why countries borrow from certain creditors but instead laid out the likely consequences of those choices for aid negotiations. Existing research has demonstrated how domestic interest group politics or the ideological orientation of the ruling party can explain the choice of certain creditors over others.[14] The case study analysis suggests additional considerations for the choice to pursue Chinese loans or private market finance, namely how these interact with a country's relations with traditional donors. In Kenya's case, a large loan from China not only enabled a popular railway project but also lent greater credence to the government's broader "Look East" foreign policy pivot. In Ghana, the government was an enthusiastic and early adopter of Chinese loans, experimenting with this new source of financing, but ultimately chose to rely more on private market finance and traditional donor funds when the Chinese loans came under domestic political fire.

8.2 Other Cases of Debt-Based Financial Statecraft

To further illustrate how alternative finance affects negotiations with donors in countries beyond those featured in the three case studies,

---

[13] Interview 29. Bilateral donor official. Nairobi, Kenya. February 2, 2027.
[14] Bunte 2019; Cormier 2022, 2023.

I present some brief vignettes of debt-based financial statecraft in other developing countries. While Kenya, Ghana, and Ethiopia borrowed both from China and private markets, I show with the examples of Uganda and Senegal that countries were able to partially enhance their negotiation leverage with only one of these two sources. The case of Laos provides an illustration of debt-based financial statecraft outside of sub-Saharan Africa.

Uganda diversified its portfolio of external finance by borrowing from China but chose not to enter international bond markets. Nevertheless, observers indicate that loans from China have increased the Ugandan government's negotiating leverage with its traditional donors. With respect to the moderating variables, Uganda has only limited donor trust in its budgeting institutions and control of corruption, but donors, especially the US, have attached considerable strategic importance to security cooperation with Uganda in the Great Lakes region.[15] On Transparency International's corruption perception index, Uganda ranked 134th in 2010, declining to 149th by 2018. Uganda has been governed since 1986 by Yoweri Museveni and the National Resistance Movement (NRM), but increasing electoral competition and internal instability and jockeying within the NRM drives spending pressures.[16] The ESID political settlement data used in Chapter 3 classifies Uganda as having a competitive-clientelist or broad-dispersed political settlement in the years between 2010 and 2018, transitioning away from vulnerable-authoritarianism in 2005. Similar to Kenya, I would expect that Uganda has had an uneven track-record with debt-based financial statecraft, helped by donors' interest in maintaining a close relationship but hindered by low levels of donor trust.

In fact, Uganda does appear to have used its new borrowing relationship with China to make more assertive requests for infrastructure financing and to secure greater lenience on governance issues. Comparing Uganda's development plan from the first half of the 2010s to one for the second half of the decade, Davies et al. find that the Ugandan government became more assertive in singling out public investment in infrastructure as a key priority, which the authors attribute to the large increase in Uganda's borrowing from China in 2014 and 2015,

[15] Fisher 2012; Omach 2017.
[16] Collord 2016; Makara et al. 2009.

when Uganda's parliament approved $1.96 billion in loans from Chinese lenders.[17] Traditional donors responded by using more innovative financing structures, including blending aid with loan financing, to support infrastructure projects. Moreover, observers note that "China's growing presence" has "enabled the Government of Uganda to pay less attention to the governance concerns of OECD-DAC donors."[18] However, domestic political circumstances made financial statecraft more difficult. Booth and Golooba-Mutebi observe that "corruption under [Uganda's President] Museveni is primarily a system for maintaining loyalty to a particular political regime."[19] As in Kenya and Ghana, limited donor trust undermined the government's efforts to deploy alternative finance to obtain greater flexibility from traditional donors.

Senegal's experience illustrates a different combination of alternative finance. Senegal borrowed repeatedly in international markets, issuing dollar-denominated bonds in 2009, 2011, 2014, and 2017. However, Senegal has been slower to borrow from Chinese lenders than other countries in the region. Until 2005, Senegal did not have official diplomatic relations with Beijing, instead recognizing the government in Taiwan. After Senegal switched its recognition to the People's Republic of China in 2005, it took some time for Senegal to borrow from the latter in sizable quantities. With respect to the moderating variables in the theory, Senegal sits in a different position than Uganda. The country performs fairly well on indicators of donor trust, with an average score on the World Bank Country Performance and Institutional Assessment budgeting measure that is above the African and global average, and lower levels of perceived corruption than regional or global peers. The ESID political settlement data classifies Senegal as a strong-dominant or broad-concentrated political settlement, illustrating how such a political settlement can coexist with multiparty electoral competition. Concerning significance to donors, Senegal has a broadly similar status as Ghana, with only limited geopolitical significance to donors but considerable stability and predictability that has historically made it an attractive partner for Western donors, especially for France. For many donors, however, Senegal is of limited

---

[17] Davies et al. 2016, p. 19.
[18] Davies et al. 2016, p. 26.
[19] Booth and Golooba-Mutebi 2009.

importance, making it an interesting complement to the cases considered in depth in this book, since it combines higher levels of donor trust with a relatively low level of significance for most traditional donors.

Anecdotal evidence suggests that Senegal was able to use private finance and its limited but growing relationships with emerging creditors to shift its relationship with traditional donors. Particularly under the presidency of Abdoulaye Wade (2000–2012), Senegal adopted a more assertive stance toward traditional donors, taking advantage of the available alternative financing sources.[20] Wade made frequent public statements pressuring donors to increase the flexibility of their financing in line with the resources provided by private lenders and emerging creditors. In a report on the new development financing landscape drawing on case study evidence from Ghana and Senegal, the OECD concludes that alternative finance, including private finance, is associated with "more policy space in negotiations with ... traditional international gatekeepers such as the IFIs and their former colonial powers."[21] Though it is of course conceivable that the anticipated threat of greater future Chinese financing tilted bargaining leverage in Senegal's favor, this vignette suggests that private finance can also be an important basis for debt-based financial statecraft.

Laos offers an example of debt-based financial statecraft outside of Africa. The country has received large volumes of finance from its neighbor, China, as well as borrowing in international markets, issuing Thai baht-denominated bonds on the Bangkok exchange in 2013 and 2015, and a dollar-denominated bond on the Singapore exchange in 2019.[22] Since 2000, Chinese finance has come to make-up 28 percent of Laos' external finance, on average. Laos is small and landlocked and likely less important to most traditional donors than other countries in Southeast Asia, since donors from outside Asia may prioritize their relationships with larger countries in the region, such as Vietnam, Thailand, or Cambodia. Moreover, Laos has a mixed performance on measures of institutional quality and corruption, suggesting only limited donor trust. On the World Bank's Country Performance and Institutional Assessment, Laos' 2010–2018 average score for budgetary institutions was above the global and regional averages, but

---

[20] Haussaire 2019.
[21] OECD 2014, p. 29.
[22] Mustapha and Greenhill 2016, p. 20.

corruption was perceived to be widespread, with the country ranking 132nd on Transparency International's ranking.

The greater diversity of external finance in Laos does appear to have increased the government's bargaining power with traditional donors. For instance, a study of traditional donors' aid to Laos' education sector in the 1990s concludes that donors were the ones to set broad priorities for the sector, as well as determining the focus of individual projects. The authors explain that "those imbalances have come from the limited resources of the country, particularly in the contexts of high dependency on donors' financial support and expertise."[23] By the late 2000s, however, the government had a greater variety of funding options available. Government officials explained that their pursuit of alternative financing was partly driven by the desire to have a counterbalance to the expectations of traditional donors, saying, "we need to have an alternative choice in case we do not agree with the terms and conditions attached to aid provided by some other donors."[24] As a result, the government was able to exercise greater influence in negotiations, especially in achieving its priority of funding more infrastructure projects. Khennavong's study of aid relations in Laos describes negotiations with the World Bank over a hydroelectric project, during which "the Lao Government had internal discussions about turning to China if agreement with the World Bank could not be reached. In the end, Laos did not need to exercise this option but having it available helped the Government's leverage in relation to the World Bank"[25]

The Lao government was not able to able to use alternative finance to achieve its preferred negotiations with all donors, however. The government had a stated preference for more concessional finance and grant aid.[26] Nonetheless, it has been unable to persuade some grant-specialized donors to remain active in the country after the country's 2011 transition to lower-middle-income status. In part, this withdrawal reflects traditional donors' reluctance to continue providing grant aid when a government is able to access market-rate finance from

---

[23] Phommalangsy and Honan 2017.
[24] Laos government official, quoted in Khennavong 2014, p. 147.
[25] Khennavong 2014, p. 147.
[26] Mustapha and Greenhill 2016, p. 27.

other sources. Yet, grant donors have not exited from all lower-middle-income countries (such as Kenya), and the fact that some donors proved unwilling to meet the Lao government's preference for grant aid may also reflect the relatively lower value that donors placed on this relationship and the lack of trust in the government.

The examples of Uganda, Senegal, and Laos suggest that the mechanisms of debt-based financial statecraft hold outside of the cases explored in-depth in this book and supports the broader cross-national findings in Chapter 3. They invite future case study research investigating how portfolios of external finance impact aid negotiations.

8.3 Implications

The findings of the book have implications for scholarship on foreign aid, international finance, and international political economy more broadly. I first describe these, before detailing implications for policymakers in developing countries and in donor agencies.

Implications for Research

Beginning with the implications for the study of development finance, the findings on the financial statecraft of borrowers lend credence to the idea that new donors and creditors have fundamentally altered the global context for foreign aid. Over the last decade and a half, scholars, practitioners, and commentators have observed that a more diverse landscape of donors supports a more diverse set of development priorities. While much of the analysis has focused on the motivations of new lenders and what they mean for traditional donors, a number of contributions – such as Bunte (2019) or the policy-oriented work of the Overseas Development Institute's "Age of Choice" project – have considered the consequences for developing countries themselves.[27] This book reinforces research in foreign aid that understands the donor–recipient relationship as a negotiation, with an awareness of the respective negotiating power of recipients and donors.[28] In particular, the financial statecraft of borrowers implies that scholars studying development aid ought to consider how alternative sources of external finance can rebalance the relationship between recipients and donors. Moreover, by focusing on the potential for alternative

[27] Bunte 2019; Greenhill et al. 2013.
[28] Swedlund 2017b; Whitfield and Fraser 2009.

finance to enhance the negotiating position of recipient governments in sub-Saharan Africa, the book joins a strand of literature highlighting African agency in international relations,[29] and specifically in relations with creditors.[30]

While the insight that outside options enhance negotiating leverage, including in aid negotiations, is not new, the explanation for how different forms of alternative finance – including private loans – can strengthen the negotiating power of recipient governments is well-suited to an era in which developing countries have a choice of lenders. Future work that considers the balance of influence between recipient governments and donors, such as evaluating the level of conditionality of foreign aid, recipient compliance with conditionality, or the alignment between foreign aid and domestic development priorities, ought to consider the diversity of a country's portfolio of external finance as a factor strengthening the recipient government's hand. Such studies commonly account for a country's oil wealth as an independent source of funding[31] or, more recently, the level of Chinese finance,[32] but the findings of this book suggest that future work ought to consider a country's access to private finance and, more generally, the overall composition of a country's portfolio of external finance.

An implication of debt-based financial statecraft for the broader study of international political economy is that changes in financial interdependence at the level of the global economy have consequences for developing countries. Recent work in international political economy – particularly on finance – has emphasized the importance of global interdependence.[33] This research stresses that cross-border loans, investments, supply chains, or trade create global structures that directly influence domestic outcomes, such as regulatory choices or monetary policy. Empirical applications of this approach have often focused on the core of the global financial system, for instance, analyzing how interdependence affects financial regulation in the United States and the European Union.[34]

---

[29] W. Brown 2012; W. Brown and Harman 2013.
[30] Mohan and Lampert 2012; Soule-Kohndou 2018.
[31] Girod and Tobin 2016.
[32] Clark and Dolan 2020.
[33] Farrell and Newman 2016; Oatley 2019.
[34] Newman and Posner 2018.

By contrast, the financial statecraft of borrowers highlights how financial interdependence affects developing countries at the periphery of the international financial system. Previous studies of how financial interdependence affects developing countries have emphasized that global financial interdependence imposes considerable constraints on developing and emerging economies.[35] The analysis in this book underscores that developing countries gain and lose access to external finance for reasons outside of their control while also demonstrating that countries can use asymmetric financial relationships to their advantage.

Moreover, the financial statecraft of borrowers reveals the value of examining the consequences of interdependence in the financial periphery. While bond market access has been very important for African governments, African sovereign debt is a small fraction of the global bond market. An analysis of how global liquidity in the 2010s pushed capital into frontier and emerging markets would register African sovereign debt as a mere blip on the radar of global lending. But, by beginning with countries in the financial periphery and asking how they are integrated into the international financial system, this analysis reveals that relationships that are far from systemically important can nevertheless be enormously important from a borrower's perspective. Research in international political economy benefits from taking financial interdependence "from below" seriously, recognizing the outsize effects that changes in the international financial system can have for developing countries.

Implications for Policy

The findings from this study offer insights for policymakers, both in developing countries and in donor agencies. For policymakers working in the developing world and navigating the range of possible creditors, the research highlights the benefits of using the country's portfolio of external finance as a negotiating tool, cultivating donor confidence, and learning from other countries that effectively triangulate among creditors.

First, the study demonstrates the potential of a diversified portfolio of external finance to improve a country's bargaining position with

---

[35] Bauerle Danzman et al. 2017.

traditional donors. Governments in developing countries may initially be attracted to borrowing from nontraditional sources because they offer a different type of financing than traditional donors, providing large volumes of funding or funding for specific infrastructure projects. However, the analysis shows that this additional financing from alternative creditors can also potentially improve the terms of traditional donor aid, and policymakers may benefit from a deliberate internal strategy to turn alternative finance into greater negotiating leverage. Such a strategy might involve identifying which traditional donors especially value the relationship with the government and then presenting these donors with priority projects when diversity in the portfolio of external finance has enhanced the government's bargaining leverage.

To increase the likelihood that this strategy of financial statecraft will be successful, policymakers may seek to cultivate donors' confidence in their credibility, perhaps focusing on particular areas of development policy. At first glance, the findings may suggest there is little policymakers in developing countries can do to increase the likely success of debt-based financial statecraft, since success varies with donors' *perceptions* of recipient importance and credibility. Governments often have little control over how donors see the strategic significance of their country, though countries may be inclined to align their foreign policy with significant partners to curry their favor. The case studies suggest a less intrusive means for developing countries to enhance the likely success of debt-based financial statecraft, namely, to cultivate their credibility with donors. Since the perception of credibility ultimately rests with donors, policymakers do not have direct control over how they are perceived, but they can increase their room to maneuver by cultivating this donor confidence, which may come from strong development performance in particular sectors or clear priorities that are consistently pursued. I have argued that donors' assessment of government credibility can be driven by the underlying political settlement in the country, which individual policymakers are unable to shift. However, policymakers can cultivate "pockets of effectiveness,"[36] which in addition to helping to achieve development objectives may have the added benefit of attracting greater donor confidence in the government's credibility, strengthening the government's position in aid negotiations.

---

[36] Hickey 2019.

Moreover, the research suggests that policymakers may benefit from the experiences of other countries navigating the diversity of external finance and using it to their advantage. The case studies exhibit clear variation in the impact of alternative finance on donor negotiations. Some of these differences were due to factors outside of policymakers' control, but others, such as Ethiopia's deliberate triangulation among creditors and clear development priorities, might be possible to emulate, even on a smaller scale. Other research has pointed to examples of countries effectively navigating the terrain of diverse external finance, which could offer lessons to emulate. In 2017, the Accra-based African Center for Economic Transformation (ACET) concluded a project studying how six African countries mobilized and managed external development finance in a time of diverse finance.[37] Among the six cases, the ACET study singled out Rwanda for being uniquely effective at negotiating with diverse creditors to secure development finance that directly supported the government's main objectives. Learning from the strategies of these successful cases can be helpful for policymakers in developing countries. While this book has focused on negotiations between developing countries and traditional donors, learning from negotiating best practices may be especially useful when policymakers negotiate with Chinese lenders, which do not use standard DAC approaches to development assistance.[38]

On the other side of the negotiating table, the findings also suggest implications for policymakers working in traditional donor agencies seeking to maintain productive and close relationships with developing countries in an era of diverse financing options. The analysis indicates that developing countries, and African countries in particular, have been drawn to Chinese loans and private finance for the flexibility, volume of funding, and infrastructure focus they offer. In countries that have many options available, donor agencies may need to consider what they can offer in order to remain relevant. Policymakers in donor countries may be reluctant to make the concessions on governance and democratization that occurred in the Ethiopian and Kenyan cases and may therefore want to consider what other forms of aid they can provide to remain an attractive partner for developing countries. Certainly, G7 countries' efforts to mobilize finance for infrastructure in

---

[37] African Center for Economic Transformation 2017.
[38] Soule-Kohndou 2018.

the Partnership for Global Infrastructure and Investment announced in 2022 appear to respond to developing countries' demands for greater infrastructure financing and the competitive pressure of China's Belt and Road Initiative. Especially for donor agencies that do not have the resources to meet developing countries' appetite for infrastructure projects, an alternative strategy may be to specialize in distinctive "market niches" that offer attractive aid to recipient countries. As discussed earlier, evidence from the cases indicates that smaller donors appear to have adopted this strategy, building on existing strengths in health or education to offer unique aid that allowed them to enjoy a continued close relationship with the recipient government.

8.4 The Financial Statecraft of Borrowers and Debt Crises

In closing, I would like to offer some reflections on the relevance of debt-based financial statecraft for the management of debt crises, given the debt distress in many developing countries that has been exacerbated by the COVID-19 pandemic. My reflections on the likely trajectory of debt-crisis management in the near future are necessarily speculative, since the outcomes of current debt crises are still uncertain at the time of writing in 2024. Nonetheless, considering what the diversity of external finance means for the resolution of debt crises and the global governance of sovereign debt casts arguments about debt-based financial statecraft into sharper relief. For developing countries, the time of plenty in external finance came to an abrupt end in 2020, when the global economic shutdown prompted by the pandemic led investors on a "flight to safety," withdrawing capital from developing countries. Not only did developing-country governments find fewer creditors willing to lend to them, the slowdown in their economies and the costs of combating the pandemic made it more difficult for them to service their debts. Soon thereafter, matters became even worse as advanced economies raised interests rates to counteract rising inflation, further raising the costs of borrowing for developing countries. Unsurprisingly, these conditions pushed many countries into debt distress, and some into default. Whereas in 2015 the IMF assessed roughly 30 percent of low-income countries to be in or at a high risk of debt distress, by 2022 this number had doubled to 60 percent.[39]

---

[39] IMF 2022a.

At its most basic, the current period of debt distress highlights the risks of debt accumulation associated with debt-based financial statecraft. Loans that increase a country's leverage can, over time, erode autonomy if higher indebtedness makes the government more reliant on concessional finance or even leads to a debt crisis that makes the country dependent on emergency loans. While the events of the early 2020s fall outside the study period, earlier fluctuations in borrowers' access to finance give an indication of the likely consequences of higher indebtedness and reduced market access. In Ethiopia, access to alternative finance initially increased the government's autonomy, but the buildup of commercial debt, together with a foreign exchange shortage caused by poor export performance, made the government more reliant on concessional finance from 2015 onward. In Ghana, this dynamic was even more pronounced during the period under study. The government's growing non-concessional debt burden left it particularly vulnerable when it was hit by a commodity price shock in 2013. The government became yet again more dependent on concessional forms of finance and, especially, on the seal of IMF approval to enable its return to the markets.

These vulnerabilities have only increased in recent years. Since 2021, two of the three case study countries, Ghana and Ethiopia, have defaulted on their debts and requested debt relief from creditors. Though their defaults were precipitated by the pandemic and, in Ethiopia's case, civil war, the debt crises underscore the risks of debt accumulation in preceding years. Chinese loans and private-market finance allowed developing-country governments to fund developmentally and politically important projects, cover budget shortfalls, and increase their bargaining leverage with traditional donors. However, these loans were expensive, with bonds priced at market rates and Chinese loans often at similar rates. The flexibility of non-concessional debt came with the financial cost of higher interest rates, which also made these debts more difficult to service, with interest rate costs eating up an increasing amount of government revenue. Debt-based financial statecraft may turn out to be a strategy for which medium- and long-term success is uncertain. By building up large amounts of expensive external debt, governments make themselves vulnerable to debt crisis in the event of shocks, leaving them more reliant on concessional sources of finance.

When it comes to negotiating with creditors over debt relief and crisis management, the diversity of creditors appears to be a burden, rather than a benefit. For countries that have defaulted on their debts and requested debt restructuring, including Chad, Ethiopia, Ghana, and Zambia, negotiating separately with different categories of creditors has led to difficulties and delays in accessing emergency finance from the IMF and debt relief from creditors.[40] In particular, the lack of coordination among creditors and lack of harmonization on shared standards have become stumbling blocks in negotiations. The distinctive features of Chinese and private market finance and the lack of coordination between alternative creditors and traditional donors was helpful to recipient countries when they allowed governments to push donors to offer more attractive aid. In negotiations over debt relief, however, lack of coordination among creditors can lead individual creditors to worry about free-riding, fearful that others will not provide the same level of relief. Those concerns about free-riding can cause creditors to withhold debt relief, prolonging the crisis for the borrower. An initial comparison of the first countries to have gone through these debt relief negotiations suggests that those with a more homogeneous portfolio of external finance, such as Chad, will fare somewhat better than those with more diversified portfolios of external finance, such as Ghana or Zambia. Moreover, countries that relied more heavily on private finance, such as Ghana, appear to have had similar difficulties coordinating among their creditors to those experienced by countries that relied more heavily on Chinese loans, such as Zambia.

Developing countries' difficulties in coordinating among creditors in the debt crises of the early 2020s, together with this book's emphasis on the impact of countries' full portfolios of external finance, suggest several implications for the global architecture for managing sovereign debt crises. Most importantly, the institutions governing sovereign debt need to become more comprehensive. Over the preceding five decades, coordination between public lenders has taken place in the Paris Club, an informal grouping of the world's leading bilateral creditors.[41] However, China has yet to join the Paris Club, despite multiple efforts to include it in the membership.[42] With China outside of the

---

[40] Do Rosario 2023; Ferry and Zeitz 2024; Setser 2023.
[41] Blackmon 2017; Josselin 2009; Rieffel 2003.
[42] Chen 2023; Wang 2014.

Paris Club, the debt vulnerabilities of developing countries have been managed through various ad hoc solutions. Early in 2020, the G20, including China, agreed to suspend debt payments on their outstanding debts, ultimately extending the Debt Service Suspension Initiative (DSSI) until the of 2021. To provide longer-term debt relief, the G20 agreed in November 2020 on the Common Framework for Debt Treatments beyond the DSSI, spelling out the procedures that G20 countries, including China, would follow in negotiating debt relief. Finally, the IMF, World Bank, and G20 have been convening the Global Sovereign Debt Roundtable since early 2023 to address continued disagreements over sovereign debt among public creditors and between public and private creditors, as well as with borrowing countries.

Given the full range of creditors in developing countries' portfolios of external finance, the emergence of the DSSI and the Common Framework are positive developments for the sovereign debt architecture. The DSSI marks the first time that China has participated in a multilateral debt restructuring initiative, and it is a sign that the debt architecture may change to better reflect the composition of developing-country debt.[43] However, more would need to be done to bring the sovereign debt architecture in line with developing countries' diverse portfolios of external finance.

In particular, borrowing countries would benefit from all Chinese public lenders committing to providing comprehensive debt relief in line with assessments of debt sustainability. Moreover, since much of the expansion of developing countries' debt burdens, especially in lower-middle-income countries, has come from private finance, borrowers would benefit from private creditors being more tightly integrated into the sovereign debt architecture. Sovereign debt governance has long been a patchwork, with separate procedures for different categories of creditors.[44] However, in the last decade, low-income developing countries entered international bond markets in significant numbers. Improbable though it is, given likely resistance from leading creditors and some middle-income borrowers,[45] developing countries would ideally have access to a resolution mechanism that is binding for both private and public creditors. The sovereign debt regime has begun

[43] Brautigam and Huang 2023.
[44] Gelpern 2016.
[45] Helleiner 2008.

to undergo changes, and recent research has examined how creditors, especially China, are shaping these reforms.[46] Future work should consider the leverage, if any, that borrowing countries have to shape these reforms, especially in venues that give borrowing countries access, and therefore potential to triangulate among creditors, such as the Global Sovereign Debt Roundtable.

Events of the recent decades raise questions for the governance not only of sovereign debt but also of development finance. Although many developing countries are confronted with the risk of debt crisis, some observers suggest that developing countries as a whole face a problem of too little finance, rather than too much.[47] In a 2022 policy paper, the IMF estimated low-income countries to have external financing needs of $440 billion in 2022–2026 to address the effects of the pandemic and to return to a path of income growth that converges on the incomes of advanced economies.[48] The transition to a low-carbon economy, in particular, will require large amounts of financing; estimates from the UN Conference on Trade and Development and the International Energy Agency indicate an annual financing need of $2.6 trillion to meet the Sustainable Development Goals by 2030 and achieve the objective of a net-zero society by 2050.[49] These large funding gaps mean that developing countries will continue to rely on external finance.

Given the large sums required and the nature of projects to be financed, the financing gap will not be met only with concessional or grant financing. Traditional donors have expanded programs to "crowd in" private investment, using concessional finance to "de-risk" projects and attract greater amounts of private finance.[50] One interpretation, consistent with debt-based financial statecraft, is that traditional donors are innovating to meet developing countries' needs, responding to their own reduced importance relative to commercial lenders. However, given the debt burdens accumulated by low- and middle-income countries, the financial risks of market-rate finance

---

[46] Brautigam and Huang 2023; Chen 2023; Lang et al. 2023; Rodriguez-Toribio and Zeitz 2023; Setser 2023.
[47] Lippolis and Verhoeven 2022.
[48] IMF 2022b, p. 35.
[49] Zelikow and Savas 2022.
[50] Bayliss et al. 2020.

need to be carefully considered. As a donor official in Ethiopia put it, commenting on the expansion of "blended" programs combining concessional finance with market-rate loans, "It's a strange position, because for the last years we've been pushing countries to reduce their debt after the HIPC efforts, but now we are developing ways to lend to them."[51] These concerns about relying on market-rate finance are why calls for the reform of development finance by low- and middle-income countries, such as the Bridgetown Initiative championed by Prime Minister Mia Mottley of Barbados, have stressed the importance of expanding concessional and official sector finance in addition to marshaling more private finance.[52]

Building on the financial statecraft of borrowers, a question going forward will be the extent of influence that developing countries have in any moves to reform global governance of sovereign debt and development finance. What sources of leverage can countries draw on in these negotiations, and how much do sources of bargaining leverage at the donor–recipient level transfer to a context of global negotiations? With private finance in retreat and Chinese lending declining and changing given China's own economic transitions, developing countries may have few outside options to use to their advantage in these negotiations. Nevertheless, in line with the core argument of this book, future research should consider how differences among donors and creditors over the governance of sovereign debt and development finance create both constraints and unexpected opportunities for borrowers.

---

[51] Interview 160. Multilateral donor official. Addis Ababa, Ethiopia. August 15, 2017.
[52] Government of Barbados 2022; UN 2023.

Appendices

Appendix A
Interview Appendix

The majority of the evidence in the three case studies stems from interviews conducted during fieldwork in Addis Ababa, Nairobi, Accra, New York, and Washington D.C. in August–October 2013 and January–August 2017. Chapter 4 describes how I identified interviewees and conducted the interviews. In this appendix, I provide further details on response rates and saturation, interview practice, as well as the interview questionnaires used in conducting the interviews. In Tables A.1–A.3, I provide an anonymized register of all respondents I contacted. Following the advice of Bleich and Pekkanen (2013), I include not only the dates of interviews I conducted but also record which contacts ignored or declined interview requests, giving the reader a better sense of the representativeness of the interview data. Across the most important categories of respondents, I achieved high response rates, increasing confidence in the interview data.

A.1 Sample Frame, Response Rates, and Saturation

I established a sample frame for interviewees by deciding the relevant categories of respondents and using public information about the organizational structure of institutions to identify particular individuals within those categories. The four essential categories in each case study country were bilateral donors, multilateral donors, the resource mobilization office within the ministry of finance, and the debt management division. Additional categories of respondents were other government officials, journalists, private sector representatives, and think tank or academic analysts working on the government's foreign policy and relations with donors. I contacted individuals within my sample frame, and also used contacts and referrals to reach additional interviewees. Combining a sample frame with this "snowball" sampling can avoid some of the bias that may arise from drawing interviewees primarily from referrals.

Tables A.1–A.3 note responses to individual requests for interviews. The response rate, especially among donor representatives and government officials, was generally high, above 70%. When individuals declined requests to be interviewed, they most often referred me to others in their organization. Notable exceptions to this were "nontraditional" donors. Though my focus on negotiations between recipient governments and traditional donors primarily required the perspectives of traditional donor representatives, I attempted to speak with Chinese representatives in each of my case study countries, as well as Turkish, Indian, and Brazilian representatives in some cases. In keeping with the reputation of emerging donors as being less transparent, but also likely due to the smaller staffs maintained by these embassies and development agencies, I received far fewer responses to these requests for interviews. This did not substantially hamper my access to information about relations between traditional donors and governments.

Saturation refers to the point at which no new information is gleaned from additional interviews within a particular category of respondents.[1] It suggests that the researcher has reached a comprehensive picture from the perspective of a particular category of respondents and that no additional interviews are necessary. Except for one category in Ethiopia, I was able to reach saturation in the four most important categories in each case study, giving greater confidence in the validity of the data. I note in Tables A.1–A.3 whether I obtained saturation within a given category of respondent.

A.2 Interview Practice: Format, Length, and Recording Method

Almost all interviews were semistructured, conducted in person and in English, and lasted an average of forty minutes. Even in Ethiopia, where the primary official language is Amharic, using English was not a barrier to interviews with government respondents, who are accustomed to negotiating with donors in English. I used a set of questions (see Sections A.3 and A.4) to guide the conversation with respondents, leaving time for follow-up questions on topics close to the specific

[1] Bleich and Pekkanen 2013.

expertise of individual interviewees. Most interviewees were only willing to speak with me on the condition of confidentiality. This also meant most of these respondents would not allow me to record the interviews, so I took detailed handwritten notes during the interview, which I then filled in with supplementary notes immediately following the interview and while typing up the notes within the next day or two.

A.3 Interview Script: Government Respondents

A.3.1 The Relationship with Traditional Lenders/Development Partners

- How would you describe [Ethiopia/Kenya/Ghana's] relationship with traditional development partners?
  - What about particular partners, for example, the World Bank, USAID, JICA, or AfDB?
  - Have these relationships changed over time? How?
- How important do you think [Ethiopia/Kenya/Ghana] is for traditional donors, for example, the World Bank?
- In negotiations over development finance [with the World Bank or other traditional donors], what have been particular areas of disagreement/difference?
  - How have these changed since the early 2000s?
- When there are disagreements with traditional development partners, how are these resolved?
- What **specific** examples can you think of where the government was successful in achieving its preferred outcome? Why was that?
- When you negotiate with traditional development partners, how free are you to set priorities? How much are you constrained by the [executive/parliament/public opinion/the opposition]?

A.3.2 The Relationship with New Bilateral Partners

- Since [the early/mid/late 2000s], the government has borrowed more from China. What is attractive about this financing? What is less attractive?
- How would you describe the government's relationship with China as a creditor?

- How have you found traditional donors reacting to these new relationships?
  - Was there a change in interactions with traditional donors because of these new lending relationships?
- When would the government prefer to finance a project with China rather than with traditional donors?
- How do you see the public/parliament/the opposition reacting to these new partnerships?

A.3.3 Borrowing in International Bond Markets

- In [2007/2014], the government issued its first Eurobond. What was the decision-making process behind the issue of the bond?
- What are the benefits of bond financing, compared to other sources of finance?
- Does the Eurobond open the government up to greater market scrutiny?
- How did traditional donors react to the bond[s]? Has this changed over time?
- When would the government prefer to finance a project with a Eurobond rather than with traditional donor funding?
- How do you see the public/parliament/the opposition reacting to market finance?

A.3.4 Connecting different types of financing

- Does access to Chinese finance/Eurobond markets affect the kind of agreements concluded with the World Bank/USAID/the EU? How?
- When does the government choose one form of finance over another?
- Do you think these changes are lasting/permanent?

A.4 Interview Script: Donor Respondents

A.4.1 The Relationship with the Government

- How would you describe your [agency/government's] relationship with the government? How has this changed over time, since the late 2000s?

- In negotiations over development finance, what have been particular areas of difference? Sticking points? Have these changed over time?
- When there are disagreements with the government, how are these resolved?
- Do you think of the government representatives that you interact with as strong negotiators?
- Of the relationships that you [agency/government] maintains, how important is the one with [Ethiopia/Kenya/Ghana], compared to other developing countries?
  - How important is [Ethiopia/Kenya/Ghana] to officials at head-quarters?
  - Why? What is distinctive about [Ethiopia/Kenya/Ghana]?

A.4.2 *The Government's New Partnerships/Lenders*

- Since [the early/mid/late 2000s], the government has increased its borrowing from China. How do you view that relationship?
- Why do you think the government has chosen to borrow from China?
- Has the government's borrowing from China affected your [agency/government's] relationship with the government? If yes, how so?
- Do you think the government is tactical in its choice of financing?

A.4.3 *The Government's Borrowing in International Bond Markets*

- One other option for the government has been to borrow in international bond markets. What did you think of the choice to turn to markets in [2007/2014]?
- Has the Eurobond issue affected your interactions with the government. If so, how so?

A.4.4 *Connecting Different Types of Financing*

- What do you see as the role of your [agency/government] in [Ethiopia/Kenya/Ghana] now that the government has access to more sources of finance?

A.5 Interview Registers

Table A.1 *Ethiopia interviews*

#	Interview date or request outcome	Source
Bilateral donors		*Saturation: yes*
124	13.07.2017	Sample frame
125	13.07.2017	Sample frame
127	14.07.2017	Sample frame
130	17.07.2017	Sample frame
132	18.07.2017	Sample frame
141	26.07.2017	Sample frame
142	26.07.2017	Sample frame
143	27.07.2017	Sample frame, referred by interviewee # 125
144	28.07.2017	Sample frame, referred by interviewee # 125
149	04.08.2017	Sample frame
151	07.08.2017	Sample frame
153	07.08.2017	Sample frame
166	17.08.2017	Sample frame
168	18.08.2017	Referred by interviewee # 141
169	18.08.2017	Sample frame
170	19.08.2017	Sample frame, referred by interviewee # 149
172	10.08.2017	Sample frame
NA	Referred me on, no interview	Sample frame
NA	No reply	Sample frame
NA	No longer in position	Sample frame
NA	No reply	Referred by interviewee # 143
NA	Referred me on, no interview	Sample frame
NA	No reply	Sample frame
NA	No reply	Sample frame
Multilateral donors		*Saturation: yes*
49	27.02.2017	Sample frame, referred by interviewee # 51
52	27.02.2017	Sample frame, referred by interviewee # 51
119	10.07.2017	Sample frame, referred by interviewee # 52

Table A.1 *(cont.)*

#	Interview date or request outcome	Source
122	11.07.2017	Sample frame, referred by interviewee # 52
123	12.07.2017	Sample frame, referred by interviewee # 52
131	17.07.2017	Sample frame, referred by interviewee # 122
137	25.07.2017	Sample frame
138	25.07.2017	Sample frame
160	15.08.2017	Sample frame
164	16.08.2017	Sample frame
NA	On leave, no interview	Sample frame
NA	Out of the country	Sample frame
NA	Referred me on, no interview	Sample frame
Ministry of Finance – resource mobilization		*Saturation: yes*
128	17.07.2017	Sample frame
129	17.07.2017	Sample frame
135	19.07.2017	Sample frame
152	07.08.2017	Sample frame
NA	No longer in position	Sample frame
Ministry of Finance – debt management		*Saturation: partial*
134	19.07.2017	Sample frame
Ministry of Finance – other		*Saturation: yes*
133	19.07.2017	Sample frame
159	15.08.2017	Sample frame
162	16.08.2017	Sample frame, referred by interviewee # 120
163	16.08.2017	Sample frame
National Bank of Ethiopia		*Saturation: partial*
126	14.07.2017	Sample frame, referred by personal contact

Table A.1 *(cont.)*

#	Interview date or request outcome	Source
Government – other		*Saturation: partial*
165	17.08.2017	Sample frame
171	18.06.2017	Sample frame, referred by personal contact
NA	No reply	Sample frame, referred by interviewee # 140
NA	No reply	Sample frame, referred by interviewee
Ethiopian Investment Commission		*Saturation: yes*
140	26.07.2017	Sample frame
148	03.08.2017	Sample frame, referred by interviewee # 140
Journalists		*Saturation: yes*
139	25.07.2017	Sample frame
161	15.08.2017	Sample frame
NA	Contacted, no reply	Sample frame
Academics		*Saturation: yes*
120	10.07.2017	Referred by personal contact
121	10.07.2017	Referred by personal contact
136	24.07.2017	Referred by personal contact
145	28.07.2017	Referred by personal contact
146	28.07.2017	Referred by personal contact
150	04.08.2017	Referred by personal contact
154	09.08.2017	Referred by personal contact
156	10.08.2017	Referred by personal contact
157	10.08.2017	Referred by personal contact
158	14.08.2017	Referred by personal contact
167	17.08.2017	Referred by interviewee # 162
Private sector		*Saturation: partial*
147	31.07.2017	Sample frame, referred by interviewee
155	09.08.2017	Referred by personal contact
NA	No interview scheduled	Sample frame, referred by interviewee

Table A.2 *Kenya interviews*

#	Interview date or request outcome	Source
Bilateral donors		*Saturation: yes*
1	18.01.2017	Referred by personal contact
23	31.01.2017	Sample frame, referred by interviewee # 3
25	01.02.2017	Sample frame, referred by interviewee # 1
29	02.02.2017	Sample frame, referred by interviewee # 19
34	08.02.2017	Sample frame, referred by interviewee # 1
36	09.02.2017	Referred by interviewee # 34
41	13.02.2017	Sample frame, referred by interviewee # 32
46	14.02.2017	Sample frame, referred by interviewee # 19
NA	Interview declined	Sample frame, referred by personal contact
NA	Interview declined	Sample frame, referred by personal contact
NA	No reply	Sample frame
Multilateral donors		*Saturation: yes*
2	18.01.2017	Referred by personal contact
11	23.01.2017	Sample frame
12	23.01.2017	Sample frame
18	27.01.2017	Sample frame, referred by personal contact
30	02.02.2017	Sample frame
32	06.02.2017	Sample frame, referred by interviewee # 1
37	09.02.2017	Sample frame, referred by interviewee # 18
44	14.02.2017	Referred by interviewee # 37
45	14.02.2017	Sample frame
50	27.02.2017	Sample frame, referred by interviewee # 51
53	28.02.2017	Sample frame, referred by interviewee # 51

Table A.2 *(cont.)*

#	Interview date or request outcome	Source
54	05.04.2017	Sample frame, referred by interviewee # 32
NA	No reply	Sample frame
NA	No reply	Sample frame
NA	No reply	Sample frame
NA	Out of the country	Sample frame
Ministry of Finance – resource mobilization		*Saturation:* yes
5	20.01.2017	Sample frame
6	20.01.2017	Sample frame
15	25.01.2017	Sample frame
20	30.01.2017	Sample frame
28	01.02.2017	Sample frame
35	08.02.2017	Sample frame
38	10.02.2017	Sample frame
39	10.02.2017	Sample frame
42	13.02.2017	Sample frame
Ministry of Finance – debt management		*Saturation:* yes
16	25.01.2017	Sample frame
19	27.01.2017	Referred by interviewee # 24
43	13.02.2017	Sample frame
NA	No reply	Sample frame
NA	Referred me on, no interview	Sample frame
Ministry of Finance – other		*Saturation:* yes
31	03.02.2017	Referred by interviewee # 14
33	07.02.2017	Referred by interviewee
48	15.02.2017	Referred by Ministry of Finance interviewee
NA	No reply	Sample frame, referred by personal contact
NA	No reply	Sample frame
NA	No reply	Sample frame

Table A.2 *(cont.)*

#	Interview date or request outcome	Source
Central Bank of Kenya		*Saturation: no*
40	13.02.2017	Sample frame, referred by personal contact
Parliament		*Saturation: no*
47	15.02.2017	Referred by interviewee # 24
Attorney General's Office		*Saturation: no*
21	30.01.2017	Referred by Ministry of Finance interviewee
Journalists		*Saturation: yes*
8	21.01.2017	Sample frame
9	23.01.2017	Sample frame
10	23.01.2017	Sample frame
14	25.01.2017	Sample frame
NA	No interview scheduled	Referred by personal contact
NA	No reply	Referred by interviewee # 13
NGO		*Saturation: yes*
24	01.02.2017	Referred by interviewee # 10
Think tanks		*Saturation: yes*
7	20.01.2017	Referred by personal contact
26	01.02.2017	Referred by interviewee # 14
Academic		*Saturation: yes*
17	26.01.2017	Referred by interviewee # 8
NA	No reply	Sample frame
NA	Interview declined	Referred by personal contact
Private sector		*Saturation: yes*
3	19.01.2017	Referred by personal contact
4	19.01.2017	Referred by personal contact
13	25.01.2017	Sample frame
22	31.01.2017	Referred by personal contact
27	01.02.2017	Referred by personal contact
NA	Out of the country	Referred by interviewee # 13
NA	No reply	Referred by personal contact

Table A.3 *Ghana interviews*

#	Interview date or request outcome	Source
Bilateral donors		*Saturation: yes*
60	19.04.2017	Sample frame
61	20.04.2017	Sample frame
62	20.04.2017	Sample frame
67	24.04.2017	Sample frame
70	27.04.2017	Sample frame, referred by interviewee # 70
71	27.04.2017	Sample frame, referred by interviewee # 61
72	28.04.2017	Sample frame, referred by interviewee # 60
74	02.05.2017	Sample frame
75	02.05.2017	Sample frame
83	04.05.2017	Sample frame
94	09.05.2017	Sample frame
104	27.09.2013	Sample frame
106	30.09.2013	Sample frame
107	30.09.2013	Sample frame
112	07.10.2013	Sample frame
116	08.10.2013	Sample frame
NA	No reply	Sample frame
NA	No reply	Sample frame
NA	No interview scheduled	Sample frame
NA	Referred me on, no interview	Sample frame
NA	Out of the country	Sample frame, referred by interviewee # 34
NA	No reply	Sample frame, referred by interviewee # 70
Multilateral donors		*Saturation: yes*
55	04.04.2017	Sample frame
56	16.03.2017	Sample frame, referred by interviewee # 51
57	06.04.2017	Referred by personal contact
80	02.05.2017	Sample frame, referred by interviewee # 57
81	03.05.2017	Sample frame
84	04.05.2017	Sample frame

Table A.3 *(cont.)*

#	Interview date or request outcome	Source
85	04.05.2017	Sample frame
93	08.05.2017	Referred by interviewee # 71
95	10.05.2017	Sample frame
98	01.08.2013	Referred by personal contact
99	02.08.2013	Referred by personal contact
100	12.08.2013	Referred by personal contact
101	12.08.2013	Referred by personal contact
102	13.09.2013	Referred by personal contact
111	04.10.2013	Sample frame
Ministry of Finance – resource mobilization		*Saturation: yes*
64	21.04.2017	Sample frame, referred by interviewee # 58
68	25.04.2017	Sample frame
69	25.04.2017	Sample frame
78	02.05.2017	Sample frame, referred by interviewee # 58
79	02.05.2017	Sample frame, referred by interviewee # 58
97	10.05.2017	Sample frame
108	02.10.2013	Sample frame
109	03.10.2013	Sample frame
110	03.10.2013	Sample frame
115	07.10.2013	Sample frame
118	09.10.2013	Sample frame
NA	No interview	Sample frame
Ministry of Finance – debt management		*Saturation: yes*
58	07.04.2017	Sample frame, referred by personal contact
65	21.04.2017	Sample frame, referred by interviewee # 58
91	05.05.2017	Sample frame
92	05.05.2017	Sample frame
113	07.10.2013	Sample frame
114	07.10.2013	Sample frame

Table A.3 *(cont.)*

#	Interview date or request outcome	Source
Ministry of Finance – other		*Saturation: yes*
63	20.04.2017	Sample frame, referred by interviewee # 58
73	28.04.2017	Sample frame
NA	No reply	Referred by interviewee # 71
NA	Referred me on, no interview	Sample frame
Bank of Ghana		*Saturation: yes*
86	05.05.2017	Sample frame
87	05.05.2017	Sample frame, referred by interviewee # 86
88	05.05.2017	Sample frame, referred by interviewee # 86
89	05.05.2017	Sample frame, referred by interviewee # 86
National Development Planning Commission		*Saturation: partial*
105	27.09.2013	Sample frame
NA	Interview declined	Sample frame
NA	No reply	Sample frame
Parliament		*Saturation: yes*
59	07.04.2017	Sample frame
66	24.04.2017	Sample frame
96	10.05.2017	Sample frame
117	09.10.2013	Sample frame
NA	No reply	Sample frame
NA	No reply	Sample frame
NA	No reply	Sample frame
Think tanks		*Saturation: yes*
76	02.05.2017	Sample frame
77	02.05.2017	Sample frame
82	03.05.2017	Referred by interviewee # 61
90	05.05.2017	Sample frame
103	25.09.2013	Sample frame

References

Abdu, Brook (2017). "Unchartered Waters: Public Private Partnerships." *The Reporter.* www.thereporterethiopia.com/655/

Abdulai, Abdul-Gafaru and Sam Hickey (2016). "The Politics of Development under Competitive Clientelism: Insights from Ghana's Education Sector." *African Affairs* 115, pp. 44–72.

Abegaz, Berhanu (2015). "Aid, Accountability and Institution Building in Ethiopia: The Self-limiting Nature of Technocratic Aid." *Third World Quarterly* 36.7, pp. 1382–1403.

African Center for Economic Transformation (2017). "Synthesis Report: Mobilizing and Managing External Development Finance for Inclusive Growth: Six Countries' Experiences and Lessons."

African Development Bank (2000). "Ethiopia: Structural Adjustment Programme – Project Performance Evaluation Report (PPER)."

African Development Bank Group (2022). *Country Policy and Institutional Assessment.* African Development Bank Group. https://cpia.afdb.org/.

Alesina, Alberto and David Dollar (2000). "Who Gives Foreign Aid to Whom and Why?" *Journal of Economic Growth* 5.1, pp. 33–63.

Amnesty International (2006). *Amnesty International Report 2006 – Ethiopia.*

Anderson, David M. and Jacob McKnight (2014). "Kenya at War: Al-shabaab and Its Enemies in Eastern Africa." *African Affairs* 114.454, pp. 1–27.

Ansu, Yaw (2013). "Industrial Policy and Economic Transformation in Africa: Strategies for Development and a Research Agenda." *The Industrial Policy Revolution II.* Ed. by Joseph E. Stiglitz, Justin Lin Yifu, and Ebrahim Patel. New York: Palgrave Macmillan, pp. 492–528.

Apter, David E. (1968). "Nkrumah, Charisma, and the Coup." *Daedalus* 97.3, pp. 757–792.

Armijo, Leslie Elliott (2019). "Financial Statecraft." *The Palgrave Handbook of Contemporary International Political Economy.* Ed. by Timothy M. Shaw, Laura C. Mahrenbach, Renu Modi, and Xu Yichong. London: Palgrave Macmillan. Chap. 2, pp. 27–41.

Armijo, Leslie Elliott and Saori N. Katada (2014). *The Financial Statecraft of Emerging Powers: Shield and Sword in Asia and Latin America.* International Political Economy Series. Basingstoke: Palgrave Macmillan.

— (2015). "Theorizing the Financial Statecraft of Emerging Powers." *New Political Economy* 20.1, pp. 42–62.

Arriola, Leonardo R. (2013). *Multi-ethnic Coalitions in Africa: Business Financing of Opposition Election Campaigns.* Cambridge Studies in Comparative Politics. Cambridge: Cambridge University Press.

Azeem, Vitus, Biship Akolgo, Lilian Breakell, Maria Paalman, Derek Poate, and Ines Rothman (2006). *Evaluation of DFID Country Programmes: Country Study Ghana 2000–2005.* Report.

Bach, Jean-Nicolas (2011). "Abyotawi Democracy: Neither Revolutionary nor Democratic, a Critical Review of EPRDF's Conception of Revolutionary Democracy in Post-1991 Ethiopia." *Journal of Eastern African Studies* 5.4, pp. 641–663.

Bailey, Michael A., Anton Strezhnev, and Erik Voeten (2016). "Estimating Dynamic State Preferences from United Nations Voting Data." *Journal of Conflict Resolution* 61.2, pp. 430–456.

Baldwin, David A. (1985). *Economic Statecraft.* Princeton, NJ: Princeton University Press.

Ballard-Rosa, Cameron, Layna Mosley, and Rachel L. Wellhausen (2019). "Contingent Advantage? Sovereign Borrowing, Democratic Institutions and Global Capital Cycles." *British Journal of Political Science* 51.1, pp. 353–373.

Barkan, Joel D. (2004). "Kenya after Moi." *Foreign Affairs* 83.1, pp. 87–100.

Barthel, Fabian, Eric Neumayer, Peter Nunnenkamp, and Pablo Selaya (2014). "Competition for Export Markets and the Allocation of Foreign Aid: The Role of Spatial Dependence among Donor Countries." *World Development* 64, pp. 350–365.

Bauerle Danzman, Sarah, William Kindred Winecoff, and Thomas Oatley (2017). "All Crises Are Global: Capital Cycles in an Imbalanced International Political Economy." *International Studies Quarterly* 61.4, pp. 907–923.

Bawumia, Mahamudu and Håvard Halland (2017). "Oil Discovery and Macroeconomic Management: The Recent Ghanaian Experience." *WIDER Working Paper.*

Bayart, Jean-François (2000). "Africa in the World: A History of Extraversion." *African Affairs* 99.395, pp. 217–267.

— (2009). *The State in Africa: The Politics of the Belly.* 2nd ed. Cambridge: Polity.

Bayliss, Kate, Bruno Bonizzi, Ourania Dimakou, Christina Laskardis, Farwa Sial, and Elisa Van Waeyenberge (2020). "The Use of Development Funds for De-risking Private Investment: How Effective Is It in Delivering Development Results?" *EU Policy Department for External Relations*.

BBC (2006). "Ethiopian Protesters 'Massacred'." http://news.bbc.co.uk/2/hi/africa/6064638.stm

Bennett, Andrew and Jeffrey T. Checkel (2015). "Process Tracing: From Philosophical Roots to Best Practices." *Process Tracing: From Metaphor to Analytic Tool*. Ed. by Andrew Bennett and Jeffrey T. Checkel. Cambridge, UK: Cambridge University Press, pp. 3–38.

Bermeo, Sarah Blodgett (2017). "Aid Allocation and Targeted Development in an Increasingly Connected World." *International Organization* 71.4, pp. 735–766.

— (2018). *Targeted Development: Industrialized Country Strategy in a Globalizing World*. New York, NY: Oxford University Press.

Berthélemy, Jean-Claude (2006). "Bilateral Donors' Interest vs. Recipients' Development Motives in Aid Allocation: Do All Donors Behave the Same?" *Review of Development Economics* 10.2, pp. 179–194.

Berthélemy, Jean-Claude and Ariane Tichit (2004). "Bilateral Donors' Aid Allocation Decisions – A Three-Dimensional Panel Analysis." *International Review of Economics & Finance* 13.3, pp. 253–274.

Betley, Mary, Andrew Bird, and Adom Ghartey (2012). *Evaluation of Public Financial Management Reform in Ghana, 2001–2010: Final Country Case Study Report*. Technical Report. Joint Evaluation (Sida, Danida, and AfDB).

Birdsall, Nancy, John Williamson, and Brian Deese (2002). *Delivering on Debt Relief: From IMF Gold to a New Aid Architecture*. Washington, DC: Center for Global Development, Institute for International Economics.

Blackmon, Pamela (2017). *The Political Economy of Trade Finance: Export Credit Agencies, the Paris Club and the IMF*. Abingdon, New York, NY: Routledge.

Blas, Javier (2014). "Investors Pile into Ethiopia's $1bn Debut Debt Sale." *Financial Times*. www.ft.com/content/0efe83f2-7bbb-11e4-a695-00144feabdc0

Bleich, Erik and Robert Pekkanen (2013). "How to Report Interview Data." *Interview Research in Political Science*. Ed. by Layna Mosley. Ithaca, NY: Cornell University Press. Chap. 4, pp. 84–105.

Booth, David (2012). "Aid Effectiveness: Bringing Country Ownership (and Politics) Back In." *Conflict, Security & Development* 12.5, pp. 537–558.

Booth, David and Frederick Golooba-Mutebi (2009). "The Political Economy of Roads Reform in Uganda." *ODI Working Paper.*

Borchgrevink, Axel (2008). "Limits to Donor Influence: Ethiopia, Aid and Conditionality." *Forum for Development Studies* 35.2, pp. 195–220.

Brautigam, Deborah (2011). *The Dragon's Gift: The Real Story of China in Africa.* Oxford: Oxford University Press.

Brautigam, Deborah and Yufan Huang (2023). "Integrating China into Multilateral Debt Relief: Progress and Problems in the G20 DSSI." *China Africa Research Initiative Briefing Paper.*

Brautigam, Deborah and Jyhjong Hwang (2016). "Eastern Promises: New Data on Chinese Loans in Africa, 2000–2014." Report. *China-Africa Research Initiative.*

Brechenmacher, Saskia (2017). "Surveillance and State Control in Ethiopia." *Civil Society under Assault: Repression and Responses in Russia, Egypt, and Ethiopia.* Ed. by Saskia Brechenmacher. Washington, DC: Carnegie, pp. 65–90.

Briggs, Ryan C. (2021). "Why Does Aid Not Target the Poorest?." *International Studies Quarterly* 65.3, pp. 739–752.

Brown, Stephen (2001). "Authoritarian Leaders and Multiparty Elections in Africa: How Foreign Donors Help to Keep Kenya's Daniel Arap Moi in Power." *Third World Quarterly* 22.5, pp. 725–739.

(2009). "Donor Responses to the 2008 Kenyan Crisis: Finally Getting It Right?" *Journal of Contemporary African Studies* 27.3, pp. 389–406.

Brown, Stephen and Jonathan Fisher (2020). "Aid Donors, Democracy and the Developmental State in Ethiopia." *Democratization* 27.2, pp. 185–203.

Brown, William (2012). "A Question of Agency: Africa in International Politics." *Third World Quarterly* 33.10, pp. 1889–1908.

Brown, William and Sophie Harman, eds. (2013). *African Agency in International Politics.* Abingdon, OX; New York, NY: Routledge.

Brownsell, James (2013). "Kenya: What Went Wrong in 2007?" *Al Jazeera.* www.aljazeera.com/features/2013/3/3/kenya-what-went-wrong-in-2007

Bueno de Mesquita, Bruce and Alastair Smith (2009). "A Political Economy of Aid." *International Organization* 63.2, pp. 309–340.

(2016). "Competition and Collaboration in Aid-for-Policy Deals." *International Studies Quarterly* 60.3, pp. 413–426.

Bundervoet, Tom, Arden Jeremy Finn, Shohei Nakamura, Berhe Mekonnen Beyene, Pierella Paci, Nataliya Mylenko, and Carolyn Turk (2020). *Ethiopia Poverty Assessment – Harnessing Continued Growth for Accelerated Poverty Reduction.* Technical Report. World Bank Group.

Bunte, Jonas B. (2018). "Sovereign Lending after Debt Relief." *Review of International Political Economy* 25.3, pp. 317–339.

(2019). *Raise the Debt: How Developing Countries Choose Their Creditors*. New York, NY: Oxford University Press.

Busby, Joshua William (2007). "Bono Made Jesse Helms Cry: Jubilee 2000, Debt Relief and Moral Action in International Politics." *International Studies Quarterly* 51.2, pp. 247–275.

Bush, Sarah Sunn (2015). *Taming of Democracy Assistance: Why Democracy Promotion Does Not Confront Dictators*. Cambridge: Cambridge University Press.

Caporaso, James A. (1978). "Dependence, Dependency, and Power in the Global System: A Structural and Behavioral Analysis." *International Organization* 32.1, pp. 13–43.

Chandy, Laurence (2011). "It's Complicated: The Challenge of Implementing the Paris Declaration on Aid Effectiveness." *Brookings Institution Policy Brief*.

Checkel, Jeffrey T. (2008). "Process Tracing." *Qualitative Methods in International Relations*. Ed. by Audie Klotz and Deepa Prakash. New York, NY: Palgrave Macmillan, pp. 114–127.

Cheeseman, Nic, Karuti Kanyinga, Gabrielle Lynch, Mutuma Ruteere, and Justin Willis (2019). "Kenya's 2017 Elections: Winner-Takes-All Politics as Usual?" *Journal of Eastern African Studies* 13.2, pp. 215–234.

Cheeseman, Nic, Gabrielle Lynch, and Justin Willis (2014). "Democracy and Its Discontents: Understanding Kenya's 2013 Elections." *Journal of Eastern African Studies* 8.1, pp. 2–24.

Chellaney, Brahma (2017). "China's Debt-Trap Diplomacy." *Project Syndicate*. www.project-syndicate.org/commentary/china-one-belt-one-road-loans-debt-by-brahma-chellaney-2017-01

Chen, Muyang (2023). "China's Rise and the Reshaping of Sovereign Debt Relief." *International Affairs* 99.4, pp. 1755–1775.

CitiFM (2011). "NDC Government Deceiving Ghanaians with $3bn Chinese Loan – NPP." *CitiFM*. www.peacefmonline.com/pages/politics/politics/201111/79762.php

Clapham, Christopher (1996). *Africa and the International System: The Politics of State Survival*. Cambridge: Cambridge University Press.

(2005). "Comments on the Ethiopian Crisis." www.ethiopians.com/Election2005/ChristopherClapham_CommentsonEthiopianCrisis.htm

(2009). "Post-war Ethiopia: The Trajectories of Crisis." *Review of African Political Economy* 36.120, pp. 181–192.

(2017). "The Ethiopian Developmental State." *Third World Quarterly* 39.6, pp. 1151–1165.

Clark, Richard and Lindsay R. Dolan (2020). "Pleasing the Principal: U.S. Influence in World Bank Policymaking." *American Journal of Political Science* 65.1, pp. 36–51.

Cohen, John M. (2003). "Foreign Aid and Ethnic Interests in Kenya." *Carrot, Sticks and Ethnic Conflict: Rethinking Development Assistance.* Ed. by Milton J. Esman and Ronald J. Herring. Ann Arbor, MI: University of Michigan Press. Chap. 4, pp. 90–112.

Collier, David (2011). "Understanding Process Tracing." *PS: Political Science & Politics* 44.4, pp. 823–830.

Collier, David and James E. Mahon (1993). "Conceptual 'Stretching' Revisited: Adapting Categories in Comparative Analysis." *American Political Science Review* 87.4, pp. 845–855.

Collord, Michaela (2016). "From the Electoral Battleground to the Parliamentary Arena: Understanding Intra-elite Bargaining in Uganda's National Resistance Movement." *Journal of Eastern African Studies* 10.4, pp. 639–659.

Copelovitch, Mark S. (2010). *The International Monetary Fund in the Global Economy: Banks, Bonds, and Bailouts.* Cambridge; New York: Cambridge University Press.

Coppedge, Michael, John Gerring, Carl Henrik Knutsen, Staffan I. Lindberg, Jan Teorell, David Altman, Michael Bernhard, Agnes Cornell, M. Steven Fish, Lisa Gastaldi, Haakon Gjerløw, Adam Glynn, Allen Hicken, Anna Lührmann, Seraphine F. Maerz, Kyle L. Marquardt, Kelly McMann, Valeriya Mechkova, Pamela Paxton, Daniel Pemstein, Johannes von Römer, Brigitte Seim, Rachel Sigman, Svend-Erik Skaaning, Jeffrey Staton, Aksel Sundström, Eitan Tzelgov, Luca Uberti, Yi-ting Wang, Tore Wig, and Daniel Ziblatt (2021). "V-Dem Codebook v11.1." *Varieties of Democracy (V-Dem) Project.*

Cormier, Ben (2022). "Chinese or Western Finance? Transparency, Official Credit Flows, and the International Political Economy of Development." *The Review of International Organizations* 18.2, pp. 297–328.

— (2023). "Partisan External Borrowing in Middle-Income Countries." *British Journal of Political Science* 53.2, pp. 717–727.

Cowhey, Peter F. (1993). "Domestic Institutions and the Credibility of International Commitment: Japan and the United States." *International Organization* 47.2, pp. 299–326.

Crawford, Gordon, Coleman Agyeyomah, Gabriel Botchwey, and Atinga Mba (2015). "The Impact of Chinese Involvement in Small-Scale Gold Mining in Ghana." *IGC Report* E-33110-GHA-1.

Davies, Fiona, Cathal Long, and Martin Wabwire (2016). "Age of Choice: Uganda in the New Development Finance Landscape." *ODI Report.*

Dejene, Melisew and Logan Cochrane (2019). "Ethiopia's Developmental State: A Building Stability Framework Assessment." *Development Policy Review* 37.S2, pp. O161–O178.

Devlin, Robert (1990). *Debt and Crisis in Latin America: The Supply Side of the Story*. Princeton, NJ; Chichester: Princeton University Press.

DFID (2010). "Building Peaceful States and Societies." *A DFID Practice Paper*.

   (2017). *Annual Review – Summary Sheet – Ethiopian Investment Advisory Facility (EIAF)*. Technical Report. UK Department for International Development.

Dietrich, Simone (2013). "Bypass or Engage? Explaining Donor Delivery Tactics in Foreign Aid Allocation." *International Studies Quarterly* 57.4, pp. 698–712.

   (2016). "Donor Political Economies and the Pursuit of Aid Effectiveness." *International Organization* 70.1, pp. 65–102.

   (2021). *States, Markets, and Foreign Aid*. Cambridge: Cambridge University Press.

Dissanayake, Ranil, Charles Kenny, and Mark Plant (2020). "What Is the Role of Aid in Middle-Income Countries?" *CGD Policy Paper*.

Do Rosario, Jorgelina (2023). "Analysis: Cash-Strapped Countries Face IMF Bailout Delays as Debt Talks Drag On." *Reuters*. www.reuters.com/business/finance/cash-strapped-countries-face-imf-bailout-delays-debt-talks-drag-2023-03-02/

Dreher, Axel and Andreas Fuchs (2015). "Rogue Aid? An Empirical Analysis of China's Aid Allocation." *Canadian Journal of Economics* 48.3, pp. 988–1023.

Dreher, Axel, Andreas Fuchs, Bradley Parks, Austin Strange, and Michael J. Tierney (2022). *Banking on Beijing: The Aims and Impacts of China's Overseas Development Program*. Cambridge: Cambridge University Press.

Dreher, Axel, Andreas Fuchs, Bradley Parks, Austin M. Strange, and Michael J. Tierney (2018). "Apples and Dragon Fruits: The Determinants of Aid and Other Forms of State Financing from China to Africa." *International Studies Quarterly* 62.1, pp. 182–194.

Dreher, Axel, Stephan Klasen, James Raymond Vreeland, and Eric Werker (2013). "The Costs of Favoritism: Is Politically Driven Aid Less Effective?" *Economic Development and Cultural Change* 62.1, pp. 157–191.

Dreher, Axel, Peter Nunnenkamp, and Rainer Thiele (2011). "Are 'New' Donors Different? Comparing the Allocation of Bilateral Aid between Non-DAC and DAC Donor Countries." *World Development* 39.11, pp. 1950–1968.

Dreher, Axel, Jan-Egbert Sturm, and James Raymond Vreeland (2009a). "Development Aid and International Politics: Does Membership on the UN Security Council Influence World Bank Decisions?" *Journal of Development Economics* 88.1, pp. 1–18.

(2009b). "Global Horse Trading: IMF Loans for Votes in the United Nations Security Council." *European Economic Review* 53.7, pp. 742–757.

Drezner, Daniel W. (1999). *The Sanctions Paradox: Economic Statecraft and International Relations*. Cambridge: Cambridge University Press.

(2001). "Globalization and Policy Convergence." *International Studies Review* 3.1, pp. 53–78.

ESID (2022). "Political Settlements." www.effective-states.org/political-settlements/

EU and World Bank (2017). *Joint Evaluation of Budget Support to Ghana (2005–2015): Final Report*. Technical Report. European Commission (DG DEVCO's Evaluation Unit) and the World Bank's Independent Evaluation Group.

Fantini, Emanuele and Luca Puddu (2016). "Ethiopia and International Aid: Development between Highmodernism and Exceptional Measures." *Aid and Authoritarianism in Africa: Development without Democracy*. Ed. by Tobias Hagmann and Filip Reyntjens. London, UK: Zed Books, pp. 91–118.

Farrell, Henry and Abraham L. Newman (2014). "Domestic Institutions beyond the Nation-State: Charting the New Interdependence Approach." *World Politics* 66.2, pp. 331–363.

(2016). "The New Interdependence Approach: Theoretical Development and Empirical Demonstration." *Review of International Political Economy* 23.5, pp. 713–736.

(2019). "Weaponized Interdependence: How Global Economic Networks Shape State Coercion." *International Security* 44.1, pp. 42–79.

Ferry, Lauren L. and Alexandra O. Zeitz (2024). "China, the IMF, and Sovereign Debt Crises." *International Studies Quarterly*.

Feyissa, Dereje (2011). "Aid Negotiation: The Uneasy 'Partnership' between EPRDF and the Donors." *Journal of Eastern African Studies* 5.4, pp. 788–817.

Fisher, Jonathan (2012). "Managing Donor Perceptions: Contextualizing Uganda's 2007 Intervention in Somalia." *African Affairs* 111.444, pp. 404–423.

(2013). "'Some More Reliable than Others': Image Management, Donor Perceptions and the Global War on Terror in East African Diplomacy." *The Journal of Modern African Studies* 51.1, pp. 1–31.

Fisher, Jonathan and Meressa Tsehaye Gebrewahd (2018). "'Game Over'? Abiy Ahmed, the Tigrayan People's Liberation Front and Ethiopia's Political Crisis." *African Affairs* 118.470, pp. 194–206.

Fleck, Robert K. and Christopher Kilby (2010). "Changing Aid Regimes? U.S. Foreign Aid from the Cold War to the War on Terror." *Journal of Development Economics* 91.2, pp. 185–197.

Fourie, Elsje (2015). "China's Examples for Meles' Ethiopia: When Development 'Models' Land." *The Journal of Modern African Studies* 53.3, pp. 289–316.

Fraser, Alastair (2007). "Zambia: Back to the Future?" *GEG Working Paper*.

Frieden, Jeffry A. (1981). "Third World Indebted Industrialization: International Finance and State Capitalism in Mexico, Brazil, Algeria, and South Korea." *International Organization* 35.3, pp. 407–431.

— (1991). *Debt, Development, and Democracy : Modern Political Economy and Latin America, 1965–1985*. Princeton, NJ: Princeton University Press.

Fuchs, Andreas, Axel Dreher, and Peter Nunnenkamp (2014). "Determinants of Donor Generosity: A Survey of the Aid Budget Literature." *World Development* 56, pp. 172–199.

Fuchs, Andreas, Peter Nunnenkamp, and Hannes Öhler (2015). "Why Donors of Foreign Aid Do Not Coordinate: The Role of Competition for Export Markets and Political Support." *The World Economy* 38.2, pp. 255–285.

Fuchs, Andreas and Marina Rudyak (2019). "The Motives of China's Foreign Aid." *Handbook on the International Political Economy of China*. Ed. by Ka Zeng. Cheltenham, UK: Edward Elgar. Chap. 23, pp. 392–410.

Furtado, Xavier and W. James Smith (2009). "Ethiopia: Retaining Sovereignty in Aid Relations." *The Politics of Aid: African Strategies for Dealing with Donors*. Ed. by Lindsay Whitfield. Oxford: Oxford University Press. Chap. 5, pp. 131–155.

Garrett, Geoffrey (1998). "Global Markets and National Politics: Collision Course or Virtuous Circle?" *International Organization* 52.4, pp. 787–824.

Gaulier, Guillaume and Soledad Zignago (2010). *BACI: International Trade Database at the Product-Level: The 1994–2007 Version*. Working Papers 2010–23. CEPII.

Gelpern, Anna (2016). "Sovereign Debt: Now What?" *The Yale Journal of International Law* 41.2, pp. 44–95.

Gerster, Richard (2010). *Developing a Performance Assessment Framework of Development Partners ("DPs' PAF") in Ghana*. Report.

Gilmore, Inigo (2006). "Ethiopia Condemns Aid Pull-Out." *The Guardian.* www.theguardian.com/society/2006/jan/01/internationalaidanddevelo pment.hearafrica05

Girod, Desha M. and Jennifer L. Tobin (2016). "Take the Money and Run: The Determinants of Compliance with Aid Agreements." *International Organization* 70.1, pp. 209–239.

Government of Barbados (2022). "Urgent and Decisive Action Required for an Unprecedented Combination of Crises: The 2022 Bridgetown Initiative for the Reform of the Global Financial Architecture."

Government of Ethiopia (2014). *Growth and Transformation Plan II (2015–2019).*

Government of Ghana (2005). *Growth and Poverty Reduction Strategy (GPRS II) (2006–2009).*

(2013). *Ghana: Public Expenditure and Financial Accountability (PEFA) Performance Review.* Government of Ghana.

(2016). *Ghana's Turnaround Story.*

(2019a). "Ghana beyond Aid Charter and Strategy Document." https:// dohaembassy.gov.gh/wp-content/uploads/2020/02/Ghana-Beyond-Aid-Charter-and-Strategy-Document-April-2019_Agricinghana-Media-Copy.pdf

(2019b). *The Annual Public Debt Report for the 2018 Financial Year.* MoFEP.

Government of Kenya (2014). *Kenya External Resources Policy.* Resource Mobilization Department, National Treasury.

Green, Daniel (1995). "Ghana's 'Adjusted' Democracy." *Review of African Political Economy* 22.66, pp. 577–585.

Greenhill, Romilly, Annalisa Prizzon, and Andrew Rogerson (2013). *The Age of Choice: How Are Developing Countries Managing the New Aid Landscape?* Report. ODI.

Gulrajani, Nilima and Rachael Calleja (2019). "Understanding Donor Motivations: Developing the Principled Aid Index." *ODI Working Paper.*

Gunu, Kofi (2023). "Capital Power: Borrowing Governments, Structural Power, and the Puzzle of IMF Programme Participation." *Working Paper.*

Hagmann, Tobias and Filip Reyntjens (2016). *Aid and Authoritarianism in Africa: Development without Democracy.* London: Zed Books.

Haussaire, Mélissa (2019). "La fabrique de l'État sous régime d'aide. Construction d'une administration extravertie au Sénégal." PhD thesis. Université de Lille.

Helleiner, Eric (2008). "The Mystery of the Missing Sovereign Debt Restructuring Mechanism." *Contributions to Political Economy* 27.1, pp. 91–113.

Herbst, Jeffrey Ira (1993). *The Politics of Reform in Ghana, 1982–1991*. Berkeley; Oxford: University of California Press.

Hernandez, Diego (2017). "Are 'New' Donors Challenging World Bank Conditionality?" *World Development* 96, pp. 529–549.

Hickey, Sam (2019). "The Politics of State Capacity and Development in Africa: Reframing and Researching 'Pockets of Effectiveness'." *ESID Working Paper*.

Hirschman, Albert O. (1945). *National Power and the Structure of Foreign Trade*. Berkeley: University of California Press.

Hoeffler, Anke and Verity Outram (2011). "Need, Merit, or Self-interest – What Determines the Allocation of Aid?" *Review of Development Economics* 15.2, pp. 237–250.

Horn, Sebastian, Carmen M. Reinhart, and Christoph Trebesch (2021). "China's Overseas Lending." *Journal of International Economics* 133, 103539.

Human Rights Watch (2007). *Human Rights Watch World Report 2007 – Ethiopia*.

  (2016). *Ethiopia: Events of 2016*.

Humphrey, Chris and Katharina Michaelowa (2019). "China in Africa: Competition for Traditional Development Finance Institutions?" *World Development* 120, pp. 15–28.

IDA-IMF (2011). *Joint IDA-IMF Staff Advisory Note on the Growth and Transformation Plan (GTP) (2010–11 to 2014–15)*. Technical Report. World Bank International Development Association and International Monetary Fund.

IMF (2002). "Press Release: Ghana to Receive $3.7 Billion in Debt Service Relief: The IMF and World Bank Support Debt Relief for Ghana under the Enhanced HIPC Initiative."

  (2015). "Federal Democratic Republic of Ethiopia: 2015 Article IV Release."

  (2018). "Macroeconomic Developments and Prospects in Low-Income Developing Countries – 2018." *IMF Policy Paper*.

  (2022a). "Crisis upon Crisis: IMF Annual Report 2022."

  (2022b). "Macroeconomic Developments and Prospects in Low-Income Countries – 2022." *IMF Policy Paper*.

Independent Commission for Aid Impact (2020). *The Changing Nature of UK Aid in Ghana: Country Portfolio Review*. Technical Report. ICAI.

India Exim Bank (2023). "Government of India – Lines of Credit Statistics." www.eximbankindia.in/lines-of-credit-GOILOC.aspx

Irungu, Geoffrey (2016). "Kenya Accounted for Eurobond, Says IMF." *Daily Nation.* https://nation.africa/kenya/news/kenya-accounted-for-eurobond-says-imf-1197492

Jablonski, Ryan S. (2014). "How Aid Targets Votes: The Impact of Electoral Incentives on Foreign Aid Distribution." *World Politics* 66.2, pp. 293–330.

Jensen, Nathan M., Glen Biglaiser, Quan Li, Edmund Malesky, Pablo M. Pinto, Santiago M. Pinto, and Joseph L. Staats (2012). *Politics and Foreign Direct Investment.* Ann Arbor, MI: University of Michigan Press.

Jerven, Morten (2013). "For Richer, for Poorer: GDP Revisions and Africa's Statistical Tragedy." *African Affairs* 112.446, pp. 138–147.

Jones, Lee and Shahar Hameiri (2020). "Debunking the Myth of 'Debt-Trap Diplomacy': How Recipient Countries Shape China's Belt and Road Initiative." *Chatham House Research Paper.*

Josselin, Daphné (2009). "Regime Interplay in Public-Private Governance: Taking Stock of the Relationship between the Paris Club and Private Creditors between 1982 and 2005." *Global Governance* 15, pp. 521–538.

Kahler, Miles (1992). "External Influence, Conditionality and the Politics of Adjustment." *The Politics of Economic Adjustment: International Constraints, Distributive Conflicts, and the State.* Ed. by Stephan Haggard, Robert R. Kaufman, and Peter B. Evans. Princeton: Princeton University Press. Chap. 2, pp. 89–139.

— (1993). "Bargaining with the IMF: Two-Level Strategies and Developing Countries." *Double-Edged Diplomacy: International Bargaining and Domestic Politics.* Ed. by Peter B. Evans and Harald K. Jacobson. Los Angeles: University of California Press. Chap. 12, pp. 363–395.

Kaplan, Stephen B. (2016). "Banking Unconditionally: The Political Economy of Chinese Finance in Latin America." *Review of International Political Economy* 23.4, pp. 643–676.

— (2021). *Globalizing Patient Capital.* Cambridge: Cambridge University Press.

Katada, Saori N., Cynthia Roberts, and Leslie Elliott Armijo (2017). "The Varieties of Collective Financial Statecraft: The BRICS and China." *Political Science Quarterly* 132.3, pp. 403–433.

Keller, Edmond J. (1988). *Revolutionary Ethiopia: From Empire to People's Republic.* Bloomington, IN: Indiana University Press.

Kelsall, Tim, Nicolai Schulz, William D. Ferguson, Matthias vom Hau, and Sam Hickey (2022). *Political Settlements and Development. Theory, Evidence, Implications.* Oxford: Oxford University Press.

Kentikelenis, Alexander E., Thomas H. Stubbs, and Lawrence P. King (2016). "IMF Conditionality and Development Policy Space." *Review of International Political Economy* 23.4, pp. 543–582.

Keohane, Robert O. and Joseph S. Nye (2001). *Power and Interdependence.* 3rd ed. New York, NY: Longman.

Kersting, Erasmus and Christopher Kilby (2014). "Aid and Democracy Redux." *European Economic Review* 67, pp. 125–143.

Khan, Mushtaq H. (2010). "Political Settlements and the Governance of Growth-Enhancing Institutions." Working paper. https://eprints.soas.ac.uk/9968/1/Political_Settlements_internet.pdf

Khennavong, Phanthanousone (2014). "Aid to Laos in the Twenty-First Century: Engagement and Change." PhD thesis. Australian National University.

Kilby, Christopher (2009). "The Political Economy of Conditionality: An Empirical Analysis of World Bank Loan Disbursements." *Journal of Development Economics* 89.1, pp. 51–61.

Kilby, Christopher and Axel Dreher (2010). "The Impact of Aid on Growth Revisited: Do Donor Motives Matter?" *Economics Letters* 107.3, pp. 338–340.

Killick, Tony (2005). "The Politics of Ghana's Budgetary System." ODI Report. Overseas Development Institute.

Killick, Tony and Andrew Lawson (2007). "Budget Support to Ghana: A Risk Worth Taking?" ODI Briefing Paper. Overseas Development Institute.

Knack, Stephen (2013). "Aid and Donor Trust in Recipient Country Systems." *Journal of Development Economics* 101, pp. 316–329.

Koeberle, Stefan and Zoran Stavreski (2006). "Budget Support: Concepts and Issues." *Budget Support as More Effective Aid?: Recent Experiences and Emerging Lessons.* Ed. by Stefan Koeberle, Zoran Stavreski, and Jan Walliser. Washington, DC: World Bank. Chap. 1, pp. 1–26.

Kragelund, Peter (2012). "The Revival of Non-traditional State Actors' Interests in Africa: Does It Matter for Policy Autonomy?" *Development Policy Review* 30.6, pp. 703–718.

— (2014). "Donors Go Home: Non-traditional State Actors and the Creation of Development Space in Zambia." *Third World Quarterly* 35.1, pp. 145–162.

Kumi, Emmanuel (2020). "From Donor Darling to beyond Aid? Public Perceptions of 'Ghana Beyond Aid'." *The Journal of Modern African Studies* 58.1, pp. 67–90.

Lancaster, Carol (2007). *Foreign Aid: Diplomacy, Development, Domestic Politics.* Chicago; London: University of Chicago Press.

Lang, Valentin, David Mihalyi, and Andrea F. Presbitero (2023). "Borrowing Costs after Sovereign Debt Relief." *American Economic Journal: Economic Policy* 15.2, pp. 331–358.

Lavers, Tom (2023). *Ethiopia's "Developmental State."* Cambridge; New York, NY: Cambridge University Press.

Lefort, René (2013). "The Theory and Practice of Meles Zenawi: A Response to Alex De Waal." *African Affairs* 112.448, pp. 460–470.

Lippolis, Nicolas and Harry Verhoeven (2022). "Politics by Default: China and the Global Governance of African Debt." *Survival* 64.3, pp. 153–178.

Lischer, Sarah Kenyon (2017). "The Global Refugee Crisis: Regional Destabilization & Humanitarian Protection." *Daedalus* 146.4, pp. 85–97.

Lynch, Gabrielle (2011). *I Say to You: Ethnic Politics and the Kalenjin in Kenya*. Chicago, IL: University of Chicago Press.

— (2013). "Electing the 'Alliance of the Accused': The Success of the Jubilee Alliance in Kenya's Rift Valley." *Journal of Eastern African Studies* 8.1, pp. 93–114.

Lynch, Julia F. (2013). "Aligning Sampling Strategies with Analytic Goals." *Interview Research in Political Science*. Ed. by Layna Mosley. Ithaca, NY: Cornell University Press. Chap. 1, pp. 31–44.

Lyons, Terrence (2006). "Avoiding Conflict in the Horn of Africa: U.S. Policy toward Ethiopia and Eritrea." *Council on Foreign Relations*.

MacCarthy, Mavis (2016). *Mobilizing and Managing External Development Assistance for Inclusive Growth: Ghana Country Report*. Technical Report. African Center for Economic Transformation.

Makara, Sabiti, Lise Rakner, and Lars Svåsand (2009). "Turnaround: The National Resistance Movement and the Reintroduction of a Multiparty System in Uganda." *International Political Science Review* 30.2, pp. 185–204.

Manson, Katrina and Javier Blas (2014). "Kenya's Debut $2bn Bond Breaks Africa Record." *Financial Times*. www.ft.com/content/4397a32a-f572-11e3-be21-00144feabdc0

Mawdsley, Emma (2012). *From Recipients to Donors: Emerging Powers and the Changing Development Landscape*. London; New York: Zed Books.

Mecagni, Mauro, Jorgen Ivan Canales Kriljenko, Cheikh Anta Gueye, Yibin Mu, Masafumi Yabara, and Sebastian Weber (2014). *Issuing International Sovereign Bonds: Opportunities and Challenges for Sub-Saharan Africa*. Report. International Monetary Fund.

Mihretu, Mamo and Gabriela Llobet (2017). *Looking beyond the Horizon: A Case Study of PVH's Commitment to Ethiopia's Hawassa Industrial Park*. Report. World Bank.

Milner, Helen V. (2006). "Why Multilateralism? Foreign Aid and Domestic Principal-agent Problems." *Delegation and Agency in International Organizations*. Ed. by Darren G. Hawkins, David A. Lake, Daniel L. Nielson, and Michael J. Tierney. Cambridge; New York, NY: Cambridge University Press. Chap. 2, pp. 107–139.

Mohan, Giles and Ben Lampert (2012). "Negotiating China: Reinserting African Agency into China-Africa Relations." *African Affairs* 112.446, pp. 92–110.

Molenaers, Nadia (2012). "The Great Divide? Donor Perceptions of Budget Support, Eligibility and Policy Dialogue." *Third World Quarterly* 33.5, pp. 791–806.

Morris, Scott, Bradley Parks, and Alysha Gardner (2020). "Chinese and World Bank Lending Terms: A Systematic Comparison across 157 Countries and 15 Years." *Center for Global Development Working Paper*.

Mosley, Layna (2000). "Room to Move: International Financial Markets and National Welfare States." *International Organization* 54.4, pp. 737–773.

— (2003). *Global Capital and National Governments*. Cambridge: Cambridge University Press.

Mosley, Layna, Victoria Paniagua, and Erik Wibbels (2020). "Moving Markets? Government Bond Investors and Microeconomic Policy Changes." *Economics & Politics* 32.2, pp. 197–249.

Mosley, Layna and B. Peter Rosendorff (2023). "Government Choices of Debt Instruments." *International Studies Quarterly* 67.2, pp. 1–13.

Mosley, Paul (1986). "The Politics of Economic Liberalization: USAID and the World Bank in Kenya, 1980–1984." *African Affairs* 85.338, pp. 107–119.

— (1987). *Conditionality As Bargaining Process: Structural-Adjustment Lending, 1980–86*. Essays in International Finance. Princeton, NJ: International Finance Section, Department of Economics, Princeton University.

Moss, Todd and Stephanie Majerowicz (2012). *No Longer Poor: Ghana's New Income Status and Implications of Graduation from IDA*. Report. Center for Global Development.

Mueller, Susanne D. (2008). "The Political Economy of Kenya's Crisis." *Journal of Eastern African Studies* 2.2, pp. 185–210.

Munnion, Christopher (2004). "Envoy's Dressing Down over Kenya Corruption Claim." *The Telegraph*.

Mustapha, Shakira and Romilly Greenhill (2016). "Age of Choice: Lao People's Democratic Republic in the New Development Finance Landscape." *ODI Report*.

Muthoo, Abhinay (2000). "A Non-Technical Introduction to Bargaining Theory." *World Economics* 1.2, pp. 145–166.

Naim, Moises (2007). "Rogue Aid." *Foreign Policy*.

Naqvi, Natalya (2018). "Manias, Panics and Crashes in Emerging Markets: An Empirical Investigation of the Post-2008 Crisis Period." *New Political Economy*, 24.6, pp. 759–779.

Nelson, Stephen C. (2014). "Playing Favorites: How Shared Beliefs Shape the IMF's Lending Decisions." *International Organization* 68.2, pp. 297–328.

Newman, Abraham L. and Elliot Posner (2011). "International Interdependence and Regulatory Power: Authority, Mobility, and Markets." *European Journal of International Relations* 17.4, pp. 589–610.

(2018). *Voluntary Disruptions: International Soft Law, Finance, and Power*. Oxford: Oxford University Press.

Ngirachu, John (2018). "Audit of First Sh204bn Eurobond 'Still Ongoing'." *Daily Nation*. https://nation.africa/kenya/news/audit-of-first-sh204bn-eurobond-still-ongoing-18548

Nugent, Paul (1996). *Big Men, Small Boys and Politics in Ghana: Power, Ideology and the Burden of History, 1982–1994*. Pinter Pub Ltd.

Oatley, Thomas (2019). "Toward a Political Economy of Complex Interdependence." *European Journal of International Relations* 25.4, pp. 957–978.

Oatley, Thomas, W. Kindred Winecoff, Andrew Pennock, and Sarah Bauerle Danzman (2013). "The Political Economy of Global Finance: A Network Model." *Perspectives on Politics* 11.1, pp. 133–153.

Odoom, Isaac (2017). "Dam In, Cocoa Out; Pipes In, Oil Out: China's Engagement in Ghana's Energy Sector." *Journal of Asian and African Studies* 52.5, pp. 598–620.

OECD (2005). *The Paris Declaration on Aid Effectiveness: Five Principles for Smart Aid*. Report.

(2014). "The New Development Finance Landscape: Developing Countries' Perspective." Report Prepared for the OECD Workshop on Development Finance. June 25, 2014. www.oecd.org/dac/financing-sustainable-development/The%20New%20Development%20Finance%20Landscape_19%20June%202014.pdf

(2021). "What Is ODA?" https://issuu.com/oecd.publishing/docs/what-is-oda/1

Olabisi, Michael and Howard Stein (2015). "Sovereign Bond Issues: Do African Countries Pay More to Borrow?" *Journal of African Trade* 2.1–2, pp. 87–109.

Omach, Paul (2017). "Uganda in the Great Lakes Region: Obstacles to Peace and Security." *War and Peace in Africa's Great Lakes Region*. Ed. by Gilbert M. Khadiagala. Cham: Palgrave Macmillan, pp. 69–83.

Oqubay, Arkebe (2015). *Made in Africa: Industrial Policy in Ethiopia*. Oxford: Oxford University Press.

Osei, Anja (2015). "Elites and Democracy in Ghana: A Social Network Approach." *African Affairs* 114.457, pp. 529–554.

Peiffer, Caryn and Pierre Englebert (2012). "Extraversion, Vulnerability to Donors, and Political Liberalization in Africa." *African Affairs* 111.444, pp. 355–378.

Phillips, Jon, Elena Hailwood, and Andrew Brooks (2016). "Sovereignty, the 'Resource Curse' and the Limits of Good Governance: A Political Economy of Oil in Ghana." *Review of African Political Economy* 43.147, pp. 26–42.

Phommalangsy, Phouvanh and Eileen Honan (2017). "An Analysis of Donor Engagement with Education Policy Development in Lao PDR from 1991 to 2000." *Development Policy Review* 35.6, pp. 823–838.

Prizzon, Annalisa (2013). "The Age of Choice: Zambia in the New Aid Landscape." ODI Report. Overseas Development Institute.

Prizzon, Annalisa and Tom Hart (2016). "Age of Choice: Kenya in the New Development Finance Landscape." ODI Report. Overseas Development Institute.

Public Finance Focus (2013). "Ghana Pledges to Increase Revenue as Deficit Swells to 12%." www.publicfinancefocus.org/news/2013/03/ghana-pledges-increase-revenue-deficit-swells-12

Queralt, Didac (2022). *Pawned States: State Building in the Era of International Finance*. Princeton, NJ; Oxford: Princeton University Press.

Rakner, Lise (2012). "Foreign Aid and Democratic Consolidation in Zambia." *UNU-Wider Working Paper Series*.

Reuters (2014a). "Ghana Will Not Draw Second Half of $3 Billion China Loan – Govt." *Reuters*. www.reuters.com/article/idUSKBN0FL1WX/

— (2014b). "Kenya Raises $750 Million at "Favorable" Rate from Eurobond Tap – Official." *Reuters*. www.reuters.com/article/world/africa/kenya-raises-750-million-at-favourable-rate-from-eurobond-tap-official-idUSL6N0TP1YT/

— (2015). "Kenya Says Rate on Its $750 mln Syndicated Loan below 6 pct." *Reuters*. www.reuters.com/article/markets/commodities/kenya-says-rate-on-its-750-mln-syndicated-loan-below-6-pct-idUSL8N12F12X/

Rieffel, Alexis (2003). *Restructuring Sovereign Debt: The Case for Ad Hoc Machinery*. Washington, DC: Brookings Institution Press.

Roberts, Cynthia A., Leslie Elliott Armijo, and Saori N. Katada (2018). *The BRICS and Collective Financial Statecraft*. New York: Oxford University Press.

Rodriguez-Toribio, Isabel and Alexandra O. Zeitz (2023). "Layering of Informal Organizations in International Regimes: Causes and Consequences of the G20 Common Framework." *Working Paper*.

Roessler, Philip G. (2005). "Donor-Induced Democratization and the Privatization of State Violence in Kenya and Rwanda." *Comparative Politics* 37.2, pp. 207–227.

Rogerson, Andrew (2005). "Aid Harmonisation and Alignment: Bridging the Gaps between Reality and the Paris Reform Agenda." *Development Policy Review* 23.5, pp. 531–552.

Rotberg, Robert I. (2008). *China into Africa: Trade, Aid, and Influence*. Washington, DC: Brookings.

Sammy, Wambua (2016). "Raila Cautions Lenders against Taking Part in Second Eurobond." *Daily Nation*. https://nation.africa/kenya/news/raila-cautions-lenders-against-taking-part-in-second-eurobond-317220

Schraeder, Peter J., Steven W. Hook, and Bruce Taylor (1998). "Clarifying the Foreign Aid Puzzle: A Comparison of American, Japanese, French, and Swedish Aid Flows." *World Politics* 50.2, pp. 294–323.

Schulz, Nicolai and Tim Kelsall (2021). *The Political Settlements Dataset: An Introduction with Illustrative Applications*. ESID Working Paper No. 165. Effective States and Inclusive Development (ESID).

Setser, Brad W. (2023). "The Common Framework and Its Discontents." *Development and Change* 54.5, pp. 1065–1086.

Sjöstedt, Martin (2013). "Aid Effectiveness and the Paris Declaration: A Mismatch between Ownership and Results-Based Management?" *Public Administration and Development* 33.2, pp. 143–155.

Smith, Elliot (2020). "Zambia Becomes Africa's First Coronavirus-Era Default: What Happens Now?" *CNBC*. www.cnbc.com/2020/11/23/zambia-becomes-africas-first-coronavirus-era-default-what-happens-now.html

Soule-Kohndou, Folashade (2018). "Bureaucratic Agency and Power Asymmetry in Benin-China Relations." *New Directions in Africa-China Studies*. Ed. by Chris Alden and Daniel Large. Abingdon, OX; New York, NY: Routledge. Chap. 12, pp. 189–204.

Steil, Benn and Robert E. Litan (2006). *Financial Statecraft: The Role of Financial Markets in American Foreign Policy*. New Haven, CT; London: Yale University Press.

Stiglitz, Joseph (2001). "Thanks for Nothing." *Atlantic Monthly*.

Stone, Randall W. (2008). "The Scope of IMF Conditionality." *International Organization* 62.4, pp. 589–620.

Strange, Austin M., Axel Dreher, Andreas Fuchs, Bradley Parks, and Michael J. Tierney (2017). "Tracking Under-Reported Financial Flows: China's Development Finance and the Aid-Conflict Nexus Revisited." *Journal of Conflict Resolution* 51.5, pp. 935–963.

Strange, Austin M., Bradley Parks, Michael J. Tierney, Andreas Fuchs, Axel Dreher, and Vijaya Ramachandran (2013). *China's Development Finance to Africa: A Media-Based Data Collection Approach*. Report. Center for Global Development.

Svensson, Jakob (2003). "Why Conditional Aid Does Not Work and What Can Be Done about It?" *Journal of Development Economics* 70.2, pp. 381–402.

Swedlund, Haley J. (2017a). "Is China Eroding the Bargaining Power of Traditional Donors in Africa?" *International Affairs* 93.2, pp. 389–408.

(2017b). *The Development Dance: How Donors and Recipients Negotiate the Delivery of Foreign Aid*. Ithaca, NY: Cornell University Press.

Tansey, Oisín (2007). "Process Tracing and Elite Interviewing: A Case for Non-Probability Sampling." *PS Online* October, pp. 765–772.

Taylor, Ian (2011). *The Forum on China-Africa Cooperation (FOCAC)*. Routledge Global Institutions. London: Routledge.

(2014). *Africa Rising? BRICS – Diversifying Dependency*. Oxford: James Currey.

Terrefe, Biruk (2020). "Urban Layers of Political Rupture: The 'New' Politics of Addis Ababa's Megaprojects." *Journal of Eastern African Studies* 14.3, pp. 375–395.

The Economist (2000). "Dancing in Kenya to the Donors' Tune." *The Economist*. www.economist.com/international/2000/08/03/dancing-in-kenya-to-the-donors-tune

Turse, Nick (2018). "U.S. Military Says It Has a 'Light Footprint' in Africa: These Documents Show a Vast Network of Bases." *The Intercept*. https://theintercept.com/2018/12/01/u-s-military-says-it-has-a-light-footprint-in-africa-these-documents-show-a-vast-network-of-bases/

Tyson, Judith E. (2015). *Sub-Saharan Africa International Sovereign Bonds: Part I Investor and Issuer Perspectives*. ODI Report. Overseas Development Institute.

UN (2023). "With Clock Ticking for the SDGs, UN Chief and Barbados Prime Minister Call for Urgent Action to Transform Broken Global Financial System."

Vaughan, Sarah (2011). "Revolutionary Democratic State-building: Party, State and People in the EPRDF's Ethiopia." *Journal of Eastern African Studies* 5.4, pp. 619–640.

Verhoeven, Harry (2009). "The Self-fulfilling Prophecy of Failed States: Somalia, State Collapse and the Global War on Terror." *Journal of Eastern African Studies* 3.3, pp. 405–425.

Verhoeven, Harry and Michael Woldemariam (2022). "Who Lost Ethiopia? The Unmaking of an African Anchor State and U.S. Foreign Policy." *Contemporary Security Policy* 43.4, pp. 622–650.

Vine, David (2019). "Lists of U.S. Military Bases Abroad, 1776-2019." *American University Digital Research Archive*.

Vreeland, James Raymond (2007). *The International Monetary Fund: Politics of Conditional Lending*. Routledge Global Institutions. London: Routledge.

Vreeland, James Raymond and Axel Dreher (2014). *The Political Economy of the United Nations Security Council: Money and Influence*. New York: Cambridge University Press.

Wade, Robert Hunter (2001). "Capital and Revenge: The IMF and Ethiopia." *Challenge* 44.5, pp. 67–75.

Wafula, Paul (2019). "Why You'll Never Know All the Truth about Eurobond." *The Nation*. https://nation.africa/kenya/news/why-you-ll-never-know-all-the-truth-about-eurobond-160762

Wang, Hongying (2014). "China and Sovereign Debt Restructuring." *CIGI Papers*.

Weis, Toni (2015). "Vanguard Capitalism: Party, State and Market in the EPRDF's Ethiopia." DPhil Thesis. University of Oxford.

— (2017). "Raising a Vegetarian Tiger: The Politics of Banking Regulation in Ethiopia." Working Paper.

Wheatley, Jonathan (2022). "Poorest Countries Face $11bn Surge in Debt Repayments." *Financial Times*. www.ft.com/content/4b5f4b54-2f80-4bda-9df7-9e74a3c8a66a

Whitfield, Lindsay (2009a). "'Change for a Better Ghana': Party Competition, Institutionalization and Alternation in Ghana's 2008 Elections." *African Affairs* 108.433, pp. 621–641.

— (2009b). *The Politics of Aid: African Strategies for Dealing with Donors*. Oxford: Oxford University Press.

— (2018). *Economies after Colonialism: Ghana and the Struggle for Power*. Cambridge: Cambridge University Press.

Whitfield, Lindsay and Alastair Fraser (2009). "Negotiating Aid." *The Politics of Aid: African Strategies for Dealing with Donors*. Ed. by Lindsay Whitfield. Oxford: Oxford University Press. Chap. 1, pp. 27–44.

Whitfield, Lindsay, Ole Therkildsen, Lars Buur, and Anne Mette Kjær (2015). *The Politics of African Industrial Policy: A Comparative Perspective*. New York, NY: Cambridge University Press.

Wibbels, Erik (2006). "Dependency Revisited: International Markets, Business Cycles, and Social Spending in the Developing World." *International Organization* 60.2, pp. 433–468.

Woods, Ngaire (2008). "Whose Aid? Whose Influence?" *International Affairs* 84.6, pp. 1205–1221.

World Bank (2006a). *Ghana: Public Finance Management Performance Reports and Performance Indicators*. Report No. 36384-GH. World Bank.

(2006b). "IDA Countries and Non-concessional Debt: Dealing with the 'Free Rider' Problem in IDA14 Grant-Recipient and Post-MDRI Countries." IDA Report No. 36563. https://documents1 .worldbank.org/curated/en/459861468138861852/pdf/36563.pdf

(2013). "Ethiopia's Productive Safety Net Program (PSNP): Integrating Disaster and Climate Risk Management: Case Study." Report No. 80622. https://documents1.worldbank.org/curated/en/893931468 321850632/pdf/806220WP0P12680Box0379812B00PUBLIC0.pdf

(2014). *IDA's Non-Concessional Borrowing Policy – The Case of Ethiopia*. Report.

(2015a). "Information on World Bank Policy-Based Guarantees." Factsheet. https://thedocs.worldbank.org/en/doc/920781440595372327-0290022015/original/PolicyBasedGuaranteesFactsheet2015.pdf

(2015b). "Poverty in Ethiopia Down 33 Percent since 2000." *Press Release*.

(2015c). *Project Appraisal Document: On a Proposed Credit in the Amount of SDR 32.7 Million to the Republic of Ghana for a Public Financial Management Reform Project*. World Bank.

(2015d). "World Bank Group Support Improved Livelihoods of Urban Poor." Press Release. December 16, 2015. www.worldbank.org/en/ news/press-release/2015/12/16/world-bank-group-supports-improve-livelihoods-of-urban-poor

(2015e). "Ethiopia Poverty Assessment 2014."

(2017a). "CPIA Criteria 2017." Washington, DC: World Bank.

(2017b). *Program Appraisal Document on a Proposed Credit in the Amount of EUR 131.6 Million to the Republic of Kenya for a Program the Strengthen Governance for Enabling Service Delivery and Public Investment in Kenya*. World Bank.

(2018). *Program Appraisal Document on a Proposed Credit to the Federal Democratic Republic of Ethiopia for a Program-for-Results Investment Project Financing Economic Opportunities Program*. World Bank.

(2019a). *Addressing Debt Vulnerabilities in IDA Countries: Options for IDA19*. International Development Association.

(2019b). *IDA's Non-Concessional Borrowing Policy: 2019 Review*. Development Finance Corporate IDA and IBRD (DFCII).

(2020a). "Implementation Status & Results Report: Program to Strengthen Governance for Enabling Service Delivery and Public Investment in Kenya (GESDeK)." *World Bank*.

(2020b). *World Development Indicators*.

(2020c). *Country Policy and Institutional Assessment Database*.

Wrong, Michela (2009). *It's Our Turn to Eat: The Story of a Kenyan Whistleblower*. London: Harper Perennial.

Wynne, Andy (2005). *Public Financial Management Reforms in Developing Countries: Lessons of Experience from Ghana, Tanzania, and Uganda*. Research rep. 7. The African Capacity Building Foundation.

Yanguas, Pablo (2017). "The Role and Responsibility of Foreign Aid in Recipient Political Settlements." *Journal of International Development* 29.2, pp. 211–228.

Yanguas, Pablo and David Hulme (2015). "Barriers to Political Analysis in Aid Bureaucracies: From Principle to Practice in DFID and the World Bank." *World Development* 74, pp. 209–219.

Younas, Javed (2008). "Motivation for Bilateral Aid Allocation: Altruism or Trade Benefits." *European Journal of Political Economy* 24.3, pp. 661–674.

Younger, Stephen D. (2016). "Ghana's Macroeconomic Crisis: Causes, Consequences, and Policy Responses." *IFPRI Discussion Paper*.

Zeitz, Alexandra O. (2021a). "Emulate or Differentiate? Chinese Development Finance, Competition, and World Bank Infrastructure Funding." *The Review of International Organizations* 16, pp. 265–292.

(2021b). "Global Capital Cycles and Market Discipline: Perceptions of Developing Country Borrowers." *British Journal of Political Science* 52.4, pp. 1944–1953.

Zelikow, Daniel and Fuat Savas (2022). "Mind the Gap: Time to Rethink Infrastructure Finance." *World Bank Blog*.

Index

Printed in the United States
by Baker & Taylor Publisher Services